ETHNICITY AND GOVERNANCE IN THE THIRD WORLD

T0346592

Contemporary Perspectives on Developing Societies

JOHN MUKUM MBAKU, Series General Editor, Weber State University
MWANGI S. KIMENYI, Series Associate Editor, The University of Connecticut &
KIPPRA, Kenya

Between 1989 and 1991, there were several changes in the global political economy that have had significant impact on policy reform in developing societies. The most important of these were the collapse of socialism in Eastern Europe, the subsequent disintegration of the Soviet Union, the cessation of superpower rivalry, and the demise of apartheid in South Africa. These events have provided scholars a new and challenging research agenda: To help the peoples of the Third World participate more effectively in the new global economy. Given existing conditions in these societies, the first line of business for researchers would be to help these countries establish and maintain transparent, accountable and participatory governance structures and, at the same time, provide themselves with more viable economic infrastructures. The *Contemporary Perspectives on Developing Societies* series was founded to serve as an outlet for such policy relevant research. It is expected that books published in this series will provide rigorous analyses of issues relevant to the peoples of the Third World and their efforts to improve their participation in the global economy.

Also in this series

Hope, K. R., Sr. (ed.) (1997), *Structural Adjustment, Reconstruction and Development in Africa.*
Mbaku, J. M. and Ihonvbere, J. O. (eds.) (1998), *Multiparty Democracy and Political Change: Constraints to Democratization in Africa.*
Kimenyi, M. S., Wieland, R. C. and Von Pischke, J. D. (eds.) (1998), *Strategic Issues in Microfinance.*
Magnarella, P. J. (ed.) (1998), *Middle East and North Africa: Governance, Democratization, Human Rights.*
Mbaku, J. M. (ed.) (1999), *Preparing Africa for the Twenty-First Century: Strategies for Peaceful Coexistence and Sustainable Development.*
Magnarella, P. J. (2000), *Justice in Africa: Rwanda's Genocide, Its Courts, and the UN Criminal Tribunal.*
Ngoh, V. J. (2000), *Southern Cameroons, 1922–1961: A Constitutional History.*
Udogu, E. I. (ed.) (2001), *The Issue of Political Ethnicity in Africa.*

Ethnicity and Governance in the Third World

Edited by
JOHN MUKUM MBAKU
Department of Economics
Weber State University
Ogden, Utah, USA

PITA OGABA AGBESE
Department of Political Science
University of Northern Iowa
Cedar Falls, Iowa, USA

MWANGI S. KIMENYI
Department of Economics
The University of Connecticut
Storrs, Connecticut, USA
&
The Kenya Institute for Public Policy Research and Analysis (KIPPRA)
Nairobi, Kenya

Routledge
Taylor & Francis Group

LONDON AND NEW YORK

First published 2001 by Ashgate Publishing

Reissued 2018 by Routledge
2 Park Square, Milton Park, Abingdon, Oxon OX14 4RN
711 Third Avenue, New York, NY 10017, USA

Routledge is an imprint of the Taylor & Francis Group, an informa business

Publisher's Note
The publisher has gone to great lengths to ensure the quality of this reprint but points out that some imperfections in the original copies may be apparent.

Disclaimer
The publisher has made every effort to trace copyright holders and welcomes correspondence from those they have been unable to contact.

A Library of Congress record exists under LC control number: 2001086755

ISBN 13: 978-1-138-73612-2 (hbk)
ISBN 13: 978-1-138-73610-8 (pbk)
ISBN 13: 978-1-315-18609-2 (ebk)

Contents

List of Tables

List of Appendices

List of Figures

List of Contributors

PITA OGABA AGBESE is Professor of Political Science at the University of Northern Iowa. His research has appeared in journals such as *Africa Today, The Journal of Commonwealth and Comparative Politics, Journal of Asian and African Studies, The Journal of International Studies, Third World Perspective, Journal of Peace Research, International Journal of Comparative Sociology, Bulletin of Peace Proposals*, and the *Journal of Third World Studies*. He is the co-author (with Julius O. Ihonvbere) of *Structural Adjustment and the Nigerian State* (Howard University Press, 1999).

KINGSLEY M. DE SILVA, holds a Ph.D. and D.Litt. from the University of London. He was Professor of Sri Lanka History at the University of Peradeniya (formerly the University of Sri Lanka) from 1969 to 1995; and has been Executive Director of the International Center for Ethnic Studies since 1982. Among his publications are *A History of Sri Lanka* (University of California Press, 1981); *Regional Powers and Small State Security: India and Sri Lanka, 1977–1990* (Woodrow Wilson Center Press and The Johns Hopkins University Press, 1995); and *Reaping the Whirlwind: Ethnic Politics, Ethnic Conflict in Sri Lanka* (Penguin Books, 1998).

NADER ENTESSAR is Professor of Political Science and Chair of International Studies at Spring Hill College in Mobile, Alabama. Dr. Entessar previously worked as a Senior Research Fellow at the Institute for International Political and Economic Studies in Tehran, Iran. He is the author and editor of several books, including *Kurdish Ethnonationalism* (Lynne Rienner Publishers, 1992), *Reconstruction and Regional Diplomacy in the Persian Gulf* (Routledge, 1992), and *Iran and the Arab World* (St. Martin's Press, 1993). Dr. Entessar has also published numerous book chapters and articles in academic journals in the United States, Europe and the Middle East.

THERESE S. GUNAWARDENA is a Ph.D. (ABD) student in the Department of Government at the University of Texas at Austin. Her research interests include South Asian diasporas, ethnonationalism, identity, and homeland politics.

MWANGI S. KIMENYI has been an Associate Professor of Economics at the University of Connecticut since 1991. Between 1987–1991, he was Assistant Professor of Economics at the University of Mississippi. He was born in Kenya and received his B.ED in chemistry from the University of Nairobi, MA in International Affairs and MA in Economics from Ohio University, and the Ph.D. in economics from George Mason University. He is Vice President and Chief Financial Controller of the African Educational Foundation for Public Policy and Market Process, Inc., and Managing Director of the African Institute for Public Policy and Market Process, Kenya. He is the author of *Economics of Poverty, Discrimination and Public Policy* (South-Western, 1995), *Ethnic Diversity, Liberty and the State: The African Dilemma* (Edward Elgar, 1998). He is the author of over 60 scholarly articles. His current research focuses on public choice and institutional reforms in developing countries. Since 1999, he has been on leave of absence from the University of Connecticut, serving as the Executive Director of The Kenya Institute for Public Policy Research and Analysis (KIPPRA), Nairobi, Kenya.

KATHLEEN R. MARTÍN is Professor of Cultural Anthropology in the Department of Sociology/Anthropology at Florida International University in Miami. She earned her doctorate at Bryn Mawr College. In 1998, she won the Sturgis Leavitt Award for the article, '"From the Heart of a Woman": Yucatec Maya Women as Political Actors.' Her current research project is a co-authored book with the Maya poet and political activist, Araceli Cab Cumi, entitled *Discarded Pages*. Dr. Martín specializes in Mexican studies with special emphasis on topics pertaining to politics, indigenous and gender issues.

JOHN MUKUM MBAKU is Willard L. Eccles Professor of Economics and John S. Hinckley Fellow at Weber State University, Ogden, Utah and Associate Editor (Africa), *Journal of Third World Studies*. He is also President of the African Educational Foundation for Public Policy and Market Process, Inc. He was born in Cameroon and received the Ph.D. degree in economics from the University of Georgia in 1985. He has previously taught at the University of Georgia and Kennesaw State University. His present research interests are in public choice, constitutional political economy, trade integration, intergroup relations, and institutional reforms in Africa. During 1994–1995, he served as the President of the Association of Third World Studies, Inc. He has traveled to several developing countries to lecture on market reforms. He is the author of *Institutions and Reform in Africa: The Public Choice Perspective* (Praeger, 1997), and *Bureaucratic and Political Corruption in Africa: The Public Choice Perspective* (Krieger, 2000); editor of *Corruption and the Crisis of Institutional Reforms in Africa* (The Edwin Mellen Press, 1998), and of *Preparing Africa for the Twenty-First Century: Strategies for Peaceful Coexistence and Sustainable Development* (Ashgate, 1999); co-editor (with Julius O. Ihonvbere) of *Multiparty Democracy and Political Change: Constraints to Democratization in Africa* (Ashgate, 1998), and (with Mwangi S. Kimenyi) of *Institutions and Collective Choice in Developing Countries: Applications of the Theory of Public Choice* (Ashgate, 1999).

EGHOSA E. OSAGHAE is Professor of Political Science at the University of Ibadan, Nigeria. Previously, he served as Professor of Political Studies and Head of the Department of Political Studies at the University of Transkei, South Africa. Osaghae is the author of several books on Nigerian political economy. His latest one is *Crippled Giant: Nigeria Since Independence* (Indiana University Press, 1999).

MOVINDRI REDDY obtained the B.A. degree from the University of Natal (Durban, South Africa), and the M.A. and Ph.D. degrees from Trinity College, Cambridge in Social and Political Science. Her Ph.D. dissertation was on Inkatha, and Zulu nationalism. She has held post-doctoral fellowships at Princeton University (Woodrow Wilson School), Yale University (Southern Africa Research Program) and the University of Chicago (Social Science Research Council/MacArthur Fellows Program).

She teaches courses on International Political Processes, International Organizations, International Theory, South African Politics, African Politics, and Comparative South Asian Politics at Occidental College in Los Angeles. Her research interests are ethnic, religious and sectarian politics that lead to intense and sustained conflicts. Her present interests are South Africa, Sri Lanka and Punjab.

WILLIAM T. VICKERS is Professor of Anthropology at Florida International University in Miami. He has conducted ethnological fieldwork in Ecuador, Peru, and Mexico, focusing primarily on the human ecology of indigenous communities, native land and civil rights, and frontier development. His books include, *Los Sionas y Secoyas: Su Adaptación al Ambiente Amazónico* (Abya-Yala, 1989 and 1996); (with Timothy Plowman) *Useful Plants of the Siona and Secoya Indians* (Field Museum of Natural History, 1984); and *Adaptive Responses of Native Amazonians* (Academic Press, 1983), co-edited with Raymond B. Hames. His articles have appeared in journals such as *Science*, *American Ethnologist*, *Human Nature*, *Human Ecology*, *Interciencia*, *Law and Anthropology*, *Cultural Survival Quarterly*, *Studies in Third World Societies*, *Latin American Research Review*, *Latin American Anthropology Review*, and *Reviews in Anthropology*. He has been a National Endowment for the Humanities Fellow, a Fulbright Fellow, and a Doherty Foundation Fellow.

Acknowledgments

Completing this book, *Ethnicity and Governance in the Third World*, required the assistance of many people and institutions. First, we thank The Ford Foundation, which provided the resources (Grant No. 995–0192) that enabled us to bring together an excellent group of scholars from all over the world to begin this important discourse on governance and peaceful coexistence of groups in the Third World. We are very grateful to the Foundation for its generous support. It is important, however, to note that The Ford Foundation's support of this project went beyond the supply of the financial resources needed to organize and hold the conference from which this book emerged. Thus, we would also like to acknowledge the encouragement and professional support given by several staff members at the Foundation, especially those associated with the *Governance and Civil Society Unit*. In particular, we acknowledge and honor Dr. Julius O. Ihonvbere for his dedication to peace and justice in the Third World. His professional support was especially critical to the completion of this project. We also commend The Ford Foundation for its continued support of projects that seek to improve governance and peaceful coexistence in developing societies.

Second, we would like to acknowledge Weber State University (Ogden, Utah), University of Northern Iowa (Cedar Falls, Iowa), and The University of Connecticut (Storrs, Connecticut) for the significant support provided to the editors of this volume. These institutions have created environments on their campuses that encourage scholarship on developing societies. We thank them for their continued support of our work and for providing us with the opportunities to meet our professional goals.

Third, we acknowledge the institutions and universities that have supported the research efforts of the other contributors to this volume—the International Center for Ethnic Studies (Sri Lanka); Spring Hill College (Mobile, Alabama); The University of Texas at Austin; Florida International University; University of Ibadan; and Occidental College of Los Angeles.

Fourth, John Mukum Mbaku would especially like to acknowledge the assistance provided this project by several faculty and staff members at Weber State University. Their help was invaluable and without it, we would not have been able to complete this project. Mbaku acknowledges Ms. Ann Poulsen, Grants & Contract Officer, Office of Grants and Contracts at Weber State University, for her unwavering support of the project. Also critical to the success of the project were the assistance provided by Dr. Michael B. Vaughan, Dean of the John B. Goddard School of Business and Economics at Weber State University; Dr. Paul H. Thompson, President of Weber State University, and Dr. Cliff Nowell, Chair of the Department of Economics at Weber State University. Ms. Lee S. Carrillo, Director of Grants & Contracts and Mr. Todd B. Nielsen, Grants & Contracts Officer, Weber State University, made sure that the budgets were prepared properly; and Ms. Elaine Thomas, secretary in the Department of Economics at Weber State University, made the travel and hotel arrangements, and carried out most of the correspondence associated with the project. We thank these efficient and very supportive staff members.

Fifth, we acknowledge the contributions of Dr. Forrest C. Crawford, a Weber State University Professor and former Chairman of the Utah Human Rights Commission, and Michael N. Martinez, Esq., a Utah civil rights attorney and present Chairman of the Utah Civil Rights Commission, both of whom have had significant experience working with civil rights groups in the US. Participants in the conference from which this volume was derived, met in Salt Lake City (June 10–13, 1999) to examine ways to improve governance in plural societies. Presenters were also expected to address the effects of existing laws and institutions on indigenous societies and communities in the Third World and how these structures can be improved to enhance the ability of these groups to participate more fully and effectively in governance. Since its founding, the US has had significant experience dealing with issues of ethnicity and governance. To provide conference participants with a view of the US experience, we invited the two veteran civil rights activists to make presentations at the conference. Since graduating from the University of Utah Law School in 1976, Martin N. Martinez has worked tirelessly as an advocate of the rights of minority citizens in Utah and the US In 1981, he was appointed by President Ronald Reagan as Deputy General Counsel to the Equal Employment Opportunity Commission. In his presentation, Mr. Martinez used a summary of census data to examine how ethnic populations are represented (or not represented) in governance both at the local and national levels. Specifically, he looked at the effects of existing governance structures and laws on ethnic populations in such critical areas as housing; employment; education; and the justice system. He also analyzed criminal activity or the perception (by greater society) of criminal activity in the indigent ethnic populations in Utah and the US. The presentation was very stimulating and provided participants with several local examples (from the metropolitan Salt Lake City, Utah area) of what he called the US's version of 'ethnic cleansing.' He described the latter as a practice in which the majority systematically passes laws and engages in practices that deny minority groups the opportunity to participate fully and effectively in governance and the economy. Through these processes, Mr. Martinez reiterated, the 'system' is 'cleansed' of the presence of certain groups in the critical domains. He argued further that while these groups may still maintain a physical presence in society, they really do not participate effectively and fully in the formulation and implementation of policies that directly affect their lives. He concluded that Utah and the rest of the US can improve minority group participation in governance and the economy through education and by adopting models and programs that focus on inclusion. Mr. Martinez argued that the US has a significant advantage over many other societies that are struggling with ethnic problems. That advantage, he went on, lies in the country's institutional arrangements—its laws and institutions, which provide adequate structures for peaceful coexistence, including the peaceful resolution of conflict. What is needed, he went on, is for the civil servants to enforce the laws rigorously, equitably and without prejudice. In addition, he argued that civil society has an important role to play in governance—civil society must remain vigilante and work continuously to make certain that government does not abuse its authority.

Mr. Martinez's presentation, which was received very enthusiastically by participants, made two very important contributions that are relevant to the research agenda on ethnicity and governance in the Third World. First, laws and institutions are very important for achieving peaceful coexistence. This re-enforces the results of research produced by several scholars regarding the importance of institutional arrangements to peaceful coexistence and sustainable development in developing societies. Second, his presentation underscored the importance of a strong and vibrant civil society to effective governance and the achievement of peaceful coexistence in any society.

Dr. Forrest C. Crawford was born in Sand Springs, Oklahoma and received the Ph.D. degree in education from Brigham Young University in 1990. Presently an Associate Professor of Teacher Education at Weber State University, Dr. Crawford has been very active in the struggle to improve living conditions for minority groups in Utah and the US. As Chairman of the State of Utah's *Martin Luther King, Jr. Human Rights Commission*, Dr. Crawford was recognized by the Salt Lake City, Utah, branch of the NAACP in 1993, for presiding over the State's 30th Anniversary Commemoration of the Historic 1963 March on Washington. He was one of eight individuals and organizations to receive the highest national honor given by the Federal King Commission and the Atlanta based King Center for Non-Violent Social Change, in a Washington, D.C. ceremony in March 1996 for his local, state and national efforts to promote the King legacy and principles of nonviolence. Dr. Crawford has taught various seminars in South Africa, France, Israel, Hungary, the Netherlands and throughout the US on non-violent approaches to the resolution of intergroup conflict.

In his presentation, Dr. Crawford reviewed America's treatment of its ethnic minorities, especially the country's struggle with slavery. As a prosperous democracy, he remarked, the US is regarded by many people around the world as a model for peaceful coexistence. On the other hand, the country has been criticized severely by others for the treatment of its minority groups. In fact, Dr. Crawford argued, some critiques have even gone as far as referring to the US as a colonial empire. However, Dr. Crawford argued that despite its many contradictions, Americans have retained their steadfast belief in the ideals that all men are created equal and enjoy certain unalienable rights, among them, life, liberty and the pursuit of happiness. Since the 1950s, significant changes have taken place in the country, resulting in, according to Dr. Crawford, (1) improved intergroup relations; (2) greater levels of participation in both political and economic markets for minority groups; and (3) a greater level of social interaction between groups. Perhaps, more important, Dr. Crawford emphasized, is the fact that the trials and tribulations of the last fifty years have actually strengthened the republic, improved governance, and paved the way for greater intergroup interaction. He concluded by saying that as the country enters the 21st century, there is evidence to indicate that it will do so with more enhanced coexistence of groups than has ever been the case in the country's history. Like Mr. Martinez, Dr. Crawford believes that such achievements are made possible by the country's institutional arrangements and the vigilance of its civil society.

We acknowledge the contributions of Dr. Forrest C. Crawford and Mr. Martin N. Martinez to this important discourse on ethnicity and governance in the Third World.

Sixth, Mwangi S. Kimenyi would like to express his gratitude to and acknowledge the support of the Earhart Foundation (Ann Arbor, Michigan), which during the last several years, has generously supported his work on ethnicity and institutions. Kimenyi also wishes to thank the Department of Economics at the University of Connecticut (Storrs, CT) for encouraging and supporting scholarship on developing societies.

Seventh, Pita Ogaba Agbese thanks the Department of Political Science at the University of Northern Iowa (Cedar Falls, Iowa), as well as the university itself, for supporting his work and for their commitment to scholarship on the Third World.

Finally, we would like to express our gratitude to our families for their patience. In our eagerness to complete this project, we may have spent a little too much time away from home. It is to them that we dedicate this volume.

The views expressed in the chapters that follow are those of the authors and should not be ascribed to the Ford Foundation or any of the institutions mentioned above or to their trustees, officers or staff.

John Mukum Mbaku
Pita Ogaba Agbese
Mwangi S. Kimenyi

Acronyms

ANC	African National Congress
BJP	Bharatiya Janata Party (Hindu nationalist political party in India)
BTS	Buddhist Theosophical Society
COE-Iwia	*Compañías de Operaciones Especiales* (elite Ecuadoran military units comprised entirely of Shuar Indians)
CONAIE	*Confederatión de Nacionalidades Indígenas del Ecuador*
COSATU	Congress of South African Trade Unions
D	Democrat (a member of the Democratic party of the US)
ENDLF	The Eelam National Democratic Liberation Front (Sri Lanka)
EPRLF	The Eelam People's Revolutionary Liberation Front (Sri Lanka)
EROS	Eelam Revolutionary Organizations for Students (Sri Lanka)
FARC	*Fuerzas Armadas Revolucionarias de Colombia* (Colombian guerrilla movement)
FMG	Federal Military Government (of Nigeria)
FMS	Federated Malay States
GNP	Gross National Product
IDB	Inter-American Development Bank
IFP	Inkatha Freedom Party (South African political party)
IMF	International Monetary Fund
IPC	International Petroleum Company (of Canada), a subsidiary of Standard Oil of New Jersey (USA)
JVP	*Janatha Vimukthi Peramuna* (Sri Lankan political party)

KLA	KwaZulu Legislative Assembly
LTTE	Liberation Tigers of Tamil Eelam (of Sri Lanka)
MB	Marginal benefit
MC	Marginal cost
MCA	Malayan Chinese Association (ethnic-based Malaysian political party)
MIC	Malayan Indian Congress (ethnic-based Malaysian political party)
NCIR	National Council on Inter-governmental Relations (Nigeria)
NEP	New Economic Policy (Malaysian economic program)
OISE	*Organización Indígena Secoyas del Ecuador*
OPEC	Organization of Petroleum Exporting Countries
PCKD	Pacific Coast Khalasa Diwan Society
PKK	Kurdistan Workers' Party
PLOTE	The People's Liberation Organization of Tamil Eelam (Sri Lanka)
PQLI	Physical Quality of Life Index (an alternative measure of economic development or the quality of life)
PRC	Provisional Ruling Council (of Nigeria)
R	Republican (a member of the Republican party of the US)
RPCC	Rivers Peace Conference Committee (Nigeria)
SGPC	Shiromani Gurdwara Parbankhak Committee (Sikh political organization founded in the 1920s)
SLFP	Sri Lanka Freedom Party
TELO	Tamil Eelam Liberation Organization (Sri Lanka)
TULF	Tamil United Liberation Front (of Sri Lanka)
UDF	United Democratic Front (South African political party)
UMNO	United Malays National Organization (ethnic-based Malaysian political party)
UN	United Nations (Organization)
UNP	United National Party (of Sri Lanka)
USS	Unfederated Malay States
VOC	Vereenigde Oost-Indische Compagnie (Dutch East India Company)

1

General Introduction

JOHN MUKUM MBAKU
PITA OGABA AGBESE
MWANGI S. KIMENYI

Introduction

Probably the most challenging issue facing developing nations today concerns the establishment of *institutional arrangements* that can effectively deal with ethnic diversity and allow *population groups* to coexist peacefully. In the past, leaders and intellectuals of these countries have proposed approaches to coexistence that involve suppressing *ethnic identity*. The assumption underlying this approach is that for the various groups to coexist peacefully, it is necessary to *homogenize* otherwise heterogeneous groups. This view of dealing with diversity is reflected by post-independence policies that included various provisions that sought to minimize or even deny group identity. For example, leaders argued that *single-party political systems* were more appropriate for uniting all groups (ethnic, religious and linguistic). The leaders warned that unity would be sacrificed if political party competition were to be introduced because different political parties would be dominated by particular ethnic and linguistic groups which in essence would politicize and promote *tribalism* (Winchester, 1986). Likewise, the elimination of *federalist* structures and traditions, and the creation of highly centralized states that greatly reduced

1

local autonomy were seen as solutions for uniting otherwise heterogeneous groups. Thus, the common response to diversity in many developing countries has been the adoption of institutional arrangements that seek to unify heterogeneous populations by limiting expressions of group differences.

To be sure, many of the peoples of the Third World had to deal with pressing problems of unity after independence that may have required them to deliberately design unifying policies. The new nations had to make crucial decisions concerning the constitutional dimensions of government activities. In selecting particular constitutional dimensions, the primary objectives included the achievement of both economic growth and of just and free societies that provided freedom from oppression of one group by another. The leaders, at least ostensibly, sought to adopt constitutions that would advance individual liberty while at the same time create unity amongst diverse populations. Concerned by the fact that the various ethnic, religious, and linguistic groups in each of the countries considered themselves distinct in various respects, the issue of unity was a primary concern. Specifically, unifying the groups into one national state was considered crucial for political stability. Nevertheless, the approaches taken by the post-independence governments to deal with heterogeneous populations have not been successful and in fact, may have been counter-productive.

Problems related to diversity are not limited to the Third World. In fact, management of diversity is a problem that is present in even the most advanced nations such as the United States, Canada, and the Western European countries. However, issues of diversity are more serious in the Third World than in other parts of the world. This is because most Third World countries have extremely heterogeneous populations. In sub-Saharan Africa, for example, there are over 2,000 distinct ethnic societies (Ayittey, 1992). These ethnic groups vary in size, with some having as few as 100,000 members and others encompassing millions of people. Other characteristics such as *language*, *religion* and *culture* make the African population even more heterogeneous. The same or similar levels of ethnic and religious diversity exist in Asia, Latin America and Caribbean, and the Middle East.

The mere number of 'ethnic units' or 'linguistic groups' may not necessarily imply serious divisions in society if individuals do not identify strongly with those groups. In many Third World societies, however, ethnic identification is quite strong. While individuals consider themselves loyal members of the nation that they belong to, they also identify strongly with particular ethnic, religious, or linguistic groups. In other words, various ethnic units do consider themselves distinct and to a large extent, want to maintain that identity. This identification is reflected in how individuals associate in social, political, and economic spheres.

Strong ethnic identification frequently results in the exclusion and marginalization of some groups from the mainstream of national politics and the economy. Groups compete to control the political machinery, and once in power adopt policies that favor some groups at the expense of others (Bates, 1983; Brough and Kimenyi, 1986; Kimenyi, 1989; and Mbaku, 1997). Absent well functioning democratic institutions, groups that are excluded may engage in violence in an attempt to gain entry into both political and economic markets. In most of the Third World, widespread internal conflicts are the norm and these conflicts almost always have a strong ethnic or religious component (e.g., India, Sri Lanka, Rwanda, Burundi, South Africa, Somalia, Ethiopia, Egypt, Democratic Republic of Congo, Mexico, to name a few). Evidence shows that just as ethnic units can be efficient in procuring benefits for their members, so too can they be efficient in organizing violence against other groups. In other words, the unit that can advance the well-being of its members also can undermine the liberty of others (Furley, 1995; Horowitz, 1994). Evidence shows that ethnic groups in many Third World countries are notorious for imposing costs on nonmembers (Ayoade, 1988; Chazan, 1988; Horowitz, 1994).

One of the clearest manifestations of *destructive ethnic rivalry* in the Third World is the military coup. For example, between 1960 and 1982, almost 90% of the 45 independent countries in sub-Saharan Africa experienced a military coup, an attempted coup, or a plot to overthrow the government (McGowan and Johnson, 1984). Since 1982, several other coups and attempted coups have taken place in the various African countries (Tordoff, 1993). While there are many factors that explain why the military intervenes to change government (Mbaku, 1994a, 1994b, 1995), the competition for the control of government by ethnic groups has played a dominant role in contributing to such political instability in Africa. In most cases, coups are organized by members of one ethnic group seeking to remove from power, leadership composed of members of other ethnic groups. As a matter of fact, most armed insurrections are aimed against ethnically based regimes (Horowitz, 1994; Furley, 1995; also see Jenkins and Kposowa, 1990, 1992).

Conclusive evidence of the ethnic orientation of most military coups is revealed by the changes in composition of members of the cabinet and senior civil servants before and after the coup. For example, before the 1966 coup in Central African Republic that deposed President Dacko, a member of the Baya ethnic group, no member of the Mbaka ethnic group was in the cabinet. After the successful coup led by J.-B. Bokassa of the Mbaka ethnic group, the composition of the cabinet changed so that 23% of the cabinet members were Mbaka. Likewise, when Kwame Nkrumah was president of Ghana, 71% of the cabinet members were from Nkrumah's Akan ethnic group. Following the coup that deposed Nkrumah, organized by members of the Ga and Ewe ethnic groups, the representation of Akan people in the cabinet dropped to 25%, that of the Ga increased from 7.7% to 25% and that of the Ewe increased from 7.7% to 38% (Morrison, et al., 1972). In almost all cases, military leaders award top government positions to members of their own ethnic groups (Kimenyi and Shughart, 1989; Breytenbach, 1976).

While military coups represent conflicts that are of short duration and often localized in urban centers, there are many other ethnic conflicts that involve large parts of the country and last for many years. Since independence, many developing countries have been involved in several such ethnic or religious conflicts. Probably the most significant in Africa was the civil war in Nigeria. That conflict reflected differences between the Ibo people in the Eastern Region and the other ethnic groups in the country. Fearing domination, the Ibo-dominated region intended to secede and subsequently form its own independent polity called Biafra. The response by the rest of the country was the use of military force that, while costly, prevented the secession.

Sudan is another example of a country where conflicts have been ongoing for decades. The conflict is one of a struggle between the northern and southern peoples. Both the northern and southern regions are themselves occupied by heterogeneous ethnic groups. However, the northerners are primarily of Arab descent and are Muslims while the southerners are of African descent and are primarily Christian. The conflict in Sudan reflects unresolved social tensions that resulted from the British colonial administration's decision to incorporate the South with its non-Muslim Nilotic and Bantu populations into a single political entity with an assertive, Islamic north oriented toward the Arab World (Copson, 1994).

The southerners for long have experienced political domination by the northerners and have attempted to rid themselves of such domination by use of violence. Northerners in turn have used force to suppress uprisings by the southerners resulting in destructive and widespread conflict. The war between northern and southern Sudan intensified during the 1960s and again during the late 1980s and continued into the 1990s. Conflicts of a similar type, between blacks and Arabs, and Christians and Muslims, have been persistent in Chad and Mauritania.

One of the most intense inter-ethnic conflicts in the Third World involves the Tutsi and Hutu tribes in Rwanda and Burundi (Greenland, 1976). The Hutu constitute a numerical majority in both countries but the Tutsi for the most part have dominated post-colonial politics. These two groups have different histories and migrated to Rwanda and Burundi at different times. In both countries, hatred is so intense that each ethnic group has attempted genocide aimed at the complete eradication of the other group. The 1972 holocaust in Burundi in which the Tutsi-controlled government killed between 100,000 and 200,000 Hutus is just one example (Meisler, 1976). Likewise, conflicts erupted in Rwanda during the early 1990s leaving thousands of people dead. Similar conflicts are continuing in Burundi though with fewer casualties.

Ethiopia provides yet another case where ethnic rivalry has persisted for hundreds of years. The country is fairly heterogeneous with over 70 languages. For a long time, the main conflict involved the people of Eritrea who sought independence from Ethiopia. Eritrea finally achieved self–determination in 1993 after a long and costly struggle. There are also other groups in Ethiopia who have waged nationalist movements. Most notable are the Somalis, who consider themselves as being colonized by the Amhara, who have for years dominated the leadership of that country. The Ogaden region of Ethiopia, where Somalis live, has on various occasions sought to secede in order to join Somalia (Henze, 1985).

Other examples include religiously-motivated struggles in Algeria; secession efforts by ethnic Tamils in Sri Lanka; the struggle between the anglophone minority and the francophone majority in Cameroon; the Tibetan independence movement in China; continued Muslim-Hindu clashes in India; Kurd nationalism in Iraq; and the Kashmiris' struggle to gain independence from India, to name a few. Some of these conflicts are discussed in greater detail in subsequent chapters of this book.

Ethnicity and governance in the Third World

Peaceful coexistence of various groups of people that exhibit distinct identity differences is a necessary condition for effective governance and for social and economic advancement. It is probably the failure to achieve this condition in many developing countries that explains these societies' low rates of economic growth. Economic crises and the extreme violations of civil liberties that characterize the majority of many Third World countries are to a large extent the product of institutions that are not suited to dealing with heterogeneous populations. The failure of political institutions to accommodate diverse interest groups (ethnic, religious, and linguistic) has generated conflict situations that adversely affect political and economic outcomes. It is the failure of political institutions to effectively balance the interests of different groups that we consider the primary cause of the pathetic conditions in many developing countries today. In other words, we believe that a primary cause of the low level of social and economic development in many Third World countries is the failure to deal effectively with diversity. When political institutions adequately harmonize the interests of diverse groups, diversity contributes positively to political stability and to economic growth and development. On the other hand, failure of institutions to deal adequately with diverse interests results in political instability, civil strife, and economic stagnation.

Ethnicity is a key feature of most Third World societies. It is therefore rather surprising that few scholars are involved in studying ethnicity and its role in the organization and governance of these societies. As a matter of fact, ethnicity is rarely discussed in academic forums. To formulate viable solutions to the many institutional problems facing the Third World, it is critically important to address ethnicity from different perspectives. If we accept that expressions of ethnic, religious and cultural preferences are a natural phenomenon and consistent with expression of individual liberty, then we realize that attempts to suppress such preferences are futile and cannot lead to peaceful coexistence. Instead, we need to better understand the positive roles that ethnicity and other characteristics with which individuals strongly identify with can play in the organization of societies. While we acknowledge that there is an ugly side to 'tribalism' or 'ethnic nationalism,' we suggest that institutions that seek to suppress ethnic preferences necessarily must involve imposed order and as a result must generate conflict. Appropriate institutional arrangements must guarantee the rights of people to maintain their identity while at the same time freely choosing to form associations with others for the purposes of accomplishing common ends. Likewise, it is necessary to take into account that groups have the propensity to exclude and marginalize others and therefore it is critical that there be sufficient provisions and constraints that adequately protect all groups from oppression and discriminatory practices.

A few scholars have investigated the subject of ethnicity from various perspectives (Horowitz, 1994, 1985, 1984; Kimenyi, 1997; Landa, 1997; Mbaku, 1997; Roback, 1991). While these scholars note that ethnicity can and does pose serious problems in the organization of society, they also suggest that under appropriate institutional arrangements, cooperative solutions can be achieved. Furthermore, ethnicity can be exploited to promote competition in the provision of public goods and also in the production of goods and services. In other words, under suitable institutional arrangements, ethnicity may have natural advantages that can enhance the quality of life. Thus, these scholars view ethnicity more positively than has been the case in the past.

A starting point in the search for solutions to problems that arise due to ethnic differences is to initiate discussions amongst scholars and policy-makers. Such discussions should explore the dynamics of group identity and how best to harmonize the interests of various groups while at the same time recognizing the need for groups to express their preferences. With recent democratization efforts in the Third World and the accompanying constitutional changes, this is an opportune time to hold such discussions because the outcomes of such discourse have a much higher probability of being translated into policy than was the case just a few years ago.

From June 10–13, 1999, several scholars from around the world met at the University Park Marriott Hotel in Salt Lake City, Utah (USA) to begin this important discourse. The conference, which was sponsored by the Ford Foundation (New York City) and Weber State University (Ogden, Utah), was designed to explore new approaches to dealing with ethnicity. The primary goal of the conference was to bring together leading Third World scholars to discuss the issue of ethnicity as it relates to governance and peaceful coexistence. The goal of the conference was not only to discuss the issue but also to come up with some general statements and observations on possible approaches to dealing with the various problems related to ethnicity. The present volume builds on the discussions that took place in Salt Lake City. In addition, the editors have solicited contributions from other scholars who have an interest in peaceful coexistence in the Third World, but who, as a result of prior commitments, were unable to join them in Salt Lake City.

This volume discusses the central role that ethnicity plays in governance in developing countries. In general, the chapters emphasize the importance of institutional arrangements that accommodate the interests of various groups in countries characterized by heterogeneous populations. Specifically, the essays contained in this volume suggest that peaceful coexistence requires institutions that permit groups to express their identity and to freely organize for the provision of 'ethnic goods'. The book also focuses on marginalized indigenous population groups in various parts of the Third World and on the attempts that have been made to accommodate the aspirations of these groups.

In Chapter 2, Eghosa E. Osaghae discusses federalism and the ethnic question in Africa. He argues that even though federalism has not 'taken root' in Africa, one should not conclude that, as a political system, federalism has failed on the continent. What has happened in many of the countries that have chosen the federal option is that the latter has not been given the opportunity to entrench itself. In many of these countries, 'consultation, reciprocity, and compromise, all elements of federal political culture ... and necessary for the emergence and sustenance of federalism, are in short supply.' What has emerged in many of these countries, Osaghae argues, is 'cutthroat zero-sum political competition and politics of exclusion.' In addition, many post-independence African leaders engaged in behaviors that were inimical to the practice of federalism (e.g., presidentialism with power concentrated in the center). In several countries, some ethnic groups assumed a sense of superiority to others because of their long tenure in power (e.g., Amhara in Ethiopia, Americo-Liberians in Liberia, Hausa/Fulani in Nigeria, etc.) making the practice of federalism difficult. Osaghae argues that although the premise of inequality remains a major source of strain for Africa's embryonic federalism, the federal system remains a relatively attractive and relevant option for Africa's multiethnic societies.

In the 1960s, Osaghae continues, federalism appears to have disappeared from the African political scene. In the late 1980s and early 1990s, it returned to the political agenda of many countries as several ethnic groups in Africa took advantage of the near-universal demand for more democratic governance systems and rose to 'challenge the validity of the imperial postcolonial state and demand its reconstruction and revalidation on the bases of inclusion, equitable power and resource sharing, negotiated constitutional settlement, decentralization, and democracy.' The struggles of many historically marginalized and excluded groups during this period reinforced the 'relevance and utility of federal principles as core elements of the multiethnic or plural democracy necessary for reducing tension and conflicts in multi-ethnic states.'

By the late 1980s, as a result of the political opportunism of many of the continent's post-independence leaders, several countries in the region were on the verge of disintegration. During this period, federalism gained currency as Africans searched for new political and constitutional configurations to save states that were in the process of disintegrating. The federal debate, Osaghae argues, was 'more pungent in ethnically divided countries with a pedigree of federal ideas.' He cautions, however, that the relevance of the federal solution, 'or at least some of its consociational variants, including decentralization/segmental autonomy and power sharing, to other countries, including those torn apart by protracted civil wars, like Liberia, Angola and Somalia, and the countries of the Great Lakes region, was also debated.' As the 1990s came to an end, Osaghae asserts, federalism appeared to have a new beginning in the continent as Ethiopia adopted a constitution based on ethnic federalism and historically excluded ethnic groups in Nigeria began to question the country's non-federal trajectories and demanded a restructuring of the latter into a true federation.

Chapter 2, Osaghae argues, rests on the argument that federalism is a viable instrument for the peaceful resolution of conflict. In the second section of the chapter, he attempts to show how federalism can deal with ethnicity, which in Nigeria, has been called the 'national question.' As argued by Burgess (1993, p. 7), '[t]he genius of federalism lies in its infinite capacity to accommodate and reconcile the competing and some-times conflicting array of diversities having political salience within a state.' Although federalism does not eliminate ethnic problems, Osaghae continues, it does provide (1) 'an opportunity for self-actualization by competing groups in divided societies'; and (2) 'a legal and institutional framework for reconciling differences, reducing conflicts, and protecting the interests of groups, especially ethnic minorities, which otherwise would be marginalized, excluded and dominated.' Federalism, however, has its problems. Osaghae points out three important ones and argues that these account for the reason why federalism is a 'contested rather than a settled option.' First, it is not very relevant in situations where population groups have decided against peaceful coexistence within the same polity. Second, as a solution to the ethnic question, federalism has not always been success-ful, as is illustrated by the disintegration of the Soviet Union, Yugoslavia and the strains suffered by the Canadian system. Finally, federalism, especially in divided states, may actually cause a polity to become more divided. These problems, Osaghae asserts in this chapter, however, do not detract from the 'powers and resilience of federalism.'

Osaghae devotes the rest of the chapter to a discussion of federalism in Africa, which he argues, is still 'in search of a tradition, partly due to the discontinuities in federal experiences and what Ayoade (1978) calls the high mortality rate of federal systems ... .' He traces the evolution of the federalist tradition from the colonial period to the pro-democracy struggles of the late 1980s and early 1990s. He warns that despite the widespread use of federalism to deal with the ethnic question, it does not imply that 'there is consensus on the desirability and suitability of the federal solution in Africa's ethnically divided states.' During most of the post-independence period in Africa, federalism as a way to organize ethnically divided societies, has been highly contested between groups who oppose any division of the polity and those who believe in a highly decentralized political structure that protects the diverse interests of the different population groups within the country. During negotiations to end apartheid in South Africa, for example, the demand for a separate Afrikaner nation threatened to wreck the country's transition. The African National Congress (ANC), which was ideologically and resolutely opposed to federalism as a way to organize post-apartheid South Africa, through careful maneuvering and its willingness to concede to the expediency of the federal formula, however, was able to reduce the tension and save the country's transition program.

During the pro-democracy struggles of the 1980s and 1990s in Africa, there was an explosion in ethnic demands for self-determination. Osaghae argues that this increase in ethnic mobilization finally made the ideological uses of federalism apparent to many people. In an effort to free themselves from many years of exploitation by erstwhile one-party and military regimes, many historically marginalized and deprived groups demanded reconstruction of the post-colonial state to provide constitutional structures that offered them protection from abuse by opportunistic leaders. Most of these demands, Osaghae argues, could only be made through the application of some form of federal principles.

Finally, Osaghae examines the impediments to federalism in Africa and concludes with the observation that the success or failure of federalism largely depends on how well the central government manages diversity and the willingness of governmental operatives to abide by constitutional rules which dilute or in some cases challenge their hegemony.

In Chapter 3, John Mukum Mbaku focuses on constitutionalism and governance in ethnically diverse societies. He argues that most of the destructive conflict that has pervaded most of post-independence Africa has been due primarily to the adoption at independence, of institutional arrangements that (1) failed to adequately constrain the power of government; (2) did not guarantee economic freedoms; and (3) failed to provide procedures for the peaceful resolution of the conflicting interests of the various ethnic groups in each country. In many instances, the laws and the institutions adopted allowed some ethnic groups to dominate governance and use governmental structures to enrich themselves. Unable to become part of the ruling coalition, many of the excluded ethnic groups turned to violent mobilization as a way to minimize further marginalization.

Mbaku uses *rational choice theory* to explain some of the observed behaviors of ethnic groups. Rational choice theory, as it applies to ethnicity, is based on four pre-suppositions. First, the individual seeks to maximize his self-interest. Second, choices made at one point in time can impact and alter the alternatives available to individuals in subsequent periods. Third, individuals, through socialization, come to recognize their dependence on other members of society. Finally, to maximize their objectives, individuals may form/join groups that allow them to engage in collective decision-making.

Mbaku suggests that African countries adopted institutional arrangements that were not appropriate for their societies because constitution making during the decolonization period and immediately after independence was dominated by external groups instead of the majority indigenous Africans. The rules imposed on the indigenous peoples were alien and not particularly suited to the needs of the Africans. The institutional arrangements encouraged political opportunism, including bureaucratic corruption and rent seeking, and destructive ethnic conflict. Mbaku asserts that Africans were so eager to free themselves of European domination and exploitation that they were willing to put-off proper constitutional discourse until independence was achieved. In the post-independence period, the new African leaders were expected to engage the people in proper constitution making and design and adopt constitutional rules that reflected each country's unique conditions and the values of the majority of the people. Unfortunately, these leaders made no effort to initiate a national debate on the constitution. In addition, the new state structures enhanced the ability of the new leaders to exploit the people and plunder the economy for their own benefit. In the process, many groups, especially minority ethnic groups, were marginalized. Throughout the continent, most of the new leaders either manipulated the post-independence constitutions to increase their power and ability to monopolize political space or discarded them and ruled primarily by decree.

According to Mbaku, control of governance structures allows the controlling group to redistribute income and wealth in favor of its members and its supporters. As a consequence, ethnic groups have engaged in a bitter struggle for capture of the state. Ethnic mobilization for control of the instruments of government has contributed significantly to violent confrontations between groups. Most of these relatively unconstrained African states have suffocated civil society, abrogated individual liberties, confiscated individual property without compensation, violated the rights of individuals and groups, and have generally engaged in regulatory activities that have stunted the development of indigenous entrepreneurship and creation of the wealth that could have been used to deal more effectively with poverty. In other cases, some states have either been unable or unwilling to perform their basic functions, including the maintenance of law and order, and the provision of public goods and services.

Mbaku also uses resource competition theories to explain ethnic relations. In each society, individuals must compete for resources. Such competition can take place along ethnic or class lines. If the ethnic group is the basic organizational structure for competing for resources, then the latter can have significant impact on ethnic groups in particular and ethnicity in general. Individuals compete mostly for jobs, leadership positions and for government transfers. The competition induces individuals within a society to form groups, develop political and ideological platforms, and to engage in conflict behaviors in an effort to maximize benefits from competition. The consequences of ethnic competition for resources include increased ethnic identification and group formation, increased racism and prejudice, increased inter-ethnic conflict and increased ethnic mobilization and activism (Nagel, 1995).

Access to political markets and control of resource allocation represent other sources of ethnic competition. Thus, elites seeking public office often organize their campaigns along ethnic lines. Mbaku argues that efforts by post-independence leaders to discourage ethnic competition for both political and economic resources has failed. Therefore, to minimize destructive ethnic conflict leaders should establish institutional arrangements that provide fair and predictable rules for competition and structures for peaceful resolution of conflict.

If the nation's institutional arrangements place some ethnic groups at a competitive disadvantage in the competition for resources, then the disadvantaged group may resort to violent mobilization. On the other hand, the favored or well-placed groups may use state structures to oppress minority groups in an effort to continue to maintain a comparative advantage in the competition for resources.

Mbaku also discusses ethnicity and governance from a *public choice perspective*. He states that opportunistic behaviors such as military coups, corruption and institutional instability in Africa represent efforts by individuals and groups to subvert existing laws and institutions to generate wealth for themselves. Mbaku argues further that pubic choice theory also shows how groups that are competing for access to political and economic markets can become engaged in violent confrontations. The theory, he believes, can help African countries develop and adopt more viable institutional arrangements, as well as provide significant insights into the importance of minimizing post-contractual opportunism, and providing viable procedures for peaceful resolution of conflict.

In conclusion, Mbaku states that the most effective way to provide sustainable solutions to the problems of destructive ethnic conflict is to engage in state reconstruction to provide efficient and viable institutional arrangements and polities, which compromise optional units of collective choice. He also proposes various constitutional constraints that are necessary to prevent Africa's ruling elites and other public servants from engaging in political opportunism.

In Chapter 4, Mwangi S. Kimenyi extends the argument outlined in Chapter 3 and specifically proposes the adoption of ethnic-based federalist systems of government in Africa's multi-ethnic polities. In essence, he suggests that the ethnic group should be considered a legitimate unit of collective choice.

Kimenyi advances the argument that most of the ethnic conflicts experienced in Africa have been due to the adoption at independence of internal organizations that failed to (1) adequately contain the power of government; and (2) provide structures for the peaceful resolution of the conflicting interests of various ethnic groups within each country. After independence, the new leaders forcefully argued for unitary governments, much like the colonial governments they had just replaced. Power was concentrated in the center, supposedly to enhance national unity and integration. However, more than forty years of one-party highly centralized governments have shown that such institutional arrangements are not suited to or capable of harmonizing the interests of heterogeneous groups.

Kimenyi demonstrates that members of ethnic groups place a high value on ethnic identification and therefore devote a lot of resources to making certain that members of a group continue to identify with that group. He suggests that decisions that are made by a single ethnic unit are likely to be more representative of *individual* preferences than would be the case when many ethnic groups are involved in the decision making process. He compares ethnic organizational units with voluntary clubs that are composed of people whose preferences are fairly similar.

This chapter suggests that the establishment of ethnic governmental units that possess a fair degree of autonomy would be the most desirable way of organizing African societies. Kimenyi then demonstrates that ethnic groups may be best suited to providing some local public goods and therefore ethnicity could be used to define local political jurisdictions in a federal system. He suggests that because ethnic groups occupy specific geographic space, the ethnic units form natural units of collective choice. Finally, Kimenyi outlines various factors favoring the establishment of federal systems of government in Africa.

An examination of Nigeria's post-independence attempts to manage relations between its several ethnic, religious and linguistic groups is undertaken by Pita Ogaba Agbese in Chapter 5. He begins by providing the reader with a few quotations that describe the manipulation of ethnic identities during British rule of the territory that later became Nigeria and how such policies contributed to violent ethnic conflict in present-day Nigeria. Through their so-called policy of indirect rule, the British attempted to manipulate identity consciousness in an effort to 'divide and rule.' The differential treatment of ethnic groups by the British colonial administration created severe imbalances among groups in such areas as educational attainment, and economic and political development, and set the stage for the violent communal conflicts that have characterized most of the post-independence period in the country.

According to Agbese, 'violent communal conflicts in contemporary Nigeria reflect both the poor state of ethnic relations and the ineffective manner in which ethnic conflicts have been managed in the country.' Since independence, he explains, successive Nigerian governments (both military and civilian) have failed to properly manage the nation's diversity. Instead, many of the country's governments have pursued short-sighted and opportunistic public policies that have actually exacerbated inter-group conflict and encouraged violent mobilization by groups to either protect their existing political and economic advantages or to resist further marginalization. Agbese rejects the traditional explanation for communal conflicts in Nigeria—which posits that these conflicts are caused by age-old rivalries and competition for scarce resources. Instead, he suggests that the locus of Nigeria's ethnic conflicts can be located in the policies of the postcolonial state. Policies promulgated by the various post-independence governments, Agbese argues, have (1) provided the arena for violent ethnic conflicts; and (2) accentuated the scope and intensity of these conflicts. He notes further that the system in which the ruling classes have turned governmental structures under their control into instruments of plunder for their own benefit has encouraged the 'manipulation of ethnic and other forms of primordial identities.'

Since independence in 1960, Nigerian elites have manipulated ethnicity in order to capture and retain political power. In Nigeria, as well as in other parts of Africa, there exists a strong linkage between public policies and ethnic conflicts. Agbese, however, is surprised that students of ethnicity have failed to undertake full-scale analyses of this linkage, especially in Africa where destructive ethnic conflicts have become endemic. He cites the example of Nigeria where central government policies on the allocation of revenues from the extraction of petroleum have shaped inter-ethnic relations in the oil-producing regions. In addition, Agbese states that these policies have also provided the arena for violent confrontation between the federal government and ethnic groups in the oil-rich regions of the country. In fact, in 1995, the internationally-known environmentalist, Ken Saro-Wiwa, was executed by the military government of Sani Abacha partly because of Saro-Wiwa's persistent demand that Nigerian ethnic groups be allowed to own and control the nation's petroleum deposits instead of the federal government. Thus, Agbese argues, a proper study of ethnic conflict in Nigeria and other countries, must begin with the analysis of government policies.

Nader Entessar, in Chapter 6, provides an overview of the major factors that have 'heightened the sense of identity among national and ethnic groups in the contemporary Middle East.' He argues that throughout today's Middle East, and indeed, in most of the Third World, 'the politicization of ethnicity and the rise of nationalism have been linked with the concept of self-determination.' He begins the analysis by quoting from the controversial article by Francis Fukuyama (1989) in which the latter claimed that the tumultuous political and economic events of the late 1980s and early 1990s (the fall of the Berlin Wall; the end of the Cold War and the subsequent cessation of superpower rivalry; and the near-global demand for democracy and free markets) represented the 'end of history' and the triumph of Western liberalism. In his 1989 article, which was later expanded into a book, Fukuyama acknowledges the critical impact and importance of ethnic nationalism and religious fundamentalism on the global political economy, but asserts nevertheless that Western liberalism will overcome the challenges posed by these and other phenomena and emerge triumphant.

Next, Entessar reviews the literature and explores some of the definitions of ethnicity. For the purpose of Chapter 6, he adopts Harik's (1972, p. 303) definition, which states that an ethnic group is a 'community conscious of sharing similar characteristics such as a distinct language, a religion, a culture, or a historical experience of its own and also conscious of its differences from other communities by virtue of these same characteristics ... .' He argues that in studying the Middle East, one must keep in mind that language, religion, common historical experiences, and cultural distinctiveness are important components of ethnicity and variables that affect nationalism among the various nationalities that inhabit the region.

According to Entessar, one of the most important and salient features of the contemporary Middle East is the expanded role of the state in managing the competing claims of the several ethnic groups and nationalities that inhabit each polity. Governments, which have traditionally limited their control to the urbanized and industrialized core regions (e.g., capital cities) of their polities, have in recent years, sought to extend their reach into the heretofore neglected peripheral areas through the provision of bureaucratic, educational, health and security structures. Perhaps, more important is the fact that such governmental expansion has gone beyond taxation (to raise revenues), the maintaining of law and order, and the provision of public goods and services into the direct management of inter-ethnic relations. Entessar argues that one unintended consequence of the new globalization for the Middle East has been 'the rise of socioeconomic demands for ethnic equality and fairness.' This development has led to the emergence of conflicts among ethnic nationalities on the one hand, and between the state and minorities on the other. The state, which has managed to retain its autonomy from all the other actors in the society, despite recent challenges, continues to shape and even alter ethnic identities around the world. In the Middle East, Entessar argues, the state has been able to manipulate ethnic identities to meet its own objectives. Like the colonialists did several years earlier, the modern state in the Middle East has 'manufactured' inter-ethnic rivalries and employed 'divide-and-rule' tactics to enhance its hegemonic position over other societal actors. As examples, Entessar mentions ongoing conflicts between Arab and Iranian nationalism; Arab and Turkish nationalism; and Turkish and Kurdish nationalism in several countries in the region.

Entessar states that one can study ethnic or nationality groups in terms of 'their assimilative or dissimilative effects on the political structures and nation-building efforts of the larger unit or state.' In 1981, Yinger argued that the extent of the assimilation of an ethnic group into the larger society in which its members live is a function of (1) acculturation; (2) amalgamation; (3) integration; and (4) identification. Using these variables, Entessar examines the assimilation or the lack there of, of several ethnic groups in several polities in the Middle East. Acculturation, he argues, is the 'process of change toward greater cultural similarity brought about by contact between two or more groups.' As a consequence, there is a positive correlation between the degree of acculturation of an ethnic group and the extent of its assimilation into greater society. As an example, Entessar states that the relatively successful degree of acculturation of German-Americans or Italian Americans has 'negated any secessionist tendencies or nationalistic drives for political autonomy by these groups in the contemporary United States.' However, the poor level of the acculturation of the Kurds in modern Iraq and Turkey has contributed significantly to the rise in Kurdish nationalism. In fact, Kurds have already proclaimed an autonomous region in northern Iraq and continue to challenge the foundations of the Turkish and Iranian states.

In Iraq, the government has given official recognition to ethnic differences between the majority Arabs and the minority Kurds. The process of acculturation of the Kurds, however, has been quite difficult, especially in light of the glorification of Arabism by the government, as exemplified in the ideology of the ruling Ba'th Party. Entessar argues that Iraq's genocidal war against the Kurds in the 1980s and the post-Persian Gulf war Kurdish rebellion against the government of Saddam Hussein and the Ba'th Party represents the failure of state policies towards minority groups. In a similar manner, Entessar uses the other variables (amalgamation, integration and identification) to provide greater insights into the experiences of the Kurds in several countries in the Middle East.

Entessar concludes by asserting that the modern state system has not accommodated the demands of ethnic nationalism and has largely ignored ethnic diversity. As a consequence, a number of non-assimilating minorities have emerged to challenge the hegemony of politically dominant groups. As they began to lose their rights in the Middle East, many ethnic minorities proportionally increased their demands for self-determination. Entessar, like other contributors to this volume (e.g., Mbaku, Kimenyi, Osaghae and Agbese) believes that state reconstruction to provide more appropriate institutional arrangements can have a positive impact on the management of ethnic relations. Thus, he suggests that each state in the Middle East can lessen ethnic tensions by providing constitutional and legal arrangements that can effectively accommodate minority rights.

The book devotes two chapters to an examination of the treatment of indigenous populations in Latin America. In Chapter 7, Kathleen R. Martín examines the economic, social and political conditions faced by indigenous peoples in Mexico and in Chapter 8, William T. Vickers provides the reader with an insight into Ecuador's treatment of its indigenous populations.

Martín examines the challenges faced by indigenous groups residing in what is now the modern Mexican state. She outlines state policies towards indigenous peoples, beginning with Spanish colonial rule and ending with the present Mexican state. She then suggests policies that can be implemented to resolve conflict between the state and indigenous groups, enhance respect for indigenous peoples and their culture in particular, and for diversity in general, and improve the living conditions of the indigenous peoples, the majority of whom have historically been discriminated against, deprived and marginalized. She pays special attention to the context within which policies towards indigenous peoples must operate and the political and social actors who could effect these policies.

On the first day of 1994, a rebellion led by indigenous peoples broke out in Chiapas, one of the most impoverished regions of Mexico and one that is populated largely by indigenous peoples. The military action, led by the *Ejercito Zapatista de Liberacion National* (Zapatista National Liberation Army), demanded among other things, greater political and economic autonomy for the region, recognition and respect for the region's cultural distinctiveness, and improved material conditions for the people. Today, more than six years after the rebellion began, the Mexican state is yet to resolve it or deal effectively with the conditions that forced the indigenous peoples to engage in violent mobilization.

Martín argues that although there have been several rebellions in Mexico's history, the Chiapas action is unique in that it brought more global attention to and recognition of centuries of political and economic marginalization of the country's indigenous peoples than any other rebellion in history. At the core of the continuing conflict between the indigenous peoples of Chiapas and the Mexican state, Martín argues, are two critical issues: (1) land tenure and property rights; and (2) political rights—specifically the right of the indigenous peoples to govern themselves and participate more fully and effectively in the political life of Mexico. Thus, in response to President Zedillo's mobilization against indigenous peoples in February 1995, the latter proclaimed their now famous slogan: 'never again a Mexico without us.'

Loss of ancestral lands by indigenous peoples began with the arrival of the Spanish conquerors. After they arrived the region, the Spanish designed a pyramidal social hierarchy that placed them at the apex and the indigenous peoples at the bottom. Subsequently, economic privileges and political and civil rights were assigned based on this hierarchy, with the Spaniards receiving the lion's share of all rights and privileges and the indigenous peoples granted the least. In fact, most fertile and cultivable land was confiscated and re-assigned to or reserved for Spanish settlers. How much access an individual had to political and economic markets was determined by the individual's position in this relatively rigid social hierarchy. In addition, social mobility was also determined by the individual's assigned position, with Spaniards and people of Spanish origin being the most economically and socially mobile. The system developed by the Spanish colonizers to help them exploit the resources of the indigenous peoples for their benefit and that of Spain has remained almost intact to the present day. In recent years, the confiscation of lands belonging to indigenous populations has increased as large agricultural and cattle estates expand and encroach on land owned by the Maya and other indigenous groups. Despite constitutional guarantees against such seizures, the indigenous peoples have been unable to obtain relief from the Mexican judiciary system. State indifference towards the sufferings of the Maya, for example, has effectively deprived them of their Mexican citizenship and the protection granted them under the Mexican constitution. As a consequence, indigenous populations in Mexico remain poor and marginalized.

Throughout history, indigenous peoples have resisted conquest and exploitation. Unfortunately, attacking forces, beginning with the Spanish, have usually possessed superior military technology and as a consequence have been able to defeat and subject these people to significant levels of suffering. In addition, the diseases brought by invading Europeans, as well as war-induced famine, usually weakened the indigenous peoples' ability to fight and made them vulnerable to European exploitation.

Despite their illustrious history, one rich in achievements, Mexico's indigenous peoples remain at the bottom of the economic ladder. They are also the most likely to have little or no access to decent housing, health care, education, and jobs. In addition to the fact that they suffer from relatively high rates of material deprivation, they are also socially ostracized, discriminated against and marginalized.

Since Mexico gained independence from Spain, indigenous peoples have continued their struggle for greater access to economic and political markets. This struggle was carried out within a Mexican state that sought to suppress indigenous cultural identities—Mexican ruling elites argued that plurality was divisive and sought ways to create a more homogenous nation through the assimilation of indigenous peoples into the mainstream. The government undertook programs to incorporate the indigenous peoples into the Mexican Republic, but without their cultural distinctiveness. Thus, the assimilationist policies that had been started by Spanish colonizers were adopted by the Mexican state and used to effectively undermine the ability of the indigenous peoples to develop themselves. Throughout most of post-independence Mexico, however, indigenous peoples continued to resist the cultural 'genocide' imposed on them by the Mexican state. The government reacted with forced removals and resettlements of large populations of indigenous peoples, usually to economically peripheral and inhospitable areas of the country. In addition, the government promulgated policies (e.g., privatization of lands that were owned communally by indigenous groups) that destroyed indigenous farming practices and negatively affected the ability of these people to support themselves.

According to this chapter, the present conditions of the indigenous peoples in Mexico are a testament to the inability or unwillingness of the state to design and implement policies that can enhance the welfare of these people. The 1994 rebellion globalized the struggle of Mexico's indigenous peoples for greater access to government and to the economy. That year, Mexico also became part of a larger economic community—the North American Free Trade Area (NAFTA). Advocates for the indigenous peoples had hoped that entry into NAFTA would force Mexican authorities to pay more attention to the needs of the country's indigenous populations, which continue to suffer from very high rates of poverty and deprivation. Although the government has undertaken several institutional reforms designed to improve conditions for the indigenous peoples, Martín believes that one of them, changes in Article 27 of the Mexican Constitution, may actually spell disaster for these peoples. That part of the constitution made it very difficult for communally owned lands to be sold legally. Since the amendment makes the sale of communally owned land legal, Martín believes that this could encourage poor indigenous groups to sell their land so as to obtain the cash they need to meet the short-terms needs of their families, leaving them without a way to support themselves in the long run. Since most of them are poorly educated and support themselves and their families primarily through farming and hunting, sale of their lands to developers from the urban areas of Mexico could prove disastrous as these people are likely to end-up homeless and unable to provide for themselves.

Mexico, which recently elected a new president—Vincente Fox, faces a lot of problems with respect to management of diversity. In order to deal effectively with these problems, the new government must engage in genuine dialogue with the indigenous peoples, while at the same time undertaking institutional reforms to (1) improve access to political and economic markets for indigenous populations; (2) enhance the ability of these people to govern themselves; (3) end discrimination against the indigenous peoples; (4) respect and value indigenous cultures; and (5) provide structures for the indigenous peoples to truly become part of Mexican society without giving up their identity.

In Chapter 8, William T. Vickers continues the study of indigenous peoples started by Martín in Chapter 7. Vickers' study, however, deals with politically sensitive border regions of Ecuador. In this brief study of the conditions affecting indigenous groups in Ecuador, Vickers begins by looking at the policies developed by the Ecuadorian military for dealing with indigenous communities in the Amazonian Ecuador, locally known as the *Oriente*. The treatment of the indigenous communities in the Oriente by the Ecuadorian state is influenced significantly by (1) the continuing border conflict between Ecuador and Peru; (2) the discovery of large oil deposits in the region; (3) the need for soldiers capable of living and fighting successfully in the extremely hostile and inhospitable equatorial climate; and (4) the Shuar Indians' reputation as fierce warriors and 'head hunters' with a long established military history. The army has successfully established linkages with the resident Indian populations in the Amazonian region that have helped the country tremendously in its border war with Peru.

The second area that Vickers examines is the northern Oriente, an area that borders Colombia. Small communities of Kofán, Siona, and Secoya Indians occupy this area. In this region of the country, however, the military mistrusts the indigenous populations and rarely uses them for military purposes as it defends Ecuador's oil fields against incursion by so-called 'subversive elements' and drug dealers from Colombia.

The southern Oriente is considered the ancestral homeland of the Jivaroan speaking peoples, among whom are the Shuar and Achuar. Today, the population of the two groups is estimated at between 20,000 and 30,000. Across the border in Peru, one can find several other Jivaroan speaking peoples, among whom are the Aguaruna and the Huambisa. As a result of tradition and historical accomplishments, the Shuar and Achuar are considered legendary and fierce warriors, highly respected not only in their communities but also by professional soldiers of the Ecuadorian military. Their strategic location along the disputed southern frontier, their relatively large population, and their aforementioned military fame, has made them desirable allies to the Ecuadorian army in its war against Peru. Thus, in the 1980s, military officers from Ecuador initiated and implemented a program to train elite Shuar units for use in further battles with Peru. Such linkages significantly improved state treatment of the Shuar. In addition to the fact that the government, through the military, has provided Shuar communities with medicines, food, educational facilities (mainly to train soldiers), and other amenities, the Ecuadorian state has also legalized Shuar land claims, a process that enhances property rights and decreases the chances of the appropriation of their lands by outside groups (e.g., multinational companies prospecting for oil and other environmental resources). Many Shuar leaders, however, are apprehensive of such close relationships with the state for fear that the government's concept of development may not be in line with theirs. In fact, in 1995, the Shuar of Bomboiza were fighting a Canadian company that was about to begin gold-mining operations in nearby communities. Of course, the Ecuadorian government had approved such operations, seeing them as an opportunity to develop the area and generate revenues that could be used for further development. The Shuar prefer projects that enhance indigenous organizations and the ability of the people to govern themselves and manage their own environment.

In the rich oil fields of the northern Oriente, the Ecuadorian army sees a different set of problems. First, the army must guarantee the security of the oil fields, which represent the country's most important source of wealth. Second, there does not appear to be any immediate threat of invasion by conventional forces. However, there are significant threats from drug dealers seeking a place to hide from Colombian anti-drug forces; Colombian anti-government guerillas; and illegal immigrants. As a result of the existence of these 'unconventional' threats, the military has adopted a cautious attitude toward the civilian population in the region since it is relatively difficult to recognize criminals and guerillas among the general population. The army, however, does not consider the small communities of Kofán, Siona and Secoya Indians in the northern Oriente as good allies.

In this area, traditional Indian territories do not coincide with Ecuador's boundaries with Colombia and Peru. In other words, the Indians who inhabit what is Ecuadorian territory may have relatives in Peru and/or Colombia. Unfortunately, the Ecuadorian army does not allow Indians within the country's borders to visit relatives across the border in Peru or hunt and gather food along the Peruvian frontier. On many occasions, the army has accused Secoya Indians of spying for Peru since Peru captured their homeland on the Santa María River during the 1941 war. The Secoya, Siona and Kofán consider the international boundaries between Ecuador, Peru and Colombia artificial creations of the European colonizers, designed primarily to serve their own objectives and not those of the indigenous peoples. In fact, many indigenous groups often prefer to ignore these boundaries while they conduct their activities in what they consider to be their ancestral lands. As a result of the relatively poor relations between the army and the Indians of the northern Oriente, the latter have been treated very poorly by the state. Quite often, many of them are denied permission to travel to traditional hunting and fishing grounds. In 1993, relations between Indian groups in the northern Oriente and the government of Ecuador reached an all-time low when the Indians joined several groups to file a law suit against Texaco for environmental damage caused by oil spills and the dumping of petroleum waste.

In conclusion, Vickers argues that Ecuador's policies toward the indigenous peoples are based on strategic economic and military interests and not necessarily on respect for these people or concern for their welfare. In the southern Oriente, Ecuador treats the Shuar and other indigenous groups relatively well because of their contributions to the nation's military struggle against incursions by Peru. Here, the indigenous groups have managed to retain a significant portion of their communal lands. In the northern Oriente, where there has been widespread displacement of indigenous peoples in order to give way for oil exploitation, indigenous groups are neglected, abused, marginalized and treated with scorn. In 1998, Ecuador adopted a new constitution, which declared the country a 'plural-cultural and multiethnic state' with the state charged with the job of promoting and enhancing national unity in diversity. This move is considered an important symbolic act that could signify greater respect for the country's indigenous peoples and their cultures. Whether the Ecuadorian state will use this instrument to improve the treatment of the indigenous peoples, provide them with structures to govern themselves and control the allocation of their resources, remains to be seen.

The end of the Cold War has brought with it increased demands, by many nationalist factions within many of the world's polities, for self-determination. The sudden disintegration of the Soviet Union and Yugoslavia and the sectarian violence that followed these monumental events seemed to support the long-held belief by some students of ethnicity that political maps should coincide with ethnic ones. By the dawn of the new millennium, Therese S. Gunawardena argues in Chapter 9, violent ethnic mobilization had become pervasive in several regions of the world. In an effort to stem the flood of secessionist aspirations, many governments have resorted to draconian methods to control so-called recalcitrant ethnic, religious and linguistic minorities within their borders.

Gunawardena argues that although there is a significant literature that studies the domestic context of both ethnic conflict and ethnonationalism, few researchers have ventured into the analysis of transnational factors that affect the dynamics of nationalist movements. Specifically, she argues, scholars of ethnic conflict have generally neglected the study of coethnic groups operating from abroad (i.e., diasporan groups) on nationalist and ethnopolitical conflicts. Thus, this chapter is devoted to an examination of the influence of the Sikh Diaspora on political developments in the Punjab in particular and in India in general. To accomplish this task and help the reader appreciate the motivation behind diasporan support for 'homeland' politics and the mechanisms employed to render such assistance, Gunawardena examines the historical development of two important ethnopolitical movements in India—Ghadar and Khalistan.

The Ghadar movement was a struggle to decolonize India and rid the territory of British influence. Khalistan, on the other hand, is an ongoing movement to carve out a separate Sikh state out of what is now Indian Punjab. Although there exists several similarities between the two movements, Gunawardena cautions that the Ghadar movement was a pan-Indian struggle that brought together Sikhs, Muslims and Hindus to free India from colonial rule. The Khalistan movement, on the other hand, is supported and underwritten exclusively by Sikh nationalists. She also adds that about half a century ago, Sikh participation in Ghadar helped secure independence for India; today, however, Sikh involvement in the Khalistan struggle is designed to destroy India's present territorial form. Further analysis of political developments in the Punjab are provided by Movindri Reddy in Chapter 11, where she undertakes a comparative study of ethnic conflict and violence in South Africa, Punjab and Sri Lanka.

In several sections of the chapter, Gunawardena reviews the history of Sikh migration, which ultimately resulted in the founding of significant Sikh communities in North America (notably in the US and Canada) and Europe (primarily in the UK). However, before providing the reader with an overview of the history of Sikh migration from India, she attempts to define the term 'Sikh.' Among several definitions contained in the literature for the term, 'ethnoreligious community' appears to be a relatively popular one. Based on that definition, Gunawardena states that there are presently about sixteen million Sikhs with about 8%–10% of that number living outside India. In some countries, Sikhs comprise a majority of the South Asian population (for example, in Britain, Sikhs make up more than 50% of all Indian immigrants). Of all Sikhs leaving outside India, most of them are concentrated in the UK, Canada and the US.

Since independence, India's internal and external political relations have been shaped significantly by the country's emigrant communities. Gunawardena argues that 'this phenomenon is exemplified in the case of overseas Sikhs whose specific migrant experience highlights the extent to which expatriates can exert leverage on and be influenced by the political conditions in their erstwhile homelands.'

According to Gunawardena, the founding of many Sikh institutions in North America is directly linked to the sociopolitical events that were taking place in both North America and in India at the time. One of the most important issues confronting Sikh immigrants in North America during the early years of settlement was the increasing racism and hostility they faced from white society. Also of concern to Sikh immigrants were the deteriorating economic, political and religious conditions in their homeland. Thus, many of the early Sikh institutions that were founded in North America were designed to (1) improve political and economic conditions for Sikhs living in Canada and the US; (2) provide structures for the education of Sikh children, in an effort to preserve their culture; (3) maintain Sikh religious and educational institutions in India; and (4) support the struggle against British colonialism in India.

In this thorough examination of the Ghadar and Khalistan movements, Gunawardena has provided the reader with important insights into how diasporas based on enduring ethnic affinities embrace political struggles in their homeland and in the process, influence political developments in the latter. The Ghadar movement, she concludes, shows how migrants have historically played a significant role in the politics of their homelands. The Khalistan movement, on the other hand, illustrates the way in which this role has been significantly expanded in this age of globalization.

Throughout history, ethnicity has played two important roles—a powerful constructive agent in state building and also a potent destabilizing one. Kingsley M. de Silva argues in Chapter 10 that 'in its most constructive phase, nationalism in alliance with ethnicity, was one of the principal driving forces in the successful agitation for independence against colonial rule, an integral part of the historical anti-colonial struggles of the post-second world war era.' Although ethnicity gave legitimacy to many of the nationalist struggles against European colonialism, it has proven to be one of the most important obstacles to the peaceful consolidation of power by these same nationalist forces in the post-colonial period. In Chapter 10, de Silva reviews the recent history and politics of Sri Lanka and Malaysia, two countries which he considers to be excellent case studies on the dual conflicting roles ethnicity plays.

When Sri Lanka gained independence from Britain, de Silva argues, nationalist leaders either underestimated or ignored the importance of ethnicity as a destabilizing force to power consolidation and state construction. Many of them felt that ascriptive ethnic identities were most likely to disappear in the face of the deliberate social change that was expected to accompany the construction of a new and modern Sri Lankan nation.

Unfortunately, these predictions did not come true as the optimistic phase lasted only ten years and the nation found itself overwhelmed by violent ethnic mobilization.

Malaysia's passage to independence was more violent as independence was won through a Communist insurgency directed at the colonial government and led by Malaysia's Chinese minority. Unlike the case in Sri Lanka at independence, there was little optimism for peaceful coexistence of ethnic groups in post-independence Malaysia.

According to de Silva, in colonial societies, once independence is achieved, there is then a struggle to determine who should rule the country. These struggles for capture of the apparatus of government are usually based on ethnicity and religion and not class. He argues that in Sri Lanka, where independence came through a negotiated settlement instead of through an armed rebellion, the struggle for control of the state was postponed for nearly ten years. The absence of violent mobilization in the immediate post-independence period in Sri Lanka, de Silva argues, can be attributed to (1) the leadership of the country's first prime minister, D. S. Senanayake; (2) the highly efficient and professional civil service inherited from the British; (3) a democratic system based on universal suffrage; and (4) a dynamic judiciary system and a well established social-welfare system. In fact, before independence in 1948, three successful general elections had been held in the territory.

De Silva argues that one need only study the policies pursued by the Sri Lankan government during the 1940s and 1950s to see how a multi-ethnic polity should be managed. One of the most important actions taken by Senanayake to improve governance in the country was his active recruitment into the government of members of minority ethnic groups in an effort to emphasize the multi-ethnic nature of the government. Later governments, unfortunately, were to ignore this inclusive approach to governance and force minority ethnic groups to engage in violent mobilization, creating the instability that has characterized Sri Lankan society since the early 1980s. According to de Silva, the country's descend into political violence was influenced significantly by (1) the government's unilateral change in language policy; (2) the policies of the Bandaranaikes (S. W. R. D. and Sirimavo), 1965–1970 and 1970–1977, which marginalized the minority Tamils; and (3) the destruction of the country's democratic system and tradition by Mrs. Bandaranaike's government.

In examining the case of Malaysia, de Silva begins by asking the following question: How did Malaysia succeed in maintaining a stable political structure and relatively harmonious relations between potentially antagonistic if not hostile ethnic groups while Sri Lanka failed to do so? Like his counterpart in the immediate post-independence period in Sri Lanka (S. D. Senanayake), Malaysia's first prime minister, Tunku Abdul Rahman, adopted a shrewd, pragmatic and inclusive approach to governance. Rahman, however, had a much more difficult environment to work with in post-independence Malaysia than was the case with Senanayake in Sri Lanka. Despite the fact that Rahman was presented with a country that went through a lot of structural changes during the first few years of independence, he was still able to build a governing coalition that allowed for peaceful state construction. One of his most important achievements was the formation of a political coalition consisting of ethnic political parties, which in various forms, has ruled the country to this day.

In the case where an ethnic conflict erupts and threatens to destroy peaceful coexistence in a country, de Silva argues, it takes extraordinary political skills to deal effectively with it. Malysian politicians, he states, have performed more effectively than their counterparts in Sri Lanka or even India in this regard. He goes on to say that of all the many reasons advanced to explain the successful management of ethnic relations in Malaysia and the fact that the country has been able to maintain peaceful coexistence of groups during most of its post-independence period, the 'evolution of a pragmatic political bargain between the principal ethnic groups in the country, the Malays and the Chinese' is the most important. He gives two other factors that explain the ability of Malaysia to sustain a stable and peaceful political system—the country's electoral system and the fact that there are no territories in Malaysia in which ethnic minorities form the majority of the population. Unlike Sri Lankan minorities, Malaysia's minority groups do not have territorial bases, which can serve as a homeland and thus, encourage separation aspirations. In addition, there is no regional power in the vicinity that seeks to exercise its influence on behalf of an ethnic minority as India has done in Sri Lanka.

In conclusion, de Silva states that the moral of Sri Lanka's experience is that hastily organized policies can destroy chances for peaceful coexistence and that once this is done, it is very difficult to remedy the situation and restore the peace. Evidence from Sri Lanka shows that violent ethnic mobilization is most likely to occur whenever the government decides to ignore, neglect or pay little attention to the legitimate interests and concerns of minority groups. The Malaysian experience, on the other hand, demonstrates how political stability and peaceful coexistence of groups can be assured if not guaranteed in polities with multi-ethnic populations. This can be done, as de Silva and other contributors to this volume have demonstrated, by providing the society with institutional arrangements that enhance the ability of minority groups to participate in governance and the allocation of resources. It is critical, for example, that existing laws and institutions provide minority groups relatively effective access to the highest levels of government.

In the final chapter of the book, Movindri Reddy undertakes a comparative analysis of ethnic conflict and violence in South Africa, Punjab and Sri Lanka. Her analysis complements the work done by K. M. de Silva (on Sri Lanka and Malaysia) and Therese S. Gunawardena (on the Punjab). Reddy, in Chapter 11, concentrates her analysis on gross human rights violations by the Zulu-dominated Inkatha Freedom Party (IFP) in apartheid South Africa; the activities of the Liberation Tigers of Tamil Eelam (LTTE) against the Sinhalese-led government of Sri Lanka; and Sikh battles for secession in the Punjabi region of India.

Like other contributors to this text, Reddy spends some time examining definitions for ethnicity and ethnic identities. Then, she examines the influence of colonialism on ethnic identities and the formation of ethnic associations. For example, she argues that soon after educated Zulus, Tamils, Sinhalese and Sikhs discovered that British colonial authorities were unwilling to see them as educated, skilled and competent *individuals* but viewed them primarily as 'modernized ethnics', they sought to enhance their political and economic power by forming more coherent ethnic organizations. In all three colonies (India, South Africa and Sri Lanka), the British used racial categories to analyze the non-European populations, drawing distinct hierarchical differences between the local people based on ethnicity. The Anglo-Saxon and his culture were placed at the pinnacle of this hierarchical social structure and provided with a lot of privileges.

South Africa gained independence in 1910 and established a government based on a racist constitution that effectively excluded the nation's black majority from participating in governance. In 1948, the apartheid state came into being and proceeded to formally restructure the nation's population into categories based on ethnicity and race. Under the new system, ethnic segregation was perfected and developed into an all-encompassing political agenda. It is within the social, political and economic environment created by the apartheid state that the Inkatha Freedom Party emerged and found a niche to operate.

In the case of Sri Lanka, Reddy argues that policies promulgated by D. S. Denanayake and S. W. R. D. Bandaraniake disenfranchised the Indian Tamils and pushed them to the periphery of Sri Lankan society. As already mentioned by de Silva, Reddy argues that the unilateral enactment of the

Official Language Act, which replaced English with Sinhala as the official language, had a significantly damaging effect on ethnic relations in the country. Later governments set geographic quotas on admission to the universities and higher entrance requirements for Tamils that had a negative effect on their educational attainment. Eventually, Sinhalese students came to monopolize higher education the same way that their parents were dominating the government. These developments set the stage for the violent mobilizations by the Tamils that started in the early 1980s.

At independence in 1947, Punjab was divided between India and Pakistan. In independent India, Sikhs made up about 2% of the population and were officially categorized as Hindus. Sikh leaders, however, have consistently argued that they are a distinct ethnoreligious group, separate from Hindus and Muslims. In the state of Punjab, Sikhs formed a majority (54% to 44% for the Hindus). Although leaders of the most important Sikh political party, the Akali Dal, thought they would dominate the political economy of the state because of the Sikh's population advantage, they soon discovered that the Congress party actually commanded more support among many Sikh voters than the Akali Dal. While the Akali Dal based its political fortunes on the notion of Sikh separateness and identity, the Sikh community in the Punjab believed that they stood to gain more by aligning themselves with the Hindu-dominated Congress party. Unable to capture more than 30% of the vote, the Akali Dal sought to portray the Indian government as an intrusive-absent state.

In all three cases, Reddy argues, identity is the basis of violence within the ethnic group. She concludes the chapter by arguing that violent ethnic mobilization is not only the result of immediate local causes and conditions, but is also the outcome of certain kinds of governance structures, and of the particular ways in which some governments deal with civil society.

In line with the title of this book, the contributors have sought to shed some light on the role played by ethnicity in governance in the Third World, using a few countries and regions as case studies. We have learned that ethnicity helped provide the legitimacy to many of the struggles against European colonialism in Africa, Latin America and Caribbean, Asia and the Middle East. Unfortunately, in the post-independence period, ethnicity became an important constraint to state construction and the consolidation of political power by the same ethnic-based coalitions that had fought for independence. Part of the problem comes from the activities of so-called 'ethnic entrepreneurs', who resorted to ethnicity in order to consolidate their political power and enhance their ability to monopolize political spaces indefinitely. Thus, the subsequent domination of political spaces and the allocation of resources by some ethnic groups forced locked-out groups to resort to violent mobilization either to gain access to political and economic markets or to secede and form their own polity. Today, many countries in the Third World are faced with deteriorating ethnic relationships. In many of these societies, inter-ethnic conflict, as well as conflict between ethnic nationalities and the state, are on the rise.

The contributors to this volume have made several policy relevant suggestions on how to better manage ethnic relations and improve peaceful coexistence. The most important suggestion, and the one that appears to be universal, is state reconstruction to provide institutional arrangements that (1) guarantee the rights of individuals to maintain their own identity; (2) accommodate the interests, aspirations and legitimate concerns of the various groups that inhabit the polity; (3) adequately constrain the state and prevent government officials from engaging in opportunism; (4) provide fair and predictable rules for competition and structures for the peaceful resolution of conflict; and (5) enhance the ability of minority groups to participate in governance.

References

Ayittey, G.B.N. (1992), *Africa Betrayed*, St. Martin's Press: New York.

Ayoade, J. A. A. (1988), 'States Without Citizens: An Emerging African Phenomenon', in Rothchild, D. and Chazan, N. (eds.), *The Precarious Balance: State and Society in Africa*, Westview Press: Boulder, CO.

Bates, R. H. (1983), 'Modernization, Ethnic Competition, and the Rationality of Politics in Contemporary Africa', in Rothchild, D. and Olorunsola, V. A. (eds.), *State Versus Ethnic Claims: Africa Policy Dilemmas*, Westview Press: Boulder, CO.

Breytenbach, W. J. (1976), 'Inter-Ethnic Conflict in Africa', in Veenhoven, W. A. (ed.), *Case Studies on Human Rights and Fundamental Freedoms*, Martinus Nijhoff: The Haque.

Brough, W. T. and Kimenyi, M. S. (1986), 'On the Inefficient Extraction of Rents by Dictators', *Public Choice*, Vol. 48, pp. 37–48.

Burgess, M. (1993), 'Federalism and Federation: A Reappraisal', in Burgess, M. and Gagnon, A.-G. (eds.), *Comparative Federalism and Federation: Competing Traditions and Future Directions*, Harvester Wheatsheaf: Hertfordshire, UK.

Burke, F. (1991), *Africa*, Houghton Mifflin: Boston, MA.

Chazan, N. (1988), 'Patterns of State-Society Incorporation and Disengagement in Africa', in Rothchild, D. and Chazan, N. (eds.), *The Precarious Balance: State and Society in Africa*, Westview Press: Boulder, CO.

Copson, R. W. (1994), *Africa's Wars and Prospects for Peace*, M. E. Sharp: Armonk, NY.

Fukuyama, F. (1989), 'The End of History?', *The National Interest*, No. 16 (Summer), pp. 3–18.

Furley, O. (ed.) (1995), *Conflict in Africa*, I.B. Tauris Publishers: London.

Greenland, J. (1976), 'Ethnic Discrimination in Rwanda and Burundi,' in Veenhoven, W. A. (ed.), *Case Studies on Human Rights and Fundamental Freedoms*, Vol. IV, Martinus Nijhoff: The Haque.

Harik, I. F. (1972), 'The Ethnic Revolution and Political Integration in the Middle East', *International Journal of Middle East Studies*, Vol. 3, No. 3 (July), pp. 303–323.

Henze, P. (1985), 'Rebels and Separatists in Ethiopia: Regional Resistance to a Marxist Regime', Report Prepared for the Office of the Under Secretary of Defense for Policy, Santa Monica: Rand Corporation.

Horowitz, D. (1984), 'Democracy in Divided Societies', in Diamond, L. and Plattner, M.F (eds.), *Nationalism, Ethnic Conflict and Democracy*, The Johns Hopkins University Press: Baltimore, MD.

Horowitz, D. (1985), *Ethnic Groups in Conflict*, University of California Press: Berkeley, CA.

Horowitz, D. (1994), 'Democracy in Divided Societies', in Diamond, L. and Plattner, M. F. (eds.), *Nationalism, Ethnic Conflict, and Democracy*, The Johns Hopkins University Press: Baltimore, MD.

Jenkins, J. C. and Kposowa, A. J. (1990), 'Explaining Military Coups d'État: Black Africa, 1957–1984', *American Sociological Review*, Vol. 55, pp. 861–975.

Jenkins, J. C. and Kposowa, A. J. (1992), 'The Political Origins of African Military Coups: Ethnic Competition, Military Centrality, and the Struggle Over the Postcolonial State', *International Studies Quarterly*, Vol. 36, pp. 271–292.

Kimenyi, M.S. (1989), 'Interest Groups, Transfer Seeking and Democratization: African Political Stability', *The American Journal of Economics and Sociology*, Vol. 48, pp. 339–349.

Kimenyi, Mwangi S. (1997), *Ethnic Diversity, Liberty and the State: The African Dilemma*, Edward Elgar: Aldershot.

Kimenyi, Mwangi S. and Mbaku, John M. (eds.) (1999), *Institutions and Collective Choice in Developing Countries: Applications of the Theory of Public Choice*, Ashgate Publishing Limited: Aldershot, UK and Brookfield, VT.

Kimenyi, M. S. and Shughart, W. F. (1989), 'Political Successions and the Growth of Government', *Public Choice*, Vol. 62, pp. 173–179.

Landa, Janet Tai, (1997), *Trust, Ethnicity and Identity*, The University of Michigan Press: Ann Arbor.

Mbaku, J. M. (1994a), 'Bureaucratic Corruption and Policy Reform in Africa', *Journal of Social, Political and Economic Studies*, Vol. 19, pp. 149–175.

Mbaku, J. M. (1994b), 'Military Coups as Rent-Seeking Behavior', *Journal of Political and Military Sociology*, Vol. 22, pp. 241–284.

Mbaku, J. M. (1995), 'Military Intervention in African Politics: Lessons from Public Choice', *Konjunkturpolitik*, Vol. 41, No. 3, pp. 268–291.

Mbaku, J. M. (1997), *Institutions and Reform in Africa: The Public Choice Perspective*, Praeger: Westport, CT.

Mbaku, J. M and Kimenyi, M. S. (1995), 'Democratization in Africa: The Continuing Struggle', *Coexistence*, Vol. 32, pp. 119–36.

McGowan, P. and Johnson, T. (1984), 'Military Coups d'État and Underdevelopment: A Quantitative Historical Analysis', *The Journal of Modern African Studies*, Vol. 22, pp. 633–666.

Meisler, S. (1976), 'Holocaust in Burundi, 1972', in Veenhoven, W. A. (ed), *Case Studies on Human Rights and Fundamental Freedoms*, Vol. V, Martinus Nijhoff: The Haque.

Morrison, D. G., et al. (1972), *Black Africa: A Comparative Handbook*, Free Press: New York.

Nagel, J. (1995), 'Resource Competition Theories', *American Behavioral Scientist*, Vol. 38, No. 3 (January), pp. 442–458.

Roback, J. (1991), 'Plural But Equal: Group Identity and Voluntary Integration', *Social Philosophy and Policy*, Vol. 8, No. 2, pp. 60–80.

Tordoff, W. (1993), *Government and Politics in Africa*, Indiana University Press: Bloomington, IN.

Winchester, N.B. (1986), 'Africa Politics Since Independence', in Martin, P. and O'Meara, P. (eds.), *Africa*, Indiana University Press: Bloomington, IN.

Yinger, J. M. (1981), 'The Dialectics of Cultural Pluralism: Concept and Reality', in Young, C. (ed.), *The Rising Tide of Cultural Pluralism: The Nation-State at Bay?*, The University of Wisconsin: Madison, WI.

2

Federalism and the Ethnic Question in Africa

EGHOSA E. OSAGHAE

Introduction

Of all the attempts to resolve ethnic problems by constitutional means, federalism stands out clearly as the most prescribed option for divided societies (Watts, 1970; Ordeshook and Shvetsova, 1997). This should, *prima facie,* make sub-Saharan Africa, with its catalog of state-challenging and stability-threatening ethnic conflicts one of the world's leading centers of federalism. But this is not the case, as federalism has failed to take firm roots on the continent. This does not amount to saying that federalism has failed, but that it has not been really or properly applied. This has been attributed to a number of factors. One is that consultation, reciprocity, and compromise, all elements of federal political culture and what Horowitz (1993) calls multi-ethnic democracy, and necessary for the emergence and sustenance of federalism, are in short supply. What predominates is cutthroat zero-sum political competition and politics of exclusion.

Another is the entrenchment of presidentialism, personal autocratic rulership and attendant informalization of politics, scant regard for constitutional rules, and (over)centralization of power, which are not conducive to federalism and constitutional rule in general (cf. Chabal and Daloz,

1999). There is also the psychological premise of inequality defined by Dent (1989, p. 176) as 'the sense of inherent superiority to others that several African ethnic groups [for example the Amhara in Ethiopia, Americo-Liberians in Liberia, Hausa/Fulani and other major ethnic groups in Nigeria] possess as a result of their long tenure of dominant power'. The premise of inequality has been a major source of strain and instability in the Nigerian federation and is also likely to be the case in Ethiopia where Amhara domination has been at the core of the country's political problems. But all these have not made the federal solution less alluring or less relevant in Africa (for strong arguments in this regard, see Elaigwu and Olorunsola, 1983; Dent, 1989; Adamolekun and Kincaid, 1991).

The 1980s and 1990s were particularly notable for the return of federalism to the political agenda of several countries after it disappeared from the scene in the early 1960s. These were the years of unprecedented economic and social crises, political conflict and instability, when aggrieved ethnic groups rose to challenge the validity of the imperial post-colonial state and demand its reconstruction and revalidation on the bases of inclusion, equitable power and resource sharing, negotiated constitutional settlement, decentralization, and democracy (cf. Joseph, 1999). The forces unleashed in the milieu of democratization, economic decline and reforms within which these demands were made, reinforced the relevance and utility of federal principles as core elements of the multi-ethnic or plural democracy necessary for reducing tension and conflicts in multi-ethnic states (Osaghae, 1999a).

Federalism in fact gained currency in the search for new constitutional and political configurations that could save the endangered state from disintegration (Olukoshi and Laasko, 1995). For fairly obvious reasons, the ensuing federal debate was more pungent in ethnically divided countries with a political pedigree of federal ideas (Sudan, Cameroon, Uganda, Kenya, Ethiopia, South Africa, Tanzania, Democratic Republic of Congo, and Ghana). But the relevance of the federal solution, or at least some of its consociational variants, including decentralization/segmental autonomy and power sharing, to other countries, including those torn apart by protracted civil wars, like Liberia, Angola and Somalia, and the countries of the Great Lakes region, was also debated. Federalism indeed had something of a new beginning in Africa, for in addition to the reinvigorated debate, Ethiopia became the first full-fledged post-colonial federal system. Aggrieved groups in Nigeria, the only full-fledged federation in the continent until the 1990s, also found occasion to question the non-federal trajectories of the country. They demanded the latter's restructuring into a true federation in the light of new realities and demands of the national question (Amuwo et al., 1998).

The resurgence of federalism raises a number of questions over constitutional and institutional mechanisms for managing pluralities. It also provides the opportunity to reassess the whole question of the tenability of the federal solution to ethnic problems in Africa. The key questions are: is federalism really a solution to the ethnic question? If so, why has it had such a poor run in Africa? Are African states finally ready to appropriate the much-touted curative or talismanic powers of the federal solution to ethnic problems, as suggested, for example, by the adoption of a federal constitution in Ethiopia? If so, under what conditions is the federal solution likely to work where it failed in the past? The attempt in this chapter is to provide answers to these questions.

Federalism and the ethnic question: an introduction

As the chapter hinges on the argument that federalism is a veritable instrument of conflict management,[1] we shall close this introductory section with an elaboration of how federalism attempts to deal with the ethnic question, which is also referred to as the national question. The underlying premise of the federal solution is that the most peaceful and democratic way to ensure the stability and survival of divided societies where competing ethnic, racial, cultural, religious and regional claims are fundamental to political competition and there are strong sentiments for the protection of these identities, is to offer room for self-expression and relative autonomy of the groups, while at the same time guaranteeing the groups access to and participation in power structures at the center. 'The genius of federation', Burgess (1993, p. 7) has written, 'lies in its infinite capacity to accommodate and reconcile the competing and sometimes conflicting array of diversities having political salience within a state'.

In other words, federalism presupposes that the expression of subnational claims is legitimate and not incompatible with the goal of national integration on which most divided societies place great value; that, in fact, the state is likely to face problems of separatism and instability if the claims are unacknowledged or suppressed. However, it is important to stress that federalism cannot work where the claimant groups lack a minimum consensus on coexistence, and prefer to live separately. Also, federalism of the full-fledged constitutional variety (see below) is not necessary where diversity is not so fundamental to politics as to require constitutional recognition and representation. In such cases, mild federal doses, involving basic federal principles of power sharing and decentralization, are usually enough to deal with off and on ethnic problems when they do become salient.

This is perhaps the greatest strength of the federal solution: it offers a variety of options that accord with the depth of division and degree of political accommodation required. As Daniel Elazar (cited in Kotze, 1995, p. 69) has noted,

> Utilising the federal principle does not necessarily mean establishing a federal system in the conventional sense of modern federation... federalism is a phenomenon that provides many options for the organisation of political authority and power; as long as the proper relations are created, a wide variety of political structures can be developed that are consistent with federal principles.

Although it does not solve, as in eliminating, ethnic problems—it may in fact reify differences instead—federalism does provide, firstly, an opportunity for self-actualization by competing groups in divided societies and, secondly, a legal and institutional framework for reconciling differences, reducing conflicts, and protecting the interests of groups, especially ethnic minorities, which otherwise would be marginalized, excluded and dominated (Diamond, 1999, p. 151).[2] Federalism is therefore a device for political stability in divided societies.

But federalism is not all pros when it comes to dealing with the ethnic question. It also has cons that are equally important, which is why, as we point out in the next section, federalism is a contested rather than a settled option. First is that, as was pointed out earlier, it cannot help much in situations where component groups of a state have resolved to go their separate ways—where things have so fallen apart that the center can no longer hold. Secondly, the federal solution to the ethnic question has not always worked. The collapse of the former Soviet Union and Yugoslavia, the stresses that the Canadian federal system, which is one of the oldest federal systems, continues to face with regard to Quebeçois separatism, and the so-called failure of federalism in Nigeria, are cases in point.

Third and most importantly from the point of view of divided states, which desire national integration, federalism poses the inherent danger of making a polity more divided. Some scholars believe federalism is a first step towards separation and secession as it fosters and legitimizes claims to nation-statehoods through protection of language, culture, religion, and paraphernalia of statehood such as own constitution, government, re-sources, anthem, and flag (cf. Linz, 1997). Indeed, the coupling of the resurgence of federalism with the escalation of violent ethnic conflicts in the 1980s and 1990s seemed to vindicate the argument of nationalist critics of federalism that it encourages and legitimizes state-challenging ethnic demands.

These shortfalls and dangers indicate that the federal solution, like any other human system, is not foolproof, and point to the need to be circum-spect in the application and design of federal systems. But they do not detract from the powers and resilience of federalism, which have been demonstrated time and again. For example, the collapse of the old Soviet Union was not so much a failure of federalism as it was of the weakening of federalism by unfederal socialist practices and Russian domination. Similarly, the so-called 'failure' of federalism in Nigeria, which was the basis for the clamor for political restructuring in the 1990s, was actually a failure to practice true federalism under prolonged military rule.

In both cases, the absence of democracy, which is sine qua non for federalism, severely limited the capacity of the federal system to work. The danger of deepening division and encouraging secession has been dis-missed as 'slippery reasoning' by Diamond (1999, p. 156) who argues that not only have multinational federations such as Canada, Spain, and Swit-zerland, persevered through periods of national conflict, but also that in federations like India and Nigeria, 'federalism has done more to relieve or contain secessionist pressures than to stimulate them'. Welsh (1989, p. 263) has also argued that unitary arrangements, the most commonplace alterna-tive to federal arrangements, are not strong enough to withstand the onslaught of ethnic and racial mobilization, and are not capable of 'stand-ing up to the stresses of conflict that deeply divided societies most regularly manifest' (Welsh, 1989, p. 263).

On balance then, federalism is a veritable instrument for addressing the ethnic question. Conceived in these terms, there can be no doubting the relevance of federal solution(s) to conflictual multiethnic situations in Africa, especially in view of the fact that the spate of separatist agitations and violent conflicts/wars have not altered the composition of states inherited from colonial authorities. The separatist agitations and conflicts that characterize politics in the states however indicate that the survival of these countries cannot be taken for granted, and point to more equitable politics of accommodation and compromise, which federalism in general offers, as the appropriate solution. This explains, in large part, the bringing back in of federalism in the 1980s and 1990s which witnessed the heightening of the stakes of the national question as a result of severe ethnic conflicts and civil war.

Although Ethiopia remains the only country in Africa to have adopted a federal constitution specifically to address the ethnic question, other countries, notably South Africa, Angola, and Sudan have found varieties of the federal genus expedient in the political proposals and restructuring introduced to salvage the endangered post-colonial state. All this is in addition to Nigeria where the federal solution has witnessed several experimentations and revisions to cope with the dynamics of the ethnic question, since the federal constitution was first adopted in 1954. Notwithstanding the travails and instability of Nigeria's federal system (Suberu, 1993), some studies have pointed to the remarkable gains in ethnic conflict management made possible by the federal formula (Elaigwu and Olorunsola, 1983; Ekeh and Osaghae, 1989; Osaghae, 1994; Nmoma, 1995). A few studies have suggested, on the basis of a comparison of ethnic conflict management in Nigeria and other African countries, that the multiple centers of power in Nigeria and the attendant dispersal of conflicts from the center have made for better management, in contrast to several countries in East and Central Africa where every minor conflict had the potential of becoming nationally consequential (see, e.g., Wunsch and Olowu, 1990).

Yet, federalism has had a difficult run in Africa to the extent that basic federal principles that could be taken for granted such as executive power sharing and decentralization have been difficult bargains. As a result, the ethnic management capacity of federalism has yet to be maximized and remains for the most part, a potential not yet realized. The rest of the chapter will examine how and why this has been the case.

Federalism in African political discourse and practice: an outline

In this section, we shall (i) attempt to sketch the outline of an emergent or tentative African tradition or perspective of federalism; and (ii) periscope and evaluate the experience with federalism in the continent. These provide the necessary conceptual and empirical background to the analysis of the travails of federalism in the next section.

Federalism and its political uses

The various uses to which federalism has been put (political, economic, social, intra-state and inter-state) create different paradigms of federalism which, in turn, produce varieties in definition and design (Elazar, 1987; Burgess, 1993). For example, approaching federalism as a system of government, one is likely to be overly legal-constitutional, restrictive, and inflexible. Dent (1989, p. 170) doubts if we would have any federal system to study in Africa in this case, whereas a sociological approach that relates federalism to the nature of the society it serves is likely to be more pragmatic and dynamic.

However, the differing perspectives do not detract from the essence of federalism as a political system that has more than one determinate level of government (federal, state, and local levels) and in which power is exercised by each and all the levels in a shared and cooperative manner. This essence, most students of federalism agree, is the minimum requirement that a political system has to meet in order to be considered federal. To this end, federalism may be defined, from a broad political uses/solution perspective, which is the approach in this chapter, as 'a political device for establishing viable institutions and flexible relationships capable of facilitating inter-state relations...inter-state linkages...and inter-community cooperation' (Gagnon, 1993, p. 15).

This definition emphasizes the ends-means nexus which is central to federalism, the point being that federalism is a purposive system of government designed to bring about ends that typically have to do with balancing unity and diversity. As King (1982, p. 146) points out, 'for all its institutional character, a federation is still governed by purpose, and this reflects values and commitments'. The 'viable institutions and flexible relationships' may be designed to ensure local autonomy, central power sharing, strengthen the powers of the central government or constituent governments, and so on, in so far as these are capable of meeting the desired goals, and fit the circumstances of the political society. The emphasis here is on the dynamics of federalism as a process which explains the variety in federal devices (Osaghae, 1997).

Briefly, the devices can be classified into two broad categories, which may however be fused in real federal situations. First is the category of full-fledged federal government, which involves the operation of a federal constitution and involves, guaranteed territorial dispersal of (non-centralized) power. Second is the category of federalism without federation, which mostly involves non-territorial devices for accommodating diversity.

The hallmark of this category of federalism is that although a federal constitution may not be formally adopted, federal principles (not in the singular sense of dividing power between two tiers of government emphasized by Wheare (1967)) are applied in the organization and operation of government.

The principles referred to here include decentralization and non-territorial consociational devices, notably executive power sharing, quota system, segmental autonomy and minority veto. The distinctions between the two categories are not hard and fast because as pointed out earlier, they may overlap. Federations like Nigeria, for example, have adopted consociational devices to enhance the capacity of federalism's politics of compromise. Also, Ethiopia's adoption of a federal constitution after a run of operating federal principles, and South Africa's incrementalist federalizing process, suggest that federalism without federation may be a step in the process of becoming a federation, as the paradigm of evolutionary federalism makes clear (Agranoff, 1996).

Finally, what is interesting from the African experience is that while federalism as federation is limited (Nigeria and Ethiopia are the only two in this category), federalism without federation is popular as power holders have found ethnic arithmetic formulas and more recently decentralization schemes expedient legitimization strategies. Despite their popularity and expediency however, federal or consociational principles have not produced the desired effects largely because of the prevalent contradictory pulls of over-centralization and presidentialism, which are discussed in the next section.

The evolving African tradition of federalism

The resilience of federalism is partly explained by the enduring traditions of the system of government. The two established traditions, which however have overlaps and variations, and from which newer federations have generally taken their cues, are the continental European and Anglo-American traditions (possibly a third tradition whose federal status was highly contested while it lasted was the socialist federal tradition led by the Union of Soviet Socialist Republics—USSR).[3]

Although federalism in Africa is still in search of a tradition, partly due to the discontinuities in federal experiences and what Ayoade (1978) calls the high mortality rate of federal systems, enough is known of its origins, uses and trajectories, to enable us to sketch the outline of a tentative African paradigm of federalism.[4] Federalism may not be alien to Africa, as the existence of federal-like arrangements such as the Egba and Fanti confederacies in pre-colonial Nigeria and Ghana suggests, but its contemporary existence has colonial origins. Given the arbitrariness involved in the delineation of the boundaries of the present states, and in the forced incorporation of groups into them, colonial federalism which the British led, was a device for holding together and administering the highly artificial states.[5] However, the federal formula did not operate only at the level of colony-state. It also extended to attempts at supra-state union. Once again British colonies took the lead in this, forming the Central Africa federation of Northern and Southern Rhodesia and Nyasaland, and the abortive federations of Southern Africa and Eastern Africa. The French also created supra-state federations—*Afrique Equatorial Française* and *Afrique Occidental Française*—to enhance the administration of its colonies. The French federations came to an end with the *loi cadre* of 1956, which restored autonomy to individual colonies in preparation for independence.

In the post-colonial period, the federal formula became more generalized, although it retained the state-integrating, problem-solving and administrative convenience imprint of colonial federalism. These were the major considerations that guided the federal formulas employed in the reintegration of Western (Anglophone) and Francophone Cameroon in 1961, the integration of Tanganyika and Zanzibar into Tanzania in 1964, as well as the adoption of federal constitutions by Sudan in 1972, and Ethiopia first in 1952 and more recently in 1995.

With such pedigree, federalism has been rightly regarded as a device for managing the political problems of divided multiethnic states (Beloff, 1953), as a means of state consolidation and nation building (Mckown, 1988), and as a formula for inter-state fusion, integration and cooperation.[6] We are concerned with the first two uses which relate directly to the ethnic question, although the important lesson taught by the high mortality rate of inter-state federations—that Africa's social and political structures and practices may not be conducive to the aggregative federalizing process—cannot be ignored. Indeed, Thomas-Woolley and Keller (1994, p. 418) attribute the inability to fully appreciate the utility of the federal formula to the disaggregative rather than aggregative tendencies, and suggest that some countries 'may need to split apart completely and then later decide to federate after having experienced the problems/dangers inherent in complete autonomy, or after having developed a sense of equality and mutual respect'.

A return to the uses of federalism that relate directly to the ethnic question should begin with an important caveat. The 'objective' statement of the perceived uses of federalism does not imply that there is consensus on the desirability and suitability of the federal solution in Africa's ethnically divided states. If anything, federalism has been highly contested between, on the one hand, hegemonic centralist-nationalists who are averse to divisions of any political significance and therefore favor a unitarist-assimilationist strategy of nation building and, on the other, those who insist on a multi-layered approach which holds that sub-national claims to self-determination are not incompatible with nation building and that a viable nation-state is impossible without the protection of the diverse interests of groups in the country. Ayoade's (1978, p. 6) assertion that 'perhaps the most distinguishing characteristic of African federalism is...that it is a device for providing union without unity' is therefore only partially true, as federalism would offer very little attraction to state power holders if it is solely defined in such terms.

The assimilationists, who usually control state power, are most reluctant to preside over divided polities with potential for dissolution, and accept federalism if at all, only as a temporary measure, that is, until a sufficient degree of national integration that would make federal structures redundant, is attained (Mckown, 1988). For them, federalism is at best a means to an end rather than an end in itself which Ayoade's 'union without unity', and the implied suggestion of immutability, implies.[7] The debate over federalism, which was one of the dominant issues in South Africa's transition to the post-apartheid order, provides perhaps the best illustration of this contestation. The African National Congress, which was set to take over the reins of power from the National Party, saw the demands for federalism/regionalism by the latter and its strategic allies in the transition negotiations, especially the Inkatha Freedom Party, its main rival in the liberation struggle, as part of the design to keep the country divided along apartheid lines so as to preserve the privileges enjoyed by the white minority, and weaken the ANC's control of state power (cf. Kotze, 1995; Osaghae, 1999b).

What do we make of such contestation, which goes to the very heart of the tenability of the federal solution? It is not that any of the contesting views, which can produce a matching federal design (centralized and non-centralized variants, for example), is right or wrong. The point that needs to be understood is that the mere fact of diversity is not sufficient for groups to demand the right to self-determination or the protection of diversity or, even, federalism. This is especially so in Africa where federalism has mostly come through disaggregation, and where, therefore, the central government retains a great deal of power. It is the extent to which the central government manages or mismanages diversity to accentuate or reduce injustices and inequalities of power relations which underlies demands for self-expression and self-determination, that is more important. Timing is also important, as prompt response to grievances can nip potentially explosive conflicts in the bud, and make elaborate federal solutions unnecessary.

In South Africa, for example, one of the greatest threats to the transition to the post-apartheid order was the (sometimes violent) demand for a *volkstaat* (a separate Afrikaner nation) which, the white-Afrikaner right-wing reckoned, was the only check to the expected redressive and redistribution agenda of the ANC. By conceding to the demands by the moderate arm of the right-wingers, represented by General Constand Viljoen's Freedom Front, for a Volkstaat Council (which was provided for in the 1993 interim constitution) to, amongst others, seek legitimate means and ways of actualizing the idea of a Volkstaat, the ANC managed to reduce the tension and save the country the calamity of a full scale Afrikaner war of self-determination. At least the Council was able to engage the ANC government in pursuance of Afrikaner interests, and in 1996, it organized an international conference on the right to self-determination. Although no provision was made in the 1996 (final) constitution for the council, the virtual granting of the right of self-determination to groups desiring it, the guarantee of the rights to language, religion and culture for members of all groups, and the wide-ranging powers enjoyed by the provinces, including the writing of their own constitutions, all have gone a long way to reduce the agitations for separate states, not only for white Afrikaners but also other minorities, including the Indians and Coloreds, and members of the powerful Zulu group.

One point that is not often acknowledged is that demands for self-determination, like other human rights, are a weapon of empowerment and emancipation used by weak, marginalized and excluded groups to seek redress of inequitable power configurations (Shivji, 1989; Osaghae, 1996). The struggle may even be a more fundamental one for survival and affirmation of the humanity of the group (Ake, 1993). According to this logic, tensions and conflicts arising from diversity can become less troubling—diversity cannot be eliminated—if the federal system is able to protect the interests of the composite groups and address the problems of inequality and injustice in ways acceptable to aggrieved groups. Those countries, which have adopted federal principles in Africa, expect to reap such benefits, as the alternative is secession and violent confrontations.

This brings us to the other point that because of its close association with demands for the right to self-determination, federalism is an ideology of political contestation and struggle. This may not have been so obvious because of the tendency to prescribe federalism as an 'objective' solution to problems of multi-ethnicity (cf. Welsh, 1989), but the explosion of ethnic demands in the throes of democratization in the 1980s and 1990s finally opened our eyes to the ideological uses of federalism. In the struggle to emancipate themselves from the oppression of exclusionary rule perpetrated by erstwhile one-party and military governments, minority and other previously marginalized or excluded groups demanded the reconfiguration of extant power structures and one form of constitutional protection or the other to prevent future relapse to what was in some cases internal colonialism. The demands, which could only be met through the application of federal principles, ranged from power sharing and resource redistribution to local political autonomy and other correlates of the right to self-determination, including protection of language, culture and religion.

Those who demanded outright federalism to preserve or restore (lost) power and privileges, or to enhance their capacity to contest for state power, constituted a separate category of relatively more powerful reconfiguration-seeking groups. These were groups with strong separatist histories or potential, having existed previously as independent political entities (Natal federalists in the 1910 Union of South Africa), or been displaced from power (white Afrikaners in South Africa), or previously enjoyed privileges of autonomy under federal arrangements (Anglophone Cameroon, Baganda *federos*), or were large enough to stand on their own in separate states (the Oromo and other separatists in Ethiopia), or were involved in civil wars with important self-determination dimensions (UNITA-allied groups in Angola, Mandingos and Krahns in Liberia). To this category also belonged the Rift Valley neo-majimboists in Kenya, led by Kalenjin political elites, who in typical counter-revolutionary fashion, sought a return to the majimbo or regional constitution of the early 1960s to protect their interests after Moi's demise from power, as well as Northern hegemonists who favor the federal option in Sudan, and the Southern majority groups (Yoruba mainly and Igbo to a lesser extent) in Nigeria who demanded a restructuring of the federation along confederal lines as a way of reducing the dangers of alleged domination by the North and enhancing their own access to federal power and resources.

Although state power holders manipulated and acceded to some of these demands in the bid to hold on to power at all cost, and because political stability could not be guaranteed without doing so, the fundamental weakness and powerlessness of the groups, especially minorities, demanding federal solutions meant that the emancipatory potentials of federal solutions were still highly circumscribed. For example, while many governments found decentralization expedient (in some cases it was pressure from international donors that forced them to do so), they undermined its capacity for engendering local political autonomy by starving the decentralized units of funds and any real responsibilities (the units were to function as administrative agencies of the central government), and promptly recentralized once pressure from opposition and the danger of state dissolution appeared to have eased off.

One way of summarizing all that has been said so far would be that the distinguishing mark of federalism in Africa is that it is a means to an end rather than an end it itself.[8] This is not surprising, considering that the hallmark of the federalizing process in Africa is that it has mostly been disaggregative rather than aggregative—it is in aggregative situations where formerly independent states continue to insist on their rights of relative autonomy, that federalism is likely to be an end in itself. But the larger implication of the disaggregative nature of federalism is the inherent proprietary powers it gives to the central government. This has been a major source of problems for federalism in Africa, as it has been possible for the central government to unilaterally abrogate federal constitutions and arrangements, contrary to the tenets of thoroughgoing federalism.

The recent phase of federalism in Africa

While acknowledging the utility of federal principles, evaluations of the experience have mostly been negative. Of the over nine colonial and postcolonial federations, only Nigeria managed to survive, albeit on a shoestring and sometimes only in name, until the emergence of the Ethiopian federation in 1995. The others were either abrogated by hegemonic postcolonial authorities and replaced by unitary and quasi-federal states (Ethiopia, Libya, Cameroon, Sudan, Tanzania, Uganda, and to some extent Kenya), or simply collapsed (Central African federation, Ghana-Guinea Union, Mali federation). Then there were a few others such as the Union of South Africa (1910) and Ghana where initial federal ideas could not stand the test of time.

Our immediate concern is not, however, with what might be called the old phase of federalism, which happily has received some attention in the literature (cf. Rothchild, 1966; Ayoade, 1978; Elaigwu and Olorunsola,

1983; Dent, 1989; Adamolekun and Kincaid, 1991). Federalism did not fare as well as it should have in this period because of the overly optimistic hopes about the future of the post-colonial state—what Ottaway (1999, p. 302) calls the early illusion of the movement from tribalism to nation-building. In the hurry to develop and become nations, as the dominant modernization paradigm prescribed, and the way they perceived advanced industrialized countries to have done, African states had little room, if at all, for (federal) arrangements which for them celebrated division, regionalism, ethnic (opposition) parties, and all.

Indeed, attempts were made to delegitimize ethnic politics, and subnational claims that posed even the slightest threat to the state (actually the president and the ruling party) were violently suppressed (Neuberger, 1986). It took the desperation to survive the devastating economic decline and crisis, including structural adjustment programs, and the ventilation offered by the wind of democratization that swept through Africa, beginning from the late 1980s, to realize the ineptitude of the old wisdom. The harvest of rising ethnic tensions, violent conflicts and protracted wars that rocked the foundations of the state and threatened to pull them down, finally forced state power holders to search for more accommodationist models of state-building (see for example, the movement from 'confrontation' to 'accommodation' in Zimbabwe in Sithole, 1995). Federalism was perhaps the most popular model of the new dawn, its major attraction being, once again, that it offered a dependable means of keeping the state together.

The scope of consideration of federal options was far wider than at any other time in Africa.[9] This followed demands, in virtually every country that underwent democratic transition, for equitable power sharing, redress of extant disparities and redistribution of resources, and local political autonomy as minorities and other aggrieved groups capitalized on the return of multiparty politics, the accent on good governance and human, including group, rights in the democratization process, and the support and intervention of the international community to press for reconfiguration of the post-colonial state. The responses to the demands included decentralization, executive power sharing, and the fostering of the values of tolerance, compromise, accountability and reciprocity, all federal elements, although these remained highly tentative and tokenist. In some cases, they were calculated to enable state power holders to buy time, as it were, to allow the pressure of demands to cool off, or they became strong enough to return to familiar paths of suppression and hegemony.

But the most ardent federal proposals were in countries with federal antecedents (Cameroon, Kenya, South Africa, Uganda, and Ethiopia). We shall briefly look at the cases of Kenya and Uganda, where there were moves to restore old federal orders, though for different reasons. In Uganda, Baganda *federos* held demonstrations in 1994 to back up demands for a return to a federal arrangement akin to that of the 1961 constitution that granted special federal status to the powerful Buganda kingdom. They faced stiff opposition from the majority of the unitarist Constituent Assembly delegates from other groups who have historically feared Baganda domination in a federal set up. In an important editorial, the *New Vision* (October 15, 1994) referred to the demand for a federal kingdom of Buganda as a fantasy, and argued that 'a cultural monarchy combined with decentralization of power to the districts offers the best possible solution to the problem of Buganda'.

In Kenya, it was a counter-revolutionary replay of the scenario in the period immediately after independence when the opposition coalition—led by Rift Valley Kalenjin elites who dominated KADU and white minority leaders anxious to keep land rights and other privileges—successfully fought for the *majimbo* constitution, whose guarantee of regional autonomy at least assuaged the fears of Kikuyu-KANU hegemony. That constitution was repealed and replaced with a unitary one in 1964 after KANU absorbed KADU and neutralized the opposition. Then in late 1991, Kalenjin elites, led by Nicholas Biwott, rose up to demand a return to the majimbo constitution. What was at issue, once again was the threat of Kikuyu domination, but this time, regional autonomy was being demanded to preserve the privileges enjoyed by the Kalenjins under president Arap Moi, a Kalenjin. In addition, the Kalenjins sought to avert or reduce possible reprisal against them by the Kikuyu after Moi eventually leaves office. The 'ethnic cleansing' that hallmarked the attempt to forcibly evict Kikuyu settlers from the Rift Valley in the period immediately preceding the majimbo proposals, however, suggests that the old issue of land rights was still important in the struggle between the Kikuyus and the Kalenjins (Ngunyi, 1995).[10]

In a report in *The Weekly Review* (October 7, 1994, p. 4), Biwott (a Kalenjin leader), boasted that the Kalenjin were there to stay 'even after president Moi's tenure has expired'. The former minister went on to state that the Kalenjin would not succumb to threats and harassment from any quarter and would fight for equal rights with other Kenyans.

Unlike the 1960s, however, the neo-majimbo project did not get support from other aggrieved groups. The Kikuyu who now proliferated the opposition ranks and therefore needed one form of protection or the other did not support it, neither did other small non-Kikuyu groups like the Luo, Kiisi, Embu, Meru, Luhya and Akamba, who were expected to close ranks to stop the big Kikuyu from dominating them in the post-Moi era. The intervention by president Moi who criticized the clamor for majimbo as the handwork of tribalists, and his success in securing another presidential term in 1996, put paid to the majimbo debate, at least for the time being.

While the resurgence of federalism did not result in the adoption of elaborate federal arrangements beyond decentralization in Uganda and Kenya, it did in South Africa and Ethiopia where ethnic divisions and conflicts run deep. The federal debate in South Africa dates back to the union of 1910, and featured prominently in subsequent discussions of constitutional options on account of the country's geographical, ethno-racial, cultural and religious diversity, which were manipulated by white minority hegemonists to produce highly divisive and conflictual politics (Welsh, 1989). Against this background, white minorities sought to make maximum use of the transition-pacting of the early 1990s to negotiate federal solution type devices and arrangements that were capable of keeping the exclusive privileges of the apartheid years intact, and amelio-rating the consequences of black majority rule following their transmuta-tion from political masters to minorities (Osaghae, 1998). They were joined by the IFP which sought political autonomy for its KwaZulu-Natal region (along the lines of the Indaba proposals of the 1980s) and some of the governments of the old black homelands (notably Bophuthatswana) which also desired to uphold the autonomy and privileges they enjoyed under apartheid.

The ANC, as we have seen, was ideologically and resolutely opposed to federalism—which connoted a divided South Africa in which the ethno-racial and regional inequalities and disparities of the apartheid era were frozen—but its leaders were forced by the give-and-take milieu of the negotiations, the imperatives of the country's federal situation, accentuated by the long years of division and conflict, and separatist agitations and threats of civil war, to concede to the expediency of the federal formula. This was how non-territorial consociational devices of executive power sharing involving the formation of the government of national unity at the central and provincial levels, proportional representation electoral system, protection of religious, cultural and linguistic diversity (nine languages were designated official languages), and the establishment of the Volkstaat Council; and territorial power sharing, involving the central, provincial and local governments, with the latter enjoying entrenched powers, all of which were embodied in the 1993 interim constitution, emerged as the instrumentalities of the transition to the post-apartheid order.

At that stage, and given the sunset clause that provided for the termination of executive power sharing in 1999, the federal solution seemed to be a temporary measure designed to see the country through the difficult transition period. But the 1996 (final) constitution which deepened and consolidated the federal elements in key areas of provincial powers (the renaming of the upper house of parliament as Council of Provinces and the accent on cooperative government suggest a strengthening of these powers), and the virtual granting of the right of self-determination to groups desiring it, indicated that, despite the aversion of the ANC-controlled central government to the federal label, federalism has come to stay in the country. The abiding federal basis and character of the constitution was well summarized by Dullah Omar, then South Africa's justice minister:

> [the] constitution recognises duality, namely the equal citizenship of all in one South Africa on the one hand and the diversity of South Africa's people on the other. Hence [the] constitution makes provision for equal rights at every level. And then the constitution makes provision for protection of freedom of religion, belief and opinion, language and culture...as well as cultural, religious and linguistic communities. The constitution enjoins upon the state the obligation to respect persons of different ethnic and cultural origins (Omar, 1997, p. 8).

The struggle by the provinces to wrest more powers, especially in fiscal terms, the strong desire by the IFP-controlled KwaZulu Natal province, the Colored-dominated Western Cape Province, and some of the ANC-controlled provinces to seek increased autonomy, continuing separatist agitations by Afrikaner right-wing extremists, emerging allegations of Xhosa domination of the ANC by other black minorities who subsequently demand protection, and the continuing disparities amongst the provinces, are some of the factors which are likely to make federalism relevant to South Africa for a long time to come.

Next, we turn to Ethiopia, the only country in the recent phase of federalism in Africa to adopt a full-fledged federal constitution, and one specifically aimed at addressing the ethnic question. What seems to make the Ethiopian case unique is that it is the closest to a voluntary federation in Africa's post-colonial history—the ethnic federating units reserve the right to secede from the federation. The prolonged wars of liberation fought by

Eritrea and other nationalities against Amhara hegemony and military dictatorship opened the door to a new dawn of mutual self-respect amongst the ethnic groups which underlay the accommodative, as opposed to the hegemonist approach to state-reconfiguration.

Thus, in the ensuing federal system, the ethnic states were entitled to their own constitutions, flags, anthems and languages for both educational and administrative purposes, while the states were further subdivided into zonal, *woreda* and *kebele* levels to give expression to major ethnic sub-divisions (Kefale, 1999). Such legitimization of ethnicity is unprecedented in Africa, and definitely presents a new trajectory of the federal solution to the national question. Ottaway (1999) however suggests that the goal of ethnic accommodation may very well have been only a secondary goal of the Ethiopian federation. She attributes the structuration of the federation to the manipulation of ethnicity by the minority Tigreans to keep themselves in power. Faced with the problem of governing a country already mobilized along ethnic lines, Ottaway argues, the TPLF organized Ethiopia into ethnic regions, held together by an umbrella party, the Ethiopian People's Revolutionary Democratic Front (EPRDF), composed of ethnic movements organized by the TPLF to represent the dominant ethnic group in each region. By organizing ethnic movements under its own control in each region, and keeping firm control over them through the EPRDF, the Tigrean minority could govern the country (Ottaway, 1999, p. 314).

The Ethiopian experiment may therefore not be as unique as is widely believed (Ottaway likens the ethnic manipulation involved to apartheid structuration in South Africa), but its legitimization of the ethnic question in a continent where ethnicity is an anathema is unprecedented.

This, I think, is because of the long history of separatist agitations, and the realization by the Tigreans that political stability could not be assured without the satisfaction of such aspirations. Although the point Ottaway makes is that this could not have happened if the Tigreans had not found it an expedient strategy of retaining power, its more important lesson is that it at least showed that they could not exercise central power alone (notwith-standing that they were a minority). A lot therefore depended on how far the central government was going to be able or willing to accommodate the claims of other groups because, as Kefale (1999) shows, the ethnic states still lacked any serious form of independent fiscal capacity, and depended largely on financial hand-outs from the center.

Finally, we shall briefly examine the case of Nigeria where aggrieved groups rose in the 1980s and 1990s to question and reject the extant federal arrangement that seemed unable to halt domination by ethno-regional and religious hegemonists (the country's First Republic collapsed for precisely this reason) and demanded a restructured (or 'true') federal system built on the equality and mutual self-respect of all groups (some proposals were for an ethnic federation along Ethiopian lines), and equitable access to power and resources. Although the problems and demands articulated by the various groups differed,[11] they all were provoked by the overcentralization of power in the country which was the legacy of the defederalizing consequences of prolonged rule by the military, the concentration of wealth in federal hands following the rise of the oil economy, and the failure of devices such as the federal character principle, the creation of more states and local governments, and periodic changes to the system of resource distribution, to check exclusionary tendencies and open up central power structures to the diverse ethnic claims to the satisfaction of most, if not all groups.

It was therefore not surprising that almost all the aggrieved groups demanded restructuring along confederal lines to reduce the effects of power loss due to over-centralization, and guaranteed equitable access to central power structures, including the military and other security forces. The temptation to conclude that federalism has been a failure in Nigeria must however be resisted for the simple reason that prolonged military rule has continually denied federalism some of its enabling elements, notably constitutionalism, democracy and continuous political bargain. However, considering that the over-centralized federal trajectory was encouraged, even necessitated, by the desire of Nigerians to have a more united country in the aftermath of the divisions and separatist tendencies that resulted in civil war (1967–70), the demands for a return to the non-centralized trajectory should be seen as evidence of the plasticity and adaptability of the federal formula. The overall lesson of Nigeria's experience, which is important for other federal situations in Africa, is precisely this.

Overcoming the travails of federalism

In this concluding section, we shall examine, more closely, the impediments to federalism in Africa. Now that federalism has something of a new beginning in Africa, it raises two important questions. Would the hopes of say the federal solution in Ethiopia be dashed, as those of the 1960s were? What would be the grounds for expecting that this time around, things would be different?

Perhaps the place to begin is to ask if federalism has in fact been unsuccessful in Africa. Ayoade (1978) has rightly argued that the success or failure of federalism can only be measured in relation to the purpose it was designed to serve. If this is so, the collapse or abolition of federalism in countries like Cameroon, Uganda, Sudan and Ethiopia (1952) may not amount to failure, since in the case of Cameroon and Uganda at least, it helped to integrate and stabilize the state, which was why it was adopted in the first place. Even in the case of Ethiopia and Sudan it is difficult to say that it was federalism that failed, as it is generally agreed that the systems were federal only in name, just as Nigeria was under military rule. Yet, there is abundant evidence that federalism (including federal principles) has had a difficult run in Africa, and that this has led to its abrogation and replacement by unitary systems in many cases. The point is that in the case of Cameroon and Uganda, it was not really that the countries had been well integrated or that federalism was no longer relevant (continuing agitations for federalism at least suggest that this is not so) but that federalism was not given a chance to work. This takes us to the argument advanced at the beginning of this chapter, that the uses and benefits of the federal solution remain potentials that have yet to be realized in Africa. The question is, why is this so?

From what has been analyzed in this chapter, two reasons immediately come to the fore. First, the multi-center power configuration of federalism, as well as its legitimation of diversity and the rights of groups to self-expression and self-determination, contradict the unitarist, assimilationist-exclusionary and authoritarian constitution of the ostensible nation-building projects pursued by power holders in the post-colonial state. Second, federalism, as an instrument of emancipation and empowerment or self-determination for marginalized and oppressed groups, is an ideology of political struggle, a demand to change the status quo (or, in counter-revolutionary fashion, such as that by the white Afrikaner minority in post-apartheid South Africa, the neo-majimboists in post-1991 Kenya, and the Baganda autonomy-seeking *federos* in Uganda, to preserve the status quo). It is precisely because it has been perceived and contested in such divisive and central power-diluting terms that federalism and federalist values have proven difficult to enthrone in Africa.

What is however fundamental to these explanations, and provides the key to federal problems in Africa, is the inclination toward centralization in state political organization. The trend was established, *ab initio*, by the very origins of the colonial state, which had no room for challenges or rebellion, by groups unwilling to belong to the state. Given the fragility of the state structures inherited from colonial authorities, centralization became even more pronounced after independence. Federalism under these circumstances could only be, to borrow Dent's (1989, p. 170) useful terminologies, inward-leaning (that is centralist) rather than outward leaning (that is non-centralist or confederal). The truism of Dent's contention is to be seen in Ethiopia whose so-called ethnic federation with its confederal connotations has not obliterated the virus of centralization.

Since federalism can only be at the behest of the central government, and since this confers proprietary and determinatory powers—of creation and possibly dissolution—on it, the success or failure of federalism then comes to depend greatly on the political management of diversity by the central government, and the willingness of its operatives to abide by constitutional rules which dilute or in some cases challenge its hegemony. In view of this, I think we need to re-examine the postulates of federalism in Africa along the lines of how to give the constituent groups a guaranteed share of power structures at the center. One reason for this is the fact that no matter how real decentralization schemes and local political autonomy are, constituent groups still define their belongingness to the state in terms of how much voice they have in the central government, its agencies, and the resources it controls. The efforts of the EPRDF in Ethiopia, and the reformulation of the Senate in South Africa as the Council of Provinces, give useful leads in this regard.

For those who would argue that such a proposal is likely to reify division, the simple answer is that it is precisely the division in the first place that necessitated the federal solution. The federalization of the center should not also be seen as the antithesis of non-centralized federalism, since the diversity that is politically consequential requires protection in one way or the other. The search, as the Nigerian example shows, should therefore be for how to balance the two forces to conform with the dynamics and changing nature of problems arising out of competing ethnic claims.

Notes

1.   In these terms, Gagnon (1993) has identified conflict-solving, protection of minority groups, expression of democratic practices, especially where balances are sought between centripetal and centrifugal forces, and where the politics of representation is very complex, as some of the political uses to which federalism has been put.

2.   Horowitz (1985, pp. 598–613) identifies five conflict-reducing mechanisms which are well served by federalism: proliferation of the points of power; generation of

intra-ethnic competition; generation of inter-ethnic cooperation; encouragement of alignment on non-ethnic issues; and reduction of disparities between regions through redistribution.

3.   While the emphasis in the European tradition is on the creation of representative bodies and the rule of law, the Anglo-American tradition is more oriented towards limiting central state power and allowing self-governance (Burgess and Gagnon, 1993).

4.   The fact that this paradigm shares a lot in common with paradigms of federalism elsewhere, especially the other new federations of Asia which also have colonial origins, does not make it any less African. The concern is not so much with African peculiarities, but with how federalism has been approached, employed and operated in Africa.

5.   The British were the clear leaders in this regard, not only because they established some of the largest and most ethnically divided colonies in Africa, but also because they had considerable experience with federalism in other parts of the world (Canada, Australia, India). It is instructive that most former British colonies have contemplated the federal option at one time or the other, and that countries which adopted federal (or federal-like) constitutions at independence—Nigeria, Uganda, Kenya, and South Africa—were former British colonies.

6.   Attempts at aggregative inter-state federation have included the Central African Federation of Northern and Southern Rhodesia and Nyasaland (1952), Ethiopia-Eritrea (1953), Mali federation formed by Senegal and the former French Soudan, now Mali (1960), Ghana-Guinea union, Tanzania, born out of the amalgamation of Tanganyika and Zanzibar (1964), the abortive East African federation, the federation of Egypt, Libya and Syria and the Senegambian federation. Of these, only Tanzania has survived, though the country became a unitary state in 1977.

7.   I think it is wrong to regard federalism, as Ayoade does, as an immutable balance of the forces of unity and those of diversity, and therefore an end in itself. Given its enormous variety, federalism cannot be immutable when it is related to the nature of the society it serves and the purpose for which it was adopted, a point which Ayoade himself acknowledges.

8.   Nigeria may have been an exception in this regard, as the regionalist founding fathers of the federation envisaged federalism as both ends and means, but the imperatives of nation-building won the day for federalism-as-means under military rule in the post-civil war period.

9.   In addition to countries of the Great Lakes region, former Zaire, and Zimbabwe, federal options were contemplated even in Liberia, Somalia and Sierra Leone, unlikely federal candidates on account of their small sizes, in the desperation to salvage what was left of the state from protracted wars.

10.   Other possible reasons such as the attempt by the powerful Biwott to create a 'private empire' and protect the rich mineral deposits discovered in the Rift Valley for exclusive Kalenjin use were also speculated, but what seemed to have been uppermost in the calculations of the Kalenjin elites was post-Moi security. This was especially because the majimbo proposals went against the official preference by KANU, the ruling party to which Moi's supporters belonged.

11.   For example, the minorities of the oil-rich Niger Delta (Ogoni, Ijaw, Urhobo, and others) sought greater share of the federation's resources to reflect their contribu-

tion to the country's oil-based wealth, while the Yorubas of the old Western region demanded a shift of power from the North in the aftermath of the annulment
of the presidential election of June 12, 1993 which seemed to confirm the fear that
the Northern hegemonists were unwilling to relinquish power.

References

Adamolekun, L. and Kincaid, J. (1991), 'The Federal Solution: An Assessment and
    Prognosis of Nigeria and Africa', *Publius: The Journal of Federalism*, Vol. 21,
    No. 4, pp. 173–188.
Agranoff, R. (1996), 'Federal Evolution in Spain', *International Political Science Review*,
    Vol. 17, No 4, pp. 385–401.
Ake, C. (1993), 'What is the Problem of Ethnicity in Africa?' *Transformation*, Vol. 22.
Amuwo, K., Agbaje, A.A.B., Suberu, R. and Herault, G. (eds.) (1998), *Federalism and
    Political Restructuring in Nigeria*, Spectrum: Ibadan, Nigeria.
Ayoade, J. A. A. (1978), 'Federalism in Africa: Some Chequered Fortunes', *Plural
    Societies*, Vol. 9, No. 2/3.
Beloff, M. (1953), 'The "Federal Solution" in Its Application to Europe, Asia and Africa',
    Political Studies, Vol. 1, No. 2, pp. 114–131.
Burgess, M. (1993), 'Federalism and Federation: A Reappraisal', in Burgess, M. and
    Gagnon, A.-G. (eds.), *Comparative Federalism and Federation: Competing Tra-
    ditions and Future Directions*, Harvester Wheatsheaf: Hertfordshire, UK.
Burgess, M. and Gagnon, A.-G. (eds.), *Comparative Federalism and Federation: Competing
    Traditions and Future Directions*, Harvester Wheatsheaf: Hertfordshire, UK.
Chabal, P. and Daloz, P.-J. (199), *Africa Works: Disorder as Political Instrument*, Interna-
    tional Africa Institute and James Currey: Oxford.
Dent, M. (1989), 'Federalism in Africa, With Special Reference to Nigeria', in Forsyth, M.
    (ed.), *Federalism and Nationalism*, Leicester University Press: Leicester, UK.
Diamond, L. (1999), *Developing Democracy: Towards Consolidation*, Johns Hopkins
    University Press: Baltimore, MD and London.
Ekeh, P. P. and Osaghae, E. E. (eds.), *Federal Character and Federalism in Nigeria*,
    Heinemann: Ibadan.
Elaigwu, J. I. and Olorunsola, V. A. (1983), 'Federalism and Politics of Compromise', in
    Rothchild, D. and Olorunsola, V. A. (eds.), *State Versus Ethnic Claims: African
    Policy* Dilemmas, Westview Press: Boulder, CO.
Elazar, D. J. (1987), *Exploring Federalism*, University of Alabama Press: Tuscaloosa, AL.
Gagnon, A.-G. (1993), 'The Political Uses of Federalism', in Burgess, M. and Gagnon, A.-
    G. (eds.), *Comparative Federalism and Federation: Competing Traditions and
    Future Directions*, Harvester Wheatsheaf: Hertfordshire, UK.
Horowitz, D. L. (1985), *Ethnic Groups in Conflict*, University of California Press: Berkeley,
    CA.
Horowitz, D. L. (1993), 'Democracy in Divided Societies', *Journal of Democracy*, Vol. 4,
    No. 4, pp. 17–38.
Joseph, R. A. (ed.) (1999), *State, Conflicts, and Democracy in Africa*, Lynne Rienner:
    Boulder, CO.

Kefale, A. (1999), 'Ethiopia's Experiment with Federalism: Challenges and Opportunities for Success', paper presented at the International Conference on New Directions of Federalism in Africa, Abuja, Nigeria.

King, P. (1982), *Federalism and Federation*, Croom Helm: London.

Kotze, H. (1995), 'Federalism in South Africa: An Overview', in Kotze, H. (ed.), *The Political Economy of Federalism in South Africa*, Center for International and Comparative Politics, University of Stellenbosch: Stellenbosch, South Africa.

Linz, J. J. (1997), 'Democracy, Multinationalism, and Federalism', paper presented at the International Political Science Association Conference, Seoul, Korea.

Mckown, R. (1988), 'Federalism in Africa', in Brown-John, C. L. (ed.), *Centralizing and Decentralizing Trends in Federal States*, University Press of America and Center for the Study of Federalism: Lanham, MD.

Neuberger, B. (1986), *National Self-Determination in Post-Colonial Africa*, Lynne Rienner: Boulder, CO.

Ngunyi, M. (1995), 'Resuscitating the Majimbo Project: The Politics of Deconstructing the Unitary State in Kenya', in Olukoshi, A. O. and Laasko, L. (eds.), *Challenges to the Nation-State in Africa*, Nordiska Afrikainstitutet: Uppsala.

Nmoma, V. (1995), 'Ethnic Conflict, Constitutional Engineering and Democracy in Nigeria', in Glickman, H. (ed.), *Ethnic Conflict and Democratization in Africa*, African Studies Association Press: Atlanta, GA.

Olukoshi, A. and Laasko, L. (1995), 'The Crisis of the National-State Project in Africa', in Olukoshi, A. O. and Laasko, L. (eds.), *Challenges to the Nation-State in Africa*, Nordiska Afrikainstitutet: Uppsala.

Omar, D. (1997), Opening Address at the International Conference on National Identity and Democracy, Cape Town.

Ordeshook, P. and Shevtsova, O. (1997), 'Federalism and Constitutional Design', *Journal of Democracy*, Vol. 8, No. 1, pp. 27–42.

Osaghae, E. E. (1994), *Ethnicity and Its Management in Africa: The Democratization Link*, Malthouse Press: Lagos.

Osaghae, E. E. (1996), 'Human Rights and Ethnic Conflict Management: The Case of Nigeria', *Journal of Peace Research*, Vol. 33, No. 2, pp. 171–188.

Osaghae, E. E. (1997), 'The Federal Solution in Comparative Perspective', *Politeia*, Vol. 16, No. 1.

Osaghae, E. E. (1998), 'What Democratization Does to Minorities Displaced from Power: The Case of White Afrikaners in South Africa', Report submitted to the CODESRIA Research Group on Ethnicity and Democratization in Africa.

Osaghae, E. E. (1999a), 'Democracy and National Cohesion in Multiethnic African States: South Africa and Nigeria Compared', *Nations and Nationalism*, Vol. 5, No. 2.

Osaghae, E. E. (1999b), 'South Africa and the Federalist Logic', paper presented at the International Conference on New Directions in Federalism in Africa, Abuja, March.

Ottaway, M. (1999), 'Ethnic Politics in Africa: Change and Continuity', in Joseph, R. A. (ed.), *State, Conflict and Democracy in Africa*, Lynne Rienner: Boulder, CO.

Rothchild, D. (1966), 'Federalism: The Limits of an Examination of Political Institutional Transfer in Africa', *The Journal of Modern African Studies*, Vol. 4, No. 3.

Shivji, I. G. (1989), *The Concept of Human Rights in Africa*, CODESRIA Book Series: Dakar.

Sithole, M. (1995), 'Ethnicity and Democratization in Zimbabwe: From Accommodation to Confrontation', in Glickman, H. (ed.), *Ethnic Conflict and Democratization in Africa*, African Studies Association Press: Atlanta, GA.

Suberu, R. T. (1993), 'The Travails of Federalism in Nigeria', *Journal of Democracy*, Vol. 4, No. 4, pp. 39–53.

Thomas-Woolley, B. and Keller, E. J. (1994), 'Majority Rule and Minority Rights: American Federalism and African Experience', *The Journal of Modern African Studies*, Vol. 32, No. 3, pp. 411–427.

Watts, R. L. (1970), *Multicultural Societies and Federalism*, Studies of the Royal Commission on Bilingualism and Biculturalism: Ottawa.

Welsh, D. (1989), 'Federalism and the Problem of South Africa', in Forsyth, M. (ed.), *Federalism and Nationalism*, Leicester University Press: Leicester, UK.

Wheare, K. C. (1967), *Federal Government*, 4th Edition, Oxford University Press: London.

Wunsch, J. S. and Olowu, D. (eds.) (1990), *The Failure of the Centralized State: Institutions and Self-Governance in Africa*, Westview Press: Boulder, CO.

3

Ethnicity, Constitutionalism, and Governance in Africa

JOHN MUKUM MBAKU

Introduction

In the last several years, ethnic conflict has become endemic in Africa. In many parts of the continent, inter-ethnic conflict has deteriorated into wars that have claimed the lives of hundreds of thousands of people—recent examples include Sudan, Nigeria, Burundi, Rwanda, South Africa, Ethiopia, Mozambique, Somalia, and Angola. Much has been written about such destructive ethnic conflict (see, e.g., Young, 1976; Horowitz, 1985). In this chapter, we argue that most of the destructive ethnic conflict that has pervaded most of post-independence Africa has been due primarily to the adoption at independence, of institutional arrangements that (1) failed to adequately constrain the power of government; (2) did not guarantee economic freedoms; and (3) failed to provide procedures for the peaceful resolution of the conflicting interests of the various ethnic groups within each country. In fact, in many instances, the laws and institutions adopted, allowed some ethnic groups to dominate governance and use governmental structures to enrich themselves at the expense of the rest of society. Unable to become part of the ruling coalition, and thus excluded from effective and full participation in economic and political markets, many of the excluded ethnic groups turned to violence as a way to minimize further marginaliza-tion. We then advance reconstruction of the post-colonial state through proper constitution making as the most effective way to deal with the 'ethnic problem' in Africa.

Theories of ethnicity and governance

One of the most important theories of ethnic relations within sovereignties is a collection of propositions called *resource competition theories.* Competitive resource allocation systems are characteristic of the capitalist mode of production (see, e.g., Marx, 1957, 1959). Competition, as a way to allocate scarce resources, can also be found as a basic assumption in many contemporary theories of socio-political interaction, including game theoretic models of international relations (Brams and Kilgour, 1988; Myerson, 1991) and rational choice theory (Banton, 1983, 1985; Hechter, 1987, 1992). The modern application of the concept of competitive re-source allocation to the study of ethnicity first appears in the seminal work of Fredrik Barth (1969) and his colleagues. In their view, one can see ethnicity as a system of boundaries between groups whose power and relevance are determined primarily by the nature and scope of contact and competition for scarce resources among ethnic cleavages (see, Nagel, 1995, p. 442). They argue, then, that ethnicity is not a permanent trait (e.g., skin color) but a changing group characteristic—implying that the boundaries of an ethnic group, as a social category, can change.

As has been made evident by economists, scarcity is a universal problem. In each society, individuals must compete for resources. Such competition can take place along ethnic lines, class, gender, age, race, and religion, just to name a few. If the ethnic group is the basic organizational structure for competing for resources, then the latter can have significant impact on ethnic groups in particular, and ethnicity in general. According to Nagel (1995, p. 443), resource competition in a society in which the ethnic group is an important organizational structure for competing for scarce resources can affect (1) ethnic identification; (2) racism and prejudice; (3) interethnic conflict; and (4) ethnic mobilization.

The ethnic group as an organizational structure for competing for scarce resources

The European social thinker, Max Weber, defined ethnic groups as 'human groups (other than kinship groups) which cherish a belief in their common origins of such a kind that it provides a basis for the creation of a community' (cited in Runciman, 1978, p. 364). Weber's definition of ethnic groups places emphasis on a set of beliefs, instead of biological traits such as race or objective group characteristics such as language and religion. Nagel (1995, p. 443), however, sees ethnicity as referring to 'differences in language, religion, color, ancestry, and/or culture to which social meanings are attributed and around which identity and group formation occurs.' Barth (1969) argues that ethnicity can result from *choice* or *ascription.* An individual living in the U.S. can, for example, choose to be an American or a Mexican (as in Mexican-American), an African (as in African-American), white, etc. On the other hand, membership in a certain ethnic group can be imposed on an individual by the greater society. For example, the demand by society that an individual of African ancestry be categorized as 'black.' In other words, while individuals can choose their ethnicity, such a choice must be acceptable to society. Ethnicity is a combination of individual choice and social imposition or designation (see, for example, Davis, 1991; Harris, 1964; also see Bunting, 1986 for a discussion of the social imposition of ethnicity in apartheid South Africa).

Nagel (1995, p. 444) states that historical differences in ancestry, religion, and language form the foundation for ethnic choices and impositions. He cautions, however, that 'the extent of ethnic self-awareness and the level of external ascription can vary a great deal over time, with ethnic differences quite prominent at some points in history and relatively unimportant at others.' For example, Africa's cultural and linguistic diversity is extensively documented (see, for example, Morrison, Mitchell and Paden, 1989; Young, 1976). Nagel (1995, p. 444) goes on to argue that despite the continent's significant level of ethnic and linguistic diversity, there does not appear to have been much interethnic conflict until the era of state formation following independence. Decolonization and independence appear to have significantly increased ethnic competition in the continent and resulted in the emergence of the ethnic group as an important organizational structure for resource competition.

During the decolonization process in the continent, individuals organized themselves along ethno-regional lines to compete for capture of the evacuated structures of colonial hegemony. (It is important to note that some of these ethno-regional groupings resulted from colonial legal administrative regions that had been developed in an effort to improve control of Africans and enhance exploitation of their resources by the resident Europeans.) Several scholars, including Nagel (1995), believe that the supply of military hardware to these groupings by the Cold War protagonists—the U.S. and its allies and the Soviet Union and other Eastern bloc countries, increased destructive ethnic conflict and effectively militarized ethnic conflict in Africa (see, Young, 1976). Of course, before independence became a reality, there was ethnic conflict in the continent, and individuals did organize along ethnic lines to compete for resources. Unfortunately, the level and extent of the African's participation in governance and the economy was severely constrained (and to a certain extent predetermined) by colonial laws designed to maximize European exploitation of African resources. However, the impending departure of the Europeans opened a window for greater levels of political and economic participation for Africans and thus, significantly changed the nature of interethnic conflict. Thus, there is significant variation in 'the level of ethnic self-awareness, ethnic political mobilization, and interethnic conflict in even the most ethnically fractionalized regions of the world' (Nagel, 1995, p. 444). In fact, while many African ethnic groups might have cooperated in their struggle against colonialism—fighting to rid themselves of a common enemy, the European colonizer, many of these groups were to become bitter enemies after the departure of the Europeans, as each struggled to monopolize governance and resource allocation.

Although language, culture, and religion are usually identified as important building blocks of ethnicity, it is often not certain which of these would become the defining variable for a group, the one that identifies and distinguishes it from all others during periods of intense conflict. For example, today, religion is no longer an important basis for ethnic identification or conflict in the U.S. However, in many regions of the world (e.g., Northern Ireland, the Middle East, North Africa, and South Asia), religion remains a very important source of discrimination and mobilization (Young, 1976, 1986, 1993). Language remains an important source of conflict in many countries and regions of the world (e.g., Cameroon—anglophones vs. francophones; Canada; Spain; and Belgium). However, in most of Africa with its enormous linguistic diversity (for example, Sudan has more than 170 distinct languages; Nigeria has between 200 and 400; and Cameroon has more than 250 languages), most ethnic conflict 'is framed not as a language dispute but more in religious or cultural terms' (Nagel, 1995, p. 445). In South Africa (during the apartheid regime), Zimbabwe (during the colonial period and the Ian Smith regime), and Namibia (during the colonial period and South African occupation), race or skin color, and ethnic group/language were used as the major sources of discrimination or conflict.

Evidence now shows that variations in language, religion, and culture and traditions do not necessarily result in strong ethnic identification and the formation of (closed) ethnic communities. Nagel (1995, p. 445) argues that these differences can serve as the basis for 'ethnic identification, the rationale for interethnic conflict, or the logic of ethnic collective action.' However, one may wonder when ethnicity will become an important tool for economic competition or for mobilization to capture governance structures. Resource competition theories of ethnicity attempt to provide answers to these and other questions.

What causes ethnic competition?

The need to compete for jobs, leadership positions in society's political institutions, and for government transfers forces individuals to organize themselves (e.g., as interest groups) in order to minimize their transaction costs and maximize benefits accruing to them. In other words, competition for scarce resources induces individuals within a society to form groups, develop political and ideological platforms, and to engage in conflict behaviors (e.g., through peaceful constitutionally prescribed methods, or through violence) in an effort to maximize benefits from competition. Individuals can form groups based on age, class, gender, religion, region, race, etc. When, however, will individuals prefer to be organized along ethnic lines in order to compete for resources? Researchers have identified two major conditions that make organization along ethnic lines the most preferred option for individuals competing for resources. These are *historical* and *emergent* factors that promote ethnic competition. A critical form of social organization that has the ability to generate ethnic conflict and the preference for ethnic discrimination is what has been termed the *cultural division of labor* (see, for example, Nagel, 1995; Hechter, 1978; Hechter and Levi, 1979). In these types of social systems, one or a few distinct groups are dominant and exploit others politically, economically, and socially. According to Nagel (1995, p. 446), '[c]ultural divisions of labor tend to produce segregated ethnic communities characterized by great inequalities of wealth, power, and status.' Although there are many examples in Africa, South Africa under apartheid represents an excellent example of the cultural division of labor. During this period of the country's history, whites in general, and Afrikaners in particular, dominated African ethnic groups and forced them to live on non-viable peripheral areas called homelands, and in urban preserves (townships) that served as labor reservoirs for white commercial, agricultural and industrial activities (Fredrickson, 1981; Nattrass, 1981; Magubane, 1979; Mbaku, 1993). According to proponents of the cultural division of labor theory, conflict in these societies tends to be organized along ethnic instead of class or ideological lines. It is important to note that while conflict in cultural divisions of labor may emerge along ethnic lines, some ethnic groups may compete not to capture the apparatus of government and maximize benefits to group members through economic and political exploitation of other groups, but to effect dispensations that provide *all groups* with an opportunity to maximize their values (i.e., these groups seek to provide society with competitive political and economic systems that enhance the ability of *all* citizens to participate in both governance and development). As pointed out by Nagel (1995, p. 454, fn. 5), Nelson Mandela and the African National Congress' approach to competition for resources in South Africa was to rid the society of the policy of apartheid and establish a nonracial democratic society (see, for example, Mandela, 1990).

There is no agreement among cultural division of labor theorists regarding the conditions under which mobilization by ethnic groups (i.e., competition along ethnic lines) will occur in cultural divisions of labor. Hechter (1975), for example, has argued that ethnic conflict or mobilization may result from the geographic isolation of certain groups—usually from the core industrial and economic centers of the country. Ragin (1986) and Nielsen (1986), however, argue that shocks (either external or internal) that increase or improve opportunities for economic and political competition enhance the probability of ethnic mobilization. In Africa, such shocks include decolonization and independence; the end of the Cold War; and the demise of apartheid in South Africa. The evidence seems to indicate that ethnic mobilization has increased significantly in Nigeria every time the country's extant military dictatorship has announced a program to transfer power to civilians. In the 1970s, when OPEC (Organization of Petroleum Exporting Countries) increased the price of oil, Nigeria, a net exporter of petroleum, saw a significant increase in its export revenues. The huge windfalls from oil induced nation-wide ethnic mobilization as groups sought ways to maximize their share of the increasing public budget.

The *split labor market* has also been offered as another structural factor enhancing ethnic mobilization. Split labor markets are said to exist when two ethnic groups compete for jobs in the same labor market and one is paid a lower wage. Ethnic boundaries are reinforced by the competition for employment opportunities, increasing the possibility of conflict between the groups. Color bar legislation in apartheid South Africa created split labor markets and increased ethnic mobilization (see, e.g. Hutt, 1964; Doxey, 1961).

Ethnic competition is also being promoted by *contemporary factors*. New immigrants are seen as competitors for jobs, educational opportunities, and public goods and services. Some countries often provide new immigrants with assistance to secure jobs, loans to finance education, etc. Some of these immigrants may form ethnic enclaves that compete with existing ethnic groups for resources. If seen as successful and exclusionary (e.g., the perception of Koreans and Vietnamese by inner-city blacks in the U.S.; and the view by 'native' Ugandans that government policies favored Indian and other Asian business owners in that country), tensions can arise between these new groups and existing ethnic societies (see, e.g., Cohen, 1974; Nagel, 1995). In those countries or societies in which interethnic conflict already exists, the new immigrants may be forced to integrate into existing patterns of ethnicity and ethnic mobilization. During the civil war in Nigeria, Ibo refugees arriving neighboring Cameroon easily integrated themselves into existing Ibo enclaves in such places as Kumba and Victoria (now Limbe) that had high concentrations of members of this ethnic group. In many African urban areas, it is very common for individuals arriving from the rural areas to seek and settle in areas occupied primarily by members of their own ethnic group. As noted by Nagel (1995, p. 448), antagonism may arise if the new immigrants are perceived to be favored by public programs that provide special services to refugees or new immigrants.

Access to political markets represents another source of ethnic mobilization. In post-independence Africa, where the state is the most important and biggest actor in the economy, access to political markets and control of resource allocation represent important sources of ethnic competition. In fact, in many African countries, elites seeking public office often organize their campaigns along ethnic lines. Factors contributing to the preference of ethnicity as a basis for political organization include (1) common language and culture, and the existence of ethnic organizational structures that can allow contenders for political office to minimize transaction costs; (2) possession of large deposits of exploitable environmental resources (e.g., petroleum, natural gas, diamonds and other minerals, etc.) by an ethnoregional group; and (3) historical domination of some groups by others. The existence or discovery of exploitable resources, as Nagel (1995, p. 449) argues, may 'reinforce ethnic self-awareness and sensitize ethnic groups to the possibility of exploitation by other groups' (also see Nafziger, 1983). The decision by the Ibos to secede from Nigeria in the mid-1960s and form the Republic of Biafra can partly be explained by the discovery of large deposits of oil on land occupied by Ibos and minority ethnic groups that the Ibos expected to dominate in the new country (St. Jorre, 1972). Discrimination against or political domination of other ethnic groups by a group favored by historical events (e.g., colonialism) can motivate disadvantaged ethnoregional groups to become politically active. Examples include post-independence ethnic mobilization against groups that were either favored by the colonial system or, as a result of several factors, fared relatively well during the period. Of course, one must include the struggle by black groups against apartheid in South Africa as an example of ethnic mobilization induced by historical discrimination. In addition, conflict involving the Bamiléké in Cameroon, the Ibos in Nigeria, the Silks in India, and the Kikuyus in Kenya are examples of post-independence ethnic political mobilization against groups that had fared *relatively* well under colonial rule (see, e.g., Laitin, 1986; Schermerhorn, 1978; Horowitz, 1985; Young, 1976). Many of the groups that were disadvantaged during colonialism formed ethnoregional political parties to compete against the advantaged groups for political and economic positions in the post-independence society.

At independence, the African state was granted significant power over the economy and the allocation of resources. In fact, as a result of the choice of statism as the post-independence development model in most African countries, the state came to represent the most important single organization in the national economy. In most countries in the continent, the state is the largest employer, investor, and supplier of goods and services (Ihonvbere and Ekekwe, 1988; Agbese, 1992). The group that captures the state has control of an enormous amount of resources and thus, can reward its supporters, provide for group members, and proceed to install barriers to entry into political and economic markets (Mbaku, 1997). If the government engages in the redistribution of income and wealth in favor of historically marginalized and deprived groups (i.e., the state attempts to develop and implement so-called affirmative action programs), other groups that consider themselves disadvantaged but have not been designated as such by the state, may mobilize in an effort to capture the same or similar benefits. Majority groups, or those considered to have been favored (and thus, advantaged) by past public policies may also mobilize to prevent any erosion in their benefits and subsequently, their standard of living. The recent backlash against affirmative action programs in California and several other states in the U.S. is an example of mobilization by majority groups against what they perceive to be special privileges for minority groups (Schermerhorn, 1978; Simmons, 1982; Darnell and Parikh, 1988; Lopez and Espiritu, 1990). In South Africa, white groups, especially the Afrikaners, who were favored by apartheid, have already begun to mobilize against policies of the new post-apartheid government. These groups believe that the new policies, which are designed to reduce income and wealth inequalities and improve living conditions among the nation's historically marginalized and deprived groups, could significantly reduce their wealth positions (see, e.g., Mbaku, 1997).

Both historical and contemporary factors promote ethnic competition for scarce resources. Public policies that seek to reduce inequities caused by historical discrimination can promote mobilization by groups that seek to be designated by the government as disadvantaged—so that they can benefit from the public programs, or by those that believe that the new programs will reduce their wealth position (i.e., they will become the suppliers of wealth transfers) and consequently, their standard of living.

The literature (see, e.g., Nagel, 1995) has identified four major consequences of ethnic competition for resources. These are 'increased ethnic identification and group formation, increased racism and prejudice, increased interethnic conflict, and increased ethnic mobilization and activism' (Nagel, 1995, p. 452). The question to ask here is: when will ethnic conflict or ethnic competition for resources become destructive or result in savage attacks on other groups as occurred in places such as Rwanda, Burundi, and the Balkans? If the nation's institutional arrangements place some ethnic groups at a competitive disadvantage in the competition for resources, then the disadvantaged groups may resort to violence. On the other hand, the favored or well-placed groups may use state structures to oppress 'minority' or weaker groups in an effort to continue to maintain a comparative advantage in the competition for resources (e.g., Afrikaners in apartheid South Africa; whites in some parts of the U.S. and several dominant ethnic groups in the African countries). Throughout Africa, ethnicity remains durable as a basis for social organization. In fact, despite significant efforts by post-independence leaders to discourage ethnic competition for both political and economic resources, ethnic identification remains as strong as it was during colonialism. Many of these leaders have come to realize that the multiethnic state is likely to remain the rule not the exception in Africa for a long time. As will be argued later in this chapter, the most effective way to minimize destructive ethnic conflict is not to prevent ethnic identification but to establish institutional arrangements that provide fair and predictable rules for competition, structures for peaceful resolution of conflict, and enhance the ability of groups to coexist peacefully. Under such institutional arrangements, economic freedoms will be constitutionally guaranteed, and the state adequately constrained so that civil servants cannot use state structures as instruments of plunder to benefit one group at the expense of others (see, e.g., Kimenyi, 1997).

The rational choice perspective on ethnicity

Rational choice theorists define rationality as the maximization of well defined objective functions (e.g., wealth, profit, and utility). Alternatively, rationality can also be viewed as the *minimization* of costs (including transaction costs) and other associated disutilities (Williamson, 1994; Zafirovski, 1999). According to rational choice theory then, the activities of rational individuals are basically optimizing behavior. In rational choice theory, individuals are seen as purposeful actors, seeking to maximize their self-interest (Hechter, 1989). Thus, rational choice theory can be seen to be based on the concept of *rational action*, taken from neoclassical economic theory (Coleman, 1986). Rational action as used in economics, implies the maximization of well-defined objectives or goals (e.g., profit, wealth, or utility). Market participants, then, can be seen as utility maximizers (Abell, 1989) whose behavior or activities in the market are designed to maximize well-defined objective functions, for example, expected utility (Coleman, 1986); private benefits (Hardin, 1997); wealth (Wittman, 1995); rent (Tollison, 1997); or money income (Opp, 1989). It is important to note that rational choice theory posits that maximizing behavior is not restricted to economic agents (e.g., consumers and business firms) but applies to all participants in both political and economic markets. Thus, 'families, social movements, political parties and officials, governments, racial and ethnic groups, churches or scientists are assumed to optimize their utility functions' (Zafirovski, 1999, p. 48). In other words, according to rational choice theory, maximizing behavior is universal, applying to actors in both economic, as well as political markets.

   The theory of rational choice can offer guidelines for studying economic and social behavior. By providing a well-defined objective to be pursued, rational choice theory can help elucidate how individuals should behave (Zafirovski, 1999, p. 49). Accordingly, the objective function of, for example, wealth, is then said to define rationality (Hey, 1993). Viewing rationality as utility maximization implies that actors or market participants attempt to reach the point where 'their optimally chosen actions generate best outcomes' (Zafirovski, 1999, p. 49). Since it is assumed that the primary interest of the individual's actions is his personal welfare, rational choice postulates actors to be self-interested—that is, actors engage in self-regarding behaviors (Abell, 1992). Rational choice theory depends upon the belief that individuals are utilitarian or self-interested. Hechter (1989, pp. 60–66) argues that rational choice theory is 'based upon the concept that individuals are rational egoists.' The 'principle of utilitarian action' is considered 'the hallmark of rational choice theory in the sense that all social behavior is seen as explicable by what is called a generalized calculus of utility-maximizing behavior' (Zafirovski, 1999, p. 49; also see, Stigler and Becker, 1977, pp. 76–77). In political markets, rational choice theorists would argue that politicians seek power in order to use it to maximize their individual interests (Coleman, 1986). Individuals within a society act purposefully, deliberately, and intentionally, within the given set of constraints (i.e., market incentive structures) made possible by the society's institutional arrangements, to maximize well-defined objective functions (Elster, 1979). The theory of rational choice, then 'is grounded on the neoclassical economic model of rationality with its basis in the concept of utility function positing that social action is guided by the goal of maximizing or (satisficing with respect to) utility' (Zafirovski, 1999, p. 50).

In each society, people create structures that allow them to more effectively maximize their individual interests. Thus, people create social norms and values, as well as taboos, to help them achieve their objectives. As a consequence, one can see taboos and societal values as merely tools to enhance the ability of individuals to engage in optimization. In this light, one can see actions in the 'interest of the public' as a form of investment designed to enhance extraction of individual economic benefits and allow the individual to achieve a given set of objectives.

It has been argued that ethnic violence is an instrument to secure real benefits (e.g., political and economic resources) for group members. In Africa, ethnic conflict, especially in the post-independence period, is seen as a mobilization tool used by emerging ethno-regional elites to either consolidate existing political positions or gain new ones. Rational choice theory refines this 'strategic view' of violence as a modality of political action (Mehta, 1998, p. 377). If there is a breakdown in existing institutional arrangements, creating uncertainty, institutionalized mechanisms for security may breakdown or cease to function effectively, forcing groups to take preemptive action against other groups. Under these conditions, writes

Mehta (1998, p. 377) 'violence can be analyzed in terms of cost benefit analysis, theories of bargaining, game theory and rational choice.' Ethnic violence in places such as Rwanda can be interpreted as preemptive action by one group against the other in view of the collapse of existing enforcement mechanisms. Ethnic violence can also occur even when institutional arrangements have not collapsed but have become instruments of plunder of some groups (by dominant ones) or are the source of violence directed at some groups. For example, in apartheid South Africa, governance structures had not broken down, but were being used by the state to oppress and marginalize African groups. In fact, during this period, the state had become the source of most of the violence directed at African ethnic groups. As a consequence, many of these groups mobilized and became engaged in violence in an effort to defend themselves and at the same time bring about a more democratic dispensation to the country.

Viewed from the rational choice perspective, such violence is a response to existing incentive structures and thus, can be managed effectively only by providing the appropriate types of incentive structures through rules design (i.e., constitution making to provide the appropriate institutional arrangements, including well-specified and enforceable property rights regimes). The assumption of rationality implies that individuals engaging in ethnic conflict do so after determining this to be the least cost alternative to mobilize and maximize their values. But why this particular form of violence? Why did Africans prefer ethnic to other forms of violent confrontation? One can answer this question by examining specific examples from Africa's violent ethnic history. Under the apartheid regime in South Africa, existing institutional arrangements made organization along ethnic lines the only option for many of the country's citizens. The state and its agencies were used to oppress and marginalize African groups. Africans were expected to remain *permanently* inferior and subordinate to whites. Eventually, Africans came to realize that they could never change their welfare under existing institutional arrangements. They subsequently engaged in efforts to change governance structures within the country. They appealed to the government for reforms of the country's laws and institutions, but their pleas were ignored or rejected. In fact, the government instead passed additional laws to make certain that blacks could not *legally* (i.e., constitutionally) change the existing dispensation to one that enhanced their ability to maximize their values. For example, in 1968, the apartheid government passed the Prohibition of Political Interference Act—a law that specifically prohibited the formation of political parties whose membership was made up of people from more than one *officially designated* population group—making it impossible for liberal white opposition groups to recruit Africans as legal members and for black groups to form political parties. Thus, efforts by blacks to change the *status quo* and improve their ability to participate in governance, faced two major problems. First, institutional forms of participation were foreclosed to them. Second, Africans were not allowed by law, to participate in constitutional forms of regime change (e.g., they were not allowed to vote or compete for leadership positions in the nation's political system). As a consequence, organization and mobilization along ethnic lines and violence became the only avenues opened to them.

Apartheid South Africa was not the only country in Africa whose institutional arrangements forced citizens to engage in ethnic mobilization. At independence, leaders of many of the new African countries argued that in order to maintain peaceful coexistence among the multitude of ethnic groups in each country, required strong central governments. Concentration of political power in the center was considered a *sine qua non* for maintaining the peaceful coexistence of ethnic groups. Governance structures that were characterized by multiple political parties—that is, competitive political systems—were said to present opportunities for the politicization of ethnicity, endangering peaceful coexistence and national integration. In fact, former Sierra Leone president, Siaka Stevens, argued that multiparty politics would encourage and enhance ethnic warfare and make it difficult for the new countries to pursue the goals of national development (see, e.g., Decalo, 1992). As a consequence, shortly after independence, many of the new countries adopted one-party political systems with relatively strong central governments. According to Julius Nyerere of Tanzania, the single political party was expected to represent 'all streams of opinions and societal groups' (Decalo, 1992, p. 10). However, instead of giving voice to all 'political opinions' and 'societal groups', the single political party became an instrument used by those who had captured the evacuated structures of colonial hegemony, to monopolize political power and the allocation of resources. Since most of these single parties were usually dominated and controlled by one or a few ethnic groups, most of the deprived (or excluded) groups came to see ethnic mobilization as the only way to avoid permanent marginalization and relegation to the periphery of society. During the last forty years, most of the African countries that adopted single political parties have been characterized by civil strife, military coups and wars. Most of the conflicts that have resulted in war have usually been between heterogeneous population groups. While the argument for establishing single party political systems was that such structures would enhance peaceful coexistence, through the unification of ethnic groups, Africa's post-independence experience has confirmed the argument that such institutional arrangements are not appropriate for the harmonization of the interests of heterogeneous groups (Kimenyi, 1998, pp. 43–63).

Rational choice theory, as it applies to ethnicity, is based on four presuppositions. According to the first one, in his relations with other members of society, the individual seeks to maximize his self interest—that is, the individual engages in optimizing behavior. The second presupposition states that choices made earlier can impact and alter the alternatives available to individuals in subsequent periods. According to the third presupposition, individuals, through socialization, come to recognize their dependence on other members of society. As a consequence, individuals may, from time to time, forego some of their 'selfish' interests in order to promote 'group' goals. Group identification—for example, with an ethnic group—can be seen as part of the traditions passed down from one generation to another. Finally, to maximize their objectives, individuals may form or join groups that allow them to engage in collective decision-making. It must be understood that individuals may have many goals to pursue and as such, may join more than one group. For example, an African intellectual who plans to run for public office may identify strongly with his ethnic group in order to secure the required votes to win the position, while at the same time maintaining a strong presence in a scholarly organization representing his discipline. Ethnic identification is expected to help his political ambitions, while participation in the scholarly organization will advance his professional career. Thus, individuals will usually align themselves with groups which they believe can provide them with the most efficient and effective way to maximize their individual objectives (see, e.g., Banton, 1995).

As mentioned earlier, in seeking to maximize their self-interest, individuals may form groups, quite often, by exploiting physical and cultural differences. The boundaries for ethnic groups are drawn through inclusive processes while those for racial groups are arrived at through exclusion. Interaction between groups (e.g., through trade) can have a significant impact on the boundaries that define them. During colonialism in Africa, the Europeans—the colonizers—categorized Africans into a separate part of the colonial population and denied them most of the rights of citizenship. Africans were easily identified by the color of their skin—the majority of Europeans were white and Africans, black. For example, France's colonial policy, called association (*politique d'association*), divided the population of each colony into two social categories: *français* or *européen* and *African* or *indigène*. As a category, *européen* included any *white* Frenchman or non-African. Most of the rights of citizenship were enjoyed only by French citizens and other Europeans (*européens*). Since there often were not enough French citizens to serve in all the various administrative positions in the colony, the colonial government engaged in selective social promotions of Africans into the *européen* category. Africans, through education in French language and culture, could become *assimilé* (assimilated). An indigenous person who had evolved to the European cultural ideal could then apply and be granted French citizenship and subsequently become *citoyen* or citizen (of France). The law protected the person and property of citizens, but provided little or no benefits to natives (*sujets indigènes*). Under this policy, citizens even if they were *black* Africans, were not subject to forced labor, and as a consequence, had more secure property rights (see, for example, LeVine, 1964; Mbaku, 1991). The system of social promotions, however, was not designed to enhance the ability of the indigenous peoples to improve their welfare but to provide France with an effective tool to manage its colonial possessions. Thus, Africans who had 'properly evolved' but were considered a threat to the colonial regime were not granted promotion to the status of *citoyen* (Thompson and Adloff, 1969; Gardinier, 1971).

In apartheid South Africa, whites re-organized the country's population into several categories based primarily on skin color and reserved the bulk of the rights of citizenship to themselves. Two major categories—whites and blacks—were identified. Whites were sub-divided by language and culture into Afrikaners (Europeans of Dutch-German-French ancestry) and English (Europeans of British origin). Blacks were sub-divided into colored (consisting of seven sub-categories, see Mbaku, 1997, p. 145; IDAF, 1991); African (consisting of several indigenous ethnic/language groups); and Asian (mainly Indian). Through several forms of legislation, the apartheid government created and sustained many privileges for whites while forcing blacks to live in extreme poverty and deprivation (Fredrickson, 1981; Magubane, 1979; Nattrass, 1981; Hutt, 1964). Despite the collapse of the apartheid government in 1994 and the establishment of a multi-party/multiracial democracy under the leadership of Nelson Mandela and the African National Congress, blacks remain severely impoverished as whites, who make up less than 20% of the population, continue to control virtually all the country's agricultural and industrial wealth.

If members of an ethnic group are discriminated against, say by the larger society, the likelihood increases that the discriminated group will engage in collective action to (1) reduce the discrimination; (2) improve the welfare of group members; and (3) promote the group's other interests. It is important to note that the marginalized ethnic group—that is, the one that is being discriminated against, may also mobilize to change the existing dispensation in order to increase participation in markets not only for itself but also for all groups within the country. In other words, the marginalized group may seek to establish a competitive and more inclusive dispensation that enhances the ability of *all* citizens to participate in both political and economic markets. This is evidenced by the struggle against apartheid in South Africa—during the long struggle, Nelson Mandela and other ANC members argued persistently that their aim was not to replace 'white racism' with 'black racism' but to establish in the country, institutional arrangements that enhanced the ability of all South Africans, including those who had oppressed blacks, to maximize their values. Thus, they referred to the new dispensation as an all-inclusive and 'non-racial' democracy.

During the struggle for independence in the African colonies, many ethnic-based political parties argued along the same lines, claiming that the struggle was for independence of the colony and the establishment of governance structures and resource allocation systems that allowed all population groups full participation. Unfortunately, the laws and institutions adopted at independence allowed bargaining to become a zero-sum game in which politically dominant groups benefited at the expense of others—that is, dominant groups captured virtually all the benefits of independence, forcing minority or non-dominant groups to live in poverty and deprivation. In fact, in many countries, the indigenous ethnic groups that had captured the evacuated structures of colonial hegemony proceeded to monopolize governance structures and the economy, erecting significant barriers to entry. As a consequence, many population groups within the country were marginalized both politically, socially and economically. Since the institutional arrangements in many of the new African countries provided what amounted to situations of zero-sum competition, citizens became very conscious of their group identity. In Cameroon, for example, where ethnic coalitions controlled governmental structures, some ethnic groups were able to monopolize certain sectors of the government and the economy. As a consequence, it was difficult either for an individual to secure a job (either in the public or private sector) without an 'ethnic connection.' For example, in the early 1960s and 1970s, the police force in West Cameroon was dominated by one ethnic group and as a consequence, those who did not belong to that group were rarely accepted into the police academy. Members of the relevant group that aspired to become police officers identified very strongly with the group, hoping to use their membership to gain easy entrance into the police academy. Thus, 'tribalism' came to dominate hiring into many public agencies and even the private sector in Cameroon, and in fact, in many other African countries. Despite arguments by many of the indigenous elites in the pre-independence period that the society they were seeking to create was an inclusive one, in which all groups and all streams of opinion would be accorded equality, monopolization of political power and the allocation of resources by certain ethnic groups came to characterize post-independence society in many African countries (see, e.g., Kofele-Kale, 1986, pp. 53–82). The ethnic group that had control of the apparatus of government redistributed income in favor of its members and supporters and used national resources to defend its control of governance structures. Ethnic or ethno-regional mobilization intensified as groups controlling the state fought to retain their lucrative positions, while locked-out or marginalized groups struggled to gain entry into markets through the capture of the government. Given the absence of constitutional methods for regime change, most of this competitive mobilization degenerated into violent confrontations between ethnic groups or ethno-regional coalitions (e.g., Rwanda, Zaire, South Africa, Burundi, and Nigeria).

Strong ethnic identification should not necessarily become a constraint to peaceful coexistence. In addition, mobilization along ethnic lines should not endanger peaceful coexistence and proper governance either. Market competition improves resource allocation, increases national wealth and enhances the quality of life for the people. However, in order for this to occur, market participants in each society must be provided with the appropriate incentive structures. If the latter place some ethnic groups at a competitive disadvantage, making it relatively difficult or impossible for them to participate in markets, then ethnic violence would become inevitable. Of course, some ethnic groups might become opportunistic and refuse to 'play by the rules' in an effort to generate additional benefits for themselves. However, with the appropriate institutional arrangements, such post-contractual opportunism can be minimized (see, e.g., Ostrom, Schroeder and Wynne, 1993).

Ethnicity and governance in Africa: the public choice perspective

Public choice theory is well suited to examining and explaining pervasive behaviors such as military coups, corruption and institutional instability in Africa (see Mbaku, 1997 for a review of the literature) and destructive ethnic violence. (It is important to note that public choice theory is a subset of what is generally referred to as 'rational choice theories'.) The public choice paradigm has also been used to study apartheid in South Africa (Mbaku, 1993; Dollery, 1990; Dollery, 1989). First, the opportunistic behaviors mentioned above (e.g., corruption and military coups) represent efforts by individuals and groups (some of them based on ethnicity) to subvert existing laws and institutions to generate wealth for themselves, or to change the extant rules and adopt institutional arrangements that enhance their ability to plunder the economy for their own benefit (see, e.g., Mbaku and Paul, 1989; Mbaku, 1994). Second, the public choice perspective can also show how groups that are competing for access to both political and economic markets can become engaged in violent confrontation and other regime-destabilizing behaviors (Mbaku, 1995). Third, public choice theory can help African countries develop and adopt more viable institutional arrangements—those that effectively constrain the exercise of government agency and provide a fair and equitable system of resource allocation, and enhance the ability of groups to co-exist peacefully. Finally, public choice theory can provide significant insights into the importance of rules—including well defined property rights—to peaceful coexistence of groups. It places significant emphasis on rules and their importance in minimizing post-contractual opportunism, and providing viable procedures for peaceful resolution of conflict.

During the last several years, many studies of Africa's political economy have attributed the continent's institutional crisis—including destructive ethnic conflict—to high levels of poverty and deprivation. Studies by public choice scholars, however, provide a different explanation for endemic instability in the continent (see, e.g., Mbaku and Paul, 1989; Brough and Kimenyi, 1986; Mbaku, 1995; Kimenyi and Mbaku, 1993; Kimenyi, 1987, 1989). In these studies, the ethnic group is treated as a special interest group that competes for government transfers. According to Kimenyi (1998, p. 44), '[m]embers of a particular tribe consider themselves different from those of other groups and have an interest in increasing the welfare of their members relative to that of other tribes.' Given the fact that most African countries adopted single-party political systems at independence, with most power concentrated in the center, the incumbent leadership can redistribute income and wealth in favor of certain politically dominant groups, including groups based on ethnicity. As a consequence, there is a tendency for ethnic groups to either try to capture the apparatus of government or develop enough violence potential to force the incumbent government to favor the group in resource allocation. In fact, during the last forty years, many African governments have maintained their control of governance structures by redistributing resources in favor of specific ethnic and social cleavages (e.g., the military, urban dwellers, and specific ethnic groups; in South Africa, apartheid was maintained primarily by favoring whites in general, and Afrikaners in particular in the redistribution of wealth). Incumbents have secured the support to maintain a monopoly on power by transferring resources from politically weak to dominant groups. As already mentioned, control of governance structures allows the 'controlling' group to redistribute income and wealth in favor of its members and its supporters. As a consequence, ethnic groups have engaged in a bitter (and often destructive) competition (or mobilization) for capture of the state. Given the fact that constitutional methods of regime change either do not exist in these countries or function poorly, those groups seeking to capture the state (i.e., governance structures) are forced to resort to violence. This represents an important source of violent confrontation between ethnic groups in Africa. In other words, ethnic mobilization for the control of the instruments of government—and by implication, those of income and wealth redistribution—have contributed significantly to violent confrontations between groups. Examples include Rwanda, Sudan, Zaire, Nigeria, and apartheid South Africa.

Research by public choice scholars points to the fact that Africa's post-independence institutional arrangements (i.e., the laws and institutions adopted at independence) did not provide for *optimal units of collective choice* (Kimenyi, 1998, p. 45). At independence, the new African leaders sought ways to force the several ethnic groups within each country to unite to form unitary states. Such so-called unity was not based on *voluntary association* but on decrees that sought to force all groups to live under a single administrative and political system, with little or no devolution of power to local or ethnic units. Given the fact that the polities formed through this process were not optimal units of collective choice, the ethnic groups within each country found themselves permanently trapped in Pareto-inferior noncooperative market outcomes. Kimenyi (1998, p. 45) argues that Africa's highly centralized states, which had been formed by using state coercion to unite ethnic groups, 'resulted in outcomes that are very much like those found in stateless societies described by Hobbes

([1651] 1962).' Thus, destructive ethnic conflict in post-independence Africa represents institutional failure which can only be addressed effectively through state reconstruction. In other words, the most effective way to deal with destructive ethnic conflict is to provide each African society with appropriate institutional arrangements—those that are capable of solving prisoner's dilemma problems. To 'harmonize conflicting interests of various ethnic groups, countries characterized by high degrees of ethnic diversity should adopt institutional arrangements that utilize ethnic units as a basis for local governments' (Kimenyi, 1998, p. 45). This can easily be undertaken since most ethnic groups in Africa identify with specific geographic regions of the country. Where several ethnic groups reside in a geographic region and none has exclusive ownership rights, issues of property rights and ownership can be resolved through *proper* constitution making. To confront the problem of destructive ethnic mobilization in Africa requires proper constitution making (that is, reconstruction of the post-colonial state) to provide:

- each society with governance structures that effectively constrain the exercise of government agency, in order to minimize political opportunism (e.g., corruption and rent seeking);
- resource allocation systems that guarantee economic freedoms, enhance indigenous entrepreneurship and maximize wealth creation;
- well-defined and enforced property rights regimes (especially in environmental resources, in order to minimize overexploitation and agro-ecological degradation); and
- efficient and optimal units of collective choice (e.g., some form of constitutional federalism that utilizes the ethnic group as an autonomous political jurisdiction within the federation)—the latter would allow groups to resolve prisoner's dilemma problems and avoid subjecting themselves indefinitely to Pareto-inferior noncooperative market outcomes.

In resolving the problems of violent ethnic mobilization, public choice theory emphasizes the importance of rules to peaceful coexistence. The first line of business, thus, should be to reconstruct the post-colonial state and provide each African country with institutional arrangements (that is, a model of government) that (1) minimizes opportunism; (2) constrains the ability of interest groups (including ethnic and other social cleavages) to seize and employ governmental structures as instruments of plunder; (3) upholds the constitution and maintains law and order; (4) protects property rights and as a consequence, enhances wealth creation; (5) enforces contracts, but refrains from activities that restrain trade or exchange; (6) enforces rules against theft (and other forms of illegal redistribution of wealth, including those undertaken by the state); and (7) provides public goods efficiently and equitably. In such a society, ethnic competition and mobilization would still exist, but they will not necessarily be violent, since there would be appropriate avenues within each market for such conflict to be resolved peacefully.

The importance of rules to peaceful co-existence

In his now famous treatise titled, *Leviathan*, Thomas Hobbes (1651 [1962]) describes a stateless society in which there are no governance structures to regulate socio-political interaction, protect individual and civil liberties or enforce property rights. In such a society, individuals in an attempt to maximize their self-interest, concentrate their abilities and efforts on the exploitation of others instead of engaging in production (i.e., wealth creation). As a consequence, such a society is characterized by economic and social stagnation and chaos. To get out of this 'jungle', Hobbes suggested that individuals place constraints on their behavior through the creation and sustaining of a common authority. Thus, he considered *unlimited* government as essential for the existence of civil society.

Today, students of political economy generally agree that government can play an important and crucial role in regulating socio-political interaction in order to enhance wealth creation and peaceful co-existence of groups. However, research has determined that providing a society with a common authority is a necessary but not sufficient condition for the maintenance of civil society, peaceful coexistence and human progress. In order to maintain a viable civil society, enhance wealth creation and allow groups, including those based on ethnicity, to co-exist peacefully, government must be *constitutionally constrained*. Constraints on the exercise of government agency should be clearly stated and elaborated in the constitution.

In the late 17th century, John Locke (1690 [1988]) became one of the earliest proponents of the *limited government* or state as a condition for the maintenance of a viable civil society. Although Locke suggested that a common authority (i.e., government) was necessary for the establishment and sustaining of a civil society, he argued very forcefully that *individual liberty* (or rights) be respected and not be sacrificed to the state. Thus, he envisaged a state that would serve as an agent of the people but noted that if that government exceeded its authority, rebellion and war could break out.

Today, *contractarians,* foremost amongst them, James M. Buchanan (1975, 1989), emphasize the importance of rules to human progress. Rules regulate socio-political interaction (e.g., they prevent individuals from harming each other); and constrain the state and minimize political opportunism (e.g., bureaucratic corruption and rent seeking). In their 1985 treatise, Brennan and Buchanan argued that rules determine how individuals within a society interact with each other; provide market participants with a means to peacefully resolve conflict; provide information, allowing traders to anticipate the behavior of other market participants; and impose significant constraints on the behavior of individuals, as well as on that of the collectivity. In other words, in performing the duties assigned them by the people through the constitution, the state is constrained by the law. This contractarian view of the state is an extension of the concept or theory of exchange. Here, the emphasis is on assigning the state certain specific activities (that is, constitutionally defining the scope of state authority or power), and limiting the activities of each individual within society relative to those of other members, with wealth maximization as the ultimate goal. Thus, in Buchanan's view of the state, the major difference between totalitarian and non-totalitarian societies is that in the former, there does not exist rule-protected spheres in which individual liberties are guaranteed. It is important to note, however, that although a common governmental authority provides members of non-totalitarian societies significant gains, the latter are associated with substantial costs—the sacrifice of individual liberties (Buchanan, 1989, p. 54). Thus, when individuals within a society accept state authority, they invariably pay a price in the form of lost liberties. However, this does not imply the destruction of civil society since the laws establishing and regulating state authority guarantee the existence of a viable civil society. Proper constitution making should allow for the establishment of a state with adequate capacity to perform its functions well, but constrained well enough so that it does not endanger the existence of civil society—that is, the state is constitutionally constrained so that it does not abrogate individual liberties.

During the last forty years, destructive ethnic conflict has become a feature of many African countries. One could argue that these post-independence outcomes are due to the absence of a common governmental authority to regulate socio-political interaction or harmonize the various conflicting interests (see, e.g., Kimenyi, 1997). In post-independence Africa, however, Hobbesian 'jungle-type' outcomes appear to exist in many countries not because of the absence of a common state authority but because of relatively unconstrained governmental structures. In other words, while one could argue that Africa's chaotic political and economic situation is made possible by the absence of a common power to harmonize the various conflicting interests, the reality is that the continent's malaise is caused by poorly constrained or unconstrained governments. The post-independence state, through its activities in the economy, has contributed significantly to a lot of the violence that has pervaded the continent during the last several decades. For one thing, most of these relatively uncon-strained states have suffocated civil society, abrogated individual liberties, confiscated individual property without compensation, violated the rights of groups, and have generally engaged in resource redistributions that have stunted the development of indigenous entrepreneurship and the creation of the wealth that could have been used to deal with poverty and deprivation. In other instances, some of these states have either been unable (due to inadequate state capacity and capability) or unwilling (due to opportunism on the part of politicians and civil servants) to perform their basic functions (e.g., providing public goods and maintaining law and order). Such state neglect has been very devastating to rural communities. As a consequence, many people who live in the rural sectors of these countries are less likely than their urban counterparts to have effective access to health care and educational services. This has resulted in further marginalization of rural communities, most of which comprise ethno-regional groups, forcing the latter to engage in violent mobilization in an effort to improve their welfare.

Massive poverty and deprivation in post-independence Africa is the result of poorly specified and insecure property rights. The latter were made possible by excessive state intervention in markets. In addition to stunting entrepreneurship and wealth creation, government intervention in private exchange creates or exacerbates conflicts among groups and poses serious problems for governance. Most forms of government intervention in the African economies involve wealth and income redistributions that benefit some groups at the expense of others. One can view ethnic conflicts in the continent, thus, as a reflection of 'sub-optimal institutional arrange-ments that make it possible for governments to use discriminatory policies that seek to transfer benefits from one tribal group to another' (Kimenyi, 1997, p. 12–5). In addition, the lack of institutionalized processes for the peaceful resolution of competitive claims has forced groups to rely on armed conflict as a way to improving their participation in markets. In recent years, many social scientists have argued that deregulation or the reduction of state intervention in private exchange should significantly improve macroeconomic performance and lead to higher levels of human development. In fact, many multilateral organizations (e.g., the World Bank and the International Monetary Fund—IMF) and other African benefactors, have made similar suggestions, emphasizing the importance of deregulation to economic performance. Unfortunately, such policy reforms, even if implemented, are not likely to provide *long-term sustainable solutions* to the continent's problems of underdevelopment and destructive ethnic conflict. First, deregulation can be reversed by subsequent governments in response to pressure from interest groups within society. Second, the success of the policies prescribed depends on the country's existing institutional arrangements. The latter determine the incentive structures faced by market participants. Since deregulation does not change the country's institutional arrangements, incentive structures—which determine the behavior of market participants—remain the same, and as a consequence, the behavior of market participants is not affected. Today's African governments are notorious for (1) violating property rights—in order to redistribute income and wealth in favor of some ethnic groups and at the expense of others (cf. apartheid South Africa; and many other African countries [e.g., Cameroon, Nigeria, Rwanda, Somalia, and Zaire] where some ethno-regional coalitions dominated both governance and resource allocation and plundered the economy for their own benefit while relegating non-dominant groups to the periphery of the economy and society); and (2) abuse of individual and civil liberties. The violation of individual liberties and the attenuation or abrogation of property rights is part of the overall effort by the ruling coalition to redistribute income and wealth in favor of its members and supporters. Given the fact that most ruling coalitions in the African countries are also ethnic or ethno-regional coalitions, that implies that some ethnic groups would have to supply the transfers. In addition, given the nature of institutional arrangements—which do not provide constitutional means for regime change—some ethnic groups are likely to be forced to remain suppliers of transfers indefinitely. Many of these disadvantaged groups are likely to engage in violent mobilization in order to reduce their marginalization and improve their welfare through increased participation in markets—both political and economic.

Given the above discussion, it is evident that the solution to Africa's pervasive problems of underdevelopment and violent ethnic mobilization lies in state reconstruction to provide each society with more effective institutional arrangements. There is the possibility that Africans may have to engage in the process of redrawing their political boundaries in an effort to create more viable states—those that provide for optimal units of collective choice. However, that is not the subject of this chapter as the issue of ethnic federalism in the continent has been examined thoroughly elsewhere (see, for example, Kimenyi, 1997). In this chapter, we concentrate on state reconstruction to provide more effective and viable institutional arrangements—those that guarantee economic freedoms, limit government activity in the economy, enhance wealth creation, provide structures for peaceful resolution of conflict and guarantee the right of members of society—either as individuals or groups—to freely engage in exchange and contract. Thus, the rules will guarantee the right of persons to engage in exchange either as individuals, or as a group if doing so would enhance their welfare. Under such a system, ethnic competition for resources should not be any different from other forms of group mobilization (e.g., along class or religious lines) in order to compete for resources. Within the appropriate set of rules, no individual or group would be placed at a competitive advantage or disadvantage simply because of such special characteristics as race, ethnicity, wealth, geographic location, and so on. The idea is to establish and sustain fair, predictable and efficient mechanisms that can allow all individuals and groups to compete for both political and economic resources. Given the appropriate mechanism for resource allocation, then, ethnic mobilization need not necessarily become violent.

Decolonization and independence: improper constitution making and the adoption of inappropriate rules

During the colonial period, Africans blamed their poverty and deprivation on the exploitative and repressive institutional arrangements imposed by the Europeans. The new dispensation's primary objective in the continent was to redistribute Africa's wealth in favor of the metropolitan economies. As a consequence, the institutional arrangements imposed on the colonies enhanced the ability of the Europeans to meet their objectives; stunted indigenous entrepreneurship and the participation of Africans in wealth creation; increased inequality in the distribution of resources; and significantly marginalized the indigenous peoples. To enhance the management of the new territories, colonialists brought Africans from different ethnic groups, each with its own language, culture, religions, traditions, customs, and political and economic systems, to form a single political and administrative unit. As a consequence, each colony was made up of a gathering of indigenous groups who could only be kept together through the use of significant coercion. Peaceful co-existence of ethnic and other social cleavages was not secured through voluntary arrangements but by force. As a consequence, the colonies did not constitute optimal units of collective choice, forcing Africans to remain trapped in Pareto-inferior noncooperative outcomes (see, e.g., Kimenyi, 1998).

Many Africans saw decolonization and independence as an opportunity to dismantle the state inherited from the colonialists, reconstruct it and provide themselves with institutional arrangements that enhanced peaceful coexistence of groups; promoted indigenous entrepreneurship and maximized their ability to engage in wealth creating activities; adequately and effectively constrained the exercise of government agency (that is, institutional arrangements that provided for a constitutionally limited government); and provided structures for the peaceful resolution of conflict. It was generally believed that the new sovereign nations formed out of the colonies would represent optimal units of collective choice, allowing Africans to achieve Pareto-efficient cooperative outcomes. Unfortunately, the conditions under which they achieved their independence did not allow Africans to develop and adopt such efficient and viable institutional arrangements. In addition to the fact that they were unable to engage in *proper* constitution making, they could not readjust the political boundaries of the colonies in order to create more viable polities. Given the nature of colonization, especially regarding the arbitrary partition of the continent into colonies for the different European 'powers', decolonization should have involved an attempt to re-unite ethnic groups separated by the partition. Thus, the preparation of the British colony of Nigeria for independence, for example, should have been undertaken together with that of its neighbors—British Cameroons (Southern and Northern) to the east; the French colonies of Dahomey, Niger and Chad. Such a comprehensive approach would properly have resulted in political boundaries different from the ones that exist in these countries today, but would have allowed for the construction of more effective nations—that is states comprising optimal units of collective choice.

Kimenyi (1997, 1998, 1999) has shown that ethnicity can be used effectively to organize African societies and provide states or sovereignties that enhance peaceful coexistence. In this approach, the economic model of clubs is extended to show why organizing heterogeneous African countries along ethnic lines (that is, ethnic federalism) is efficient. According to this model, ethnic groups are allowed to organize for the provision of public goods and services. Advantages include the fact that tribal territories in the continent serve as natural boundaries which can provide stable political jurisdictions. Also, many of the factors that unite members of an ethnic group also facilitate the solving of prisoner's dilemma problems, allowing for cooperative outcomes to be achieved. In order for these groups to meet the preferences of their members, they must be guaranteed a significant level of political and economic autonomy—in other words, constitutional federalism. Of course, it is important to note that political jurisdictions will invariably have to cooperate on certain issues in order to better exploit and benefit from technological economies of scale (e.g., in the provision of public higher education several ethnic groups may find it more efficient to join together and own and operate a single institution rather than allow each to have its own university). Such cooperation, however, would be on a mutually beneficial *voluntary* basis, similar to market exchange. Thus, the 'ideal institutional arrangement that would preserve ethnic autonomy and yet permit ethnic groups to be united for some purposes is a [constitutional] federal arrangement' (Kimenyi, 1998, p. 58) with significant devolution of power to the local political jurisdictions.

As mentioned earlier, the partition of Africa split ethnic groups, placing part of the population under one European administration and the other under another. The process of decolonization should have provided these groups an opportunity to unite and form more viable political units. Had preparations for independence been handled properly, the new nations that emerged from the colonies could have been federal systems consisting of political jurisdictions formed along ethnic lines. Such an arrangement in most, but not all the African countries, would have produced more viable polities (see, Kimenyi, 1998).

In the majority of the African colonies, the process of 'transforming' the territories for independence was dominated and controlled by the colonial state; the resident European entrepreneurial and commercial class; a few urban-based Europeanized indigenous elites; and, in the case of colonies such as Algeria, Southern Rhodesia, Kenya, Mozambique, Angola, South Africa and Namibia (then called South West Africa), European settlers, the majority of whom intended to remain in the continent permanently (see, e.g., LeVine, 1964; Cowen, 1961). The African 'representatives' in the transformation process were indigenous inhabitants who had been schooled in the European languages and cultures; were employed in occupations of a European nature (as opposed to traditional African pursuits such as hunting and gathering); had most likely lived in the metropole for several years and had accepted European culture; and were attracted to European political and economic systems. In fact, during colonialism, many of these urban-based indigenous elites had served as petty officers in the colonial civil service. These individuals eventually came to represent an important and crucial link between the colonial state and the indigenous population. These groups—the colonial state, the indigenous elites, and the European entrepreneurs, including the settlers—were usually not well informed on social, economic, and political conditions in the rural areas of the colonies and did not quite understand the aspirations, needs, values, and problems of the majority of the population groups in the colony. Not only were members of these three groups not representative of each colony's diverse population, but they had not been elected by the people to represent them in the deliberations to prepare the colony for independence. Quite often, certain ethnic groups, primarily those which had had the earliest contact with colonial institutions (e.g., European languages, exchange economy, and culture and traditions), were the ones who provided most of the African representatives for the conferences that produced institutional arrangements for the post-independence society.

Many researchers have argued that the 'transition' from colonialism to independence was a reluctant, opportunistic and exploitative process in which the Europeans failed to assist the Africans to properly transform the critical domains and develop more efficient and viable institutional arrangements for the new societies (Fatton, 1990). The new African countries inherited, with little or no transformation, governance structures that had been designed to enhance the ability of Europeans to exploit Africans and their resources. Had decolonization and the preparation of the colonies for independence been a bottom-up and inclusive process that enfranchised Africans and provided them facilities to participate effectively and fully in state reconstruction, the outcome would have been more effective institutional arrangements and polities that comprised of optimal units of collective choice.

Why did the African countries adopt institutional arrangements that were not appropriate for their societies? Why were they unable to develop laws and institutions that reflected their values, traditions, customs and cultures, and aspirations? The primary reason for such outcomes was, as mentioned earlier, the fact that pre-independence constitution making and reconstruction of the colonial state was closed to all but a few Africans. The bulk of indigenous political opinion was excluded from constitutional discourse resulting in a *top-down* process in which each new nation's rules were designed externally and imposed on the people. First, almost without exception, the new nations based their institutional arrangements on European political models, producing and adopting constitutional rules that failed to reflect African realities, national specificities, and the people's historical experiences. Of course, it should be mentioned that borrowing ideas from other cultures was not the primary problem for the post-independence society. The problem lay in the fact that these borrowed models did not reflect local realities, the values of the people or those to be governed by the new rules, and were not adjusted well enough to make them relevant to the people. In the former French colonies, for example, those who had been appointed by the colonial government to select the constitution for the new countries simply adopted, almost verbatim, the Constitution of the French Fifth Republic (LeVine, 1964; Mbaku, 1997).

Second, as already mentioned, constitution making in each colony was dominated by three classes—*the colonial state, resident European entrepreneurs*, and a few *urban-based indigenous elites*, all of whom had very little information about conditions in the rural regions of the colony where most of the people lived. For example, when Britain granted independence to its colonies in South Africa in 1910, the new country's first constitution, the South Africa Act (9 Edward II, c.9) was designed exclusively by *white* representatives of the four colonies, Cape of Good Hope, Natal, the Transvaal, and the Orange River Colony. The majority of these colonies' population, which consisted of people from several African ethnic/language groups, was not provided the facilities to participate fully and effectively in constitution making. In fact, the white minority specifically made a concerted effort to make sure that the black majority did not participate in the process. In addition, the resident colonial power, Britain, did not insist on the participation of African groups (see, e.g., Cowen, 1961). As a consequence, the constitutional rules that emerged from the 1909 constitutional deliberations were designed to promote white supremacy and provide whites with the structures to exploit and marginalize the African peoples. This first constitution set the stage for the establishment of the repressive, cruel and exploitative apartheid system in 1948. Third, most of the pre-independence constitutional conferences were usually held in some metropolitan city, away from the people to be governed by the rules selected. The interests of the African peoples were represented at these conferences by urban-based indigenous elites, most of whom had been educated in Europe, lived there for many years, and had been captured by European culture, customs, and political traditions, and viewed African traditional economic and political systems as inferior, unsophisticated, not particularly 'modern' and obstacles to rapid development in the new countries. In the majority of cases, these elites were not elected by the people but were appointed by the departing colonialists, usually based on their willingness to establish a post-independence dispensation that would enhance the ability of the departing colonial power to have effective and adequate access to the resources of the new country. For example, in the French colonies, conditions for independence were often manipulated to make certain that governance structures were captured by indigenous elites who were willing to keep the new country within the French Community (LeVine, 1964). Fourth, in virtually all the cases, the final document adopted at independence was usually a thinly disguised version of the constitution of the new nation's former colonizer (see, e.g., LeVine, 1964, for a discussion of the events leading to the 'construction' and adoption of the first constitution of the *république du Cameroun*, the former UN Trust Territory of Cameroons under French administration which gained independence in 1960). This approach to constitution making cheated Africans out of an opportunity to construct, by themselves, their own constitutional rules and provide the proper foundation for the development of their institutions. Finally, it must be emphasized that the indigenous peoples were rarely consulted. The constitutional rules for the new countries were designed without the full and effective participation of Africans. According to LeVine (1997, p. 204), '[c]onstitutional debates were only rarely conducted outside the assizes of the drafting groups, and in most cases the finished product, while often the subject of intense public discussion, remained unaltered.' As a matter of fact, there does not seem to be any evidence to indicate that any post-1957 referendum on a proposed constitutional compact ever produced the rejection of the document. The outcome of constitutional deliberations is most likely to produce a viable and more effective set of rules if the process is bottom-up, participatory and inclusive—involving the extensive and full consultation of the people either directly or through their properly elected representatives. In each colony, however, the indigenous peoples were not enfranchised and provided the facilities to participate effectively in constitution making. As a consequence, the outcomes of these pre-independence deliberations were institutional arrangements that did not reflect the African people's values. Instead, the rules designed this way imposed on the indigenous peoples governance and resource allocation systems that were alien and not particularly suited to their needs. Like their colonial counterpart, the new rules (1) enhanced the ability of the state to engage in inefficient resource distributions, including the enactment of fiscally discriminatory legislation; (2) distorted economic incentives; (3) stunted indigenous entrepreneurship and discouraged wealth creation; and (4) significantly impeded economic growth and development. More important, however, is the fact that these institutional arrangements encouraged political opportunism, including bureaucratic corruption and rent seeking, and destructive ethnic conflict.

Many scholars of African political economy (see, e.g., LeVine, 1964) have suggested that the institutional arrangements that the African countries adopted at independence may have been the result of political exigency. It is argued that Africans were so eager to free themselves of European domination and exploitation and assume control of their lives that they were willing to put-off temporarily, proper constitutional discourse. Once independence was granted and governance structures were in the hands of indigenous elites, the latter could then engage the people in proper constitution making to reconstruct the post-colonial state and provide the new country with institutional arrangements that reflected not only the people's values but their unique conditions. Unfortunately, this approach had two major problems. First, the people who captured the evacuated structures of colonial hegemony made no effort to initiate a national debate on the constitution. As has been mentioned already, the state structures inherited from the colonialists were oppressive and exploitative, and enhanced the ability of the new leaders to exploit and marginalize citizens, especially those belonging to minority ethnic groups. The new leaders either manipulated the post-independence constitutions to increase and enhance their power and ability to monopolize political space or discarded them and ruled primarily by decree. Throughout the continent, post-independence leaders engaged in opportunistic reforms that legitimized their autocratic approaches to governance and enhanced their ability to monopolize the supply of legislation and the allocation of resources. Thus, as had been the case in the pre-independence period, post-independence institutional reforms were top-down, with participation limited to a few elites. The people were not enfranchised and provided the facilities to participate in the process (see, e.g., LeVine, 1979, 1997; Joseph, 1987). Second, the decolonization project did not provide Africans with the opportunity to develop polities that comprised optimal units of collective choice (see, e.g., Kimenyi, 1998).

Despite the monumental changes that have taken place in the African democratization project since the late 1980s and early 1990s, many Africans still live in societies regulated by weak, poorly designed and inappropriate institutional arrangements. In several countries, even these poorly designed rules have been abandoned in favor of rule by presidential or military decree. As a consequence, the government has been able to suffocate civil society, disenfranchise popular forces, plunder the economy for the benefit of the ruling coalition—which, in most of the African countries is made up of a few ethnic groups, and stunt the creation of the wealth that could have been used to confront poverty and deprivation. Perhaps, more important is the fact that this approach to governance has forced excluded, deprived and marginalized ethnic groups to engage in violent mobilization. As mentioned earlier, in these countries, the groups that control the apparatus of state also control access to the nation's resources. Unfortunately for deprived groups, constitutional methods for regime change either do not exist in these countries or function poorly. As a consequence, many marginalized ethnic groups have come to see violent competition as the only way for them to improve their political and economic participation. As is argued in this chapter, the effective way to provide sustainable solutions to the problems of destructive ethnic conflict is to engage in state reconstruction to provide (1) efficient and viable institutional arrangements; and (2) polities which comprise optimal units of collective choice.

Minimizing destructive ethnic mobilization: the role of the constitutionally limited government

Kimenyi (1998, 1997, 1999) has shown that the first step in minimizing destructive ethnic conflict in Africa is to engage in the restructuring of African countries in order to produce 'new' polities which comprise optimal units of collective choice. This involves some form of *constitutional federalism* in which each polity is divided into as many autonomous political jurisdictions as possible. In such a political system, the power of the central government is minimized in favor of greater political and fiscal authority to local and regional governmental units. In addition, the rights of citizens to migrate freely from one political jurisdiction to another, and to freely engage in exchange and contract should be constitutionally guaranteed. Such a constitutional arrangement effectively constrains the ability of the central or local governmental units to exploit citizens (see, e.g., Wiseman, 1990, pp. 121-122). The model advanced by Kimenyi (1998) for the African societies is based on the economic theory of clubs, and suggests that the autonomous political jurisdictions that comprise each nation be based on ethnic units. Each ethnic-based political jurisdiction would then be granted the power to supply certain public goods and services. Significant devolution of power in favor of local governmental units is essential for the success of such a governance system. It is important, however, that devolution not be seen as weakening the state. Instead, it should be recognized that permitting individuals at the local level to determine the fiscal packages that are unique to their political and economic environments actually improves and enhances governmental efficiency and the ability of the state to meet the needs of the people. Thus, decentralization, if undertaken properly and with the full and effective participation of the relevant stakeholders, will significantly improve governance and promote peaceful coexistence (World Bank, 1997). This process has two major dimensions: providing governmental units with enough authority to perform their duties effectively and efficiently; and making certain that governmental institutions are adequately constrained so that they do not become instruments of plunder. As noted by Mueller (1991, p. 342), a decentralized federal system minimizes conflict at the national level since each autonomous political unit can define 'a particular individual right in their own constitutions in those situations where agreement at the national level is not possible.' He argues further that federalism can minimize levels of conflict and allow groups to live together peacefully. Under federalism, he continues, '[c]onflicts over distributional and rights issues can be reduced, thus freeing each polity for the task of discovering and supplying a community's collective goods by drawing federalist political boundaries to separate the cultural groups that feel hostility toward one another' (Mueller, 1991, pp. 340-341).

Metropolitan areas, such as big cities, which are ethnically and politically diverse, can be allowed to enter constitutional negotiations as autonomous city-states (see, for example, Lowenberg, 1992). Since present African polities do not comprise optimal units of collective choice—due primarily to the nature of the partition of the continent by the Europeans in the late 19th century—it may be necessary to redraw some countries' political boundaries.

Constitutional federalism enhances the ability of individuals to migrate freely and at low cost to competitive political jurisdictions. If citizens can easily exit competitive political jurisdictions without incurring significant costs, then the ability of governmental units to employ coercion to exploit their citizens will be minimized. Competition between political units for tax payers should minimize the exploitation of citizens by the state and its structures (Anderson and Hill, 1986).

Placing constitutional constraints on the state in order to make sure that its agents do not engage in political opportunism in the post-contractual period is very important for the survival and proper functioning of the polity. It is important that during constitutional negotiations, the people determine an appropriate role for the state, define and elaborate it in the constitution. Research by public choice scholars has shown that an appropriate government is one that is *productive* and *protective*. In the former function, the state is expected to provide society with those goods and services that the private sector cannot organize efficiently, and in its latter function, the state should protect the lives, liberties, and property of citizens from both outside and domestic aggressors (see, e.g., Gwartney and Wagner, 1988).

As has been argued by Gwartney and Wagner (1988, p. 30), the appropriate government should be a '*consensual arrangement* designed for the *mutual betterment* of all' (emphasis added). As mentioned earlier, the institutional arrangements that the African countries adopted at independence cannot be viewed as consensual. In the post-independence period, the leaders were expected to engage the people in efforts to produce more consensual political arrangements. Unfortunately, such a process never took place, leaving the African people with oppressive and exploitative governance structures, most of which exacerbated inequalities in the distribution of resources and resulted in increased violent ethnic mobilization.

The literature on political economy in Africa now points to limited constitutional government as an effective way to deal with the problems of wealth creation, poverty, political opportunism and destructive ethnic conflict in the continent (see, e.g., Mbaku, 1998). During the last forty years, opportunism—bureaucratic corruption and rent seeking—have become endemic to the region. As Africans prepare for the new century, how can they minimize such behaviors? Many researchers have suggested that what economists call substantive constraints be incorporated into each country's constitution. Such constraints are expected to limit the ability of legislators to enact fiscally discriminatory legislation (that is, laws that allow the state to redistribute income and wealth from one group to another—in Africa, this has usually been from weak or minority ethnic groups to politically dominant ones, leading to violent mobilization by suppliers of the transfers to stop the process and by recipients to maintain the status quo). The nation's Supreme Court can then be assigned the job of enforcing compliance to the rules. A second strategy, called the procedural design approach, has also been suggested. It involves the establishment of 'political institutions and procedures which reduce the likelihood that governmental policies plundering some for the benefit of others will be adopted' (Wagner and Gwartney, 1988, p. 37). According to the latter approach, each country should establish a self-enforcing constitution, making constitutional maintenance (that is, enforcement of compliance to rules) an internal process (see Mbaku, 1997 for a discussion of the con-struction of the self-enforcing constitution).

While the substantive constraints approach is quite attractive, it does not appear to be very feasible for Africans at the present time in their political development. Today in Africa, the Supreme Court is not an independent institution, but an agency that is subordinate to the incumbent government. In most African countries, judiciary systems have been politicized and the judicial officers, including those who serve on the Supreme Court, serve at the pleasure of the incumbent head of state. In fact, many of these individuals are not elected by the people nor are they appointed by the people's dully elected representatives. Instead, those who serve in the courts are political appointees who owe their allegiance and jobs only to the nation's leaders and ruling coalition—the latter in many countries usually consists of ethnic or ethno-regional groups. Given the fact that the government retains the exclusive right to appoint and dismiss judiciary officers, it is not possible for the people to censure poorly per-forming, misbehaving and opportunistic court officials. Thus, the Supreme Court may not be an appropriate institution to enforce constitutional maintenance.

As a result of the fact that the Supreme Court may not be an appropri-ate institution to deal effectively with post-contractual opportunism, another viable option must be found. During the last several years, research by public choice scholars has pointed to the design and adoption of self-enforcing constitutions as a way to deal effectively with constitutional maintenance and political opportunism (see, e.g., Gwartney and Wagner, 1988; Buchanan and Tullock, 1962; Mbaku, 1997).

Parties to constitutional deliberations, which as we have suggested, are likely to be ethnic units, must consider the problem of opportunism by some participants. To minimize this problem and make the negotiating environment more competitive, each autonomous unit entering the negotia-tion must be guaranteed the right of exit. In constitutional negotiations, the threat of exit (and subsequent existence either as an independent polity or union with other autonomous units) can be used effectively against coer-cion and opportunism by other participants in the process. According to Lowenberg (1992, p. 310), '[t]he ability to shop around among alternative partners and alternative arrangements among autonomous groups provides the basis for efficient constitutional outcomes.' It is important to emphasize that the process of designing the constitution be as inclusive as possible, giving each unit the opportunity to secure rules that maximize its values. If, as a result of poor constitution making, the rules produced place some ethnic groups at a competitive disadvantage, violent ethnic mobilization is likely to be pervasive in the post-contractual society.

For ethnically plural societies, the voting rule is an important institutional factor that has significant impact on the degree of democracy in the country. In constitutional federalism, the voting rule will have a significant impact on representation at the federal level. As a result of colonial policies, most of the educated and highly skilled individuals in the African countries at independence were from those ethnic groups that had had the earliest contacts with colonial institutions. Despite significant efforts made by the post-independence society, this imbalance remains in many of the continent's polities. Thus, if a country adopts constitutional federalism with a majoritarian voting rule, ethnic groups with significant political skills and/or capital could dominate governance at the federal level, making it very difficult for weak and relatively less endowed groups to participate in governance. The result would be violent confrontation between the state and deprived groups. To improve the participation of all groups in governance at the federal level, federalism should be combined with a proportional electoral system (Vanhanen, 1991; Mueller, 1991).

Conclusion

As Africa and Africans prepare for the new century, they face many serious problems. The most important of them are destructive ethnic conflict and pervasive poverty and deprivation. During the last forty years, most African countries have failed to improve the living standards of their citizens. Since the 1960s, many developing countries have been able to significantly raise the quality of life of their citizens, thanks to relatively healthy rates of economic growth. The existence of structures that enhance entrepreneurship and constrain the ability of the state to engage in inefficient redistributions of income and wealth, have resulted in healthy rates of economic growth in these countries, providing them with the wealth that they need to confront mass poverty. Unfortunately, this move towards increased human progress has not been universal. Relatively poor macroeconomic performance in the majority of African countries during the last several decades has made it difficult or impossible for these societies to deal effectively with underdevelopment. Although many reasons have been advanced to explain continued poverty in Africa, the most critical determinant of the continent's continued economic deterioration is the absence of institutional arrangements that enhance entrepreneurship and wealth creation, but minimize political opportunism, including corruption and rent seeking.

In addition to poverty, destructive ethnic conflict has also become endemic in Africa. In fact, during the last several years, violent ethnic competition has resulted in bloody and growth-stunting civil wars in many African countries, including Rwanda, Somalia, Nigeria, Liberia, Zaire, and Sierra Leone. In addition, racial bigotry in apartheid South Africa caused several bloody confrontations between blacks and whites that resulted in the deaths of many people and the destruction of significant amounts of property. Basically, during the last several years, Africa's many ethnic and other social cleavages have not been able to live together peacefully. In this chapter, we have argued that the most effective way to enhance peaceful coexistence of groups is to provide each society with institutional arrangements that (1) minimize political opportunism; (2) enhance entrepreneurship and wealth creation; and (3) provide mechanisms that do not place any individual or group at a competitive disadvantage or advantage in the competition for resources—that is, institutional structures that are considered by members of society to be fair and allow all individuals and groups to compete for both political and economic resources. If each society provides itself with such institutional arrangements, then ethnic mobilization need not necessarily become violent.

References

Abell, P. (1989), 'Games in Networks: A Sociological Theory of Voluntary Associations', *Rationality and Choice*, Vol. 1, No. 2 (October), pp. 259–262.

Abell, P. (1992), 'Is Rational Choice Theory a Rational Choice of Theory?', in Coleman, J. and Fararo, T. (eds.), *Rational Choice Theory: Advocacy and Critique*, Sage: Newbury Park, CA.

Agbese, P. O. (1992), 'With Fingers on the Trigger: The Military as Custodian of Democracy in Nigeria', *Journal of Third World Studies*, Vol. 9, No. 2, pp. 220–253.

Anderson, T. L. and Hill, P. J. (1986), 'Constraining the Transfer Society: Constitutional and Moral Dimensions', *Cato Journal*, Vol. 6, No. 1, pp. 317–339.

Banton, M. (1983), *Racial and Ethnic Competition*, Cambridge University: New York.

Banton, M. (1985), 'Mixed Motives and the Processes of Rationalization', *Ethnic and Racial Studies*, Vol. 8, pp. 534–547.

Banton, M. (1995), 'Rational Choice Theories', *American Behavioral Scientist*, Vol. 38, No. 3 (January), pp. 478–497.

Barth, F. (1969), *Ethnic Groups and Boundaries*, Little, Brown: Boston, MA.

Brams, S. J. and Kilgour, M. (1988), *Game Theory and National Security*, Basil Blackwell: New York.

Brennan, G. and Buchanan, J. M. (1985), *The Reason of Rules: Constitutional Political Economy*, Cambridge University Press: Cambridge.

Brough, W. and Kimenyi, M. S. (1986), 'On the Inefficient Extraction of Rents by Dictators', *Public Choice*, Vol. 48, No. 1, pp. 37–48.

Buchanan, J. M. (1975), *The Limits of Liberty: Between Anarchy and Leviathan*, University of Chicago Press: Chicago.

Buchanan, J. M. (1989), *Explorations into Constitutional Economics*, Texas A&M University Press: College Station.

Buchanan, J. M. and Tullock, G. (1962), *The Calculus of Consent: Logical Foundations of Constitutional Democracy*, The University of Michigan Press: Ann Arbor, MI.

Bunting, B. (1986), *The Rise of the South African Reich*, International Defense and Aid Fund for Southern Africa: London.

Cohen, A. (1974), *Urban Ethnicity*, Harper & Row: New York.

Coleman, J. (ed.) (1986), *Individual Interests and Collective Action: Selected Essays*, Cambridge University Press: Cambridge.

Cowen, D. V. (1961), *The Foundations of Freedom: With Special Reference to Southern Africa*, Oxford University Press: Cape Town.

Darnell, A. and Parikh, S. (1988), 'Religion, Ethnicity, and the Role of the State: Explaining Conflict in Assam', *Ethnic and Racial Studies*, Vol. 11, pp. 263–281.

Davis, J. F. (1991), *Who is Black? One Nation's Definition*, Pennsylvania State University: University Park.

Decalo, S. (1992), 'The Process, Prospects and Constraints of Democratization in Africa', *African Affairs*, Vol. 9, No. 362, pp. 7–35.

Dollery, B. (1989), 'Capital, Labour and State: A Rent-Seeking Framework for South African Political Economy', *Journal for Studies in Economics and Econometrics*, Vol. 13, No. 2, pp. 59–70.

Dollery, B. (1990), 'Labour Apartheid in South Africa: A Rent-Seeking Approach to Discriminatory Legislation', *Australian Economic Papers*, Vol. 29, No. 54, pp. 113–127.

Doxey, G. V. (1961), *The Industrial Colour Bar*, Oxford University Press: Cape Town.

Elster, J. (1979), *Ulysses and the Sirens: Studies in Rationality and Irrationality*, Cambridge University Press: Cambridge.

Fatton, R. Jr. (1990), 'Liberal Democracy in Africa', *Political Science Quarterly*, Vol. 105, No. 3, pp. 455–473.

Fredrickson, G. M. (1981), *White Supremacy: A Comparative Study in American and South African History*, Oxford University Press: Oxford.

Gardinier, D. (1971), 'French Colonial Rule in Africa: A Bibliographical Essay', in Gifford, P. and Louis, R. (eds.), *France and Britain in Africa: Imperial Rivalry and Colonial Rule*, Yale University Press: New Haven, CT.

Gwartney, J. D. and Wagner, R. E. (1988), 'Public Choice and the Conduct of Representative Government', in Gwartney, J. D. and Wagner, R. E. (eds.), *Public Choice and Constitutional Economics*, JAI Press: Greenwich, CT.

Hardin, R. (1997), 'Economic Theories of State', in Mueller, D. (ed.), *Perspectives on Public Choice: A Handbook*, Cambridge University Press: Cambridge.

Harris, M. (1964), *Patterns of Race in the Americas*, Norton: New York.

Hechter, M. (1975), *Internal Colonialism*, University of California Press: Berkeley.

Hechter, M. (1978), 'Group Formation and the Cultural Division of Labor', *American Journal of Sociology*, Vol. 84, pp. 293–318.

Hechter, M. (1987), *Principles of Group Solidarity*, University of California Press: Berkeley, CA.

Hechter, M. (1989), 'Rational Choice Foundations of Social Order', in Turner, J. (ed.), *Theory Building in Sociology: Assessing Theoretical Comulation*, Sage: Newbury Park, CA.

Hechter, M. (1992), 'The Dynamics of Secession', *Acta Sociologica*, Vol. 35, pp. 267–283.

Hechter, M. and Levi, M. (1979), 'The Comparative Analysis of Ethnoregional Movements', *Ethnic and Racial Studies*, Vol. 2, pp. 260–274.

Hey, J. (1993), 'Rationality is as Rationality Does', in Gerrad, B. (ed.), *The Economics of Rationality*, Routledge: London.

Hobbes, T. ([1651] 1962), *Leviathan*, Collier: New York.

Horowitz, D. (1985), *Ethnic Groups in Conflict*, University of California Press: Berkeley, CA.

Hutt, W. H. (1964), *The Economics of the Colour Bar*, Institute for Economic Affairs: London.

IDAF (International Defense and Aid Fund for Southern Africa) (1991), *Apartheid: The Facts*, IDAF: London.

Ihonvbere, J. O. and Ekekwe, E. (1988), 'Dependent Capitalism, Structural Adjustment and Democratic Possibilities in Nigeria's Third Republic', *Afrika Spectrum*, Vol. 23, No. 3, pp. 273–292.

Joseph, R. A. (1987), *Democracy and Prebendal Politics in Nigeria: The Rise and Fall of the Second Republic*, Cambridge University Press.

Kimenyi, M. S. (1987), 'Bureaucratic Rent and Political Institutions', *Economia Delle Scelte Pubbliche*, Vol. 5, No. 3, pp. 189–199.

Kimenyi, M. S. (1989), 'Interest Groups, Transfer Seeking and Democratization: Competition for the Benefits of Governmental Power May Explain African Political Instability', *American Journal of Economics and Sociology*, Vol. 48, No. 3, pp. 339–349.

Kimenyi, M. S. (1997), *Ethnic Diversity, Liberty and the State: The African Dilemma*, Edward Elgar: Cheltenham, UK.

Kimenyi, M. S. (1998), 'Harmonizing Ethnic Claims in Africa: A Proposal for Ethnic-Based Federalism', *Cato Journal*, Vol. 18, No. 1 (Spring/Summer), pp. 43–63.

Kimenyi, M. S. (1999), 'Spatial Competition, Ethnicity, and the Optimal Size and Composition of Units of Collective Choice', in Kimenyi, M. S. and Mbaku, J. M. (eds.), *Institutions and Collective Choice in Developing Countries: Applications of the Theory of Public Choice*, Ashgate: Aldershot, UK and Brookfield, VT.

Kimenyi, M. S. and Mbaku, J. M. (1993), 'Rent Seeking and Institutional Stability in Developing Countries', *Public Choice*, Vol. 77, No. 2, pp. 385–405.

Kofele-Kale, N. (1986), 'Ethnicity, Regionalism, and Political Power: A Post-Mortem of Ahidjo's Cameroon', in Schatzberg, M. G. and Zartman, I. W. (eds.), *The Political Economy of Cameroon*, Praeger: New York.

Laitin, D. D. (1986), *Hegemony and Culture: Politics and Religious Change Among the Yoruba*, University of Chicago Press: Chicago, IL.

LeVine, V. T. (1964), *The Cameroons: From Mandate to Independence*, University of California Press: Berkeley.

LeVine, V. T. (1979), 'Parliaments in Francophone Africa: Some Lessons from the Decolonization Process', in Smith, J. and Muolf, L. D. (eds.), *Legislatures in Development: Dynamics of Change in New and Old States*, Durham, NC: Duke University Press.

LeVine, V. T. (1997), 'The Fall and Rise of Constitutionalism in West Africa', *The Journal of Modern African Studies*, Vol. 35, No. 2, pp. 181–206.

Locke, J. ([1690] 1988), *Two Treaties of Government*, edited by Laslett, P., Cambridge University Press: New York.

Lopez, D. and Espiritu, Y. (1990), 'Panethnicity in the Unites States: A Theoretical Framework', *Ethnic and Racial Studies*, Vol. 13, pp. 198–224.

Lowenberg, A. D. (1992), 'A Post-Apartheid Constitution for South Africa: Lessons from Public Choice', *Cato Journal*, Vol. 12, No. 2, pp. 297–319.

Magubane, B. M. (1979), *The Political Economy of Race and Class in South Africa*, Monthly Review Press: New York.

Mandela, N. (1990), *Nelson Mandela's Speeches, 1990: Intensify the Struggle to Abolish Apartheid*, Pathfinder: New York.

Marx, K. (1957), *Capital*, Vol. 2, Foreign Languages: Moscow.

Marx, K. (1959), *Capital*, Vols. 2 & 3, Foreign Languages: Moscow.

Mbaku, J. M. (1991), 'Property Rights, European Colonialism, and Rent Seeking in Africa', *The European Studies Journal*, Vol. 8, No. 1 (Spring), pp. 25–45.

Mbaku, J. M. (1993), 'Markets and the Economic Origins of Apartheid in South Africa', *The Indian Journal of Social Science*, Vol. 6, No. 2, pp. 139–158.

Mbaku, J. M. (1994), 'Military Coups as Rent-Seeking Behavior', *Journal of Political and Military Sociology*, Vol. 22 (Winter), pp. 241–284.

Mbaku, J. M. (1995), 'Military Intervention in African Politics: Lessons from Public Choice', *Konjunkturpolitik* (Berlin), Vol. 41, No. 3, pp. 268–291.

Mbaku, J. M. (1997), *Institutions and Reform in Africa: The Public Choice Perspective*, Praeger: Westport, CT.

Mbaku, J. M. (1998), 'Improving African Participation in the Global Economy: The Role of Economic Freedom', *Business & the Contemporary World*, Vol. 10, No. 2, pp. 297–338.

Mbaku, J. and Paul, C. (1989), 'Political Instability in Africa: A Rent-Seeking Approach', *Public Choice*, Vol. 63, No. 1, pp. 63–72.

Mehta, P. B. (1998), 'Ethnicity, Nationalism and Violence in South Asia', *Pacific Affairs*, Vol. 71, No. 3, pp. 377–396.

Morrison, D., Mitchell, R. C. and Paden, J. N. (1989), *Black Africa: A Comparative Handbook*, 2nd Edition, Paragon House, Irvington: New York.

Mueller, D. C. (1991), 'Choosing a Constitution in East Europe: Lessons from Public Choice', *Journal of Comparative Economics*, Vol. 15, No. 2, pp. 325–348.

Myerson, R. B. (1991), *Game Theory: Analysis of Conflict*, Harvard University Press: Cambridge, MA.

Nafziger, E. W. (1983), *The Economics of Political Instability: The Nigerian-Biafran War*, Westview Press: Boulder, CO.

Nagel, J. (1995), 'Resource Competition Theories', *American Behavioral Scientist*, Vol. 38, No. 3 (January), pp. 442–458.

Nattrass, J. (1981), *The South African Economy: Its Growth and Change*, Oxford University Press: Cape Town.

Nielsen, F. (1986), 'Structural Conduciveness and Ethnic Mobilization: The Flemish Movement in Belgium', in Olzak, S. and Nagel, J. (eds.), *Competitive Ethnic Relations*, Academic Press: New York.

Opp, K.-D. (1989), *The Rationality of Political Protest: A Camparative Analysis of Rational Choice Theory*, Westview Press: Boulder, CO.

Ostrom, E., Schroeder, L. and Wynne, S. (1993), *Institutional Incentives and Sustainable Development: Infrastructure Policies in Perspective*, Westview Press: Boulder, CO.

Ragin, C. (1986), 'The Impact of Celtic Nationalism on Class Politics in Scotland and Wales', in Olzak, S. and Nagel, J. (eds.), *Competitive Ethnic Relations*, Academic Press: New York.

Runciman, W. G. (ed.) (1978), *Weber: Selections in Translation*, Cambridge University Press: Cambridge.

Schemerhorn, R. A. (1978), *Ethnic Plurality in India*, University of Arizona Press: Tucson, AZ.

Simmons, R. (1982), *Affirmative Action: Conflict and Change in Higher Education After Bakke*, Schenkman: Cambridge, MA.

St. Jorre, J. (1972), *The Nigerian Civil War*, Hodder and Stoughton: London.

Stigler, G. and Becker, G. (1977), 'De Gustibus Non Est Disputandum', *American Economic Review*, Vol. 67, No. 2, pp. 76–90.

Thompson, V. and Adloff, R. (1969), *French West Africa*, Greenwood Press: New York.

Tollison, R. D. (1997), 'Rent Seeking', in Mueller, D. (ed.), *Perspectives on Public Choice: A Handbook*, Cambridge University Press: Cambridge.

Vanhanen, T. (1991), 'Institutional Strategies of Democratization', Paper presented at the 25th World Congress of the International Political Science Association in Buenos Aires.

Wagner, R. E. and Gwartney, J. D. (1988), 'Public Choice and Constitutional Order', in Gwartney, J. D. and Wagner, R. E. (eds.), *Public Choice and Constitutional Economics*, JAI Press: Greenwich, CT.

Williamson, O. (1994), 'Transaction Costs Economics and Organization Theory', in Smelser, N. and Swedberg, R. (eds.), *The Handbook of Economic Sociology*, Princeton University Press: Princeton, NJ.

Wiseman, A. (1990), 'Principles of Political Economy: An Outline Proposal, Illustrated by Application to Fiscal Federalism', *Constitutional Political Economy*, Vol. 1 (Winter), pp. 101–124.

Wittman, D. (1995), *The Myth of Democratic Failure: Why Political Institutions are Efficient*, University of Chicago Press: Chicago, IL.

World Bank (1997), *World Development Report, 1997*, Oxford University Press: New York.

Young, C. (1976), *The Politics of Cultural Pluralism*, The University of Wisconsin Press: Madison, WI.

Young, C. (1986), 'Cultural Pluralism in the Third World', in Olzak, S. and Nagel, J. (eds.), *Competitive Ethnic Relations*, Academic Press: New York.

Young, C. (1993), *The Rising Tide of Cultural Pluralism*, The University of Wisconsin Press: Madison, WI.

Zafirovski, M. (1999), 'What is Really Rational Choice? Beyond the Utilitarian Concept of Rationality', *Current Sociology*, Vol. 47, No. 1 (January), 47–113.

4

Harmonizing Ethnic Claims in Africa: A Proposal for Ethnic-based Federalism

MWANGI S. KIMENYI

Most African states are unitary with political power vested in the central government. Laws and decisions concerning the public sector are enacted and enforced by the central government.[1] Authority is delegated to junior officials who implement policies with rigid guidelines. Provincial and district levels of government serve administrative roles but do not make laws, collect taxes, or make spending decisions.[2] Strictly speaking, political power is centrally concentrated with heads of state holding power over all public policies affecting the polity. In most African states, no constitutional limitations constrain the central authority in its exercise of power over public activities at all levels.

The unitary states of Africa largely reflect the colonial legacy. European colonial powers subdivided the African continent among themselves, establishing boundaries that arbitrarily linked heterogeneous groups in one country and separated otherwise homogenous, or closely related populations, in another. After independence, charismatic leaders, frequently those who had led the nations during the struggles for independence, forcefully argued for unitary governments much like the colonial governments they replaced. Concentration of power was considered a necessary condition to maintain unity. In fact, even decentralization within unitary states has been considered a political risk because it could reinforce ethnic loyalty at the expense of loyalty to the nation.

Nonetheless, the presumed benefits of unitary governments have proved illusionary. In virtually all the countries, post independence has been marked by internal strife, military coups, and civil wars. Conflicts have generally been between heterogeneous population groups within the country. Thus, although an argument for establishing centralized unitary states was that such institutional arrangements would help unify the various ethnic groups, the African experience with unitary states has been disappointing. The experiment with unitary states shows that such institutional arrangements are not suited to harmonizing the interests of heterogeneous groups.

A common explanation for the institutional crisis in Africa is the extreme poverty in the continent. In other words, poverty is seen as the main cause of institutional crisis rather than the outcome of institutional failure. However, research using public choice theory provides alternative explanations for political instability, for unwholesome features of political institutions such as bureaucratic corruption, and for dismal economic performance in Africa.[3] Those studies treat ethnic groups as special interests that compete for transfers from the central government. Members of a particular ethnic group consider themselves different from those of other groups and have an interest in increasing the welfare of their members relative to that of other ethnic groups. Because of the concentration of power in unitary states, the leadership can redistribute resources from some ethnic groups to others. Consequently, a tendency exists for ethnic groups to compete for the control of the instruments of transfer because such control assures the controlling group a consistent flow of transfers. Ethnic competition for control of the instruments of transfer has had disastrous results in many African countries. The ongoing conflicts in Rwanda, Sudan, and Zaire are but a few of the cases where members of one ethnic group continue to inflict serious atrocities against members of other groups. The competition for political control results in ethnic conflicts, military coups, and civil wars. Such outcomes, plus the non-optimal public policies designed to benefit some groups at the expense of others, translate into poor economic performance. It is therefore difficult to justify the claim that unitary states unite heterogeneous populations.

There is convincing evidence showing that Africa's unitary states do not comprise 'optimal units of collective choice.' Unifying ethnic groups by decree has resulted in institutions that are not suited to achieving cooperative agreements among the various groups. Instead, more often than not, unitary states associate with Pareto-inferior outcomes whereby competing groups fail to achieve cooperative solutions in prisoner's dilemma situations. Groups in these institutions are therefore trapped in Pareto-inferior non-cooperative outcomes. Thus, in essence, highly centralized unitary states have resulted in outcomes that are very much like those found in stateless societies described by Thomas Hobbes ([1651] 1962). It is clear that the observed crises in Africa reflect institutional failures, and for Africans to emerge from this state of affairs, it will be necessary to establish institutions that facilitate the achievement of cooperative solutions in prisoner's dilemma situations.

This chapter advances the idea that the most pressing institutional problems confronting Africans have to do with the internal organization of their states. Specifically, African countries do not use political arrangements that are suited to solving prisoner's dilemma problems. The chapter argues that to harmonize conflicting interests of various ethnic groups, countries characterized by high degrees of ethnic diversity should adopt institutional arrangements that utilize ethnic units as a basis for local governments. The analysis presented here suggests that because members of each ethnic group consider themselves different from members of other groups, establishment of ethnic governmental units that possess a fair degree of autonomy would be the most desirable form of organizing African societies. Since ethnic groups associate with particular territories, African states are naturally suited for the establishment of federal systems of government.[4]

The chapter proceeds as follows: First a brief history of African countries and their institutions is discussed. Ethnicity and its implications for the organization of African societies are then examined. Ethnic groups are viewed as being analogous to voluntary clubs that perform some desirable functions for the members. It is demonstrated that ethnic groups may be best suited to provide some 'local' public goods and therefore ethnicity could be used to define local jurisdictions in a federal system. The chapter then outlines some features of African institutions that make federalism desirable followed by some concluding remarks.

Colonial rule and the creation of the African state

Institutions of collective choice emerge as solutions to minimize the transaction costs of achieving cooperative agreements. Such agreements are necessary for Pareto optimality in the presence of public goods and externalities. Absent a government, the independent self-interested actions of each member of society translate into outcomes that are Pareto-inferior.

Table 4.1   Ethnic group's dilemma

Group 1	Group 2	
	Live peacefully	Steal
Live peacefully	#1 (300, 300)	#3 (0, 400)
Steal	#2 (400, 0)	#4 (30, 30)

This result is demonstrated by the classic prisoner's dilemma matrix as shown in Table 4.1. The matrix shows the payoffs to two ethnic groups who are in a conflict situation. Members of ethnic groups can either live peacefully or steal from each other. The payoff matrix shows that both ethnic groups are better off if they live peacefully (cell #1) instead of stealing from one another (cell #4). However, each ethnic group would be better off if it succeeded in stealing from the other (cell #2 and #3) as long as the other decided to live peacefully. The situation shown in the matrix represents a dilemma because the 'steal' strategy dominates the 'live peacefully' strategy. In the absence of cooperative agreements, the ethnic groups are worse off than if they entered into such agreements. Once the ethnic groups recognize this dilemma, it is in their best interest to reach agreement and achieve the cooperative solution (cell #1).[5]

As noted, African countries are characterized by dictatorial political systems, serious internal divisions, and civil wars. Those outcomes suggest that institutional arrangements in Africa are not effective in solving prisoner's dilemma problems and are unable to facilitate the achievement of cooperative solutions. While many African countries are attempting to establish constitutional democracies, there seems to be little hope that such efforts will result in a resolution to the current crisis in the continent. To understand why institutional arrangements in Africa fail to facilitate the achievement of cooperative agreements, and why merely writing new constitutions without radical transformation of the institutions may be futile, it is necessary to look at the origin of the present day African states and their institutional arrangements.

The emergence of the modern African state is largely the result of a number of events that disrupted the traditional African way of life. The most important of these include the African slave trade, the spread of Islam, and the imposition of colonial rule. The people of North Africa, for example, readily accepted Islam and governmental institutions introduced by Arabs. Islam also had some influence on people living along the East African Coast. The slave trade, on the other hand, provided a lucrative source of wealth to Arabs, Europeans, and African Kingdoms that were involved in the trade. The slave trade also created a variety of conflict situations as slave raids spread from the coast to the interior regions of Africa and guns were introduced into African states as payment for slaves. Those events disrupted the organization of traditional societies but did not have significant lasting effects on the basic institutions of most of sub-Saharan Africa.

Probably the most important event that explains contemporary African institutions is European colonialism. During the late 1800s, Great Britain, France, Germany, Belgium, and to a lesser extent Italy and Spain, were heavily engaged in attempts to place under their control parts of the African continent—a process that is generally referred to as the 'scramble for Africa.' Between 1870 and 1880, the European powers rapidly expanded their territorial claims and as each power acquired more and more of the continent, it became apparent that competition for Africa threatened peace in Europe. In 1884, Chancellor Otto Von Bismarck of Prussia invited European nations for a conference in Berlin with the main goal of regularizing the scramble for Africa. The Berlin Act of February 26, 1885, stipulated how Africa would be partitioned into European colonies. By 1910, the partition of Africa was achieved and, for the next 45 years, only Liberia and Ethiopia (which was occupied by Italy) remained independent nations (Burke, 1991).

Colonial rule adversely affected African institutions. Indeed, many of the problematic features of current African political institutions are the product of the colonial experience (Mbaku and Kimenyi 1995).[6] Most important, in partitioning Africa among themselves across *spheres of influence*, colonial powers rarely took into consideration the issue of ethnic heterogeneity. In some countries, the boundaries were drawn in a manner that separated members of the same ethnic group by placing them in different countries while at the same time placing other, formerly separate groups in the same country. Partition was implemented without due regard to ethnicity, culture, or even the existing institutions of government. The various groups did not participate in deciding which other groups to unite with nor did they have an opportunity to agree on the nature of their relationship with these other groups. In the process, different ethnic groups were placed within the same authority and confined within the same boundaries. In other cases, members of one ethnic group were dispersed among different nations. Likewise, colonial partition disrupted long established kingdoms and ethnic governments, and also disrupted existing trade networks and other inter-ethnic linkages. Thus, the political units that were created by Europeans were not only arbitrary but also lacked any strong unifying factors.[7]

At the time of independence, the new nations had to make crucial decisions concerning the constitutional dimensions of government activities. These dimensions included such characteristics as the number of jurisdictional levels, whether the political system was to be unitary with power concentrated at one level, or federal system with power distributed between regional governments and a central government. In the case of the federal system, decisions had to be made concerning the number of levels, such as provincial, district, municipal, and local, and also the functions that would be performed at each level. Other decisions pertained to procedures and processes of selecting representatives, and the constitutional rules regulating the amendment of the constitution.

In selecting particular constitutional dimensions, the primary objectives included the achievement of both economic growth and a just and free society that provided freedom from oppression of one group by another. The leaders, at least ostensibly, sought to adopt constitutions that would advance individual liberty.

Concerned by the fact that the various ethnic, religious, and linguistic groups in each of the countries considered themselves different from other groups in various respects, the issue of unity was a primary concern. Specifically, unifying the groups into one national state was considered crucial for political stability. To be sure, Africans had to deal with pressing problems of unity after independence that may have required them to adopt unifying policies. For example, many ethnic communities existed independently. These communities frequently consisted of thousands of members and possessed well-developed cultures and languages and clear ethnic consciousness.

However, the existing national boundaries cut across those groups, ignoring the boundaries that defined previously autonomous units. For this reason, leaders advocated the establishment of unitary states with a high concentration of power. It was claimed that centralizing power allowed for the adoption of uniform policies and for the balancing of economic resources, thus uniting diverse populations.

Some leaders argued that single-party political systems were more appropriate for African countries because all groups (ethnic, religious, linguistic), regardless of their differences, would be joined together under one party. Thus, the single-party system was seen as an important unifying agent of otherwise different groups. The leaders warned that unity would be sacrificed if political party competition were to be introduced because different political parties would be dominated by particular ethnic and linguistic groups, which in essence would promote *tribalism* (Winchester, 1986). Thus, the common response to diversity was the adoption of policies and institutional arrangements that unified heterogeneous populations by limiting expressions of group preferences.[8]

Unfortunately, attempts to unify ethnic groups in Africa have largely been unsuccessful as evidenced by various ethnic rivalries that have resulted in continuous civil wars in the continent and the domination of some ethnic groups by others. Thus, evidence points to the fact that institutions of the sub-Saharan African countries are not adequate to deal with the high degree of population heterogeneity. Institutional arrangements that have sought to unify ethnic groups by denying them autonomy have not been successful in achieving cooperative agreements among the ethnic groups. These arrangements create situations whereby ethnic groups are trapped in a Pareto-inferior 'steal-steal' strategy. It appears that units of collective choice that seek to unify various ethnic groups are not optimal and therefore do not minimize the transactions costs of achieving cooperative agreements. It is contended here that for units of collective choice to minimize the costs of arriving at cooperative agreements, they must to some degree be based on ethnicity.

Ethnic clubs and units of collective choice

To appreciate the significance of ethnicity in the organization of African societies, it helps to note a number of features relating to ethnic composition of those countries. The first of these is that sub-Saharan Africa is ethnically very complex. In total, there are over 2,000 distinct ethnic groups or societies, each of which has its own language or dialect, culture and tradition (Ayittey, 1992). These ethnic groups vary in size, with some having as few as 100,000 members and others encompassing millions of people. The degree of ethnic heterogeneity varies widely across the countries. In Rwanda and Burundi, for example, there are only two primary ethnic groups and two languages. In Sudan on the other hand, there are over 170 distinct languages. In Nigeria, there are between 200 and 400 distinct linguistic groups, and in Zaire, there are about 250 ethnic groups.

The other notable feature is that Africans show a high degree of ethnic identification. By and large, identifying with one's ethnic group is highly valued. As such, resources are devoted to make certain that members of a group continue to identify with that group. In virtually all African communities, children are taught from a very young age that they should identify with and be proud of their ethnic group. Thus, children learn at early ages that it is honorable to vote for members of their ethnic group or region, and that members of some ethnic groups are not trustworthy and thus they should not do business with them. In some cases, ethnic group members are warned against associating with members of particular ethnic groups.[9] As stated by Horowitz (1985, p. 7), 'in general, ethnic identity is strongly felt, behavior based on ethnicity is normatively sanctioned, and ethnicity is often accompanied by hostility toward outgroups.'

In most areas of everyday life, there are many instances in which individuals identify with members of their own ethnic group. Thus, even in major cities where people from different ethnic groups live in close proximity, ethnic groupings emerge as individuals freely select with whom to associate. Even today, the majority of urban social welfare organizations are organized along ethnic lines. Urban soccer leagues are primarily organized along ethnic lines. Strong ethnic preference has also been in a variety of studies that seek to measure the social or political spatial 'distance' between ethnic groups. W. J. Breytenbach (1976, p. 313), for example, observed that in Zambia, ethnicity played an important role in all types of associations:

> Members of various tribes clustered together on account of their regional and cultural affinities, for instance, western and eastern tribes formed separate clusters due to their particularistic bonds and interests. Those results suggested that ethnic factors played significant roles in formation of voluntary associations among heterogeneous groups, and voluntary associations normally tend to be

specifically organized for the pursuit of special interests, be they economic or political, etc.

Likewise, Kenneth Little (1957), has observed that ethnic-oriented associations—such as the Ibo State Union, which consisted of village and clan groups—rated among the most important voluntary associations in West Africa. Identifying with one's ethnic group also dominates in participation in political parties, labor unions, and so on.

The other important feature of African societies in regard to ethnic groups is that in most cases, each group associates with a particular territory. Although the boundaries that demarcate ethnic territories are not always clearly specified, they do nevertheless exist and to a large extent they are respected by the respective groups that live next to each other.[10] Thus, the various ethnic groups have what they refer to as their territory and, in many respects, members of other ethnic groups are considered as outsiders. Thus, by and large, ethnic units do make up what could be called 'ethnic nations.'

It is well known that the most preferred choices are realized when an individual decision-maker has maximum independence. In the real world, however, individuals have to associate with others for particular matters. The more people involved in the decision-making process, the less likely that an individual's preferred choice will be selected. With more and more heterogeneous preferences, the outcomes differ markedly from each person's preferred choice. Because ethnic groups are composed of people who, as a result of their past experiences, family ties, and aspirations, have preferences that are closely related on a variety of matters, decisions that are made by the ethnic units are likely to be more representative of individual preferences than would result when many ethnic groups are involved. Thus, ethnic organizational units are in some respects analogous to voluntary clubs that are composed of people whose preferences are fairly similar.

The efficiency results of voluntary organizations such as clubs are well known and have been discussed extensively in the economic literature. James M. Buchanan (1965) was among the first to explore the efficiency properties of voluntary clubs. The economic model of clubs presented by Buchanan assumes a situation where individuals have identical tastes for both public and private goods. The optimal size of a club is determined by the marginal benefits and marginal costs. Figure 4.1 shows the marginal benefit (MB) and marginal cost (MC) from an additional member as seen by other members. The marginal benefit represents costs savings from adding new members because fixed costs are spread among more people.

Additional benefits decline as club size increases. On the other hand, marginal costs increase as club size increases. The rising marginal costs reflect increasing costs due to congestion. The optimal club size (N*) is one where the marginal benefit club members receive from adding another member equals the additional costs associated with the new member.

Central to the efficient results of voluntary clubs are conditions of entry and exit. A club member who does not like a particular club's policies is free to exit and to join clubs that better represent his or her preferences. Although such exit involves costs, individuals make decisions by comparing the benefits of exit with the costs. If expected benefits exceed the costs of exit, then the individual exits. It is this mobility property of voluntary organizations that guarantees that an individual's preferences are served even in a group setting. The freedom to select those organizations that best serve one's preferences suggests that voluntary clubs and organizations advance individual liberty.

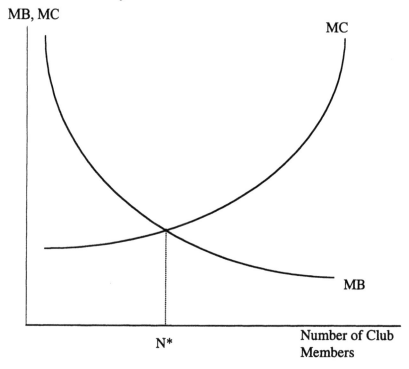

Figure 4.1   Optimal club size

What about the ethnic group? Unlike voluntary organizations, entry into a particular ethnic group, other than the one into which a person is born, is not possible. Likewise, exit from one's ethnic group is practically impossible. While limits to entry and exit may appear to undermine efficiency, I suggest that 'partial' exit and 'partial' entry are possible and serve the same goals that entry and exit serve in voluntary organizations.

Individuals can select the degree to which they identify with a particular ethnic group. This opportunity of selective identification allows persons the liberty to associate with members of their ethnic group on some matters and to disassociate from members of their ethnic group on other matters and instead to associate with members of other ethnic groups. Thus, on the one hand, the ethnic group can be viewed as an involuntary association because of entry and exit barriers. On the other hand, identifying with an ethnic group is voluntary because one can choose the degree to which one identifies with one's own or any other ethnic group.

The fact that we observe strong ethnic identification in Africa should be considered a largely voluntary choice by the individuals concerned. From an economic perspective, the expected benefits of identifying with one's ethnic group exceed the costs of such indentification.[11] When members of an ethnic group live and organize their activities without interfering with members of other ethnic groups, then the ethnic unit is an optimal form of organizing for the purpose of providing some goods and services to its members. In this respect, the ethnic unit is analogous to a private club that serves the interests of its members.

Jennifer Roback (1991) notes that one of the beneficial tasks performed by ethnic groups is that of assisting in the teaching and enforcement of social norms and behavior. Given the prisoner's dilemma situations that face individuals in making collective choices, individual members of society have an incentive to cheat because such behavior is profitable. However, if everybody cheats on every occasion on which they expect to profit, then everybody in society faces the worst possible outcome. Because people have a long-term attachment to their groups (for example, through blood or past memories), they are more likely to have continuous dealings with members of their ethnic group than with members of other ethnic groups. Continuous dealing reduces cheating in prisoner's dilemma situations and as a result ethnic groups may be more efficient in the provision of public goods than the state. Roback (1991, p. 63) observes:

> Ethnic attachments can provide significant substitute for contract law. That is, members of ethnic groups that have substantial con-

tinuous dealings with each other can develop norms of cooperation, promise-keeping and honesty. ...Thus ethnic groups can provide alternatives to government in the provision of certain public goods such as the enforcement of social norms, and in the solution of prisoner's dilemma problems. In fact, ethnic groups and other groups smaller than the modern state may actually be more efficient providers of these kinds of goods.

Benefits to members also arise from the ethnic organization of production of goods and services. An ethnic group may possess its own production technology and its own unique division of labor. Members of the ethnic group learn different types of production skills and work habits. Thus, in addition to the production of valuable social norms, the ethnic organizational unit plays a significant part in organizing the production of goods and services. Ethnic groups also provide other services such as social insurance and entertainment and act as sources of collegiality and pride (Congleton, 1992).

The club model discussed above is extended to show why organizing along ethnic lines may be efficient. If members of the same ethnic group organize particular activities such as the provision of local public goods, then the optimal ethnic club size would be at the point where MB = MC, as shown in Figure 4.1. The assumption is that members of ethnic groups have fairly close, though not identical, tastes.

Inclusion of members from other ethnic groups affects the optimal size of ethnic clubs in two ways. The first of these is that adding members from other ethnic groups creates a kink in the marginal cost curve (Figure 4.2). The cost rises because of difficulties in communicating across ethnic and linguistic boundaries. The second result of adding members from other ethnic groups is to create a kink in the marginal benefit curve at the boundary of the ethnic group (Figure 4.3). This reflects the discontinuity in the group norms, which do not extend beyond the group (Landa, 1994).

Because of discontinuities in marginal benefit and marginal costs that result from adding members from other ethnic groups, the boundary of the club is marked off by members of one's own ethnic group.[12] Given that African ethnic groups associate with clearly identifiable territorial boundaries (what is referred to as geoethnicity), then ethnic groups do form a natural basis for defining units of collective choice. Such ethnic units of collective choice are better suited to provide some local public goods. Because of the fact that members of the same ethnic group are engaged in continuous dealings, ethnic-based governments would be better at solving prisoner's dilemma problems. This then suggests that ethnicity must be taken into account in determining the optimal local jurisdictions.

So far, ethnic units have been considered analogous to voluntary clubs that are compatible with efficient outcomes. However, even voluntary clubs have problems in enforcing compliance. Mancur Olson (1965) has attacked the orthodox view that voluntary associations are always efficient in the provision of collective goods and has specifically challenged the view that the effective participation in voluntary association is virtually universal. Because voluntary associations organize around collective goals, it is often not rational for an individual member to pay for such a goal. Instead, members may pursue their interests by free-riding on other peoples' efforts.

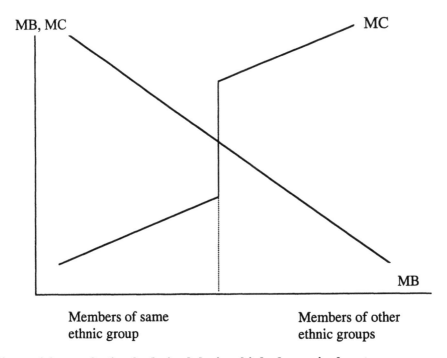

Figure 4.2   Optimal ethnic club size: kinked marginal cost

We therefore expect ethnic-based provision of collective goods and services to be undermined by free-riding. As such, members cannot be expected to pay their fair share voluntarily without some form of organized authority to enforce compliance. Because widespread free-riding lowers the well-being of all members of the ethnic group, everybody benefits when an

ethnic government is established. Notice that such a government is analogous to a club management team that enforces payments of fees and dues
and oversees that club rules are followed. The free-rider problem is likely
to be less prevalent when the group is made up of one ethnic group than
when several ethnic groups are involved.[13]

Some ethnic groups may be so large that even an ethnic government
may not be efficient in preventing free-riding. In this case, the population
exceeds the optimal club size. Organizing around such an ethnic group is
not efficient and in such cases it may be necessary to set up a number of
competing governmental units that can monitor free-riding more efficiently.
In addition to minimizing free-rider problems, such competing governments open up opportunities for 'voting with the feet' because members
have several choices of ethnic jurisdictions.

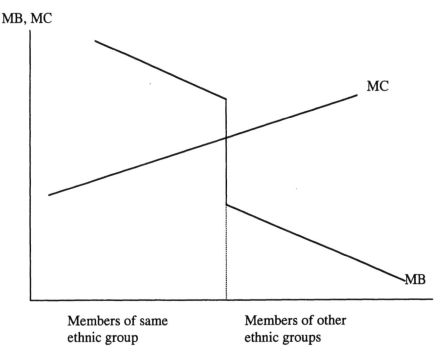

Figure 4.3   Optimal ethnic club size: kinked marginal benefit

Ethnic units have other limitations that relate to their sizes. Ethnic units
may be too large for organizing some activities. Some goods and services
require smaller political units. For example, provision of primary school

education could be more efficiently organized by the village. Just as, in some cases, individuals organize along ethnic lines, at other times they may organize into villages. As a matter of fact, the history of African communities reveals an elaborate division of activities not only by ethnic units, but also by villages and clans.

Ethnic units could also be too small to organize the provision of some goods and services. For example, it is unlikely that ethnic groups can efficiently organize for the provision of university education. In such cases, it is necessary for different ethnic units to form political associations for the purposes of accomplishing these tasks. Notice, however, that such associations take the form of market exchange—they are voluntary and thus benefit ethnic groups that enter into such associations. It is also the case that the rules that establish the relationships between such ethnic groups must be reached by agreement. Beneficial political associations will tend to be durable while those that do not benefit all the groups involved will tend to be unstable. The key then is that any form of integration should be by consent.[14]

The discussion above leads us to a similar conclusion to that reached by W. A. Lewis (1965) over three decades ago who noted that the new African governments' attempts to suppress ethnic loyalties was a futile exercise. Lewis (1965, p. 68) instead suggested the use of such loyalties as a base for establishing institutions that permitted self-expression by all ethnic groups:

> Any idea that one can make different peoples into a nation by suppressing the religious or tribal or regional or other affiliations to which they themselves attach the highest political significance is simply a nonstarter. National loyalty cannot immediately supplant tribal loyalty; it has to be built on top of tribal loyalty by creating a system in which all tribes feel that there is room for self-expression.

The primary argument advanced here is that African governments' refusal to permit ethnic groups to organize for the provision of public goods and services has resulted in the creation of units of collective choice that are not suited to achieving cooperative agreements. There are numerous advantages in relying upon the 'ethnic group' as a basis for organizing governments in Africa. For one, ethnic territories provide natural boundaries that can define stable political jurisdictions. In addition, there are various factors that unite members of an ethnic group that facilitate solving prisoner's dilemma problems such that cooperative outcomes are achieved.

Consequently, there is a strong case for defining boundaries of local units along ethnic lines. For such units to be efficient in meeting the preferences of their populations, they must possess a fair degree of autonomy. However, it must also be recognized that various groups must necessarily associate on some matters. In essence, the ideal institutional arrangement that would preserve ethnic autonomy and yet permit ethnic groups to be united for some purposes is a federal arrangement.

Conditions favoring federalism in Africa

Federal governments are fairly common and to a large extent function smoothly. Examples of federal governments include Australia, Canada, Germany, Switzerland, and the United States of America. The key characteristic of a federal system of government is the association of states or regions in which member states or regions retain a large measure of independence. Federal governments adhere to the federal principle: *The method of dividing powers so that the general and regional governments are each within a sphere, coordinate and independent.*[15]

The proposed federalist option for African countries would be one where ethnic groups in various regions would establish their own regional governments. Each region would be independent in some spheres, which would be clearly stipulated in the federal constitution. These regions would then have elected representatives to the federal legislature as is the case with other federal governments. However, for African countries, emphasis is placed on how the local jurisdictions are drawn.[16]

There are many advantages of establishing federal systems of government in Africa. Federal systems permit policy experimentation and also facilitate the achievement of efficient outcomes due to inter-jurisdictional competition.[17] However, the primary advantage of establishing federalist institutions in Africa is that such is the only system of organizing collective activities that protects groups from oppression by others and also accommodates diversity. These outcomes reflect the fact that in a federal system power is decentralized and neither the general nor regional governments possess absolute power.[18]

In the unitary states of Africa, the central governments are frequently dominated by members of some group, race, ethnic group, or religion. As a result, chances are that in countries where there are heterogeneous groups, as is typical in Africa, some groups will be excluded from the ruling coalition. Given the unlimited powers to coerce possessed by unitary states, those governments often adopt discriminatory policies that oppress groups that are outside the ruling coalition. A federal system, with the guarantees afforded to regions in regard to their independence and the fact that the general government has limited powers, offers protection to all groups in the country.

Even ethnic groups in the same countries tend to have significantly different social institutions. A main source of dissatisfaction by ethnic groups in Africa is that, more often than not, the policies adopted by the unitary governments fail to accommodate groups with widely varying preferences, customs, and norms. By attempting to unify otherwise diverse groups, unitary states fail to accommodate some groups. Thus, establishment of regional governments that possess a fair degree of autonomy allows individual groups to preserve their identity.

In addition to these benefits, several conditions exist in Africa that point to the appropriateness of federal systems of government. The high degree of ethnic heterogeneity in that continent and the fact that ethnic groups associate with particular territory have already been noted. Both of these features present natural conditions for a federal system. In addition, religious heterogeneity is important in some countries. Nigeria and Sudan are good examples of countries where religious groups have clearly expressed their desire for autonomy. More often than not, leaders of unitary states establish policies that are clearly unsuitable to some groups. This is the primary reason why Christians in the south of Sudan have sought autonomy from the Muslim north. Such differences can be accommodated by establishing a federal system.

Another feature of African countries that would make federalism desirable is the geographical isolation of some communities. Even in an otherwise homogenous nation, isolated communities develop distinct regional consciousness. Such consciousness makes the communities want to keep to themselves. When different communities in the same country develop such distinct regional awareness, they may all need to secure some degree of independence while uniting for some purposes.[19] Furthermore, when communities are isolated from the rest of the country in a unitary state, they may rightfully feel that the central government is too remote from them and fails to serve them as well as it does other communities.

Another factor that favors the establishment of federalist institutions in Africa is the size of the nations. Some of the countries are very large in terms of population and area. Nigeria has more than 100 million people, Ethiopia has a population of 54 million and Sudan has a population of 28 million. The geographical size of Sudan is one-third that of the entire United States; Ethiopia is twice the size of Texas; Mozambique is twice the size of California, and Chad, with a population of only 5.2 million is three times the size of California.[20] Somalia, which is relatively small compared with other African countries, is the size of Texas. Clearly, some of the African countries are excessively large, which makes it difficult for governments to serve local communities effectively.

Finally, many regions and communities in Africa had, at some time in the past, their own governments. Prior existence of 'ethnic' kingdoms, or chieftainships means that there are already strong ties that hold people in a particular region or community together. Furthermore, the fact that a government existed in the past implies that groups may want to regain the independence that they had before the formation of the unitary state. This has been evident in countries like Uganda, where previous kingdoms have continued to press for autonomy from the central government.

Conclusion

At the core of the analysis presented in this chapter has been the relationship between ethnic heterogeneity and the costs and benefits of organizing collective activity. It has been suggested that ethnicity is an important feature of African countries and one that economizes on organizational costs. This suggests that the provision of public goods along ethnic lines has distinct efficiency characteristics. In particular, ethnic-based institutions have a comparative advantage in solving prisoner's dilemma problems.

A primary implication of the analysis is that the optimal institutional arrangement in nations characterized with high degrees of ethnic diversity is one that allows for the establishment of local 'ethnic' jurisdictions. Each of those jurisdictions should possess a fair degree of autonomy. Naturally, this suggests the establishment of multilevel governments. Thus, it appears that the most immediate institutional reform for Africa should be the establishment of federal systems of government.

Popularizing federalism with Africans is a challenging task. Federalist proposals have been criticized by incumbent African leaders on the basis that such systems of government reinforce *tribalism*. The benefits associated with organizing along ethnic lines notwithstanding, the proposal outlined in this chapter recommending the use of geoethnicity in determining appropriate regional units of collective choice is likely to be challenged as a form of 'apartheid.' For federalism to be accepted as an ideal method of organizing society, it is necessary to emphasize the suitability of such a system particularly in creating a harmonious society.

Nonetheless, with the new democratization movements in Africa, there are signs of change. As a matter of fact, discussions by politicians and academics about the viability of federalism are going on in various countries. In Kenya, for example, a debate has emerged that focuses on proposals to change the current institutional arrangements and instead establish a federal system with provincial governments. Likewise, Ethiopia recently adopted a constitution that provides ethnic groups with a large measure of autonomy.

The federalist proposal presented in this chapter relies heavily on the fact that ethnic groups associate with specific territory and therefore calls for territorial federalism. However, territorial federalism may not solve some of the most serious ethnic rivalries in Africa. A good example is the case of the Hutu and Tutsi in Rwanda and Burundi. These two groups share the same territories and no group has exclusive rights to a specific region. Territorial federalism is therefore not feasible in these countries.[21]

A possible solution to the ethnic rivalries in Rwanda and Burundi may lie in the non-territorial federalism proposed by Gordon Tullock (1994). Non-territorial federalism involves the establishment of competing governments in the same territory, and individuals have the option of selecting which governments to belong to. Such governments operate much like private clubs, so an individual could belong to various such governments. Thus, individuals residing in the same neighborhoods could actually belong to different non-territorial states. While non-territorial federalism has some distinct advantages in dealing with ethnic conflicts, it is nevertheless a complicated institutional arrangement and not necessarily efficient from the standpoint of resource allocation. However, given the high costs associated with ethnic conflict in countries such as Rwanda and Burundi, non-territorial federalism should be given serious consideration.

Acknowledgments

This chapter was originally published in the *Cato Journal*, Vol. 18, Number 1 (Spring/Summer 1998), pp. 43-63. © Cato Institute, 1000 Massachusetts Avenue NW, Washington, D.C. 20001. Used by permission of the Cato Institute. The reader should note that the chapter was revised so it could fit more effectively in this volume. The revisions, however, did not affect the integrity of the original piece. The author would like to thank an anonymous referee of the *Cato Journal* for helpful comments. He also gratefully acknowledges the support of the Earhart Foundation.

Notes

1.   Cameroon, Nigeria, and South Africa have federal systems of government. Those states, nevertheless, have been characterized by a high concentration of decision-making authority. In Cameroon and Nigeria, dictatorial governments have not maintained the federal principle. Until recently, South Africa excluded a large number of its population from participating in the political process.

2.   Local governments in Africa do make some decisions, primarily those that deal with provision of local public goods. Nonetheless, the powers of local governments are very limited, and in most cases the local governments are under the strict supervision of a government ministry. Thus, local governments are independent only to a rather limited degree. Their lawmaking powers are minimal. In fact, the central government can dissolve a local government at will. That was the case in Kenya during the 1980s when the Nairobi City Council, composed of elected councilors, was dissolved and replaced by a City Commission whose members were appointed by the central government.

3.   Brough and Kimenyi (1986); Kimenyi (1987); Kimenyi (1989); and Kimenyi and Mbaku (1993).

4.   In some countries, different ethnic groups live in the same regions and no group can claim exclusive ownership rights. The case of Hutu and Tutsi in Burundi and Rwanda is a good example of a country where two rival groups share territory.

5.   Here we treat the ethnic group as the decision-making unit. This is realistic in the African context, and conflicts that we focus on primarily involve different ethnic groups.

6.   For a recent discussion, see Kimenyi (1997a).

7.   This is particularly true of countries in sub-Saharan Africa. This chapter primarily focuses on this part of the continent or what has been referred to by some writers as Black Africa.

8.   Until the recent democratization movements in Africa that took hold during the late 1980s, most states outlawed political party competition. Even in those that permitted entry of other parties into the political markets, the party activities were largely restricted.

9.   For example, it is not uncommon to find strong opposition to interethnic marriages.

10.   Some of the ethnic conflicts that have continued for many years are frequently due to disputes concerning the ethnic territorial boundaries. In other words, they are the result of 'poorly' defined ethnic property rights. In most cases, however, the 'ethnic' property rights are well defined.

11.   Kimenyi (1997b) presents a model of ethnic identification that shows how voluntary integration arises. In this model, the demand for identifying with one's ethnic group is shown by a downward sloping marginal benefit curve while the

supply is an upward marginal cost curve of ethnic identification. In other words, as individuals identify more and more with members of their ethnic group, additional benefits fall and additional costs rise. The intersection of the marginal benefit and marginal cost of ethnic identification determines the activities that ethnic groups should keep to themselves and the matters that they should organize with members of other ethnic groups.

12. We could envision marginal benefits and marginal costs when families, extended families, and clans organize some activities. The marginal benefit and marginal cost curves would have kinks as one moves from organizing activities from family to extended family. Likewise, including members of other clans would be marked by kinks in the benefit and cost curves. This shows why some activities are best left to the family, extended family, or clan and not the entire ethnic group. This may explain the rivalry of clans in Somalia.

13. A proposal for the establishment of ethnic governments may be considered radical. However, evidence from the history of African societies shows that such ethnic-based governmental units functioned quite well and had many features of representative governments. See for example, Ayittey (1991), Mair (1965), and Vaughan (1986).

14. This is similar to the analysis advanced by Buchanan and Tullock (1962) of mutually beneficial political exchange.

15. See Wheare (1947). For detailed discussion of the federal principle, see Lemco (1991) and MacMahon (1962).

16. A major issue in federal systems of governments is the allocation of functions between regional and the federal governments. We do not go into such details here. However, a well-functioning federal system is one that is highly decentralized so that most collective activity is left to the lower levels of government.

17. For a comprehensive treatment of the advantages of federal systems of government, see Breton (1980).

18. The powers and responsibilities of federal governments vary. But, in general, they are clearly specified. The boundary of what the federal government should do must be clearly specified. The distribution of powers between regional and federal governments is crucial to the smooth functioning of the federal union.

19. Such geographical isolation of communities played an important role in the creation of a federal system in Switzerland. Switzerland has a very rugged topography where mountains and valleys create small, isolated communities that are distinct and that have developed some degree of independence.

20. Recently, some researchers have advanced the argument that the African states are themselves not optimal. In fact, this author believes that the map of Africa will radically change as democratic institutions mature and groups freely express their self-determination goals (Kimenyi 1997c, 1997d).

21. The Hutu-Tutsi problem is complex and may require quite complex solutions. Suggestions for dealing with the ethnic rivalries in these countries have included radical proposals such as designating one country for Hutus and the other for Tutsis. Other proposals have called for incorporating these countries into neighboring countries.

References

Ayittey, G. B. N. (1991), *Indigenous African Institutions*, Transnational Publishers: Dobbs Ferry.

Ayittey, G. B. N. (1992), *Africa Betrayed*, St. Martin's Press: New York.

Breton, A. (1980), *The Design of Federations*, Institute for Research on Public Policy: Montreal.

Breytenbach, W. J. (1976), 'Inter-Ethnic Conflict in Africa', in Veenhoven, W. A. (ed.), *Case Studies on Human Rights and Fundamental Freedoms*, Maartinus Nijhoff: The Hague.

Brough, W. T. and Kimenyi, M. S. (1986), 'On the Inefficient Extraction of Rents by Dictators', *Public Choice*, Vol. 48, pp. 37–48.

Buchanan, J. M. (1965), 'An Economic Theory of Clubs', *Economica*, Vol. 32, pp. 1–14.

Buchanan, J. M. and Tullock, G. (1962), *The Calculus of Consent*, University of Michigan Press: Ann Arbor.

Burke, F. (1991) *Africa*, Houghton Mifflin: Boston, MA.

Congleton, R. D. (1992), 'Ethnic Clubs, Ethnic Conflict and the Rise of Ethnic Nationalism', Unpublished manuscript, Center for Study of Public Choice, George Mason University, Fairfax, Virginia.

Hobbes, T. ([1651] 1962), *Leviathan*, Collier: New York.

Horowitz, D. (1985), *Ethnic Groups in Conflict*, University of California Press: Berkeley, CA.

Kimenyi, M. S. (1987), 'Bureaucratic Rents and Political Institutions', *Journal of Public Finance and Public Choice*, Vol. 3, pp. 189–200.

Kimenyi, M. S. (1989), 'Interest Groups, Transfer Seeking and Democratization: Competition for the Benefits of Government Power May Explain African Political Instability', *The American Journal of Economics and Sociology*, Vol. 48, pp. 339–49.

Kimenyi, M. S. (1997a), *Ethnic Diversity, Liberty and the State: The African Dilemma*, Edward Elgar: Aldershot, UK.

Kimenyi, M. S. (1997b), 'Ethnic Rent-Seeking and Optimal Integration', Unpublished Manuscript, Department of Economics, University of Connecticut, Storrs, CT.

Kimenyi, M. S. (1997c), 'Redrawing Africa's Borders: Logical Foundations for Consensual Units of Collective Choice', Unpublished Manuscript, Department of Economics, University of Connecticut, Storrs, CT.

Kimenyi, M. S. (1997d), 'Territorial Boundaries, Constitutions, and the Demand for New States', Unpublished Manuscript, Department of Economics, University of Connecticut, Storrs, CT.

Kimenyi, M. S. and Mbaku, J. M. (1993), 'Rent-Seeking and Institutional Stability in Developing Countries', *Public Choice*, Vol. 77, pp. 385–405.

Landa, J. T. (1994), Trust, *Ethnicity and Identity*, University of Michigan Press: Ann Arbor.

Lemco, J. (1991), *Political Stability in Federal Government*, Praeger: New York.

Lewis, W. A. (1965), *Politics in West Africa*, Oxford University Press: New York.

Little, K. (1957), 'The Role of Voluntary Associations in West African Urbanization', in Van den Berghe, P. L. (ed.), *Africa: Social Problems of Change and Conflict*, Chandler: San Francisco.

MacMahon, A. W. (ed.) (1962), *Federalism: Mature and Emergent*, Russell and Russell: New York.

Mair, L. (1965), *An Introduction to Social Anthropology*, Clarendon Press: Oxford.

Mbaku, J. M. and Kimenyi, M. S. (1995), 'Democratization in Africa: The Continuing Struggle', *Coexistence*, Vol. 32, pp. 119–36.

Olson, M. (1965), *The Logic of Collective Action*, Harvard University Press: Cambridge, MA.

Roback, J. (1991), 'Plural but Equal: Group Identity and Voluntary Integration', *Social Philosophy and Policy*, Vol. 8, No. 2, pp. 60–80.

Tullock, G. (1994) *The New Federalist*, Fraser Institute: Vancouver.

Vaughan, J. H. (1986), 'Population and Social Organization', in Martin, P. and O'Meara, P. (eds.), *Africa*, Indiana University Press: Bloomington, IN.

Wheare, K. C. (1947), *Federal Government*, Oxford University Press: London.

Winchester, N. B. (1986), 'African Politics Since Independence', in Martin, P. and O'Meara, P. (eds.), *Africa*, Indiana University Press: Bloomington, IN.

5

Managing Ethnic Relations in a Heterogeneous Society: The Case of Nigeria

Identities have historically been significant in the Nigerian political process, under colonial rule as well as in the post-colonial dispensation. Under colonialism, administrative exigencies warranted 'the invention of traditions,' and the nurturing and exacerbation of an 'us' *versus* 'them' syndrome: Muslim *versus* Christian; Northerner *versus* Southerner; Hausa-Fulani *versus* Yourba *versus* Igbo, and so on. Religious, regional and ethnic differences were given prominence in conceiving and implementing social, educational and economic development projects under the indirect system of colonial administration favored by the British. Thus, the differential impact of colonialism set the context of the regional educational, economic and political imbalances which later became significant in the mobilization or manipulation of identity consciousness in order to effectively divide and rule, as well as in the politics of decolonization and in the arena of competitive politics in the post-colonial era (Jega, 2000, pp. 15–16).

125

The guns are still booming in Warri and the Niger Delta region. Ijaws versus Itsekiris; Ijaws versus Ilajes. Ogonis killed themselves and were in turn killed by the state. They soak the creeks in blood, they torch their assets with fire of hatred! Move upland to the cradle of the Yoruba race, Ile-Ife. The bloodletting between the Ifes and Modakekes have left hundreds dead, thousands maimed and billion-naira assets wasted. The war is far from over. Hoodlums have been replaying the Niger-Delta creek war in the jungles of Ifeland, since August 1997. What of the Jukuns against the Kutebs? These reflect hundreds of our new 'civil wars' North, East, West, South, etc., waiting to be exploited for partisan politics. How do we save the fatherland and remove the best attraction for military adventurers to return to power if and when they quit power in May 1999? How do we stop this carnage (*Vanguard* (Lagos), February 22, 1999, p. 1).

...Nigeria reacts to crises rather than anticipate them and take appropriate preventive action. In other words, there is no determined effort to seek to identify at the earliest possible stage, situations that could produce conflict and take corrective policy measure to remove the sources of rancor. Another important feature of conflict management in Nigeria... is the frequent resort to judicial commissions and tribunals and coercive responses rather than problem-solving techniques to ensure lasting solutions to conflicts (Imobighe, 1997, p. 277).

Introduction

Violent communal conflicts have become a common feature of contemporary Nigeria. Among the most prominent of these conflicts within the past fifteen years have been the bloodshed in Numan and parts of Adamawa State in 1986; the mass killings in Kafanchan and other parts of Kaduna State in 1987; the clashes in Wukari, Takum and other parts of Taraba State which began in 1990; the Tafawa Balewa massacres of 1991, the mass killings in Kano City in 1991, the Zango-Kataf bloodshed in 1992; and the Andoni and Ogoni bloodshed in 1993 (see, e.g., Usman and Abba, 2000, p. 86). The Toto massacres which began in 1994 and the on-going bloody feuds between the Ife and Modakake are among other violent communal conflicts which Nigeria has experienced in the past few years. Similarly, no account of bloody communal conflicts in contemporary Nigeria is complete without mention of the Aguleri and Umuleri battles of 1999 and the mass killings between the Ijaw and the Itsekiri in Warri which began in 1998.

This chapter analyzes the management of ethnic conflicts in Nigeria. Against the backdrop of several sets of dyadic conflicts among various ethnic groups (Ogoni and Okrika; Ogoni and Andoni; Hausa/Fulani and Kataf; Ijaw and Istekiri; and Jukun and Kuteb) it argues that violent communal conflicts in contemporary Nigeria reflect both the poor state of ethnic relations and the ineffective manner in which ethnic conflicts have been managed in the country. The chapter contends that the poor state of ethnic relations epitomized by bloody communal conflicts results from the failure of the Nigerian government to properly manage the nation's ethnic diversity. In addition, the chapter contends that the abysmal nature of ethnic relations in contemporary Nigeria is itself a consequence of several short-sighted federal and state governments' policies. The chapter rejects traditional explanations for communal conflicts in Nigeria which posit that these conflicts arise from age-old rivalries and struggles over scarce economic resources. Instead, it suggests that the locus for these conflicts can be located in the public policies of the Nigerian state. In other words, the chapter argues that various policies of the Nigerian government not only constitute an arena for ethnic struggles, they also accentuate the scope and intensity of resultant ethnic tensions and conflicts. In particular, the state-based pattern of capital accumulation in which the ruling classes use their access to state power as a mechanism for private appropriation of wealth encourages the manipulation of ethnic and other forms of primordial identities.

Government policies and communal conflicts

As Attahiru Jega has aptly observed, 'there has been [a] growing global sensitivity and concern with regards to the resurgence of identity politics, especially negative forms of identity politics, in many countries in the contemporary international system' (Jega, 2000, p. 11). Part of the new interest in identity politics springs from the horrendous genocide in Rwanda and the violent ethnic conflicts in Eastern Europe. In part, the resurgence in scholarly analyses of ethnicity also represents the growing phenomenon of ethnic mobilization in many parts of the world. In several African countries, major challenges to the legitimacy of the continent's many corrupt, dictatorial and inefficient states took the form of ethnic and regional mobilization. For instance, it was essentially the onslaught by largely ethnic armies that led to the demise of dictators such as Samuel Doe of Liberia. In public policy terms, the international interest in identity politics can be traced to the dilemma which international organizations such as the United Nations confront in attempting to respond to the violence unleashed by ethnic conflicts.

Several factors which have led to the new scholarly and policy interest in pluralism and ethnicity can be easily identified. First, the end of the Cold War has pushed issues of democratization, popular participation, account-ability into the forefront of political praxis and scholarly discourse. Pluralism is implicated in the general discourse on democracy and democratization in the Third World. The end of the Cold War helped to create a political space in which ethnic, cultural and religious groups that had been dis-empowered, dispossessed and marginalized could assert and reassert their identities. Second, ethnic and religious conflicts have become quite rife in many parts of the Third World and the attempt to understand the genesis and contours of these conflicts has entailed the use of pluralism as an analytical framework. Third, the re-emergence of civil society as a serious political phenomenon in many parts of the developing countries has accentuated the importance of pluralism. Fourth, the post-Cold War international system features new ways of negotiating reality and frequently, pluralism constitutes one of these novel ways of negotiating reality. Fifth, the magnitude of contemporary ethnic violence requires regional and international response and effective response requires comprehensive understanding of the nature and dimensions of the conflict. Finally, the demise of autocratic governments that had looked upon pluralism with deep suspicion is another factor that has led to the current intellectual discourse on pluralism. In the past, autocratic and authoritarian governments tried to suppress certain forms of identities. As these governments began to lose their iron-grip on societies, the ability to keep ethnic or other forms of identities under lock-and-key became untenable.

Scholars have examined ethnic issues from various vantage perspec-tives. While some scholars stress the primordial nature of ethnic identities, others place strong emphasis on the modernity of ethnicity. In particular, in examining ethnic conflicts, some analysts emphasize the importance of resources, particularly economic factors in instigating or intensifying ethnic conflicts. Other scholars examine the use of ethnicity as a manipulative tool in the hands of ethnic entrepreneurs. Okwudiba Nnoli's *Ethnic Politics in Nigeria*, for instance, sought to show how Nigerian elites utilize ethnicity as a ploy for acquiring political power. In the wake of ethnic violence in Eastern Europe, Rwanda and other parts of the world, there was a recourse to explaining these conflicts in terms of age-old rivalries. Explanations of these conflicts that are structured within the context of age-long inter-ethnic rivalries are however inadequate for several reasons. First, the identities that provide the fulcrum for these conflicts are a modern, rather than ancient phenomena. Second, the objects of many of these conflicts do not have origins in the past. Instead, they are the outcomes of contempo-rary political and economic systems. Third, these conflicts are waged with modern methods, tools and strategies even when conflicts are couched in supposed ancient ideologies. Finally, even if some of these conflicts hack back to ancient times, it is the contemporary economic and political realities which tend to provide their contexts, contours and meanings.

It is important to provide alternative explanations for ethnic conflicts. An alternative explanation that suggests itself can be located within the framework of national constitutions and government policies. The linkage between government policies, actions and pronouncements on ethnic relations deserves greater scrutiny. For instance, there is little doubt that the genesis of so many of Africa's ethnic conflicts can be traced to govern-ment policies and/or governments' nonchalant attitude to long-simmering ethnic tensions. While ethnic relations are influenced by a myriad of factors such as demography, history, the economy and competition over resources, government policies do exert a great impact on how ethnic groups view themselves and in how they relate to each other. Government policies may also constitute an arena for ethnic conflicts. Similarly, public policies shape the distribution of resources and the allocation of values. As such, their impact on the contours and substance of ethnic struggles can be substantial. Michael Brown and Sumit Ganguly have aptly noted that government policies are relevant to ethnic relations since such policies 'almost always have a significant impact on the course and trajectory of ethnic relations' (Brown and Ganguly, 1997, p. 1). Among other things, public policies affect ethnic relations through the differential impact of policies on ethnic groups. In addition, perceptions of relative privileges or deprivation are also shaped by government policies. Even in circumstances in which particular ethnic conflicts cannot be directly traced to public policies, the government may nevertheless be implicated in the conflict since its responses or even non-responses to the conflict affect not just the scope of the conflict but its trajectory and duration.

Despite substantial empirical evidence from Asia and other parts of the world that there is a direct relationship between government policies and ethnic relations, scholars of ethnicity have largely failed to undertake full-scale systematic analyses of the linkage between public policies and ethnic conflicts in Africa.[1] This is surprising given that the continent has been afflicted for decades by authoritarian rule. Despite the absence of rigorous data on public policies and ethnic conflicts in Africa, existing anecdotal evidence suggests that the link between public policies and ethnic relations in Africa is quite strong. Policies on language, religion, affirmative action and the economy stimulate or aggravate ethnic tensions. State policies also determine access to economic and political resources. Policies designed to reduce socio-economic and cultural disparities may generate tensions or may engender political stability. Ethnic assertiveness may also spring from public policies. The state may design policies and measures deliberately aimed at reducing ethnic tensions. Such policies may, however, aggravate ethnic tensions. For instance, quotas could be used to give greater access to state power and resources to previously disadvantaged ethnic groups. This could lead to resentment. There may also be preferential state policies that favor certain groups to the detriment of others.

Not only do government policies shape how ethnic groups relate to one another, they also determine the relationship between the state and its constituent ethnic groups. For example, in Nigeria, government policies on revenue allocation and the extraction of crude petroleum have not only shaped inter-ethnic relations in the petroleum-producing regions, they have also become arenas of friction and contestation between the federal government on the one hand and the ethnic groups on the other. The well-known environmentalist, Ken Saro-Wiwa, was for instance, executed in 1995 partly as a result of his demand that Nigerian ethnic groups, rather than the Nigerian national government, should own and control petroleum. State policies on oil and revenue allocation also shape intra-ethnic relations in Nigeria's oil producing regions.

In-depth analysis of ethnic conflicts requires examination of government policies. Institutional failures on the part of the state may instigate or aggravate ethnic conflicts. Similarly, public policies may have direct bearings on ethnic conflicts since the state itself is as an arena for political struggles. In some cases, officially-sanctioned ethnic or regional mythologies may create the incentive or at least the rationalization for ethnic conflicts just as access to state power and resources on ethnic basis or the distribution of power and economic resources along ethnic or regional lines may be implicated in ethnic conflicts. In short, governments create conditions that may precipitate conflicts. Ethnic groups in power may use their control of the state apparatus to effect measures that create ethnic animosities. For instance, it has been shown in the case of some African states that genocide was used to consolidate some ethnic groups' grip on state power (Lemarchand, 1998, p. 7). Even when the state instruments are not used to aggravate or instigate ethnic conflicts, state policies are indispensable to ethnic relations. For instance, when conflicts do break out, the state may be a central organ for the pursuit of peace, reconciliation and justice.

Government policies also shape the contours, scope and magnitude of ethnic relations. As Bruce Berman has rightly observed:

> The state in colonial Africa, within the broader context of the intrusion of capitalist modernity, was the central institutional force in the organization, production and distribution of social resources. It also shaped the accompanying changes in the social criteria for access to those resources; and the resulting social differentiation between individuals and communities. By authoritatively defining rules of behavior that specified for Africans what was required, prohibited and permitted, the colonial state structured the choices of individuals by constructing social, economic and political situations; assigning individual roles and identities; and defining the choice of goals, strategies and behaviors. In so doing, that delineates the strategic contexts in which ethnicity was or was not salient, and molded the choices of political actors with regard to both the ascriptive markers of ethnicity and the organizational forms in which it was expressed. This shaped, in turn, the scope of ethnic politics, its relationship with other social cleavages, and the complex interaction of ethnic identities and interests (Berman, 1998, p. 313).

In the colonial era, divide and rule tactics were employed by the colonial state to maintain European control and domination. Such policies shaped ethnic relations in many African countries during colonial rule. The legacies of such policies have continued to shape post-colonial ethnic relations (sometimes with tragic consequences as in Burundi, Rwanda and several other African countries) (Ndikumana, 1998, pp. 29–47).

State power and economic resources may be used to protect the material interests of particular groups and this is bound to shape group relations in a most profound way. Policies may institutionalize and reify economic and political hierarchies. Similarly, ethnic exclusion may be promoted directly by public policies.

In cases where the integrity of the state has been compromised because it is viewed as a tool of ethnic control and domination, its efficacy in addressing ethnic conflicts is greatly curtailed. Leonce Ndikumana has noted the inability of the Burundian state to resolve ethnic tensions because of the widely-held belief that it is a tool for ethnic domination. As he notes:

> The Burundian state has degenerated into a private institution, which makes it unsuited for fulfilling its role of third-party enforcement agent in social exchange. Individuals, ethnic and regional entities that control the state are able to shape and influence the way in which the basic functions of the state—the provision of law and order—are designed and implemented. Specifically, political leverage allows privileged groups to mold and bend the law to facilitate accumulation of power and wealth (Ndikumana, 1998, p. 40).

Interestingly, South Africa under apartheid, demonstrated quite vividly, the impact of state policies on ethnic and race relations. Under apartheid, not only did the state establish a firm system of racial and ethnic preferences, it also encouraged ethnic consciousness among the black population. The apartheid government recognized that racial discrimination against black South Africans could create black consciousness and black solidarity and the white rulers feared that black solidarity would constitute a threat to apartheid. Thus, the state found it necessary to create ethnic and sub-racial identities within the black population as part of apartheid's divide-and-rule strategy. Although not on the same grand scale as apartheid in South Africa, political and other advantages were deliberately constructed on the basis of ethnic or racial identities in such African countries as Liberia, Rwanda, Mauritania, and Sudan.

Just as government policies shape ethnic relations, the national constitution may have profound impacts on group relations. A constitution is a crucial device for the management of group relations because it establishes the institutions, parameters, and processes through which governments can operate effectively to ensure the welfare of its citizens. For instance, in a multi-ethnic society, ethnic units may be recognized by the constitution as the unit of representation. Linguistic affinity, under which people who speak the same language are grouped together in a state or province of their own may be another constitutional device aimed at managing group relations. Thus, the constitution, through devices such as language policies and territorial demarcation of administrative units, has various ways of addressing the ethnic question. General ethnic relations are also influenced by national constitutions. A constitution can also retard or frustrate societal socio-political and economic goals either by its rigidity or its patent partisanship.

Part of the importance of constitutions to group relations derives from the fact that constitutions reflect how issues of tomorrow are formulated in the context of the political and social conflicts of today. In addition, the constitution may be directly implicated in ethnic conflicts if it fails to develop viable representative institutions for all groups. Constitutions are equally important to ethnic relations because they affect how ethnic minorities perceive themselves. For instance, the revenue allocation formula enshrined in the Nigerian constitution is perceived by some of the country's ethnic minorities as a device for perpetuating domination by ethnic majorities. Accordingly, various ethnic minorities in Nigeria view the state as an instrument of ethnic domination. Similarly, the entrenchment of the Land Use Decree in the 1979 Nigerian Constitution has been viewed with suspicion as the Decree is said to confer undue advantages to some Nigerians.

Constitutions shape ethnic relations because they are not neutral documents. On the contrary, constitutions are part of the contested arena of politics. They shape how people interpret their place in society. Constitutions also allocate real values and they structure not just the relationship between the people and the state or government but inter-ethnic relations as well. They establish and/or constrain claims to rights and entitlements. Another factor that makes constitutions relevant to group relations derives from the fact that the constitution may provide a legal basis for differential access to economic and educational resources. Thus, economic, social or cultural policies that flow directly from constitutional provisions may totally exclude or marginalize some ethnic minorities. Internal power-sharing arrangements as embodied in the constitution may help to minimize antagonistic divisions among ethnic groups. Alternatively, if the constitution reflects socio-political inequities, it can aggravate group tensions.

The constitution may also aggravate ethnic tensions by granting official status to some languages, ethnic groups or religious organizations while denying such status to others. Worse, the constitution may be used as the basis for the creation of an ethnic hierarchy. Even the political rights enshrined in the constitution may shape inter-ethnic relations. For instance, the constitution may be exclusionary through the non-recognition of the rights of some groups as full citizens. In addition, not only does the constitution shape the type of responses to perceived inequities, it also creates the context for ethnic rivalries and competition. Moreover, the constitution influences the political strategies that groups may employ to address their grievances. For example, ethnic minorities may resort to violence if they perceive that the constitution does not provide them any non-violent recourse. Alternatively, if they perceive that the constitutionally mandated procedures are not likely to address their grievances, they may adopt a more militant strategy.

Constitutions also provide a window into how political leaders interpret political issues. Similarly, debates over constitutional provisions may themselves illuminate the nature of inter-ethnic relations. The types of political compromises reached during constitutional assemblies may be important to the degree of political stability in the country. If due recognition is given to ethnic expression in the constitution, that may inhibit the resort to violent ethnic conflicts. On the other hand, constitutional recognition of ethnic claims may give greater saliency to dormant ethnic problems.

Just as the constitution can be used to achieve amicable settlement of political disputes, it can equally constitute a barrier to the resolution of national problems. In 1973, King Sobunza II of Swaziland, in a royal proclamation following a period of unrest in his kingdom, declared that the Swazi 'Constitution is indeed the cause of growing unrest, insecurity, dissatisfaction with the state of affairs of our country and impediment to free and progressive development in all spheres of life' (Blaustein and Flanz, 1991, p. 109).

Even the symbolic aspects of constitutions cannot be underestimated in their political significance. Symbolically, the constitution may be used to mark a transition to a new social order. For example, when the African colonies changed their status from colonies to independent nations, their constitutions served as marker of their new status. Symbolically, the constitution can also serve as tool for political hygiene. Part of the political ritual in transitions from military dictatorships to civilian rule in Africa is the promulgation of new constitutions. Such documents are designed to underpin the supposed new moral basis of the new government. Similarly, the constitution may serve as a reflection of a new social order. For instance, the transition from socialism in the former Soviet Union and Eastern Europe has been marked by the enactment of new constitutions. Such constitutions not only reflect the new distribution of power, but also embody the new ethos of the societies.

Despite open hostilities to the expression of ethnic identities in Africa,

Africa is still beset with ethnic tensions. Recent conflicts in Rwanda, Sierra Leone, Liberia and in many other African countries have vividly demonstrated that ethnicity is not just a form of cultural expression, it can also be transformed into a deadly instrument. African leaders now seem to acknowledge that ethnicity is an important form of identification and that people may attach so much importance to it as an expression of group identity that they are willing to commit horrible atrocities in its name. In addition, there seems to be a greater recognition of the harm done to Africa by the colonial *divide-and-rule* tactics. Such tactics have intensified ethnic identities particularly, in light of African dictators' penchant for using the same tactics as a survival mechanism. Contemporary economic and political crises in Africa have also revived ethnic claims and have reinforced strong perceptions of discrimination and oppression. The rather simplistic assumption that nation-building projects would eradicate vestiges of ethnicity is no longer tenable. In the hands of ethnic entrepreneurs, ethnic identity is a very potent force. As such, ethnicity has refused to become a thing of the past.

Some African governments have now openly embraced their ethnic diversities. The new Ethiopian constitution, for instance, divides the country into ethnic federations. This is designed to give the country's ethnic groups greater salience in governance. While an ethnically-based federation may represent the Ethiopian government's acknowledgment of the nation's ethnic diversity, there is great danger in using ethnicity as the sole basis of political representation. As Yusufu Bala Usman and Alkasum Abba have pointed out in response to the agitations for ethnic federalism in Nigeria, 'family, clan, ethnic and religious affinities and ties, cannot be the basis of the representation of any citizen or, groups of citizens, in a democracy. Democratic representation is solely derived from the exercise by the citizens of the freedom of political association with other citizens in the country and the exercise of the freedom of political choice between alternative candidates and parties' (Usman and Abba, 2000, pp. 9–10).

Nigeria's ethnic diversity

Nigeria is estimated to have over 250 ethnic groups. The fact that neither the precise number of ethnic groups nor the numerical strengths of each group is known is quite telling about the nature of the management of ethnic relations in the country. Even though it is assumed that ethnicity constitutes the fundamental basis for identity and diversity in the country, there is a schizophrenic attitude on the part of the Nigerian state to ethnicity and ethnic identity. It is feared that a full recognition of the nation's ethnic diversity would threaten national unity. At the same time, government policies on state and local government creation, languages and political representation are based on a tacit recognition of the multiplicity of the nation's ethnic groups. Ironically, despite the fact that ethnicity constitutes a major part of Nigeria's political discourse, categorization of people on the basis of ethnicity is considered such a sensitive political matter that Nigerians are not enumerated by ethnicity. Accordingly, census questions do not include identification of Nigerians on the basis of ethnic identity.

As in other African countries, an important assumption that underlay post-colonial political practices in Nigeria was that constructing a political arrangement on the basis of ethnicity would engender political chaos and national disunity. Thus, the immediate post-independence elites were decidedly hostile against acknowledging the validity of ethnicity and ethnic identity. Instead, ethnicity was viewed as a major stumbling bloc to the national project. Interestingly, the regionalization of politics in the colonial era, encouraged the ethnicization of political parties. Nonetheless, the nationalist movements of the colonial era in both Nigeria and other African states sought to create a single, national identity out of ethnically, regionally and religiously diverse peoples. It was assumed that the vision of a single, united people under which the struggle against colonial rule was being waged would falter badly if recognition was given to Africa's ethnic heterogeneity. Thus, vigorous attempts were made to suppress ethnic or other forms of parochial identities.

The sheer number of ethnic groups in Nigeria is baffling enough but what further complicates the picture are the regional, cultural, and religious differences among the ethnic groups. In addition, despite the lack of precise figures, it is clear that three ethnic groups, Hausa/Fulani, Igbo and Yoruba, constitute a decisive numerical majority. The other ethnic groups are collectively referred to as the minorities. Thus, despite the existence of multiple bases of minority identities in the country, minorities are defined almost exclusively in ethnic terms. Even at that, minorities are not defined in absolute numbers but merely in reference to the three dominant ethnic-nationalities of Hausa/Fulani, Igbo and Yoruba.

Furthermore, there are multiple forms of ethnic minorities. As Eghosa Osaghae (1991) notes, some ethnic minorities in the northern part of the country are Moslems who, using their Islamic religious affinity with the dominant Hausa and Fulani groups, tend to be less disadvantaged than their non-Moslem minority counterparts. In effect, their religious identity as Moslems in a pre-dominantly Islamic Northen Nigeria acts as a shield against their ethnic minority status. Some ethnic groups such as the Igbos and the Yorubas are clearly majorities within the national context but are minorities within the regional (or later, state) contexts. Peter Ekeh (1972) refers to those who are majorities within the larger Nigerian context but are ethnic minorities within particular states as marginals (Ekeh, 1972, pp. 95–98).

Since 1967, the federal government has balkanized the country into several states. The state creation exercise has accentuated ethnic minority consciousness in several significant respects. First, some groups such as the Tiv and the Urhobo who are minorities in the larger national contexts constitute ethnic majorities in their respective states. The same charges of domination and marginalization which such groups level against the three dominant groups at the national level are hurled at them when they constitute ethnic majorities at the state level. The Idoma of Benue State, for instance, accuse the Tiv of using their numerical superiority to dominate and side-line them in the allocation of resources in the state. Secondly, the state creation exercise is frequently interpreted by ethnic minorities as a political device to increase economic and political prerogatives of the majorities. This accusation derives from the practice of sharing federal resources on state basis. Thus, from this perspective, the Yoruba with six states and the Igbo with five states get six and five shares respectively instead of one share each that would have accrued to them if states were created on ethnic basis. Aper Aku, the first elected governor of Benue State, has argued that 'the creation of states has however been accepted, as of now, as a right so much that the majority tribes are scrambling for states more than minorities. As a result, the gains that may have been made by minorities who got their states have been lost again to majority tribes' (Aku, 1982). Ken Saro-Wiwa shares the same sentiment on state creation. According to him, under the military formulation of state creation, 'the ethnic majorities in Nigeria are split into several majorities each with an assembly and a bloated bureaucracy, while the ethnic minorities continue to live in poly-ethnic states run on a unitary basis' (Saro-Wiwa, 1990, p. 192).

Osaghae (1991) recognizes that the issue of ethnic minorities had been a part of the political equation since the inception of Nigeria as a country. However, he points out that it became a salient political issue only after the regionalization of politics in the 1950s. As Osaghae (1991, p. 239) sees it, regionalization is 'the cradle of ethnic minority problems in Nigeria.'

Regionalization accentuated minority ethnic consciousness because it grouped various ethnic nationalities within three regions. Each of the three original regions (North, East, and West) was dominated by a major ethnic group, Hausa, Igbo and Yoruba respectively. Accordingly, all other Nigerians invariably became ethnic minorities.

Of the several factors that have complicated the state of ethnic relations in Nigeria, autocratic and corrupt military governance is the most important. Kleptocratic military regimes have looted the national treasury and in the process, have caused economic and social havoc for the country. It has become increasingly apparent that the military's dominance of state and society poses a major threat not only to the military institution itself, but to the very survival of the country as a viable single political entity. The naked quest for power among military officers which military rule tends to engender has decimated the ranks of the military. Numerous coups, coup attempts and even 'rumors' of coups have led to wanton killings and execution of unsuccessful and alleged coup plotters. In addition, coups have destroyed the hierarchical chain of command in the Nigerian armed forces. Junior officers who succeed in staging coups are automatically promoted over and above their erstwhile superior officers. This practice not only damages the chain of command, it results in deep resentment with its attendant negative consequences to discipline. Military rule is also detrimental to the corporate existence of the military because it creates two sets of military personnel: officers with and officers without political appointments. Those officers who hold political appointments use their political positions as a gateway to enrich themselves. On the other hand, officers without political appointments continue to perform purely military duties. Without access to state power, they do not get much opportunity to enrich themselves. This, too, breeds deep resentment with negative consequences on military discipline. The resentment felt by officers without political position is deepened by the tendency of officers who have corruptly enriched themselves to openly flaunt their ill-gotten riches.

Military rule has created wide polarization and factionalization in the Nigerian armed forces. Senior officers constantly dread junior officers for fear that the latter would one day carry out their long-expected bloody coup. On their part, junior officers live in constant fear of their senior officers. They are apprehensive that they could become victims of witch-hunts designed to wipe out potential coup plotters. Several years ago, General Ibrahim Babangida, the then head of state, raised an alarm over this state of affairs in the armed forces. He reminded his fellow officers that the Nigerian military used to have 'good old days' when officers 'really cared for their men' (Babangida, 1991, p. 186). As he put it: 'It was the days of dedicated and committed senior officers who saw their primary duties as one of producing honorable, disciplined, healthy and loyal officers and men' (Babangida, 1991, p. 186). General Babangida lamented that the 'good old days' had disappeared from military barracks. Babangida noted that instead of commonalities of interests between senior and junior officers, a wide 'communication gap' had developed between the two sets of officers. Continuing, Babangida pointed out that

> there seems to be a lack of commitment on the part of some of our officers and NCOs to the military profession...Many of us as senior officers hardly relate to our juniors. Often the gap between senior and junior officers has widened, thus making dangerously manifest generational cleavages. I expect that the military involvement in politics has had a hand in this. Also I think that the threat of witch-hunting under the guise of plotting to overthrow government is responsible for this (Babangida, 1991, p. 186).

Military officers have not been able to effectively combine governance and military preparedness. Governance has come at the expense of military training and military readiness. High-ranking officers' failure to look after their men has forced some soldiers to take up armed robbery on the side. Other soldiers are hired on a private basis by landlords who use them to collect rents from recalcitrant tenants. Yet, other soldiers set up illegal toll-booths on high-ways to extort money and other valuable goods from motorists. Illegal and sordid activities such as these have further discredited the military in the eyes of many Nigerians. Consequently, many soldiers get demoralized and lose confidence in the military as a profession. Babangida and other military officers have openly admitted that military rule has had a debilitating impact on professionalism and morale. For instance, in an address to senior military officers, he noted that:

> the morale of our men is sometimes at a discount. Welfarism is in the doldrums. Those facilities that will enable the men to function and which include medical care, accommodation, clothing, feeding and mobility are in acute short supply. We all must stand to blame for not ordering our priorities to assure that the man is well looked after and sufficiently motivated to utilize the resource available to him to achieve our final objective (Babangida, 1991, p. 187).

Military rule has fundamentally transformed the socio-political dynamics of Nigeria. Among other things, the incursion of the military into the political process in January 1966 has led to the increasing politicization of the military and the militarization of politics. It has also changed the nature of civil-military relations in Nigeria. Military intervention has abrogated the doctrine of civilian supremacy. In place of the doctrine that civilian political leaders have supremacy over the military and over security policy, military rule in Nigeria has helped to entrench a strong belief among military officers that they are supreme. After all, virtually every major political decision in Nigeria over the past thirty years has been made by the military or those closely associated with the institution. Today, the military has taken it upon itself to determine the form, nature and contents of political participation. It has arrogated to itself, not only who could rule Nigeria, but the terms and circumstances of such governance. Military rule has not only facilitated military supremacy over state and society in Nigeria, it has also allowed the military to appropriate an ever widening array of roles and responsibilities to itself—often with disastrous consequences. Babangida has listed a wide range of roles and responsibilities which the military has assumed in the last few years. He noted that:

> We [military officers] are the government of the day and, as such, are responsible for the normal day-to-day running of the affairs of the nation. We are the defenders of our territorial integrity. We are the planners and implementers of the political program of transition from military to civil rule. We are the reformers of the institutions and organizations of power in the polity as evidenced by the exercise of creating new states and local governments. We are the reformers of the existing battered economy through the Structural Adjustment Program. We are the re-directors of the political process and the architect of the institutions of civil political power. We are the planners and implementors of the process of social reorientation of the civil values in the polity as illustrated in the activities of MAMSER and DFRRI... These responsibilities define a collective system; they present an institution which organizes every facet of the societal life of the Nigerian nation. They leave no room for a contesting authority or power group; they reduce all non-military leadership groups to pressure groups whose efficacy depends upon influencing but not dictating the course of decisions by the military (Babangida, 1991, p. 154).

The military's control of state power facilitated its ability to devise new roles for itself. The tragedy for Nigeria is that the more roles the military appropriates for itself, the greater the degree of its ruination of state and society. Thus, the more roles the military appropriates, the less successful its overall management of Nigeria becomes. The military's spirited attempt to carve out new responsibilities for itself has been particularly significant in the Babangida and Abacha years (1985–1997) when the military embarked upon a wholesale program of frontal transformation of both the economy and the political system.

One of the most pernicious legacies of military rule is the culture of violence that it has created in the country. Autocratic governance as personified by military rule places high premium on force and violence. Dialogue, bargaining, compromise—all essential elements of effective governing style are de-emphasized by military officers. Instead, Nigerians are asked to submit to military dictate. Even speech patterns in Nigeria seem to have been militarized. In the absence of dialogue and compromise, inter-ethnic and intra-ethnic conflicts have been exacerbated in many parts of the country. Military officers do not seem to have any answer. In fact, the perception that the military takes sides in these conflicts has made their resolution more problematic. In general, military rule has increased the level of regional, ethnic, and religious polarization in the country.

Contemporary ethnic violence in Nigeria

While inter-ethnic and inter-communal violence is not new in Nigeria, the current spate of ethnic violence has assumed new dimensions. First, neighboring ethnic groups that had lived peacefully for centuries are at the heart of contemporary ethnic violence. Second, the ferocity and sheer scale of destructiveness of these conflicts are unprecedented. Third, many of the conflicts have their roots in government policies made far away from the theaters of the conflict. Finally, traditional political institutions such as the police and the judiciary that used to handle ethnic conflicts have broken down and ethnic groups tend to rely increasingly on self-help measures.

The 1992 Zango-Kataf crisis that resulted in the death of hundreds of people and millions of naira in property damages ostensibly was caused by the local government's decision to relocate the Zango-Kataf market to a new site. However, the decision to relocate the market was itself part of a long-simmering tension between the Hausa/Fulani ethnic group and the Kataf ethnic group. Like many other places in the old Sokoto Caliphate of

Nigeria, the political hierarchy of Zango-Kataf was dominated by an aristocracy of Hausas and Fulanis. The Katafs resented this domination arguing that they were the original indigenes of the area and should therefore not be economically and politically marginalized by the aristocracy. The creation of new local governments gave the Kataf and similar other minority groups, a greater leverage of political power. It was the attempt to use this new political power to over-turn the status quo that sparked the violent conflict in 1992.[2] According to *Citizen*, a weekly magazine, Juri Babang Ayok, the chairman of the Zango-Kataf local government council issued an order on January 30, 1992 demanding that the Zango-Kataf market must relocate to a new site within seven days.

> On the day Babang Ayok issued his relocation order, the new site was being leveled with bulldozers. There wasn't a single stall or toilet facility at the new market, and pieces of land for traders to erect stalls were first given out on the day of the commissioning itself, February 6. There were other problems too. Juri Babang Ayok had not obtained an approval from the full local council before he issued the proclamation (*Citizen*, June 15, 1992, p. 11).

The decision to move the market was informed by the fact that Hausa traders owned most of the stalls in the market and 'there was little space for emergent Kataf traders to partake in it...Hausa traders in Zango resented the council's action and saw in it a political vendetta, especially since the official reason given for the relocation was shortage of stalls in the old market; they were quick to point out that the new one had not a single stall' (*Citizen*, June 15, 1992, p. 11). The Hausa traders decided to boycott the new market and they obtained a court injunction restraining the council from relocating the market. Despite the injunction, the council decided to go ahead with the relocation.

Clashes between Ijaws and Itsekiris, Ogoni and Andoni, Ogoni and Okrika are among the new spate of ethnic conflicts in Nigeria's oil delta. While specific local grievances may be responsible for some of these crises, the roots of the crises can be traced to government policies on oil and oil revenues. As Ucheome Nwagbara has pointed out:

> The Niger Delta is Nigeria's mineral colony, which the authorities and oil companies have exploited. It is a region of a sad paradox: it is an area with great mineral wealth, an area that produces more than 90 percent of Nigeria's foreign exchange earnings, while re-

maining poor itself. The Niger Delta is the chief source of Nigeria's affluence; provides the energy that runs Nigerian industries, power plans, automobiles and airplanes. Yet, in the Niger Delta one finds abject poverty, lack of amenities, poor health, underdevelopment, and isolated people, while those who gain their wealth from the region invest their profits elsewhere and live elsewhere (Nwagbara, in *Vanguard*, February 1, 1999).

The 1994 Ogoni and the Okrika violent clashes that left many people dead occurred over contests for 'over the ownership of several waterfronts in the city...The Ogoni and the Andoni, their neighbors further to the south, are also feuding. When they clashed last August, hundreds of people were killed and several villages were destroyed...The Nembe and Kalabari have been fighting over fishing rights in the area' (Gahia in *Newswatch*, April 18, 1994, p. 10). Similarly, contests over oil-rich lands have pitted the Ijaws and the Ilajes. As *Newswatch*, a weekly magazine, has observed:

Igbokoda, the headquarters of the Ilaje Ese Odo Local Government Area of Ondo State used to be a vibrant commercial center. But last week, it was a deserted town following an outbreak of hostilities between the Ijaws and the Ilajes, two rival ethnic groups in the riverine areas of the state. The fighting was over the ownership of Obe Apata, an oil-rich area being claimed by the two communities. The bloody clashes are said to have resulted in the death of 500 persons. The Ilajes claimed that about 58 towns and villages with a population of over 1,000 have been captured and laid waste by rampaging Ijaw warriors (Adeyanju in *Newswatch*, April 18, 1994, p. 11).

The on-going violent clashes between the Ijaws and the Itsekiris had their immediate cause in the government's decision to relocate the headquarters of a Warri local government. The decision to remove the council headquarters from Ogbe-Ijoh to Ogidigben was arbitrarily made and without any consultations. In fact it was announced by fiat through the network of the Delta State broadcasting service.

Several factors make the Niger Delta a politically volatile place. First, the environmental destruction associated with oil exploration and production activities and the belief by the inhabitants that neither the oil companies nor the federal government is willing to clean up the environment causes a lot of resentment. Second, the wrenching economic crisis in the country—and in particular, the extremely high unemployment, estimated at 90 percent among youths in the Delta, is a major factor in the current volatile situation. In the wake of such high unemployment, it is easy to recruit volunteers among the army of unemployed young people (Zuokumor in *Vanguard,* January 19, 1999). Henry Alapiki contends that most of the ethnic conflicts in the state were due to 'the people angling for economic empowerment and cashing in on the general atmosphere of mass discontent to mobilize their kinsmen against strange elements or perceived traditional enemies' (Gahia in *Newswatch,* April 18, 1994, p. 10).

There is also a strong belief that neither the federal nor the state governments can be trusted to help resolve ethnic conflicts. For example, a communique issued by the General Conference of Itsekiri Patriots in January 1999, noted that because of 'the Ijaw high representation in the top echelon of the Nigerian military hierarchy, the Federal Military Government (FMG) looked elsewhere and allowed the Ijaw militias to kill and maim the Itsekiris (*Vanguard,* January 31, 1999). Admiral Mike Akhigbe buttressed this belief when he wondered why the Ijaws would not channel their grievances to 'Ijaw sons and brothers in the PRC (Provisional Ruling Council)' (see *Vanguard,* January 31, 1999).

Ethnic mobilization used to be viewed quite negatively. However, as has been shown by the Ogonis of Nigeria, ethnic entrepreneurs can positively utilize ethnic mobilization to draw attention to societal inadequacies. The Ogonis have, for instance, used ethnicity to rally people against environmental destruction caused by the extraction of crude oil in Nigeria. They have succeeded in using their political mobilization and the destruction of their environment as a metaphor for all that is wrong with Nigeria.

Government response to ethnic conflicts

The usual response of the Nigerian government to outbreaks of ethnic violence is to deploy the police to suppress the disturbances and to maintain peace. Shortly after that, a commission of inquiry is set up to investigate the root and remote causes of conflicts and recommend solutions. For instance, in the case of the clashes between the Ijaws and the Itsekiris, the government set up a commission of inquiry headed by Justice Alhassan Idoko in May 1997. Similarly, the Rahila H. Cudjoe Commission was set up after the Zango-Kataf riots. The Commission had the following terms of reference:

- Inquire into, investigate and identify the immediate and remote causes of the Zango-Kataf disturbances.
- Assess the extent of damage caused by the disturbances.
- Ascertain and identify the roles played by individuals and groups in causing tension and outbreak of violence.
- Determine the extent of loss of lives and properties.
- Examine any other matter incidental to the aforementioned terms of reference.
- Recommend appropriate penalties for culprits as well as measures to forestall future disturbances (*Citizen* (Kaduna, Nigeria), June 15, 1992, p. 14).

In other cases, those arrested after ethnic clashes were tried under the Civil Disturbances (Special Tribunal) Decree no. 2 of 1987. Two tribunals headed by Justice Benedict Okadigbo and Emmanuel Adegbite were used for the Zango-Kataf riots. They sentenced 14 people to death and many others to various terms of imprisonment.

In the case of the Ogoni conflict with the Andoni, a new strategy was tried. A peace agreement was negotiated between leading members of the two ethnic groups under the auspices of the Rivers Peace Conference Committee (RPCC) and the National Council on Inter-governmental Relations (NCIR). Ken Saro-Wiwa and some Ogoni leaders refused to sign the agreement because they disagreed with items four and six of the peace resolution. Under the two items, it was stated: 'That the Rivers State government along with the federal government, the affected local governments and all security agencies with the support of community leaders and all other individuals should ensure safe passage for all persons on all roads, waterways within Ogoni and Andoni areas. Furthermore, it is in the interest of the Ogoni and Andoni and all governments in Nigeria to ensure an immediate resumption of full economic and social activities within Ogoni and Andoni areas' (*Newswatch*, April 18, 1994).

One of the reasons why both the federal and the state governments have been unable to deal with recent outbreaks of ethnic violence in the country is the collapse of the traditional institutions for managing conflicts. The privatization of the state under military rule has created a situation in which governmental institutions are used primarily for self-aggrandizement by government personnel. Thus, when policemen are deployed to areas of conflict to suppress rioting and violence, they take bribes from both sides to the conflict. For instance, *Citizen* related the following story during the Zango-Kataf crisis.

Even in the midst of the carnage, some police personnel tried to extract bribes from victims. Sarkin Fulani Hussaini Muturba told the Cudjoe panel that when he went to the police post in Zango on the afternoon of February 6 to report that Alhaji Aruwa and his family had been killed by the Kataf, the police demanded money to buy the paper [on which] to record his statement. Muturba later collected money from another Fulani man and gave the police ten Naira, after which they recorded his statement and went with him to retrieve the corpses. By then it was dark and the corpses could not be found, so the police locked up Muturba for bringing 'false information' and demanded another 2,000 Naira to release him (Jega in *Citizen*, June 15, 1992, pp. 15–16).

Similarly, during the clashes in Warri, *African Concord* observed as follows:

In the last two weeks, units of naval and mobile policemen hang out everywhere or move all over with wailing siren. They search people, hit or beat up others. They also 'obtain'—a Warri slang for bribe (Ishaka in *African Concord*, April 14, 1997, p. 12).

Government policies also tend to create the impression that the government takes sides in ethnic conflicts. For example, when the legitimacy of the two tribunals set up to try those arrested during the Zango-Kataf crisis was challenged by the Katafs, the federal government promulgated Decree 55 of December 1992 which ousted the power of regular courts from making orders against actions of the tribunals even in cases where such actions constitute a violation of constitutional provisions on human rights. The Katafs had contended that the tribunals were not properly constituted since they were composed of seven, instead of five members each.

Conclusion

While Nigerian leaders extol and celebrate the nation's ethnic and regional diversities, decades of brutal, corrupt and oppressive military regimes have created mutual suspicions and animosities among the different ethnic groups in the country. In the past few years, these animosities have exploded with devastating consequences on many communities. Inter-ethnic and intra-ethnic conflicts have led to the needless death of thousands of Nigerian citizens. Yet, while the frequency of communal explosions has made it fairly easy to predict the next occurrence and even the trajectory of ethnic or communal violence, the Nigerian government appears unable to come to grips with the reality of the country's ethnic tensions. It lacks effective tools for managing ethnic relations. Of even greater concern is the federal and state governments' failure to address the root causes of these frequent outbursts of ethnic animosities. More often than not, governments' response to ethnic conflicts has been episodic, ad hoc and ineffective. Even more troubling is the fact that government policies by omission and commission, frequently accentuate the country's ethnic and communal conflicts.

The ethnic issue will remain an important issue in Nigeria for a long time to come. Compounding the problem of ethnic conflicts in Nigeria is the fact communal conflicts are taking place within the context of intense struggles to democratize state and society in the country. A long-term solution to Nigeria's ethnic conflicts may lie in concrete strategies designed to rebuild trust among the nation's ethnic groups. Piece-meal, ad-hoc and half-hearted approaches which have been the hall-mark of the Nigerian government's responses to communal conflicts in the country, have failed to deal with the crisis and are unlikely to be successful as a strategy of dealing with the issues generated by the country's ethnic and regional plurality.

Notes

1. For evidence from Asia and the Pacific, see the collection of excellent essays and analyses in Brown, M. E. and Ganguly, S. (eds.) (1997), *Government Policies and Ethnic Relations in Asia and the Pacific*, MIT Press: Cambridge, MA.
2. For a detailed analysis of the Zango-Kataf conflict, see Suberu, R. T. (1996), *Ethnic Minority Conflicts and Governance in Nigeria*, Spectrum Book: Ibadan, Nigeria.

References

Adeyanju, R. (1994), 'Who Owns the Land?', *Newswatch*, April 28.

Aku, A. (1982), 'Zoning, Rotation and the Stability of Nigeria', Text of a Lecture at the Institute of Administration, Ahmadu Bello University, Zaria, Nigeria, April 27.

Babangida, I. (1991), *For Their Tomorrow We Gave Our Today: Selected Speeches of IBB*, Safari Books: Ibadan, Nigeria.

Berman, B. (1998), 'Ethnicity, Patronage and the African State: The Politics of Uncivil

Nationalism', *African Affairs*, Vol. 97, No. 388 (July), pp. 305–341.

Blaustein, A. P. and Flanz, G. H. (eds.) (1991), *Constitutions of the Countries of the World: Swaziland*, Oceana Publications: Dobbs Ferry, NY.

Brown, M. E. and Ganguly, S. (1997), 'Introduction', in Brown, M. E. and Ganguly, S. (eds.), *Government Policies and Ethnic Relations in Asia and the Pacific*, Cambridge University Press: Cambridge.

Citizen (Kaduna, Nigeria), June 15, 1992.

Ekeh, P. (1972), 'Citizenship and Political Conflicts: A Sociological Interpretation of the Nigerian Crisis', in Okpaku, J. (ed.), *Nigeria: Dilemmas of Nationhood*, Third Press: New York.

Gahia, C. (1994), 'Tribes at War', *Newswatch*, April 18, 1994, p. 10.

Imobighe, T. A. (1997), 'Conflict Management in Nigeria', in Bello-Imam, I. B. (ed.), *Governance in Nigeria: Economy, Politics and Society in the Adjustment Years 1985–1995*, Stirling-Horden Publishers: Ibadan, Nigeria.

Ishaka, P. (1997), 'Flames in Oil City', *African Concord*, April 14, p. 12.

Jega, A. (2000), 'Identity Transformation and the Politics of Identity Under Crisis and Adjustment', in Jega, A. (ed.), *Identity Transformation and Identity Politics Under Structural Adjustment in Nigeria*, Nordiska Afrikainstitet: Uppsala.

Jega, M. (1992), 'Zango Kataf Riots: The Road to Hell', *Citizen*, June 15, 1992, pp. 15–16.

Lemarchand, R. (1998), Genocide in the Great Lakes: Which Genocide? Whose Genocide?', *African Studies Review*, Vol. 41, No. 1 (April), pp. 3–16.

Ndikumana, L. (1998), 'Institutional Failure and Ethnic Conflict in Burundi', *African Studies Review*, Vol. 41, No. 1 (April), pp. 29–47.

Newswatch, April 18, 1994.

Nwagbara, U. (1999), 'Peace for Ethnic Nationalities: Oil Producing States and Private Mineral Rights', *Vanguard*, February 1, 1999.

Osaghae, E. E. (1991), 'Ethnic Minorities and Federalism in Nigeria', *African Affairs*, Vol. 90, No. 359 (April), pp. 237–258.

Saro-Wiwa, K. (1990), *On a Darkling Plain: An Account of the Nigerian Civil War*, Saros International: London.

Suberu, R. T. (1996), *Ethnic Minority Conflicts and Governance in Nigeria*, Spectrum Book: Ibadan, Nigeria.

Usman, Y. B. and Abba, A. (2000), *The Misrepresentation of Nigeria: The Facts and the Figures*, Center for Democratic Development, Research and Training (CDDRT): Zaria, Nigeria.

Vanguard (Lagos, Nigeria), January 31, 1999.

Vanguard (Lagos, Nigeria), February 22, 1999.

Zuokumor, F. (1999), 'Create an Ijaw State', *Vanguard*, January 19.

6

Ethnicity and Ethnic Challenges in the Middle East

NADER ENTESSAR

Introduction

In a controversial article on the Cold War, whose theme was later expanded in a book, Francis Fukuyama, then deputy director of the State Department's policy planning staff and a policy analyst at the Rand Corporation, suggested that with the apparent triumph of Western liberalism over Soviet communism, most, if not all, underlying causes of conflict in the world have been eliminated. As Fukuyama puts it, what we 'may be witnessing is not just the end of the Cold War, or the passing of a particular period of history, but *the end of history* [emphasis added] as such: that is the end point of mankind's ideological evolution and the universalization of Western liberal democracy as the final form of human government' (Fukuyama, 1989a, p. 4).

Although Fukuyama (1989a, pp. 14–15) in his neo-Hegelian theory acknowledges the importance of religious revivalism or fundamentalism and ethnic nationalism in global politics, he nevertheless asserts that Western liberalism will eventually prevail over the challenges presented by these and similar phenomena (also see Fukuyama, 1989b). It is beyond the scope of this chapter to examine the validity of Fukuyama's theory.

However, given the sociopolitical developments in the post-Cold War period in every region of the world, one could reasonably assert that the phenomenon of ethnonationalism will continue to pose a major challenge to the structure of the Westphalian nation-state system and will continue to be a serious source of conflict in multiethnic and multinational societies in the Middle East irrespective of the future of Western liberalism on a global scale. From the Middle East to Africa and from the Balkans to the former Soviet Union, inter- and intra-ethnic conflicts have led to a seemingly endless myriad of catastrophic strife, some of which has threatened the very existence of nation-states in their present geographic configuration.

The purpose of this chapter is to provide an overview of significant factors that have heightened the sense of identity among national and ethnic groups in the contemporary Middle East. In today's Middle East, as elsewhere in what is called the Third World, the politicization of ethnicity and the rise of nationalism have been closely linked with the concept of self-determination. Of course, self-determination has been an internationally recognized principle since the French Revolution of 1789 and its resulting product—the Declaration of the Rights of Man and of the Citizen. Self-determination has been manifested in different forms, one of which has been the revival of ethnic consciousness or ethnonationalism.

What constitutes an ethnic group or what prompts ethnonationalism among distinct groups are unsettled questions that have troubled both scholars and policy makers alike. Dov Ronen has discussed ethnic self-determination in terms of a group's identification with a set of 'linguistic, historical, or general cultural identities, which have never been totally ignored but have been relegated to "subgroup" status within the (nation-) state. These self-identities were commonly termed *ethnicity*; hence this type of self-determination may conveniently, although not always accurately, be called *ethnic* self-determination' (Ronen, 1979, p. 12). This conceptualization of ethnicity assumes or implies that an ethnic group is a subgroup of a larger society with its own common sense of identity and cultural tradition as distinct from those of the larger nation within which it lives.

Other scholars of nationalism and ethnicity, such as Walker Connor, have asserted that an ethnic group is not merely a subgroup of a larger society (as is a minority group) but a basic human category 'characterized by unity of race and culture' (Connor, 1973, p. 2). In other words, the Greek word *ethnos*, or nation, should be our reference point in identifying distinct ethnic or national groups. Furthermore, Connor contends that a group 'need not have acquired a sense of separate identity in order to qualify as an ethnic group in the traditional meaning..., it is *the acquisition of a sense of group identity* [emphasis added] that converts the ethnic group into a nation' (Connor, 1973, p. 3).

For our purpose in this chapter, I will rely on Iliya Harik's definition of ethnicity, which is broad enough and addresses the points brought up by Connor. Harik, who focuses on the Middle East in his study of ethnicity and nationalism, defines an ethnic group as a 'community conscious of sharing similar characteristics such as a distinct language, a religion, a culture, or a historical experience of its own and also conscious of its differences from other communities by virtue of these same characteristics...' (Harik, 1972, p. 303). Harik, like Connor, asserts that a high degree of ethnic awareness is not an absolute prerequisite for a group to form a distinct ethnic community, although ethnic nationalism is normally manifested among ethnically conscious communities (Connor, 1994, chapters 4 and 5). All in all, one should consider language, religion, common historical experiences, and cultural distinctiveness as important components of ethnicity and as variables affecting nationalism among various national groups in the Middle East.

Dimensions of ethnicity

Much of the current theoretical debate over the nature of ethnicity has revolved around the 'primordialist' and 'instrumentalist' approaches to the scientific study of ethnicity (Connor, 1994, pp. 103–108; Smith, 1991, pp. 19–42; Brass, 1994, pp. 83–89). The primordialists view ethnic identities as having been formed through deeply rooted historical experiences and cultural formations. These communal solidarities are 'cultural givens' and form the ethnic distinctiveness or a sense of 'we-ness' (Ringer and Lawless, 1989, pp. 1–17). Thus a shared history, a common language, a perceived common lineage, distinctive shared cultural values, a territorial attachment to a specific area, and an overall sense of solidarity constitute essential components of what Anthony Smith has called an 'ethnie' or an ethnic community (Smith, 1986, pp. 22–30). The interplay of these characteristics provide an overall meaning, or a *mythomoteur*, to an ethnic community without which a group 'cannot define itself to itself or to others, and cannot inspire or guide collective action' (Smith, 1986, p. 25).

The instrumentalist approach, on the other hand, defines the boundaries of an ethnic group as situational. That is, ethnic groups can change their group identities and group boundaries with immediate exigencies. By the same token, ethnic nationalism and ethnic relations can be defined not so much in terms of rigid, primordial identities but instead through rational choices made by members of an ethnic group to change their existing boundaries or acquire new ones (Banton, 1980, pp. 475–499; Young, 1993, pp. 21–23). Therefore, instrumentalists argue that the status needs of members of an ethnic group prevail over the primordialists' concepts of ethnic solidarity if the former advance the material and security needs of a group (Esman and Rabinovich, 1988, p. 13).

The primordialist and instrumentalist approaches to the study of nationalism and ethnic collective movements should not be viewed as mutually exclusive. While primordialism allows us to study ethnonationalism from a cultural prism, instrumentalism compels us to shift attention away from purely cultural attributes and toward political and socioeconomic factors. As Crawford Young has noted, ethnic identities should be studied not as a set of fixed, objective attributes, but in terms of changing, overlapping, and interlocking subjective phenomena (Young, 1976, p. 49).

An intellectually challenging approach to the study of ethnic national movements, and nationalism in general, has been provided by Benedict Anderson. He defines a nation not so much in terms of primordial or instrumental attributes, but as a subjective entity, or as Anderson (1983, p. 15) calls it, 'an imagined political community... Communities are to be distinguished not by their falsity-genuineness, but by the style in which they are imagined.' In other words, national or ethnic groups can be perceived as an imagined political community irrespective of the strength of the actual primordial or instrumental identities that may exist among the members of their respective communities. That is, on the strength of subjective (i.e. imagined) feelings, any group can transform itself into a nation with rights of self-determination. It is this emotional attachment to an imagined political community that has fueled ethnic drives for self-determination in the modern Middle East.

State and ethnic self-determination

One of the most salient features of the contemporary Middle East has been the expansion of the role of the state as an independent variable in shaping the balance of societal forces, including managing competing socioeconomic and political claims of ethnic and nationality groups. Many Middle Eastern countries, like other multiethnic states of the Third World, which 'formerly attained only spasmodic and limited control outside their core regions and capital cities have sought increasingly systematic control over peripheral regions through the expansion of their traditional administrative bureaucracies, armies, and educational systems. At the same time, the range of governmental interference has expanded beyond the concern with raising revenues and maintaining order, as the need to direct, train, and motivate labor has increased' (Brown, 1989, p. 8). Furthermore, the challenge of globalization has accelerated the need to incorporate an ever increasing number of the citizenry, irrespective of one's ethnicity, into the labor pool. Perhaps one unintended consequence of globalization in the Middle East has been the rise of socioeconomic demands for ethnic equality and fairness. This, in part, has led to ethnic conflicts among sub-national groups and between the state and minorities in several Middle Eastern countries. However, as Yahya Sadowski and John Bowen, among others, have shown, we need to be cautious about overgeneralizing the dangers of ethnic conflicts and global chaos in the post-Cold War era (Sadowski, 1998, pp. 145–169; Bowen, 2000, section 2).

Notwithstanding recent challenges to the primacy of the state as the dominant player in international relations, the pervasive role of the state in the post-World War II era has allowed it to develop into an institution that is autonomous from all other actors in the society while maintaining monopoly control over coercive forces that enable the state to shape, *inter alia*, class formations and ethnic relations. The relative independence of the state vis-a-vis other social forces has allowed the state to shape and alter ethnic identities in multiethnic societies. In the Middle East, the state has been instrumental in fostering and/or altering ethnic identities to suit its own policy objectives, legitimize its authority, promote national unity, generate interethnic rivalries and devise a 'divide-and-rule' strategy to enhance its hegemonic position over individuals or groups in society. The ongoing conflict between Arab and Iranian nationalism, Arab and Turkish nationalism, Turkish and Kurdish nationalism, and the like are illustrative of this point. The statist paradigm, which I believe is most appropriate in understanding the dynamics of national movements in the post-Cold War Middle East, does not necessarily negate the role played by dominant classes or groups and outside forces in shaping the contours of politicized ethnicity and nationalism in today's Middle East. Nor does it downgrade primordial and instrumentalist variables in explaining the phenomenon of ethnonationalism in the region. It simply affirms the supremacy of the state as the manager and controller of competing national claims.

Lastly, with the establishment of modern nation-states in the Middle East, rights of people became increasingly intertwined with those of the sovereign and centralized nation-states. However, identification of the rights of people with those of the state has had a built-in limitation in that the nationalism of dominant groups (e.g., Arabs in Iraq, Turks in Turkey, Persians in Iran) tends to overwhelm the nationalism of other ethnic groups in the state, and the dominant groups' nationalism has tended to present itself in an aggressive and sometimes hegemonic fashion.

Assimilative vs. dissimilative trends

The characteristic features of ethnic or nationality groups can be studied in terms of their assimilative or dissimilative effects on the political structures and nation-building efforts of the larger unit or the state. As J. Milton Yinger notes, the extent of assimilation of an ethnic group into the larger unit in which its members live is a function of the strength of four independent variables: (1) acculturation, (2) amalgamation, (3) integration, and (4) identification (Yinger, 1981, pp. 249–262).

Acculturation is the process of change toward greater cultural similarity brought about by contact between two or more groups (Yinger, 1981, p. 251). Thus, there exists a positive correlation between the degree of acculturation and the extent of assimilation of an ethnic group into the mainstream of the larger society. The high degree of acculturation of the German-Americans or Italian-Americans has negated any secessionist tendencies or nationalistic drives for political autonomy by these groups in the contemporary United States. On the other hand, a low level of Kurdish acculturation in modern Turkey or Iraq has contributed to the rise of Kurdish nationalism that has already led to the establishment of an autonomous Kurdish region in northern Iraq and has challenged the foundation of the Turkish and Iranian states for eighty years.

The Kurdish acculturation process in Iran, Iraq, and Turkey has taken several forms. In prerevolutionary Iran, the monarchy was used as a centripetal force and a channel through which acculturation of Iranian ethnic nationalities was to take place. Glorification of the ancient Iranian empires and the historic contributions of various ethnic groups to Iran served as a rallying point and a reminder of their cultural affinity with the Persians (Entessar, 1992, pp. 23–29). Following the overthrow of the Pahlavi monarchy in 1979, the new Iranian regime based its policies towards Muslim minorities on the 'imperative of Islamic unity' (Dekmejian, 1980, p. 11) in order to assimilate the country's ethnic groups into the fabric of the new Islamic state. However, religious sectarianism, such as the conflict between Sunni and Shi'a Muslim Kurds, as well as the negation of the ethnic uniqueness of the Kurds and other Iranian nationalities by the new regime, prevented the government authorities from using Islam as an effective tool of sociopolitical assimilation of these minorities. A doctrine of political unity based solely on narrowly interpreted Islamic doctrine would require a complete disregard for any geographic, linguistic, racial or other ethnic considerations among the Muslim *umma*, or community. In practice, we have witnessed not a blurring of ethnic distinctiveness with the rise of Islamic revivalism but a 'coincidence of Islamic revival and ethnic consciousness' (Dekmejian, 1980, p. 11) in much of the Muslim Middle East. Similarly, Islam has not been able to overcome the countervailing social, political and economic forces which have persistently undermined the realization of ethnic demands for self-determination in the region.[1]

In Iraq, despite the fact that ethnic differences between the majority Arabs and minority Kurds have been given official recognition, the process of acculturation has been no less tortuous than the one experienced in Iran. The Iraqi government's glorification of Arabism and Arab nationalism as represented by the ideology of the Ba'th Party has hindered the development of a truly national Iraqi political culture. The genocidal campaigns against the Kurds in the 1980s and the massive Kurdish rebellion in 1991 against President Saddam Hussein and his Ba'thi government following the defeat of Iraqi forces by the U.S.-led coalition in the Persian Gulf war clearly represented the failure of the Iraqi government's policies towards the country's Kurdish minority (see, for example, Entessar, 1992, pp. 68–80; Gunter, 1992; Hazelton, 1994, chapters 2, 3, and 7; Salih, 1996, pp. 81–94).

Similarly, the Turkish government's attempts to acculturate the Kurds have been a failure as the Turks have, in general, sought to deny the existence of a separate Kurdish identity in Turkey.[2] As I have argued elsewhere, the Turks have implemented the most repressive policies towards the country's 15 million Kurdish citizens. Even after the 1999 capture of Abdullah Ocalan and the near disintegration of his Kurdistan Workers' Party (PKK), which fought a guerrilla war against the Turkish army for over 15 years, the Kurdish predicament continues in today's Turkey. The country's inability to come to terms with its Kurdish citizens is largely due to modern Turkey's Kemalist legacy (named after the founder of modern Turkey Mustfa Kemal Attaturk), which sought to create a unified Turkish state free from the ethnic sectarianism and conflict that contributed to the downfall on the multiethnic and multinational Ottoman Empire after World War I.

The second variable in the process of ethnic assimilation is amalgamation. This is a biological process which recognizes that 'groups which are biologically distinct from each other (have few common ancestors) and are distinguishable by appearance or genealogy as separate in inheritance are less likely, other things being equal, to experience psychological, cultural, or structural assimilation' (Yinger, 1981, p. 254). Amalgamation often occurs late in the process of assimilation and usually after extensive acculturation and integration of an ethnic group has taken place. The case of the Azeri minority in Iran is illustrative of this point. The Turkic-speaking Azeris, whose population of 17 million comprises close to one-third of Iran's total population, have been an integral element of the Iranian political, economic and cultural milieu for centuries. Turkish-speaking dynasties that ruled Iran from the 11th century until the advent of the Pahlavi monarchy in 1925 made the total assimilation of the Azeris in Iran a fact of life.[3] Notwithstanding the Azeri assimilation in Iran, 'the Azerbaijanis tenaciously preserve and adhere to their linguistic distinctiveness. In a gathering of Azerbaijanis, when non-Turkish speaking countrymen are not present, Turkish is almost invariably used as a language of communication' (Kazemi, 1988, p. 213). This is true not only in case of Azores, but it also applies to many other Iranian ethnic groups, like Gilanis or Mazandaranis, who use different vernacular languages than Persian. The attachment to one's dialect or language has sometimes been interpreted erroneously by certain observers as a primordial manifestation of political autonomy or secessionism. Whereas in reality language distinctiveness in this context may indeed be an expression of what Fredrik Barth has called boundary maintenance between group members and outsiders (Barth, 1969, p. 14; also see Eriksen, 1993).

The third assimilative factor, integration, refers to the 'process of structural assimilation of persons from two or more formerly separate sub-societies into a set of shared interactions' (Yinger, 1981, p. 254). Integration could take place at both individual and group levels. Group integration, also called pluralism, occurs when two or more ethnic communities, while maintaining their distinct group identities, are accorded 'the same rights and public privileges, the same access to political and economic advantages, and share the same responsibilities as citizens and members of the total society...' (Yinger, 1981, p. 254). In the case of individual integration, the foregoing criteria apply to some individuals from various ethnic communities but not to those groups as a whole. In Iran, Iraq and Turkey, for example, the integration of the Kurds seems to have taken place at the individual rather than group level. Even today, only partial integration has occurred in these three countries. That is, only prominent Kurds have attained high-level positions in the Iranian, Iraqi and Turkish governments, and many of these individual Kurds have been integrated into the dominant cultural groups within their respective societies. In general, most multiethnic Middle Eastern countries have had a high degree of success at the individual but a rather poor record at the group level of ethnic integration.

The last variable on the assimilative-dissimilative continuum is identification. This refers to a psychological process whereby individuals from separate groups 'may come to think of themselves as belonging to the same society—a new society blended from their societies of origin' (Yinger, 1981, p. 252). For this to happen, a high degree of common bond must exist among subgroups of a larger nation. But even then, submerging one's own ethnic group identity in favor of a new set of broader identities might be a transitory phenomenon. For example, Islam was thought to provide a new basis of identity for Indian Muslims who created a separate state of Pakistan after India's independence from Great Britain. Soon after the establishment of the multiethnic Muslim Pakistan, some groups began to emphasize their own ethnic identities over the new Pakistani identity. As a result of strong ethnic demands from the Bengalis in East Pakistan, the country experienced disintegrative secessionism which led to the creation of the Bengali-dominated independent state of Bangladesh. In more recent times, the Palestinians seem to have succeeded in forging a strong sense of collective national identity that has withstood sectarian differences among them (see Murphy, 1996, pp. 55–66). On the other hand, the Kurds, which are the largest national group without a state in the Middle East, have yet to forge a new national consciousness to supersede parochial loyalties that have kept them politically divided and isolated in the region. Even among the Iraqi Kurds who now have their own autonomous administration and regional government in northern Iraq, divisiveness has prevented cooperative arrangements between the two major parties, namely between the Kurdish Democratic Party of Massoud Barzani and Jalal Talebani's Patriotic Union of Kurdistan (Gunter, 1999, pp. 67–109).

Variables affecting ethnic consciousness: the case of the Kurds

As the largest non-state nationality in the Middle East, the Kurds present a unique challenge to a number of major states in the region. The overwhelming majority of the estimated 25 million Kurds reside in the territory of Kurdistan whose 500,000 square kilometers encompass areas in Iran, Iraq, Turkey and Syria. Exceptions to this geographic concentration are found in the case of the Kurds who have been moved from northern to southern Iraq, and the Kurds in the Khorassan province in northeastern Iran. The Kurds of southern Iraq are the legacies of a policy of forceful removal of the Kurds from their ancestral homeland and their dispersal to the south—a policy which was exercised at varying intervals by different Iraqi governments from 1958 to the early 1990s. This policy was pursued more vigorously by Saddam Hussein since his accession to the presidency of Iraq in the late 1970s. Both the eight-year Iran-Iraq war and, to a lesser extent, the 1991 U.S.-led war against Iraq, have led to the dispersion of the Kurds from their homeland by the Ba'thi government in Baghdad. The case of the Iranian Kurds of Khorassan dates back to the sixteenth century when the Safavid king, Shah Abbas the First, transferred several Kurdish tribes from Ardalan in northwestern Iran to Khorassan in the northeast. These new Kurdish settlers were used as a buffer to protect the country from further encroachments by Turkoman and Turani invaders (Arfa, 1966, p. 19). The majority of transplanted Kurds have become Shi'a Muslims and have, for all practical purposes, lost contact with their fellow Kurds in other parts of the Middle East. In some respects, the Khorassan Kurds have even changed many of their traditional customs and habits and have emulated the way of life of other inhabitants of Khorassan, such as the Persians, Turks, Tajiks and Turkomans. They have also developed a dialect which is a mixture of Turkish, Persian and Chagatay, an east Turkish dialect spoken by many Uzbeks and Turkomans. The southeastern regions of Turkey have been the heartland of Turkish Kurdistan and the site of the most severe Kurdish resistance to Turkish military ventures in the region. However, many Turkish Kurds have over the years moved to major Turkish cities, such as Istanbul. Notwithstanding the dispersal of the Kurds, Kurdistan as both a distinct geographic entity and for some as a state of mind remains a powerful force for the maintenance of Kurdish ethnic consciousness in the Middle East.

The degree of shared experience, especially in language, and to a lesser extent in religion, has been recognized as a principal contributor to the development of ethnic consciousness and ethnonationalism in the Middle East. Kurdish belongs to the family of Iranian languages, and like other Iranian languages, has an Indo-European origin. Therefore, Kurdish is more akin to Persian than to Arabic or Turkish. Nevertheless, Kurdish is distinct from Persian and other Iranian languages and is generally unintelligible to the speakers of Persian. Unlike many other minority and/or nationality groups in the Middle East, the Kurds have failed to adopt a standard language or a Kurdish *lingua franca*. As I have argued elsewhere, the reasons for the heterogeneity of Kurdish languages are threefold:

> First, the rugged, mountainous terrain of Kurdistan has historically impeded communication between Kurdish tribes and clans. Second, the absence of a strong, centralized administrative structure to unify the many rival Kurdish groups encouraged the development of diverse languages among the Kurds. Finally, the emergence in the twentieth century of a sovereign nation-state system in the Middle East further fragmented the Kurds and placed them under the jurisdiction of countries which themselves displayed linguistic diversity (Entessar, 1989, p. 86).

Kurdish nationalists have long contended that what appears to the outsiders as distinct Kurdish languages are in fact dialects of a single Kurdish language. However, other scholars, both Kurds and non-Kurds, have contended that variations among Kurdish languages are 'far too great by any standard linguistic criteria to warrant the classification of these tongues as simply dialects of the same language. To the discomfort of any lay Kurdish patriot, and the gratitude of prudence, one should speak of Kurdish languages' (Izady, 1998, p. 13). Irrespective of semantic differences, the Kurdish language remains the most important unifying factor among contemporary Kurdish nationalists and serves as an important catalyst for the development of a common Kurdish identity.

In addition to territorial and linguistic attachments, a common religion has also been recognized as a binding force toward the development of ethnic identity. Although, as Amir Hassanpour (1992, p. xxiv) has noted, Kurdish nationalism is essentially secular in nature, religion, in a very broad sense, has affected intra- and inter-Kurdish relations in recent years. In Iran, for example, at least two-thirds of the Kurds are followers of Sunni Islam. The overwhelming majority of the Kurds residing in the Kermanshah region of Iran are followers of Shi'a Islam, which is also the predominant religion of other Iranians as well as the official state religion of the country. There are also pockets of various Sufi orders of Nagshbandi and some Ali-Allahis (those who deify Ali, the first Shi'a Imam).

The Sunni and Shi'a Kurds have not exhibited major religious hostility against each other. The Sunni-Shi'a tensions, however, have erupted into clashes between the Sunni Kurds and Shi'a Azores. Also, conflicts have arisen in the Islamic Republic of Iran between various Kurdish religious personalities. However, these conflicts have occurred not over religious disputes and doctrinal differences between Sunni and Shi'a Islam; they have occurred over the degree of loyalty to the Iranian government. Again, territorial and linguistic attachments are by far the most important determinants of ethnic national consciousness among not only the Kurds but also many other nationality groups in the Middle East today.

Conclusion

The emergence of the modern nation-state system and the concomitant rise of territorially-based nationalism in the Middle East have profoundly affected interethnic relations in the region. In general, the rise of centrally-controlled and highly stratified states in the contemporary Middle East has not accommodated the demands of ethnic nationalism. In general, the state bureaucracy that emerged in the countries of the region tended to largely ignore ethnic diversity and structured the political system to the benefit of the dominant ethnic group. As a result, a number of nonassimilating minorities, to use Crawford Young's terminology, have emerged to challenge the hegemony of the dominant group(s) in the society (Young, 1976, pp. 402–407).

    The extension of the European-designed nation-state system to the Middle East followed either a period of European colonization or indirect domination of these states. As Charles Tilly has noted, this meant that the European-drawn boundaries, which in most cases had been imposed 'without regard to the distribution of peoples became defended frontiers of post-colonial states; only rarely did the new states accommodate to their cultural heterogeneity by partition or by reordering of administrative subdivisions' (Tilly, 1991, p. 39). As the state's power increased, and as the primacy of the state as the dominant actor on the international scene was solidified, the world became 'more tolerant of a state's massacre or displacement of its own residents on the ground of their disloyalty to the regime in power, ...' (Tilly, 1991, p. 39). The extreme form of this behavior has been reflected in the treatment of the Kurds in the region, especially in modern Turkey and Iraq.

    As the ethnic minorities began to lose their rights in the new-state systems in the Middle East, their demand for self-determination increased proportionally. The right of self determination has been recognized by various international covenants in the twentieth century. The exact nature of this principle and how it applies to different entities has been a matter of juridical contention and differing interpretations. There is no question that rights of minorities, including ethnic groups, to protection from extreme discrimination, genocide or expulsion from their lands, are a universally recognized set of international rights. But does the principle of self-determination give ethnic groups in the Middle East a legal right to demand a sovereign state of their own? How does one reconcile the right of people to self-determination and the right of the existing states to maintain their territorial integrity? Neither the international community nor the existing states in the Middle East favor minority rights if such rights threaten the disintegration of the existing nation-state systems. For example, the United States, as the linchpin of support for the Kurdish Regional Government in northern Iraq, has time and again expressed its commitment to the territorial integrity of Iraq and against the establishment of an independent Kurdish state. In the words of Francis J. Ricciardone, the U.S. State Department's Special Representative for Transition in Iraq during the Clinton administration, there is no overreaching U.S. policy towards the Kurds: 'We support the territorial integrity and unity of Iraq as necessary for regional peace and stability. We would oppose the creation of separate states or statelets either for the Kurds or for any Iraqi ethnic or sectarian community' (Ricciardone, 2000, p. 4). Even the human rights community seems to have accepted the balance that needs to be struck between the right of self-determination of people and the international commitment to maintaining the integrity of the nation state system. Thus in the June 1993 Vienna Declaration, the World Conference on Human Rights recognized the right of peoples to 'take any legitimate action, in accordance with the Charter of the United Nations, to realize their inalienable right of self-determination... this shall not be construed as authorizing or encouraging any action which would dismember or impair, totally or in part, the territorial integrity or political unity of sovereign and independent states ...' (Quoted in Hadden, 1996, p. 15).

The foregoing discussion clearly demonstrates the limitations of international behavior and practices towards ethnic rights in light of legal ambiguities associated with the principle of self-determination of minorities. However, law can be effectively used to promote constitutional and legal arrangements that can lead to the accommodation of minority rights and lessening of ethnic tensions in multiethnic countries of the Middle East. For example, constitutional and legal reforms can be implemented with the specific intention of promulgating antidiscrimination statutes to protect the status of ethnic minorities through constitutionally-mandated changes. Nondiscrimination statutes have been enacted in several Third World settings, such as India, with a fair degree of success. Even external pressures can bring about such changes if they are done properly. For example, Turkey's proposed membership in the European Union will require that country to finally devise an equitable system to deal with its Kurdish minority. In other words, membership in the European Union can serve as a catalyst for Turkey to revise its draconian legal codes with respect to the Kurds and to improve its overall human rights practices.

A carefully crafted constitutional scheme leading to the establishment of a genuine pluralistic polity is the most ideal solution to ethnic problems in the Middle East. These can take the form of federalism, as has been suggested by many parties for Iraq, or they could take different indigenously-designed structures. After all, the Middle East has historically been able to accommodate peoples of different ethnic, religious, and cultural backgrounds. In a pluralistic setting, the multiplicity of ethnic groups can act as a hedge against authoritarianism and domination of state apparatus by one group.

Notes

1. Some scholars have argued that, contrary to conventional wisdom, religion has not been a unifying sociopolitical force in the Middle East. For example, see Khan, R. A. (1979), 'Religion, Race and Arab Nationalism', *International Journal*, Vol. 34, No. 3 (Summer), pp. 353–368.
2. For a good discussion of the Kurdish predicament in Turkey, see Gunter, M. M. (1997), *The Kurds and the Future of Turkey*, St. Martin's Press: New York; Olson, R. (1998), *The Kurdish Question and Turkish-Iranian Relations: From World War I to 1998*, Mazada Publishers: Costa Meca, CA; Bowring, B. (1996), 'The Kurds in Turkey', in Schulze, K. E., Stokes, M. and Campbell, C. (eds.), *Nationalism, Minorities and Diasporas: Identities and Rights in the Middle East*, I. B. Tauris Publishers: London, pp. 81–94.
3. For a succint analysis of Azeri nationalism, see Entessar, N. (1993), 'Azeri Nationalism in the Former Soviet Union and Iran', in Young, C. (ed.), *The Rising Tide of Cultural Pluralism: The Nation-State at Bay?*, University of Wisconsin Press: Madison, WI, pp. 116–137.

References

Anderson, B. (1983), *Imagined Communities: Reflections on the Origin and Spread of Nationalism*, Verso: London.

Arfa, H. (1966), *The Kurds: An Historical and Political Study*, Oxford University Press: London.

Banton, M. (1980), 'Ethnic Groups and the Theory of Rational Choice', in UNESCO (ed.), *Sociological Theories: Race and Colonialism*, UNESCO: Paris.

Barth, F. (1969), 'Introduction', in Barth, F. (ed.), *Ethnic Groups and Boundaries: The Social Organization of Culture Difference*, Little Brown: Boston, MA.

Bowring, B. (1996), 'The Kurds in Turkey', in Schulze, K. E., Stokes, M. and Campbell, C. (eds.), *Nationalism, Minorities and Diasporas: Identities and Rights in the Middle East*, I. B. Tauris Publishers: London.

Bowen, J. R. (2000), 'The Myth of Global Ethnic Conflict', in O'Meara, P., Mehlinger, H. D. and Krain, M. (eds.), *Globalization and the Challenges of a New Century: A Reader*, Indiana University Press: Bloomington, IN.

Brass, P. R. (1994), 'Elite Competition and Nation-Formation', in Hutchison, J. and Smith, A. D. (eds.), *Nationalism*, Oxford University Press: New York.

Brown, D. (1989), 'Ethnic Revival: Perspectives on State and Society', *Third World Quarterly*, Vol. 11, No. 4 (October), pp. 1–16.

Connor, W. (1973), 'The Politics of Ethnonationalism', *Journal of International Affairs*, Vol. 27, No. 1, pp. 1–21.

Connor, W. (1994), *Ethnonationalism: The Quest for Understanding*, Princeton University Press: Princeton, NJ.

Dekmejian, R. H. (1980), 'The Anatomy of Islamic Revival: Legitimacy Crisis, Ethnic Conflict and the Search for Islamic Alternatives', *Middle East Journal*, Vol. 34, No. 1 (Winter), pp. 1–12.

Entessar, N. (1989), 'The Kurdish Mosaic of Discord', *Third World Quarterly*, Vol. 11, No. 4 (October), pp. 83–100.

Entessar, N. (1992), *Kurdish Ethnonationalism*, Lynne Rienner: Boulder, CO.

Entessar, N. (1993), 'Azeri Nationalism in the Former Soviet Union and Iran', in Young, C. (ed.) (1993), *The Rising Tide of Cultural Pluralism: The Nation-State at Bay?*, The University of Wisconsin Press: Madison, WI.

Eriksen, T. H. (1993), *Ethnicity and Nationalism: Anthropological Perspectives*, Pluto Press: London.

Esman, M. J. and Rabinovich, I. (1988), 'The Study of Ethnic Politics in the Middle East', in Esman, M. J. and Rabinovich, I. (eds.), *Ethnicity, Pluralism, and the State in the Middle East*, Cornell University Press: Ithaca, NY.

Fukuyama, F. (1989a), 'The End of History?', *The National Interest*, No. 16 (Summer), pp. 3–18.

Fukuyama, F. (1989b), *The End of History and the Last Man*, Free Press: New York.

Gunter, M. M. (1992), *The Kurds of Iraq: Tragedy and Hope*, St. Martin's Press: New York.

Gunter, M. M. (1997), *The Kurds and the Future of Turkey*, St. Martin's Press: New York.

Gunter, M. M. (1999), *The Kurdish Predicament in Iraq: A Political Analysis*, St. Martin's Press: New York.

Hadden, T. (1996), 'The Rights of Minorities and Peoples in International Law', in Schulze, K. E., Stokes, M. and Campbell, C. (eds.), *Nationalism, Minorities and Diasporas: Identities and Rights in the Middle East*, I. B. Tauris Publishers: London.

Harik, I. F. (1972), 'The Ethnic Revolution and Political Integration in the Middle East', *International Journal of Middle East Studies*, Vol. 3, No. 3 (July), pp. 303–323.

Hassanpour, A. (1992), *Nationalism and Language in Kurdistan*, Mellen Research University Press: San Francisco.

Hazelton, F. (ed.) (1994), *Iraq Since the Gulf War: Prospects for Democracy*, Zed Books: London.

Izady, M. (1998), 'A Kurdish Lingua Franca?', *Kurdish Times*, Vol. 2, No. 2 (Summer), pp. 13–24.

Kazemi, F. (1988), 'Ethnicity and the Iranian Peasantry', in Esman, M. J. and Rabinovich, I. (eds.), *Ethnicity, Pluralism, and the State in the Middle East*, Cornell University Press: Ithaca, NY.

Khan, R. A. (1979), 'Religion, Race, and Arab Nationalism', *International Journal*, Vol. 34, No. 3 (Summer), pp. 353–368.

Muphy, J. (1996), 'Institutionalization as a State-Building Strategy: The Palestinian Case', in Schulze, K. E., Stokes, M. and Campbell, C. (eds.), *Nationalism, Minorities and Diasporas: Identities and Rights in the Middle East*, I. B. Tauris Publishers: London.

Olson, R. (1998), *The Kurdish Question and Turkish-Iranian Relations: From World War I to 1998*, Mazada Publishers: Costa Mesa, CA.

Ricciardone, F.. J. (2000), 'An American Diplomat's Perspectives on Kurds in the Global Arena', paper presented at the conference on 'The Kurds: Search for Identity,' Center for Global Peace, American University, Washington, D.C., April 17–18, 2000.

Ringer, B. R. and Lawless, E. R. (1989), *Race—Ethnicity and Society*, Routledge: New York.

Ronen, D. (1979), *The Quest for Self-Determination*, Yale University Press: New Haven, CT.

Sadowski, Y. (1998), *The Myth of Global Chaos*, Brookings Institution: Washington, D.C.

Salih, K. (1996), 'Demonizing a Minority: The Case of the Kruds in Iraq', in Schulze, K. E., Stokes, M. and Campbell, C. (eds.), *Nationalism, Minorities and Diasporas: Identities and Rights in the Middle East*, I. B. Tauris Publishers: London.

Smith, A. D. (1986), *Ethnic Origins of Nations*, Basil Blackwell: New York.

Smith, A. D. (1991), *National Identity*, University of Nevada Press: Reno, NV.

Tilly, C. (1991), 'War and State Power', *Middle East Report*, Vol. 21, No. 4 (July-August), p. 39.

Yinger, J. M. (1981), 'Towards a Theory of Assimilation and Dissimilation', *Ethnic and Racial Studies*, Vol. 4, No. 3 (July), pp. 249–264.

Young, C. (1976), *The Politics of Cultural Pluralism*, The University of Wisconsin Press: Madison, WI.

Young, C. (1993), 'The Dialectics of Cultural Pluralism: Concept and Reality', in Young, C. (ed.), *The Rising Tide of Cultural Pluralism: The Nation-State at Bay?*, The University of Wisconsin Press: Madison, WI.

7

Never Again a Mexico Without Us: Indigenous Peoples and the 21st Century

KATHLEEN R. MARTÍN

Brief historical background

On January 1, 1994, an indigenous rebellion broke out in Chiapas, an impoverished, largely indigenous state in southern Mexico. The indigenous rebels, the EZLN (*Ejercito Zapatista de Liberacion Nacional*, Zapatista National Liberation Army) demanded improved material conditions, regional autonomy, and recognition and respect for their cultural distinctiveness. Despite a cease fire and a signed peace accord, however, this most significant indigenous rebellion of 20th century Mexico remains unresolved, largely because of state resistance, more than 6 years after its outbreak.

From the colonial rule of the Spanish through independence, state policies have followed a contradictory path regarding indigenous peoples. On one hand, state policies have promulgated the assimilation of indigenous peoples and yet on the other, portrayed them as inferior and thus incapable of being truly assimilated. Since colonial times, indigenous peoples have resisted assimilation since such policies sought to subjugate them and destroy their cultural distinctiveness.

Mexico has more indigenous peoples than any other nation in Latin America. Mexico is also home to two of the great pre-conquest cultures of the New World, the Aztec and the Maya. Their descendants form two of the largest linguistic groups in the nation today. Consequently for Mexico, state policies regarding indigenous peoples are especially important.

In late 20th century Mexico, the official state policy has shifted from assimilation to recognition of ethnic multi-plurality. The resolution of the Chiapas rebellion will be a critical test of this multi-plural policy. Regardless of the final outcome of the Chiapas rebellion, however, it has had an enduring success by calling global attention to the movement of the indigenous peoples of Mexico for improved material conditions and their inclusion into the Mexican Republic as culturally distinct equals: 'Never again a Mexico without Us'.

This chapter outlines the history of indigenous state policy and relations from Spanish colonial rule to the modern period. The chapter also analyzes critical issues imbedded in the conflict between the Mexican state and indigenous peoples. Policies are suggested that could resolve conflict, enhance respect for cultural diversity and improve the material conditions under which indigenous peoples live. Special attention is given to the context in which these policies must operate to be effective and to the key socio-political actors who could affect policies concerning indigenous peoples.

Introduction: the Chiapas rebellion

On January 1, 1994, Mexico joined Canada and the United States to create a free trade zone called the North American Free Trade Area (NAFTA), an event that was widely heralded as Mexico's entrance into the 'First World' with its attendant wealth, power and status. The celebration, however, proved premature. On that first day of 1994, an indigenous army, the EZLN (*Ejercito Zapatista de Liberacion Nacional*, Zapatista National Liberation Army) took control of 4 major cities and towns in the impoverished southern state of Chiapas. In the declaration explaining their actions, the Zapatistas,[1] as the EZLN and its supporters are commonly called, asked for support from their fellow Mexican citizens in their struggle for '...jobs, land, housing, food, health, education, independence, liberty, democracy, and justice and peace' (Russell, 1995, p. 38).

For Mexican President Carlos Salinas, who had strongly backed his nation's entry into the NAFTA, the timing of the uprising was a bitter surprise. As a cruelly pointed political joke of the time expressed it, President Salinas thought he would wake up on January 1, 1994 in North America, instead he woke up in Guatemala.[2] The longstanding plight of the indigenous peoples of Mexico would not go away despite the gloss of modernity supposedly brought by Mexico's entrance into the NAFTA.

The January 1 Chiapas rebellion is only the most recent indigenous rebellion to arise in a region with a long history of revolts (Brown, 1997; Wasserstrom, 1983). The dramatic outbreak of the current rebellion in Chiapas, however, has brought global attention to the centuries of poverty, political exclusion and cultural destruction of Mexico's indigenous peoples as no other previous rebellion has.

The Chiapas rebellion captured headlines worldwide as many people were drawn to support the cause of the indigenous rebels. The Zapatistas, especially through their charismatic, non-indigenous spokesman, *Sub-comandante* Marcos, made judicious use of the media (particularly the Internet), as well as employing a carefully considered revolutionary imagery to keep their message before the global public.[3] After a brief period of armed conflict between the largely Maya indigenous forces of the EZLN and the Mexican Army, a cease-fire was declared. Shortly after the implementation of the cease-fire, peace negotiations began, ultimately producing the San Andres Accord, which was signed in February 1996.

At the core of the problems in Chiapas are two especially critical issues: land tenure and political rights. The indigenous peoples of Chiapas have experienced a steady loss of their communal lands since the Spanish conquest. This process, however, has accelerated in the 20th century as large agricultural and cattle estates have expanded their borders to incorporate land held by the indigenous Maya population. Despite constitutional guarantees to the contrary, indigenous peoples have had very little redress within the Mexican judicial system for the steady loss of their lands. Without state guarantees of justice, the Chiapan Maya have been deprived of their rights as Mexican citizens.

The San Andres Accord sought to address these two issues. The Accord recommended the establishment of a commission to discuss agrarian problems, particularly those linked to land tenure. It also recommended reforms that would allow indigenous peoples to run for public office independent of national political parties, thus granting them some political autonomy especially at the local and regional levels.

To date, the San Andres Accord has yet to be implemented. The greatest obstacle to its implementation appears to be the Mexican state itself which, by its inaction, appears reluctant to make any substantial commitment to the Accord. At present, the Zapatistas continue to hold fast in the mountainous areas of Chiapas where their rebellion began. Attempts by the state to dislodge the Zapatistas with massive use of force (such as occurred in February 1995) have been abandoned, at least for the present, because strong public support in Mexico and abroad for the Zapatistas has rallied against such actions.

While the Mexican state publicly appears to have relinquished the use of mass force against the Zapatistas, violence still continues in Chiapas with the collusion of the state. Paramilitary groups, sponsored by the powerful landed elite class of Chiapas and linked to the political party that has long ruled Mexico, the PRI (*Partido Revolucionario Institucional;* the Party of the Institutionalized Revolution), have continued to employ force against the Zapatistas (Harvey, 1998, p. 245). The savage massacre in Acteal, Chiapas on December 22, 1997 in which 45 Zapatista sympathizers, mostly women and children, were killed in a Catholic church, is but the best-known example of the violence practiced by these paramilitary groups.

For the present, the Mexican army has surrounded the territory held by the Zapatistas and controls access to the area. With the aid of the paramilitary groups who have used armed force against the Zapatistas, the army wages a steady war of attrition against the EZLN and its supporters. As years pass in this stalemate, public interest in and support for the Zapatistas have begun to wane. The Mexican state seems likely to wait out the Zapatistas, believing that its war of attrition will lead to the gradual dissolution of the rebellion. Thus, more than 6 years after the Chiapas Rebellion seized the center stage of Mexican politics, it remains unresolved. And the position of Mexico's indigenous peoples is once again left in limbo.

The roots of conflict: who are the indigenous peoples of Mexico?

The ongoing conflict in Chiapas is only the most recent and dramatic manifestation of a wide rift in Mexican society that extends back to the Spanish conquest and the birth of the Mexican nation. Centuries after the arrival of the Spanish in the territory that is now Mexico, the descendants of the region's original inhabitants remain poverty stricken and marginalized within the Mexican political-economic system. Subject to ethnic biases, their part in the formation of Mexican culture and their participation in Mexican society are ambiguously regarded by many Mexicans.

The current impoverished state of indigenous peoples, however, belies their great historical depth and impressive cultural achievements. Archaeological evidence of human presence in the territory that is now Mexico extends back to 40,000 BC and the existence of village settlements dates from 5000 BC. Grand cities and city-states built by indigenous peoples arose in the central highlands and southern coastal lowlands dating from 2000 BC (Meyer and Sherman, 1991, pp. 4–13).

All of the indigenous peoples of pre-conquest Mexico created vital cultures with unique achievements. Of these indigenous cultures, however, the two best known are the Aztec and the lowland Maya (Clendinnen, 1991; Freidel, Schele and Parker, 1993; Sabloff, 1997; Schele and Freidel, 1990; Townsend, 1992). In the region of what is now the world's second most populous urban area, Mexico City, the Aztecs built the capital of their far-reaching conquest state. In constructing their capital city in the middle of a large lake, they created an urban agricultural and water management system (the *chinampas*) that sustained a population of 300,000, five times larger than was London at that time (Coe, 1962, p. 161). The Aztec empire extended hundreds of miles south into present-day Guatemala and was a model of bureaucratic efficiency.

The lowland Maya were renowned for artistic and intellectual achievements. Their painting, ceramic art and architecture are still regarded as some of the finest examples of human artistic accomplishments. The lowland Maya developed a solar calendar more accurate than the European calendar of the 1500s. They also invented a numerical system including the concept of zero and developed a celestially oriented architecture based on a very sophisticated knowledge of the heavens. In addition, the lowland Maya were the only New World indigenous peoples to create a written language, one so complex that scholars have only recently been able to decipher it (Coe, 1992).

At present, Mexico has, at a minimum, 10.5 million indigenous citizens representing 56 distinct cultural groups (Wearne, 1996, p. 3). While other Latin American nations have a higher percentage of their populations who are indigenous (Bolivia with 70% and Guatemala with 50%), the 9% of the Mexican population who are indigenous represents the largest number of indigenous peoples anywhere in the Americas (Wearne, 1996, p. 3).[4]

Indigenous peoples reside in all 32 states of the Mexican Republic. The largest concentration, however, can be found in thirteen states in the central and southern regions of the nation where the Aztec and lowland Maya constructed their grand civilizations (Barry, 1992, p. 223). The modern day descendants of the Aztec and the Maya form two of the largest indigenous language groups in Mexico today, the Nahuatl and the Yucatec Maya, each with a million speakers (Wearne, 1996, p. 4).

Yet, despite their numbers, diversity, achievements and long history, Mexico's indigenous peoples suffer disproportionately from poverty, ill health, illiteracy, sub-standard housing, poor delivery of public services and the lack of educational and economic opportunities. Underlying this poverty of material resources and services are the exclusion, marginalization and discrimination indigenous peoples experience as a part of their daily lives. The disadvantaged position of indigenous peoples is rooted in the Spanish conquest of the New World with an unfortunate history that continues to the present.

The roots of conflict: conquest and colonialism

The Spanish conquest of the New World was a holocaust for indigenous peoples. Nearly everywhere, indigenous peoples, group by group, skillfully and tenuously resisted the Conquest (Diaz de Castillo, 1966). But their own lack of political unity, the superior military technology of the Spanish, the spread of infectious diseases (typhus, bubonic plague, measles, smallpox, tuberculosis and diphtheria) and the famine created by warfare ultimately defeated them. Although it took several decades for the Spanish to consolidate their rule, the Spanish colonial period began in earnest with the defeat of the most unified political entity existing in pre-conquest Mexico, the Aztec empire, in 1521.

As the Spanish consolidated their rule, surviving indigenous peoples became populations both disadvantaged and discriminated against; both resisting and culturally persistent (Farriss, 1984; Kicza, 1993; Maybury-Lewis, 1997). During the Spanish colonial period, the indigenous peoples of Mexico survived slavery, confiscation of their lands, exploitation of their labor, imposition of a new religion (Roman Catholicism), forced resettlement, depopulation and denigration of their cultures. They also actively resisted subjugation by rebellion, escaped to zones of refuge and an array of forms of 'everyday resistance' such as described by Scott (1985) for people living under colonial systems elsewhere.

As their colonial regime began to take form, the Spanish colonial powers agreed on the necessity and legitimacy of controlling indigenous peoples and their resources. They, however, did not agree on the means of colonial management. On one hand, the military conquerors and colonial settlers wished to colonize Mexico as a private enterprise with the blessing of the Spanish crown. But they also wished to preserve the power and privileges they had accrued during the conquest without royal interference (Diaz Polanco, 1997, p. 38). Opposing them were the Spanish crown, its colonial bureaucracy and the Roman Catholic clergy. Many of the clergy defended indigenous peoples because of the injustices of colonialism they had witnessed. While the Spanish crown gave ear to this defense, the royalty also sought to assert royal and clerical power over the colonizing process in order to preserve their share of the Mexican bounty, principally in the form of indigenous labor (Diaz Polanco, 1997, p. 38). As the objects of this debate in which one side prevailed and then the other, however, the oppressive conditions of colonial rule for indigenous peoples were seldom altered.

In addition to the conflicting interests of the colonists and the crown that continued throughout the colonial period, there was also a debate about the longer-range future of indigenous peoples. One view held for indigenous autonomy under the Spanish crown's protection, and perhaps more importantly, its control. Another proposed two separate republics, one indigenous, one not—an unlikely proposal to succeed given the increasingly interwoven society of colonizers and indigenous peoples (Diaz Polanco, 1997, p. 45).

But the view that prevailed promoted the assimilation of indigenous peoples, for their total absorption into the Spanish colonial system and thus their disappearance as culturally distinct peoples.

Underlying this assimilationist view was the notion on the part of the Spanish of their inherent ethnic superiority over indigenous peoples. Adhering to this idea of their superiority, the Spanish maintained a hierarchy in which those born in Spain, the *peninsulares*, were superior to all others, including those born of Spanish descent but in the New World, the *criollos*. Anyone indigenous or of mixed ethnic background, the *mestizos*, was considered inferior to all those of Spanish descent. Economic prerogatives, political rights and social mobility were all calibrated according to an individual's position on this ethnic hierarchy. Indigenous peoples, and later the African peoples brought to the New World as slaves, were at the bottom of the hierarchy and could assume that any assimilation to Spanish colonial culture and political rule would take place at that level.

Conflicting interests among political and economic elites, the prevalence of assimilationist policies and the notion of inherent superiority of European peoples formed state policy toward indigenous peoples during the

Spanish colonial regime. These factors continued to shape state policy once Mexico gained its independence from Spain in 1821.

The roots of conflict: independence and revolution

Underlying the movement for Mexican independence was the conflict for political dominance between the Spanish-born colonial elites (the *peninsulares*), on one hand, and the Spanish *criollos* and the *mestizos* on the other. During the three centuries of colonial rule, the *mestizo* population had grown considerably. The burgeoning population of *mestizos* was partly the result of unions between the indigenous population and the Spanish colonizers. But colonial Mexico also underwent a process whereby those once considered indigenous became instead *mestizo*. Assimilationist pressures caused many indigenous peoples to abandon their ethnic identity and join the growing ranks of the *mestizos* (Barry, 1995, p. 174).

Thus, the support of the growing *mestizo* population was critical for the *criollos* in order for them to gain power. Indigenous peoples and *mestizos* were active participants in the independence movement, serving as soldiers in the Mexican army and as suppliers of troop support. The eleven years of the war for Mexican independence caused heavy casualties among the *mestizo* and indigenous troops and laid havoc in the countryside throughout most of the nation.

Mexico ultimately won its independence from Spain in 1821. Nonetheless, while political independence had been achieved, release from a hierarchy in which they were positioned at the very bottom did not come for either indigenous peoples or *mestizos* despite their prominent role in winning Mexico's independence.

Once freed from Spanish colonial rule, Mexico faced the task of building a nation from a population of Spanish and indigenous peoples, coupled with smaller populations of peoples from Africa and Asia. All of these groups intermingled and over time, the African and Asian communities ceased to be distinct, joining with the Spanish and indigenous peoples to form a unique Mexican culture. Nevertheless, despite the much intermingling with non-indigenous populations that produced the large *mestizo* group and the cumulative effects of centuries of assimilationist pressures, many descendants of the original inhabitants of Mexico retained their distinctiveness as indigenous peoples. Unfortunately, they also retained their disadvantaged status within an emerging Mexican nation.

The years following independence brought little change to the lives of the third of the Mexican population that retained their indigenous identity. Many continued to live in small villages in the more marginal and inaccessible areas of the Republic where they had been pushed first by the Spanish colonizers and later by Mexican settlers. In their remote lands, indigenous peoples were isolated from the socio-economic and political mainstream of the nation. In large towns in which both indigenous peoples and *mestizos* lived, Spanish became the *lingua franca*. In smaller towns and villages, indigenous languages dominated (Meyer and Sherman, 1991, pp. 356–558).

From the founding of the Mexican Republic, the newly emerging politico-economic elites sought to suppress indigenous cultural identities because they viewed heterogeneity as divisive. In a certain respect, their concern was understandable since Mexico at independence was not integrated as a nation-state but rather divided into distinct regions with little political, economic or social infrastructure to link them together.

Underlying this equation of diversity with divisiveness, however, was the belief that indigenous peoples were backward and hence a drag on national development. Thus, national policies were geared toward incorporating indigenous peoples into the Mexican Republic but without their cultural distinctiveness. As a result, the assimilationist policies begun by the Spanish colonial regime continued in an independent Mexican nation.

After independence, indigenous peoples throughout the Republic continued to resist subjugation in the guise of assimilation with an array of tactics from armed revolt to everyday resistance. Indigenous peoples who actively resisted the state policy of assimilation were punished harshly. Military force was employed against them whenever there was an indigenous revolt (Diaz Polanco, 1997, pp. 66–67). Enslavement and relocation to inhospitable areas far from their homeland was another strategy used by the state to control resisting indigenous peoples. During the late 1800s and early 1900s, the rebellious Yaqui of the northern desert state of Sonora were exiled as slaves to the low land tropical plantations where they died by the hundreds, unaccustomed to the hot, humid climate and the demands of overwork. From 1848–1861 after the defeat of a major indigenous uprising in the Yucatan peninsula, thousands of Maya were sold into slavery to Cuban sugar producers where they died within a generation.

In addition to force, the Mexican state also fostered assmilationist policies by continuing to attack the communal subsistence base of indigenous peoples. Policies, which sought to privatize communally held resources, especially land, were devastating to the survival of indigenous peoples. Especially destructive to them was the *Ley Lerdo* (Lerdo Law) of

1856. The original intent of the *Ley Lerdo* was to divest the Roman Catholic Church, at the time the largest land owner in Mexico, of its vast holdings (Meyer and Sherman, 1991, p. 378). Yet, the Lerdo Law also served to alienate many indigenous peoples from land they had held communally since pre-conquest times and thus undermined the subsistence base of their cultures.

Independence from Spanish colonial rule did not bring political autonomy, better material conditions, nor respect for cultural distinctiveness to indigenous peoples; rather it brought only a change in those administering them as they became neo-colonial subjects within an independent Mexico.

The roots of conflict: indigenous peoples and the modern Mexican state

From 1910–1920, Mexico underwent the most cataclysmic period in its history when a revolution arose that forever altered Mexican society. Although independence had won a new political regime for Mexico, it was not a social revolution and the lives of the indigenous peoples had changed little. Ninety years later, however, a social revolution did occur that restructured Mexican society. As in the movement for Mexican independence, indigenous peoples were active participants in the revolutionary movement both as soldiers in its armies and suppliers of troop support. The Mexican Revolution ultimately brought more political openings and opportunities for socio-economic mobility for Mexican citizens. Nonetheless, indigenous peoples remained at the bottom of the socio-economic structure, in the margins of national political life and subject to continued ethnic discrimination.

The upheaval of the Mexican Revolution brought destruction and chaos to the Republic for a decade before peace was restored. After the armed struggle of the Revolution ended, Mexico gradually made the transition from the 'one man rule' that characterized the nation's politics since independence, to that of a corporatist state and a single party democracy. The emergent ruling party, the PRI, oversaw the construction of the Mexican Republic as a corporatist state by organizing key segments of Mexican society into groups such as industrial workers, peasants or government employees. The Mexican state was restructured under the PRI so that the party and the government were layered together as virtually a single entity.

Governmental agencies were set up to administer indigenous peoples, in particular the *Instituto Nacional Indigenista* (INI)—National Indigenous Institute. The agency was charged with acting on behalf of indigenous peoples. Occasionally, the INI did promulgate policies that provided educational and economic opportunities to indigenous peoples. However, since it was small and not politically powerful or influential, it was severely hampered in its efforts to aid the indigenous peoples. In conflicts with the interests of larger and more powerful state agencies, the INI had to give way and the interests of indigenous peoples suffered in this surrender. But the INI was also, like most state agencies, structured in a hierarchical and patronistic fashion which precluded indigenous peoples from having a voice within the agency (Martin and Castillo Cocom, 1995).

By the second half of the 20th century, despite some improvement in conditions and opportunities brought by the modern Mexican state, indigenous peoples remained at the bottom of the Mexican socio-economic structure, in the margins of national political life and subject to unrelenting ethnic discrimination. While nationalist rhetoric honored the indigenous past, state policy was structured as 'assimilation by neglect' since rarely were indigenous issues the focus of governmental attention. The most visible state policy concerning indigenous peoples was the marketing of their ancestral cultures and their contemporary 'picturesque' villages as tourist attractions. Archaeological sites such as Teotihuacan and Chichen Itza, together with contemporary market towns such as San Cristobal de las Casas, became internationally well-known tourist destinations as the large and highly profitable Mexican tourist industry developed throughout the 20th century.

It was in this context of unimproving material conditions, political marginalization and ethnic discrimination, that the Chiapas rebellion arose. As outlined previously, resistance by Mexico's indigenous peoples on their own behalf has a long history. None, however, in the 20th century has captured the public eye as successfully as has the Chiapas rebellion. The Zapatistas have placed the resolution of indigenous issues at the center of the nation's political debate. Whether the Chiapas rebellion leads to substantial reforms or not, the Zapatistas have had an enduring success. This indigenous rebellion has changed the consciousness of Mexico so that indigenous peoples can no longer be so easily ignored nor relegated to the margins of national life. Mexico's indigenous heritage, the worth of indigenous cultures *as indigenous cultures* and the starkly desperate conditions of life endured by contemporary indigenous peoples are now more widely acknowledged among Mexican citizens. Given the increased public awareness of indigenous issues, it seems that the 21st century might offer a new era of hope for indigenous peoples.

Indigenous peoples and the modern Mexican state: the context of transformation

Despite the hopes generated by the Chiapas rebellion, any transformation in the lives of the indigenous peoples of Mexico must take place within the context of the contemporary Mexican society and political economy. Most important in the present day context are the consequences of changing economic policies and the continuing democratization of the Mexican political system.

For nearly two decades, Mexico has been transforming itself from a social welfare state to a neo-liberal market economy. In addition, Mexico's economy has participated in global economic restructuring exemplified by the nation's entry into the NAFTA. As elsewhere in other states that have undergone such a marked change in their economy, poor people especially have borne the negative effects of changing economic policy. For indigenous peoples, many of whom are among the poorest in Mexico, the changes have been particularly burdensome (Harvey, 1999). Most of the state programs on which both the indigenous and non-indigenous poor relied for supplemental support are gone. Price supports for basic food items have been removed, and state support for health care and education decreased.

However, the most damaging effects of the new reforms to indigenous peoples have come from changes made in Article 27 of the Mexican Constitution that protected communal land holding rights. With the sale of communally held land now legal, many impoverished indigenous peoples have sold their land. The short-term profits of the land sale are often spent on immediate family needs, ultimately leaving indigenous peoples without any capital resources. The accelerated loss of their lands—a process underway since colonial times—has alienated indigenous peoples from the agricultural subsistence base that underlies their cultures. As the neo-liberal market economy takes hold in Mexico, indigenous peoples, along with the non-indigenous poor, are confronted with growing wealth differentials, failing real wages and a neglected public service sector (Barry, 1992, pp. 79–128).

Mexico's economy has long been based on oil, tourism and assembly plant manufacturing. The current economic crisis has added an economy of remittances and the illegal drug trade. As the economy has worsened, the Mexican poor have, in increasingly greater numbers, migrated to the U.S., long an economic alternative for the poor of Mexico. The income the migrants remit to their families in Mexico provides critical economic support for many. Their migration, however, has a steep social cost. Many migrants must enter the U.S. illegally and thus become prey to smugglers, as well as to employers who pay them sub-standard wages. In addition, these desperate workers often face enormous legal entanglements with U.S. authorities and must endure long periods of separation from their families and alienation from their culture.

. The illegal drug trade has brought with it increasing crime and a growing domestic market within Mexico for drugs. The criminality and violence spawned by the drug trade has become a society-wide problem. Indigenous peoples are most involved as growers of drug producing crops and as local transporters of drugs. Their involvement in the illegal drug trade is driven by their poverty, as is their international migration.

Given that the welfare of indigenous peoples has not been a priority for the Mexican state, it is unlikely that scarce resources will be allocated to them in the future unless the Mexican economy significantly improves. Until then, indigenous peoples will continue to suffer from high rates of poverty and deprivation.

Since the late 1960s, Mexico has taken gradually escalating steps to transform its decades long single party rule into a multi-party democracy. Honest elections, multi-party contestation of votes and a separation of the state from PRI political party dominance, are basic issues in the democratization of the Mexican political system.

In the July 2000 presidential elections, Mexico's transition to democratic governance took a critically important step forward. Vincente Fox of the *Partido de Accion Nacional* (PAN) became the first opposition leader to win a presidential election in Mexican history.[5]

President-elect Fox officially takes office in January 2001. Until then, there will be significant maneuvering among all sectors of the Mexican political system as the different actors react and try to adjust to this monumental change in the country's politics. In the month following the election, both the PRI and the leading leftist party, the *Partido de la Revolucion Democratica* (PRD) undertook some form of self-examination in light of their defeat at the polls. The discourse within both parties often degenerated into name-calling as party executives sought to blame particular members for the losses. Some members of the PRI and PRD formed what appear to be opportunistic alliances with the PAN, especially at the local and regional levels. Government officials, most of whom were appointed to their positions by the president, sought to ensure that they would retain their jobs after the PAN took control of the government in January 2001. Non-governmental organizations (NGOs) have also been quite busy trying to adjust to the new political environment which is expected to be ushered in when Fox and the PAN take control of the government in January 2001.

Capture of the apparatus of government by the opposition party has brought a lot of hope to indigenous groups and their supporters in Mexico. President-elect Vincente Fox has remarked several times that he will resolve the Chiapas crisis quickly by honoring the San Andreas Peace Accord. If he keeps his promise and implements the agreement, then he would provide a rare opportunity for the Mexican state to begin a system-atic process of improving the welfare of the indigenous peoples.

In August 2000, a coalition of political parties led by Pablo Salazar, a former PRI party member, won the Chiapas gubernatorial elections. Pablo Salazar had formed the coalition with the PAN, the PRD, and several minority parties with the expressed goal of ending the Chiapas crisis and creating in the region, an environment conducive to the maximization of the values of the indigenous peoples. The coalition's victory brings to an end many decades of PRI monopolization of political spaces and resource allocation in the region. The victory diminishes the political and economic dominance of powerful PRI elites who, during the last several decades, have used their public offices to exploit and marginalize the indigenous peoples. It is hoped that the new coalition government would provide the structures for the indigenous peoples to lift themselves out of poverty.

Since the country's presidential elections ended in the defeat of the PRI, Mexico's political system has continued to see profound transforma-tion. How such changes will affect the indigenous peoples is not yet clear. However, if as has been indicated by Fox, the new dispensation to be ushered in by him is more transparent, participatory and accountable to the people, then indigenous peoples are likely to benefit significantly. The Mexican economy remains in serious crisis and dealing effectively with the latter would most likely be the new president's first line of business. Already, Fox has traveled to the U.S. and Canada to solicit the cooperation and aid of his northern neighbors for the economic restructuring that he is expected to undertake when he takes office in January 2001. In Washing-ton, D.C., Fox discussed immigration matters with U.S. officials and suggested that increased U.S. investments in his country would signifi-cantly improve economic growth and development and reduce the need for Mexican nationals to leave the country in search of opportunities to earn a living. Thus, after taking the oath of office in January, Fox is most likely to be pre-occupied with economic restructuring and may not be able to place appropriate emphasis on indigenous problems. In fact, some Mexicans may see any presidential emphasis on the Chiapas crisis as divisive and not designed to foster national unity. Thus, if after assuming office in January 2001, Fox fails to make the Chiapas crisis an important national policy issue because he is pre-occupied with the country's deteriorating economic conditions or because of opposition from those who believe that national unity would be sacrificed if the problems of minority groups are given presidential attention, then indigenous peoples will again be pushed to the margins of Mexican society. Another opportunity to finally deal effectively with the economic, political and social problems that have plagued indigenous peoples for so many years will be squandered. When he takes the oath of office in January 2001, however, Vincente Fox can use the authority of his office to start a process that will finally bring indigenous peoples into Mexican society as full citizens. He can do that by fully implementing the San Andreas Peace Accord.

Policy implementation: socio-political actors

While the political-economic context for improving the lives of indigenous peoples and their position within Mexican society is not particularly favorable at present, more hope can be found among key socio-political actors. Such actors are those who can either influence public policy and consciousness regarding the indigenous peoples of Mexico or those who directly work to improve the lives of indigenous peoples.

Most important among the social actors who work on behalf of indigenous peoples are indigenous peoples themselves. Through a wide variety of activist organizations, both large and small, indigenous peoples have sought to improve the material conditions of their communities, press for some degree of political autonomy and achieve recognition of their cultural distinctiveness. It is important to note, however, that at present, an umbrella organization that links all the indigenous peoples of Mexico together and enhances their ability to negotiate with the Mexican state is still in the early stages of development. Neither in pre-conquest times nor now have indigenous peoples been organized collectively. Since there are 56 distinct indigenous cultures in Mexico, any attempts at unity must take into account the diversity among and within these groups. Accommodating this cultural and linguistic diversity adds another layer of complexity to the task of collective organizing.

Most indigenous organizations are small-scale, operating at the community level and only rarely at the regional level. Of the indigenous activist organizations, one of the largest and longest established is the *Coalicion Obrero Campesino e Estudiantil del Istmo* (COCEI)—Coalition of Workers, Farmers, and Students of the Isthmus. This organization of the Zapotec from the Isthmus of Tehuantepec in Oaxaca state, has for several decades, defended the local autonomy of the Zapotec and promoted cultural pride. It has also created sub-organizations, such as the Union of Indigenous Communities, that bring together Zapotecan communities involved in various subsistence activities, from fishing to coffee growing, to promote their mutual economic well being.

Indigenous peoples participate in the northward migration to the U.S. in search of economic opportunities. Consequently, they form migrant associations as do other poor Mexicans who work and reside in the U.S. for varying lengths of time. The indigenous Mixtec from the southern state of Oaxaca are an example. As thousands of Mixtec have migrated to southern California to find employment, they have formed their own associations to safe guard their human rights both in the United States and on behalf of those Mixtec who remain in their Mexican homeland (Kearney, 1988). When human rights violations occur in Oaxaca, the Mixtec mobilize protests in front of the Mexican consulate in Los Angeles. By drawing international media attention that places the Mexican state in an unfavorable light, the Mixtec know that the Mexican state is more likely to try to resolve issues than if they mounted a similar protest in Mexico where they would be less likely to draw the eyes and ears of the international media.

Aside from activist organizations that focus on economic or political issues, indigenous peoples have also formed organizations that foster cultural awareness and indigenous pride. Groups of intellectuals and artists of the highland Maya of Chiapas, with the help of activist Roman Catholic clergy, foreign and Mexican academics, have formed a theater group, a writer's workshop and a women's photography project (Duarte, 1996; Santiz Gomez, 1998). All of these Maya groups seek to promote their indigenous culture through their artistic works. Similarly, in many Mexican cities, indigenous peoples have formed dance groups that seek to demonstrate the spiritual power of their cultures and educate the non-indigenous public about indigenous life. On Sundays, the performances of these revivalist dance groups are very visible components of the urban landscape in which many young indigenous and non-indigenous peoples participate.

It is ultimately indigenous peoples who are the most effective proponents of making transformations in their own lives. While hundreds of grassroots indigenous organizations work within their own region to improve material conditions, gain greater political autonomy and respect for cultural distinctiveness, they face the problem of attempting to bring together very different indigenous groups. While the indigenous peoples of Mexico seldom have conflicts with each other, their differences challenge organizing efforts. Until indigenous peoples can create cohesive political organizations at the national level, their successes will remain at the grassroots level and only bring gradual, incremental change.

Indigenous peoples have allies in their movement to transform their lives and improve their position within Mexican society. Principal among these are non-governmental organizations (NGOs). In Mexico, as elsewhere, NGOs are taking on many responsibilities for social welfare and social transformation that formerly were under the auspices of the state. In Mexico, there are NGOs that focus on indigenous issues exclusively, most often organized by indigenous peoples themselves as described above. More commonly, however, in Mexico, NGOs have focused on issues such as poverty or human rights and thus incorporate indigenous peoples in their agenda without focusing on indigenous issues *per se*. While NGOs have proved to be organizationally volatile with organizations forming, splintering and reforming, they have sponsored successful grassroots, local development projects within indigenous communities. In Mexico, NGOs have proliferated in regional development planning and often serve as local think tanks focusing on the resolution of issues beginning at the grassroots level.

Another important social actor on behalf of indigenous peoples is the Roman Catholic Church. In Mexico, the Church has the force of moral suasion behind it to help transform the social consciousness of the Mexican public regarding the nation's indigenous peoples. Originating with the theology of liberation movement of the 1960s, some Roman Catholic clergy have taken the 'preferential option for the poor' and become activists for the indigenous cause. The highest profile activist clergyman for the indigenous cause has been Archbishop Samuel Ruiz of Chiapas. He has, for many years, defended the indigenous peoples of Chiapas. Monsignor Ruiz also played a pivotal part in the peace negotiations that resulted in the San Andres Accord.

Local clergy in indigenous areas have trained indigenous social leaders as community catechists and sponsored community development projects. The Roman Catholic Church, while not united in its efforts to aid indigenous peoples nor in its stance on clerical activism, is a voice of moral consciousness in Mexico. Should the Church make more of an effort to act on behalf of indigenous peoples, it could potentially benefit them especially by changing the public consciousness to eliminate ethnic discrimination. If Scott (1985) could postulate 'everyday acts of resistance' to describe the mechanisms people under colonial rule employ to combat their oppression, then 'everyday acts of decency' could describe the day to day, face to face acts of people who wish to transform the public consciousness of Mexico against ethnic discrimination.

Within the Mexican political mainstream, there are also those who seek to work on the cause of indigenous peoples, in particular, local level politicians and political activists. At the local and regional level some elected officials and activists within the partisan political system have undertaken actions that benefit or could potentially benefit indigenous peoples. In the west Mexican state of Jalisco, for example, a group of legislators has proposed a legal initiative concerning the rights of indigenous communities in their state (*Comision de Asuntos Indigenas de la LV Legislatura Estado de Jalisco,* 1999). In the three states of the Yucatecan peninsula, a region with a large population of Maya, all three of the major political parties of Mexico (PAN, PRD and PRI) have had some success in incorporating Maya into their local level political organizations as party workers, candidates and elected officials (Martín, 1998).

Thus, it is indigenous peoples themselves working alone or in concert with NGOs, the Roman Catholic Church or political parties and activists at the local level that seem to offer the best hope for any significant improvements in the welfare of this historically marginalized of Mexican citizens. Perhaps in the coming years such alliances will be able to improve the material conditions of indigenous peoples, gain some measure of political autonomy for these peoples and allow them to participate in Mexican society as culturally distinct equals.

Critical issues and their resolution—never again a Mexico without us: indigenous peoples and the 21st century

There are particular critical issues imbedded in the conflict between the Mexican state and indigenous peoples that need to be resolved in order to enhance respect for ethnic multi-plurality, improve the material conditions and the political positioning of indigenous peoples. These issues and suggestions for their resolution are detailed in the following section.

Respect and recognition: the end of ethnic discrimination

Most basic to all the policy recommendations that follow, is a change in public consciousness to end ethnic discrimination and replace it with respect and recognition of indigenous peoples as *indigenous peoples*. It is after all ethnically biased thinking that has led to discriminatory policies and actions.

To end ethnic discrimination, there must be recognition that cultural diversity is wealth. The value of indigenous cultures *as indigenous cultures* must be acknowledged and their continued relevance in contemporary times should be recognized (Bonfil Batalla, 1996). To some Mexicans, the indigenous past is unfortunately seen as unconnected to contemporary indigenous peoples. Although referring to Peru, the following statement applies equally well to Mexico, '...[the] elite perceives its indigenous patrimony as temples and walls (and not people)...' (Dworkin y Mendez, 1998, p. 5).

At the very least, indigenous peoples have much to offer in terms of teaching cultural resilience, alternative cosmovisions and management of the natural world. As an editorial from the Guatemalan Maya journal, *Nojb'el Mayab* (1994, p. 28), states, speaking of the Guatemalan Maya but also true for the indigenous peoples of Mexico:

> We are an original people with our own destiny, a people that thinks with its own mind, feels with its own heart, walks with its own feet, with its own symbols, with its ample, rich and indestructible collective memory. Perhaps this is why we have resisted five foreign invasions and systematic genocide, and our culture and identity continue to live, endlessly manifesting themselves in daily life with a bountiful capacity for starling, rebellion and ingenuity. Because of this, we assert that we have constructed an identity through the course of history. We don't accept a future without a past.

Since cultures that thrive are those that have the capacity to transform themselves, indigenous peoples should have the freedom to alter their cultures in order to preserve their indigenous identities. It is not a contradiction for indigenous peoples to transform themselves in order to remain indigenous (Nash, 1995, p. 35). French culture and French people change in order to remain French; Americans change to redefine themselves as Americans, etc. In addition, indigenous peoples who have been distanced from their cultural heritage must possess the intellectual freedom to rediscover and reclaim their indigenous cultures and identities.

In order for indigenous peoples to retain their unique cosmovisions, the rituals sacred to them as part of their spiritual and religious life should be respected by allowing their continued practice. In recognizing indigenous cosmovisions and the knowledge they have constructed over the millennia, indigenous peoples should not be romanticized as 'New Age' answers to age-old questions (Castenada, 1996). Nor should non-indigenous cultures misuse indigenous symbols for their own benefit, and prominent indigenous individuals should not be made into iconic figures such as happened with the Guatemalan Maya Nobel Peace Prize Laureate, Rigoberta Menchu (Stoll, 1999).

Education and indigenous intellectual patrimony

Educational reform is critical to assure respect for the cultural uniqueness of indigenous peoples and their successful participation in national political, economic and social life as distinct equals. In the policy recommendations discussed here, special effort should be made to assure the education of indigenous women who have often been bypassed in educational reform efforts.

Indigenous peoples should have access to an education appropriate to guarantee their economic well being and intellectual development. At present, only 14% of indigenous adults have completed primary school; 28% of children between 6–14 years do not attend school and the illiteracy rate among those 15 years and over is 46% (Barry, 1995, p. 175). Indigenous peoples need also to have access to education that grants them not only literacy but also includes them in the current technological communications revolution.

Since monolinguality constricts communication, bilingual education is necessary for all Mexican indigenous groups. With bilingual training, not only can indigenous peoples retain their own languages but they can also participate in national discourse through the use of Spanish. Literacy training in indigenous languages also should be included in the school curricula since, while many indigenous peoples speak and understand their own language, they can neither read nor write it. Ideally, Mexico's educational system should seek to preserve indigenous peoples' unique cultural heritage in the face of widespread trends toward cultural uniformity.

In addition to reforms of the educational system for indigenous peoples, changes need also to be made to the national educational curriculum for all students. Most basic to changes in the national educational system is the inclusion of an accurate and respectful depiction of indigenous cultures and the incorporation of indigenous peoples into all periods of the Mexican national history.

Strengthening democracy and preserving human rights

The Mexican Constitution guarantees basic human rights and an adherence to democratic principles for all Mexican citizens. Despite constitutional guarantees, the Mexican state has an unfortunate history of employing policies toward indigenous peoples that do not operate on notions of inclusion and fair play. The proper enforcement of national law needs to be ensured as applying to all citizens. As an urgent first step, the use of violence as a means to resolve conflict between indigenous peoples and the state must be permanently renounced.

Mechanisms should be found which assist the successful participation of indigenous peoples in a transforming Mexican democracy. Indigenous peoples should be allowed self-determination in decisions regarding the means and degrees of integration and articulation with the state as well as issues of local self-governance at the community level. While indigenous peoples will not all choose the same mechanisms of articulation with the state or the same degree of integration with it, efforts should be made to allow self-governance at the local level.

It is important to note that in their participation in the Mexican national socio-political system, indigenous peoples are taking elements of non-indigenous cultures and reformulating them to fit indigenous cosmovisions, a process of *'indigenization'*. For example, in her 1992 speech to the Yucatecan state legislature, a Yucatec Maya Congresswoman, Araceli Cab Cumi, proposed the use of Maya collective social forms as relevant to contemporary political practice within the Mexican legal system:

> The solidarity of indigenous peoples was by tradition [defined as] reciprocal aid enabling people to do productive work...Social solidarity should be based in the traditional roots of solidarity

respecting ethnic plurality and the legal precepts of the Constitution (Martín, n. d.).[6]

To assure the human rights of indigenous peoples *as indigenous peoples* within the context of democratic societies, their unique patrimony and continuing cultural distinctiveness must be honored (Greaves, 1994). To this end, indigenous archaeological sites and indigenous sacred places should be repatriated and allowed to remain within the domain of indigenous control.

Finally, appropriate mechanisms to safe guard human rights should also be made within indigenous communities themselves. Abuses against women or those that violate religious freedom cannot be allowed to persist because they are falsely depicted as practices which maintain indigenous 'tradition' (Harvey, 1999, pp. 225–226). To this end, the internal differences within indigenous communities must be recognized since wealth differentials, political party allegiances and religious differences have created fissures within formerly homogenous communities.

The eradication of poverty and the improvement of economic well being

The most basic means to eradicate poverty is to allow all citizens functional access to education, health care and necessary public services within the context of a healthy economy. Unfortunately, indigenous peoples do not have such access; 83% of indigenous majority municipalities are ranked by INI statistics as very poor (Barry, 1995, p. 175).

The dismantling of the social welfare state and its replacement by market oriented neo-liberal economic policies has negatively affected indigenous peoples in Mexico. Changes in Article 27 of the Mexican Constitution altering communal land ownership laws, and the removal of state supports on basic food items has undermined the household economies of many indigenous families. Consequently, it is critical to address the special characteristics of indigenous poverty. Intra-community struggles based on growing wealth differentials, disputes about resource management and conflicts over land ownership and distribution need to be resolved in order to allow indigenous peoples to leave behind the assaults of poverty.

Indigenous peoples should be permitted to control their own patrimony and especially their economic development. Careful consideration of the consequences to indigenous peoples of any kind of economic development should be made with indigenous peoples actively participating in this discourse. Indigenous peoples should have the final determination in any economic decisions that directly affect them at the community level.

Given that many indigenous peoples live in rural areas where they are dependent on the natural world for their livelihood, their special knowledge of the environment and their dependency on it should permit them a central role in determining environmental policy and the structure of sustainable development. Their technical and scientific knowledge should be at the core of any development plans. Since indigenous peoples '...have maintained and deliberately cultivated an intimate relationship with their ecosystem over a period of at least three thousand years' (Stitler, 1997, p. 71), they have valuable knowledge of the natural world to employ to the benefit of all Mexicans.

Since indigenous peoples have long been associated with the natural world, their religious and spiritual beliefs are intimately intertwined with their knowledge of the region's ecology. These beliefs deserve respect as they represent alternative cosmovisions to the worldviews that prevail in Western thought and practice. The knowledge of the environment that indigenous peoples possess is based on their understanding of how to live *with* this planet rather than merely *on* it.

Eco-tourism and ethnic tourism such as the '*El Mundo Maya*/the Maya World' promotion have become important developments within Mexico's large tourism industry. Because these kinds of specialized tourism affect indigenous populations especially, their development should be determined with much greater input by indigenous peoples themselves. The remains of the great stone monuments, the centuries old cultural traditions and finely developed crafts of indigenous peoples serve as a major basis of the highly profitable tourism industry in Mexico. Mechanisms must be found that allow greater participation of indigenous peoples in the development of the tourist industry and ways for them to profit from it since tourism is likely to remain an important sector of the Mexican economy.

Gender rights and indigenous women

Since among no human group is the lived experiences of women and men identical, gender should be a special consideration for any policy regarding indigenous peoples. It is important to note that many indigenous women suffer from a triple burden of discrimination as women, indigenous peoples and low income individuals. Thus, indigenous women tend to be the poorest of the poor and the most alienated of the alienated in Mexican society. Policies and practices that take differing gender experiences and needs into account will help end the triple burden borne by many indigenous women.

Conclusions: indigenous peoples and the 21st century

From Spanish colonial times through the establishment of the Mexican Republic, state policy has followed the consistent but contradictory path of trying to assimilate indigenous peoples. The history of the assimilation movement in Mexico, however, has been fraught with many contradictions. First, the state has relied primarily on force to try to bring indigenous peoples into Mexican society. Second, state policies have traditionally attempted to undermine the indigenous peoples' cultural and subsistence bases. Third, throughout most of Mexican history, state assimilation programs have not offered to bring indigenous peoples into the mainstream as full citizens with equal rights, but as people who are inferior and incapable of being fully integrated into Mexican society. Fourth, proponents of assimilation have supported programs that if successful, would strip the indigenous peoples of their culture and traditions and force them to lose their identity. Finally, during the last half century, public policy towards the indigenous peoples has failed to improve their living conditions. Instead, it has significantly impoverished them and forced most of them into the periphery of Mexican society. Today, as the country enters the new millennium with a new government, the latter appears to be leaning towards a policy of more inclusiveness and, recognition of and respect for the indigenous peoples. If this is indeed, a genuine change in public policy, then there is hope that the indigenous peoples of Mexico will finally be able to enjoy their full citizenship rights while at the same time retaining their cultures and traditions (Barry, 1995; Diaz Polanco, 1997; Van Cott, 1994).

The Chiapas crisis presents the greatest challenge to any new policy of inclusiveness. President-elect Fox has pledged to end the crisis quickly by honoring the San Andreas Peace Accord. The latter was signed four years ago but the Mexican state, under the leadership of President Ernesto Zedillo and the PRI, refused to implement or honor it. If the new president keeps his promise and honors the Accord, that will represent a move in the right direction. Whether or not proper management of diversity in general and the plight of the indigenous peoples in particular, remain central policy concerns in Fox's administration, however, is unclear. What is clear, however, is that the EZLN has been quite successful in informing the global community of the misery and exploitation suffered by the indigenous peoples of Mexico. In addition, the Zapatistas have also made the average Mexican more aware of the plight of the indigenous peoples. If such efforts are continued, indigenous issues are most likely to remain a central concern of Mexican policymakers for the next several decades.

Although the summer 2000 elections, in which Vincente Fox was elected president and the PRI lost its ability to continue to monopolize political spaces in the country, promise to bring in leadership that is more sympathetic to indigenous issues, there is no guarantee that the new government will actually undertake institutional reforms to improve the welfare of the indigenous peoples. Organizations representing indigenous peoples must remain vigilant in order to make certain that the new government keeps its promise and implements reforms to enhance the quality of life for the country's impoverished and deprived citizens.

Western intellectuals may debate the presence or absence of cultural continuity between the indigenous past and the indigenous present (Cook and Joo, 1995; Farriss, 1984). Latin American policymakers may debate the wisdom of maintaining ethnic distinctiveness, claiming that such a practice leads to ethnic divisiveness and conflict (Warren, 1998). Yet, what is not debatable is that the indigenous peoples of Mexico persist as distinct and are persistent in their desire to remain culturally distinct while becoming equal participants within Mexican society.

On February 9, 1995, President Zedillo mobilized the Mexican army to move against the Zapatistas. In response, 100,000 people marched in Mexico City against this mobilization. Placards read, 'Leave our Indians Alone' and 'We are all Marcos' (referring to the articulate and charismatic non-indigenous spokesman for the Zapatista movement). The march showed public support for indigenous causes as represented by the Zapatistas and likely prevented state violence against them. But while the 'Leave our Indians Alone' placard was intended to show support for the Zapatista cause, it also demonstrates an inappropriate sense of ownership of indigenous peoples by the wider Mexican society that is ultimately patronizing. The other placard ('We are All Marcos'), was also intended to lend public support to the Chiapan indigenous rebels. It, however, also demonstrates a hero worship of but one actor (and a non-indigenous one at that) in a broad movement with a collective leadership.

The placard with the most appropriate and meaningful slogan was the one created by indigenous peoples themselves, 'Never again a Mexico without Us'. This slogan, more than the others, seems to point the way to a Mexico that includes indigenous peoples as they wish to be included, i.e., as culturally distinct equals with an emphasis on inclusion, respect and equality.[7]

Notes

1. Emiliano Zapata was one of the great agrarian leaders during the Mexican Revolution of 1910–1920. His name has been adopted by the contemporary Zapatistas in honor of his past struggles on behalf of *campesinos* and indigenous peoples.

2. Guatemala, like all of Central America, is regarded by many Mexicans as backward. Guatemala also has a population that is at least half indigenous. Thus, the joke means that Mexico, instead of joining the First World as represented by the U.S., was drawn backward into the Third World represented by the largely indigenous Guatemala. The racist underlay of the joke demonstrates the negative view of indigenous peoples held by many.

3. During the early days of the rebellion, *Sub-comandante* Marcos became the most visible and identifiable Zapatista. Although the EZLN is directed by a communal body, the high visibility and personal charisma of Marcos led to the erroneous impression that he was the sole leader of the EZLN. Critics of EZLN have noted that a *Ladino* (non-indigenous Spanish speaking Mexican) should not play so visible a part in an indigenous rebellion (Castillo Cocom, 1998).

4. As is generally true of all of the Americas in whose nations indigenous peoples reside, the actual indigenous population figures of the official Mexican census represent an undercount. Indigenous peoples of Mexico are underrepresented in national censuses because of limiting methodologies for taking the censuses; too restricting definitions of indigenous identity; and subtle forms of bureaucratic discrimination against indigenous peoples. By underestimating their numbers, the presence of indigenous peoples, their needs and their contributions can more easily be underestimated or disregarded by the Mexican state and society. In an effort to counteract the statistical difficulties presented by attempting to include very young children in the census (because of infant morality rates), the Mexican census includes only those over 5 years of age. Since indigenous families tend to be larger than non-indigenous ones, the census misses proportionately more young indigenous peoples than it does their non-indigenous counterparts. In addition, it has proved difficult for census takers to employ appropriate measures to reach those living in remote rural areas where some indigenous peoples reside or to count those living in rapidly growing, poor urban neighborhoods where indigenous migrants tend to congregate. Too narrow definitions of indigenous identity adds to the undercount as well since the Mexico census considers only those who speak an indigenous language to be indigenous. The use of language ability as a defining ethnic marker, however, provides an inaccurate measure of indigenous identity. State educational policies and practices often exclude indigenous languages from the school curriculum. Consequently, there are those who by other markers (including self-definition) can rightfully claim an indigenous identity, but are not counted as indigenous because they cannot speak an indigenous language. Furthermore, indigenous peoples sometimes migrate to regions where few speak

their language and thus they, and their children especially, are less likely to retain their indigenous language while they may well retain claim to their identity as indigenous. Also difficult to reflect in the national census has been an accounting of the number of indigenous peoples who have fled civil war in Guatemala and sought refuge in Mexico. Despite the end of hostilities in Guatemala and the subsequent repatriotization of many indigenous peoples, an undetermined number have chosen to remain in Mexico. This indigenous, largely Maya, population in flux has not been reflected in the Mexican census. Yet this population has added to the indigenous presence in Mexico especially in its southern states. All these seemingly methodological problems of census taking leave the Mexican state open to the accusation that its policies are directed toward a subtle process of 'whitening' the nation's population so that it appears more European and less indigenous. While the state rhetoric in Mexico emphasizes dynamism of the nation's multiethnic origins, the everyday practice is to value its European heritage while denigrating its indigenous roots. As Lovell and Lutz (1994) have pointed out in the case of Guatemala, the census consistently undercounts the nation's indigenous population in what they conclude is an attempt to have the Guatemala population appears to be more European-based than it actually is. Consequently for all of these reasons, the indigenous populations of Mexico, as in other New World nations, are likely to be undercounted and thus their presence negated. By denying their numbers, the Mexican state and Mexican society in general can more easily ignore indigenous citizens, excluding them from any meaningful participation in the nation and placing their needs outside of public policy debates.

5.   Mexican presidents serve a single 6 year term of office and cannot immediately succeed themselves in the presidency. While several governors have served more than one non-consecutive term in office, as yet no Mexican president has.

6.   The translations from Sra. Cab Cumi's original text in Spanish are my own.

7.   During the Salinas Presidency (1988–1994), Article 4 of the Mexican Constitution was revised to recognize the ethnic multi-plurality of Mexican society.

References

Barry, T. (1992), *Mexico: A Country Guide*, Inter-hemispheric Education Resource Center: Albuquerque, NM.

Barry, T. (ed.) (1995), *Zapata's Revenge: Free Trade and the Farm Crisis in Mexico*, South End Press: Boston, MA.

Bonfil Batalla, G. (1996), *Mexico Profundo: Reclaiming a Civilization* (Translated by Dennis, P. A.), University of Texas Press: Austin, TX.

Brown, P. (1997), 'Cultural Resistance and Rebellion in Southern Mexico', *LARR,* Vol. 33, No. 3, pp. 217–229.

Castenada, Q. (1996), *In the Museum of Mayan Culture*, University of Minneapolis Press: Minneapolis and London.

Castillo Cocom, J. (1998), 'Personal Communication With Author.'

Clendinnen, I. (1991), *Aztecs,* Cambridge University Press: Cambridge.

Coe, M. D. (1962), *Mexico*, Ediciones Lara: Mexico, D. F.

Coe, M. D. (1992), *Breaking the Maya Code*, Thames and Hudson: New York.

Comision de Asuntos Indigenas de la LV Legislatura Estado de Jalisco (1999), 'Iniciativa de Ley sobre derechos de los Pueblos indigenas de Jalisco', LV Legislatura Estado de Jaliscio: Guadalajara, Jalisco, Mexico.

Cook, S. and Joo, J-T. (1995), 'Ethnicity and Economy in Rural Mexico: A Critique of the Indigenista Approach', *LARR*, Vol. 30, No. 2, pp. 33–59.

Diaz del Castillo, B. (1966), *The True History of the Conquest of New Spain, 1517–1521*, Penguin: New York.

Diaz Polanco, H. (1997), *Indigenous Peoples in Latin America: The Quest for Self-Determination* (Translated by Rayas, L.), Westview Press: Boulder, CO and Oxford, UK.

Dworkin y Mendez, K. C. (1998), 'Beyond Indigenism and Marxism: The Deterritorialized Borders of Jose Maria Arguela's Deep Rivers', *SELA*, Vol. 42, No. 1, pp. 1–12.

Duarte, C. (1996), 'Personal Conversation with Author.'

Farriss, N. M. (1984), *Maya Society under Colonial Rule: The Collective Enterprise of Survival*, Princeton University Press: Princeton, NJ.

Freidel, D., Schele, L. and Parker, J. (1993), *Maya Cosmos: Three Thousand Years on the Shaman's Path*, William Morrow and Company, Inc.: New York.

Greaves, T. (ed.) (1994), *Intellectual Property Rights for Indigenous Peoples: A Source Book*, Society for Applied Anthropology: Oklahoma City, OK.

Harvey, N. (1999), *The Chiapas Rebellion: The Struggle for Land and Democracy*, Duke University Press: Durham, NC and London.

International Liga Maya (1994), 'Nojb'el el Mayab—Maya Thought', *Nojb'el Mayab*, January 10, Issue No. 4. Reprinted in *Anthropology Newsletter*, May 1994, pp. 28–29.

Kearney, M. (1988), 'Mixtec Political Consciousness: From Passive to Active Resistance', in Nugent, D. (ed.), *Rural Revolt in Mexico and U.S. Intervention*, Monograph Series No. 27, Center for U.S.-Mexico Studies, University of California: San Diego, CA.

Kicza, J. E. (ed.) (1993), *The Indian in Latin American History: Resistance, Resilience and Acculturation*, Scholarly Resources: Wilmington, DE.

Lovell, W. G. and Lutz, C. (1994), 'Conquest and Population: Maya Demography in Historical Perspective', *LARR*, Vol. 29, No. 2, pp. 133–140.

Martín, K. R. (n.d.), *Discarded Pages: The Life and Works of a Maya Poet and Politician: Araceli Cab Cumi*, Unpublished Manuscript, Department of Sociology & Anthropology, Florida International University: Miami, FL.

Martín, K. R. (1998), 'From the Heart of a Woman: Yucatec Maya as Political Actors', *Sex Roles: A Journal of Research*, Vol. 39, Nos. 7/8, pp. 559–571.

Martín, K. R. and Castillo Com, J. (1995), 'Indigenous Participation in the State', Paper presented at the annual meeting of the American Anthropological Association.

Maybury-Lewis, D. (1995), *Indigenous Peoples, Ethnic Groups, and the State*, Allyn and Bacon: Boston, MA.

Meyer, M. C. and Sherman, W. L. (1991), *The Course of Mexican History*, Oxford University Press: Oxford and New York.

Nash, J. (1991), 'The Reassertion of Indigenous Identity: Mayan Responses to State Intervention in Chiapas', *LARR*, Vol. 30, No. 3, pp. 7–39.

Russell, P. L. (1997), *The Chiapas Rebellion*, Mexico Resource Center: Austin, TX.

Sabloff, J. A. (1998), *The Cities of Ancient Mexico: Reconstructing a Lost World*, Thames and Hudon, Inc.: New York.

Santiz Gomez, M. (1999), *Creencias de Nuetros Antepasados*, Centro de la Imagen, CIESAS and Casa de las Imagenes: Mexico City.

Schele, L. and Freidel, D. (1990), *A Forest of Kings: The Untold Story of the Ancient Maya*, William Morrow and Company, Inc.: New York.

Scott, J. C. (1985), *Everyday Forms of Peasant Resistance*, Yale University Press: New Haven, CT.

Stitler, R. K. (1997), 'Gaspar Pedro Gonzalez: The First Maya Novelist', *SECOLAS Annals*, Vol. 28, pp. 67–72.

Stoll, D. (1998), *Rigoberta Menchu and the Story of All Poor Guatemalans*, Westview Press: Boulder, CO and Oxford, UK.

Townsend, R. F. (1991), *The Aztecs*, Thames and Hudson: London.

Van Cott, D. L. (ed.) (1992), *Indigenous Peoples and Democracy in Latin America*, St. Martin's Press: New York.

Warren, K. B. (1998), *Indigenous Movements and their Critics: Pan-Maya Activism in Guatemala*, Princeton University Press: Princeton, NJ.

Wasserstrom, R. (1983), *Class and Society in Highland Chiapas*, University of California Press: Berkeley, CA.

Wearne, P. (1996), *Return of the Indian: Conquest and Revival in the Americas*, Temple University Press: Philadelphia, PA.

8

Ecuador's Strategic Policies Toward Indigenous Communities in Sensitive Border Areas

Introduction

On October 26, 1998, Peru and Ecuador signed a historic peace accord in Brasilia which hopefully will end the longest-running territorial conflict in Latin America. For over 150 years, Ecuadorian-Peruvian relations have been characterized by mutual suspicion, diplomatic disputes, and periodic skirmishes along their contested borders. In 1828–1829, 1904, 1941, 1981, and 1995, the fighting was of sufficient scope and intensity to be classified as 'war,' even though neither nation made formal declarations of war against the other.

The international media have largely ignored the Peru-Ecuador conflict, except in those periods when the fighting escalated or the occasional peace treaty was signed. However, the dispute has had a profound effect on Ecuadorians and Peruvians, and especially those who live in or near the contested border regions in southern and eastern Ecuador and northern Peru. These militarized areas have been a barrier to international trade and the ordinary citizen's right to freedom of travel. Deprived of normal commerce, the Ecuador-Peru border areas are among the least developed regions of their respective nations. And the private suffering of individuals has been great, as in the case of divided families and indigenous cultures who have members residing on both sides of the disputed frontiers.

The purpose of this chapter is to describe and discuss the situation of indigenous peoples residing in Ecuador's sensitive frontier regions. The story of these people, and how they have been affected by border tensions and disputes, is probably the least known aspect of the current situation. In this analysis I give particular attention to the policies and practices developed by the Ecuadorian military for dealing with indigenous communities in Amazonian Ecuador, which is locally referred to as the 'Oriente.' In the southern Oriente, the large Shuar Indian population has been recruited as a military ally in the long-running border dispute with Peru. Conversely, in the northern Oriente, along the border with Colombia, small communities of Kofán, Siona, and Secoya Indians are often treated with mistrust as the armed forces focus on the defense of Ecuador's largest oilfields and battle 'subversive elements' and a flourishing drug trade.

The 1995 conflict in the southern Oriente

The January-March 1995 undeclared war between Ecuador and Peru brought increased media attention to the situation of the Amazonian Indians who live in the zone of conflict. Some press accounts focused on the Indians as victims of war by describing the bombing of native villages, the exodus of refugees, malnutrition, and environmental destruction caused by modern weapons. Ecuadorian and Peruvian reporters also emphasized another story, that of former 'headhunters' who served as stalwart jungle fighters and scouts. In these accounts, the qualities attributed to Indian soldiers reached mythical proportions. In Ecuador, for example, Shuar soldiers were celebrated as 'jungle devils' who were invisible to the enemy, untiring, and capable of surviving many days in the forest without rations (e.g., Fernández, 1995a; Hoy, 1995a; Moreno Mendoza, 1995). Many articles and editorials also spoke of the need to give greater recognition and support to Amazonian peoples since they proved so essential to Ecuador's military effort (e.g., Espinosa, 1995; Hoy, 1995b).

In March 1995, I visited Ecuador at the request of the Pontificia Universidad Católica in Quito to join a group of scholars who would evaluate the situation of the Shuar Indians in the war zone. As a member of this group, I visited Shuar communities near the front lines and participated in meetings with native leaders such as Felipe Tsenkush, the president of the Federación de Centros Shuar-Achuar; Domingo Ankuash, the president of the Shuar community of Bomboiza; and Nina Pacari, a well-known attorney affiliated with the *Confederación de Nacionalidades Indígenas del Ecuador* (CONAIE). Our group also interviewed area residents, native teachers, military officers, reporters, and government officials, including Dr. Luis Felipe Duchicela, the Minister of Indigenous Affairs, and Dr. Carlos Larriategui, the Secretary General of President Sixto Durán Ballén's administration.

This experience allowed me to evaluate Ecuadorian military policies toward the native peoples of Ecuador's southern Amazon region, and I was struck by how different they are from the military policies practiced in Ecuador's northern Amazon, where I have conducted anthropological research since 1972. In both the northern and southern Oriente, military policy is based on national security concerns. However, the northern and southern regions present different conditions and strategic situations.

The primary military concern in the southern Oriente has been the border dispute with Peru along the Cordillera del Condor and Río Cenepa. This is a classic border conflict between two nations that has involved several incidents of conventional warfare followed by diplomatic wrangling. The Ecuador-Peru border dispute goes back to the late colonial period when a Spanish royal decree of 1802 transferred the Province of Maynas from the Audiencia of Quito to Lima (Erickson et al., 1966, p. 288). During the late 19th and early 20th centuries, rubber traders operating from Iquitos also established a *de facto* Peruvian presence in areas claimed by Ecuador, but not effectively administered by it.

In July 1941, Peruvian forces invaded Ecuador from the south and east. The eastern attacks involved units that moved up various Amazonian tributaries, including the Tigre and Napo Rivers. The numerically superior and better equipped Peruvians overwhelmed the defenders and occupied El Oro Province on the coast of Ecuador and large areas of the Oriente. The 1942 Protocol of Río de Janeiro treaty, in which Argentina, Brazil, Chile, and the United States served as guarantors, ceded one third of Ecuador's claimed national territory to Peru. The greater part of this loss was in the Amazonian lowlands.

Ecuadorian journalist, Jaime Galarza (1972, pp. 87–91), sees the 1941 Peru-Ecuador War as the result of competition for oil. He points out that the boundary established by the Río Protocol closely followed the limits of the oil concession Ecuador granted to Royal Dutch Shell in 1937. Years later, the Canadian-based International Petroleum Company (IPC), a subsidiary of Standard Oil of New Jersey, acquired a concession at the confluence of the Tigre and Corrientes Rivers, just south of the Río Protocol boundary. In short, Galarza argues that Peru invaded the Oriente to deprive Ecuador of these oil rich lands. It is not clear whether the quest for oil played a decisive role in the Peruvian government's decision to invade Ecuador in 1941. However, Royal Dutch Shell's activities in the Ecuadorian Oriente were certainly known and may have provided an incentive for war.

In 1950, Ecuador unilaterally declared the Río Protocol null and void, and the border dispute continued to sour its relations with Peru. In 1981, Ecuador and Peru fought a brief but sharp battle at Paquisha in the Cordillera del Condor in the southern Oriente. Paquisha was an Ecuadorian Army outpost located in an area claimed by both of the contending nations. Ecuadorian troops were forced to retreat from Paquisha as Peru employed helicopter gunships and artillery against the former's position.

In January 1995, the dispute again flared into open warfare along the Cordillera del Condor and in the adjacent Cenepa River Valley. This time the Ecuadorian military was better prepared as it occupied the high ground surrounding the upper Cenepa Valley and had established fortified positions with interlocking fields of fire and an effective antiaircraft defense employing surface to air missiles.

The Peruvian troops who advanced up the Cenepa River were forced to fight from the valley floor and met strong resistance from the entrenched Ecuadorians in the heights. After two months of bloody fighting, the Ecuadorians still held their positions. A ceasefire agreement was reached in March 1995 and the Río Protocol guarantor nations sent peace-keeping troops to monitor the combat zone. Although the fighting ended in a stalemate, Ecuadorians treated it as a 'victory' and the whole nation celebrated. This was the first time in modern history their armed forces had withstood the far larger Peruvian military machine.

The role of indigenous peoples in the Ecuador-Peru conflict

The southern Oriente is the ancestral homeland of Jivaroan speaking peoples, including the Shuar and Achuar. Estimates of the Shuar-Achuar population in Ecuador range from 20,000 to 30,000 individuals (see Figure 8.1). Related Jivaroan peoples known as the Aguaruna and Huambisa live in nearby Peru. The reputation of the Shuar-Achuar as fierce fighters and 'headhunters,' which is based both on cultural tradition and historic deeds

Figure 8.1   **Map of Ecuador.** Location of the Shuar, Achar, Kofán and Siona-Secoya peoples along Ecuador's borders with Peru and Colombia. The southern border area has been the scene of recent military conflicts with Peru, whereas the northern border with Colombia is subject to other national security concerns such as the protection of oil fields, guerilla infiltration, and the drug trade. Ecuadorian military strategies have impacted these native communities of the north and south in different ways.

(Harner, 1972), gives them a warrior mystique that is respected by the professional soldiers of the Ecuadorian military. With their large population and formal tribal government in the form of the Shuar Federation, these people represent a formidable ethnic and political force.

The Ecuadorian army sees the Shuar-Achuar people as desirable allies because of their strategic location along the southern frontier, their large population, and their aforementioned warrior fame. Hence the armed forces attempt to maintain good relations with Shuar-Achuar communities and often support their projects with donations of medicines, food, and other material goods.

In the 1980s, the army began to organize elite Shuar units which are now known as *Compañías de Operaciones Especiales (COE)-Iwia*. *Iwia* is the name of a Shuar demon who kills humans. Today, these *Iwia* special forces units also include Lowland Quichua Indians from the central Oriente. Shuar infantry reservists are referred to as *Arutams*. In the Shuar language, an *arutam* is a 'vision or apparition' that is often associated with the appearance of a *wakanï*, or soul (Harner, 1972, p. 135).

These linkages between the army and the southern Oriente's native population have supported Ecuador's military strategy in its conflict with Peru. The elite *Iwia* companies played a significant role in combat operations in the Cenepa Valley in 1995 (Fernández, 1995a, 1995b). The *Arutam* reservists were called up at the start of the war and also participated in the conflict. At the local level, Shuar communities like Bomboiza organized 'resistance groups' as a 'second line of defense' against possible Peruvian breakthroughs (Ankuash, 1995). Felipe Tsenkush (1995) of the Shuar Federation mentioned that many other Shuar volunteered for service when the war broke out, including some *teleauxiliares* (teaching assistants in the Shuar radio education program) who worked as scouts. He also said that 'Peru is once again threatening to divide our tribal territory.'

The Shuar presence in the upper Cenepa Valley appears to be traditional, but intermittent. The territory is used for seasonal foraging activities and in the past some families had homesteads there. The 1995 battles of Tiwintsa, Etsa, and Cueva de los Tayos occurred in places that bear Shuar names.

The upper Cenepa Valley is also a border region between the Shuar, Aguaruna, and Huambisa (Descola 1989, p. 41). All three speak Jivaroan languages. The Shuar and Aguaruna visit each other across the disputed border and there is some intermarriage between them (e.g., one bilingual teacher I interviewed in Bomboiza has an Aguaruna mother and a Shuar father). Undoubtedly, some Aguaruna and Huambisa fought for Peru in the

1995 war (Peruvian television newscasts touted the virtues of native soldiers and scouts much as the Ecuadorian media had done). According to one report, the Shuar broadcast a short-wave radio message to the Aguaruna 'asking their forgiveness because they had to go to war with them.'

Fortunately, the casualties in the 1995 conflict were relatively light for a modern war. There were reports of one Shuar killed, one missing in action, and several wounded. As of March 1, 1995, the Ecuadorian Ministry of Defense released a casualty list of 28 killed, 4 missing, and 87 wounded. Peru reported slightly higher casualties for its side. However, some unofficial estimates place the total casualties at about 500. Several Shuar villages were bombed by the Peruvian air force in the first weeks of the war, but no deaths or injuries were reported from these attacks. Ecuadorian press accounts stated that about 10,000 refugees evacuated the war zone, but Domingo Ankuash insisted that most of these were white colonists who fled to their places of origin, while the Shuar stayed because, 'we have no other place to go to.'

Many of the Shuar I talked to in 1995 see themselves as Shuar first, but also accept their status as Ecuadorian citizens. The political relationship between the Shuar and Ecuador has some characteristics of an alliance between two nations that share common strategic interests. Ecuadorian army Major Iván Borja (1995) said the Shuar had requested a military academy for Indians in the southern Oriente so they would not have to leave their homeland to pursue a military education and career. However, the high command responded that such an academy was not feasible because it would duplicate facilities already available in the sierra and coast.

Ecuador has given material assistance to Shuar communities and legalized some of their land claims, but the Shuar are wary of government development and colonization projects, and the multinational corporations that seek to exploit their region's resources. In 1995, the Shuar of Bomboiza were fighting a Canadian-owned gold mining company that was about to begin operations adjacent to their community.

In a public meeting with the Minister of Indigenous Affairs on March 5, 1995, the Shuar Federation's president, Felipe Tsenkush, stated that government and international aid should be directed to the strengthening of existing native organizations and programs rather than attempting to create new bureaucratic structures and settlement projects. He noted that native people are well adapted to the rain forest environment and are the people who are best able to serve as the 'living frontiers' desired by Ecuador.

Both Felipe Tsenkush of the Shuar Federation and Nina Pacari of CONAIE emphasized their desire for a negotiated settlement to end the border dispute and restore peace. José Juncosa, a member of our research group and manager of the indigenist Abya-Yala Press in Quito, expressed the view that there is a danger that the current goodwill of the Shuar people toward the Ecuadorian state may be transformed into a relationship that focuses too heavily on the military dimension. He cautioned that a large-scale and prolonged military presence in the region may pose serious problems for the Shuar in the future.

Military-Indian relations in the northern Oriente

In the oil producing northern Oriente, the Ecuadorian military perceives a different set of problems. First, it must guarantee the security of oil fields that are Ecuador's greatest economic resource, and provide about 50 percent of the national budget. Second, while there is no imminent threat of invasion of the northern Oriente by conventional forces, there is considerable criminal drug trafficking, infiltration by Colombian guerrillas, and illegal immigration. Because of these 'unconventional' threats of leftist subversion and crime, the military has adopted a cautious attitude toward the region's civilian population. The small communities of Kofán, Siona, and Secoya Indians in the northern Oriente are not seen as allies of the armed forces. Instead, they face a military that deals with them inconsistently and often treats them as nuisances or potential enemies.

Ecuador shares borders with both Peru and Colombia in the northern Oriente. In 1904 and 1941, Ecuador and Peru fought battles along the Río Napo, one of the two major rivers of the region. Today, the Ecuadorian post of Nuevo Rocafuerte and the Peruvian post of Pantoja face each other across the boundary that resulted from the 1942 Protocol of Río de Janeiro. As a result of Ecuador's dissatisfaction with the terms of this 'imposed' treaty, the Napo was until recently, closed to commerce and travel between the two nations. While the Napo is an important historic battlefield, it did not figure in the more recent fighting of 1981 and 1995.

In contrast to the Napo situation, the border with Colombia along the San Miguel and Putumayo Rivers is open to commerce and transportation. The economic development of the northern Oriente began in earnest in the late 1960s following the discovery of oil in the region. In 1970, a consortium of the Texaco and Gulf oil companies completed the construction of a 512 kilometer pipeline from the oil fields at Lago Agrio to the Pacific port of Esmeraldas. The new road that paralleled this pipeline became the main route of penetration into the northern Oriente. By the mid-1970s, almost all of the land along this road had been colonized by migrants from Ecuador's Andean and coastal provinces. From Lago Agrio, a short road runs north to the San Miguel River, where travelers can cross into Colombia. In the early 1980s, another road was extended from Lago Agrio in a northeasterly direction until it reached the Colombian border at Puerto El Carmen, near the confluence of the San Miguel and Putumayo Rivers.

According to Major Iván Borja (1995), an artillery officer assigned to the Ecuadorian Ministry of Defense, the military in the northern Oriente see their key missions as those of suppressing the narcotics traffic, combating guerrilla activity, and controlling illegal migration. All of these problems are related to the border with Colombia. Borja said the armed forces in this zone have adopted a cautious attitude in dealing with civilians because criminals, guerrillas, and illegal aliens are not easily recognized among the general population.

Several events illustrate the strained relationship between the military and civilians in the northern Oriente. For more than a decade, guerrillas of the *Fuerzas Armadas Revolucionarias de Colombia* (FARC) have been active in the jungle fastness of Putumayo region, where they have been relatively safe from government forces. They have also been known to take refuge on the Ecuadorian side of the border when pressed by the Colombian army, a fact that is highly discomforting to the Ecuadorian government.

In December 1993, there occurred the now infamous encounter between the FARC and an Ecuadorian patrol (*The New York Times*, 1993). Several canoes transporting an Ecuadorian anti-drug force on the San Miguel River were ambushed by guerrillas armed with machine guns and rockets. After inflicting 14 casualties, the guerrillas escaped into the forest.

Following this attack, Ecuadorian forces conducted sweeps of the communities along the San Miguel River and detained a number of people who were suspected of being guerrillas or guerrilla sympathizers. The men and women who were held denied participation or complicity in the attack, and claimed to be nothing more than poor colonists who were being subjected to military abuse and torture. This case provoked a major human rights controversy, and a Quito judge eventually ordered the release of most of the prisoners.

Major Borja related another case in which the military was betrayed by the civilian population. In an act intended to improve civilian-military relations, an army unit attempted to carry out a 'civic action' project by participating in a community work party (*minga*). The soldiers laid down their rifles to take part in the work, but when they looked up they saw that their hosts had picked up their weapons and surrounded them in a threatening manner. (Major Borja did not elaborate on how this incident ended.)

The principal city of the northern Oriente is Lago Agrio, a booming oil town located only 16 kilometers south of the Colombian border. Despite its regional importance as the capital of Sucumbíos Province, Lago Agrio is a rough frontier town with many bars, numerous houses of prostitution, and a high crime rate. Several military bases are located in the vicinity of Lago Agrio, including an air force installation and various army posts. Military patrols often pass through the town, and soldiers check the identification papers of people on the streets. On November 23, 1994, I was having a beer at a sidewalk cafe in Lago Agrio when I suddenly found myself surrounded by five soldiers carrying semiautomatic assault rifles. The officer in charge asked for my papers and I handed him my passport. When he determined that everything was in order, he warned me to be careful, because as he claimed, 'Lago Agrio is a dangerous place.' He also reminded the café owner of a law that forbids the drinking of beer at sidewalk tables. He then ordered me to take my drink into the interior dining room of the restaurant. Several days later, the cafe owner told me that she had complained to the municipal government about this new policy and was told to ignore it and that the army officer was acting without authorization.

The officer's apparent concern for my welfare may have been based on the fact that the northern Oriente has been the scene of multiple kidnappings in recent years. The victims of these kidnappings have been affluent town merchants and foreigners, including seven Canadians, four Americans, three Spaniards, and a Belgian. The first American who was kidnapped was Scott Heindal, an engineer with the Iminco gold mining company. After being abducted in April, 1990, his captors carried him across the border into Colombia and held him for ransom (*The Miami Herald*, 1990). After lengthy negotiations between the kidnappers, Heindal's family, and Ecuadorian officials, a ransom was paid and Heindal was released. In a more recent case in 1994, two American oil workers were kidnapped in the frontier town of Shushufindi in Sucumbíos Province. Newspapers reported this crime, but not its aftermath. While the fate of these men went unreported, it appears that their employer may have secretly negotiated a ransom with the kidnappers.

The most ambitious and notorious kidnapping, however, occurred on

September 11, 1999 when 12 people were abducted near kilometer 68 of the Lago Agrio-Tarapoa road (*El Comercio*, 1999a). Eight of these (including seven Canadians and one American) were employees of United Pipeline, a subsidiary of City Investing Company, which operates an oilfield at Tarapoa. The remaining four consisted of three Spaniards and a Belgian who were on an excursion to the Cuyabeno Wildlife Reserve. The kidnappers were well armed and organized. According to an Ecuadorian woman who was seized and then released, there were about 12 men and 3 women dressed in camouflage uniforms and carrying automatic assault weapons, submachine guns, and a radio for communications (El Comercio, 1999b, 1999c). This witness also reported that there was a clear chain of command within the band, and that some members spoke with Colombian accents, while others had Ecuadorian accents.

The Ecuadorian Army quickly mobilized and conducted searches, but it could not locate the kidnappers and their victims who had disappeared into the jungle. Because the kidnappings took place only 30 km from the Ecuador-Colombia border, many people theorized that the abductors were members of Colombia's FARC guerrilla organization. Others suggested that the band might be from a Colombian right-wing paramilitary group or just common criminals. After an initial release of the Spaniards and the Belgian, the eight United Pipeline workers were released on December 19, 1999. Press reports indicated that a ransom of 3.5 million dollars was paid for the oil workers (Carlos Antonio, 1999a, 1999b).

The indigenous people of the northern Oriente

Unlike the Shuar of the southern Oriente, the indigenous groups of the northern Oriente have been reduced to minuscule populations in a few scattered villages (Vickers, 1989). The traditional natives of the San Miguel, Putumayo, and Aguarico Rivers include the Kofán, Siona, and Secoya, whose combined population does not exceed 1,500 individuals. In addition, some Lowland Quichua have migrated into the Aguarico Valley from the Napo since the turn of the century, and three Shuar *comunas* have been established in the region area since the 1970s.

Relations between the Ecuadorian military and the indigenous groups of the northern Oriente are tenuous. There are no specially trained Indian battalions from this region, and only a few Siona, Secoya, and Kofán men have entered military service. Native elders report a sad history of mutual mistrust and abuse in their dealings with the army. The small army outposts along the Aguarico River have often interfered with Indian travelers and denied their access to traditional hunting and fishing grounds such as the Cuyabeno River and Lagarto Cocha. In the 1960s, soldiers stationed at the mouth of the Cuyabeno River detained and raped a Siona woman.

Siona and Secoya residents of the Cuyabeno River report that from the 1950s to the 1970s, the army periodically rounded them up and forced them to clear the military trail from the post of Puerto Montufar to the San Miguel River. In July 1974, I observed an army canoe dispensing emergency food supplies to the Siona and Secoya of San Pablo following a flood, but a few months later, another canoe passed and the soldiers fired their rifles into the air as if to threaten the people.

One problem in the northern Oriente is that the traditional Indian territories do not coincide with Ecuador's present boundaries with Colombia and Peru. Indians who wish to cross these borders to visit kin and to hunt and fish are often prevented from doing so, particularly along the Peruvian frontier. Some military personnel have accused the Secoya of being 'Peruvian spies' because their traditional homeland on the Santa María River was annexed by Peru in the 1941 war. Ironically, Ecuador still claimed this area until 1998, so it is curious that these soldiers saw the Secoya as 'spies' rather than as 'Ecuadorians' whose lands have been occupied by Peru.

In truth, many of the Secoya, Siona, and Kofán people feel their primary 'nationalities' are those of their respective indigenous cultures. They know the international boundaries between Ecuador, Peru, and Colombia are artifacts of 'white history,' and that these borders were superimposed on their ancient Indian homelands within the past 200 years.

Elías Piyauaje, a former president of the *Organización Indígena Secoya del Ecuador* (OISE), feels that there should be a special national policy concerning military service by members of tiny ethnic minorities like the Siona, Secoya, and Kofán. In his view, such service should be voluntary rather than compulsory because these groups are small and fragile. In fact, most Secoya, Siona, and Kofán youths do not enter military service. However, this causes problems because these individuals have difficulty obtaining a *cédula militar,* which is a vital document in Ecuadorian civil life. Without a *cédula militar* a man cannot travel freely within the country or obtain a passport for international travel. As a consequence, Indian men are frequently harassed and not allowed to pass military checkpoints along roads and rivers.

Another bone of contention with the government occurred when the Siona, Secoya, and Kofán joined other Indian groups and non-Indian settlers in a class-action lawsuit against Texaco seeking 1.5 billion dollars in compensation for environmental damages caused by oil spills and the dumping of petroleum waste products. This suit was filed in New York's U.S. District Court on November 3, 1993 (Salpukas, 1993, p. C3).

Texaco countered by arguing that New York was an improper jurisdiction and by offering a settlement to the Ecuadorian government in the form of a $10 million cleanup fund. Initially the Ecuadorian government under conservative President Sixto Durán-Ballén supported Texaco's proposal. Plaintiff attorney Cristobal Bonifaz (1994) commented that this sum was ridiculously low and that the proposed resolution was like 'two thieves agreeing to settle with each other while ignoring their victims.' He also argued that the federal court in New York was the proper jurisdiction since Texaco managed its Ecuadorian operations from its White Plains, New York headquarters.

After a long process of discovery and many delays, U.S. federal judge Jed Rakoff dismissed the class-action suit against Texaco in November 1996, ruling it should be tried in Ecuador. However, the new Ecuadorian administration of President Abdalá Bucaram (elected in July 1996) adopted a policy of supporting the plaintiffs and in January 1997, dispatched Ecuador's Attorney General Leonidas Plaza to New York to appeal Rakoff's decision.

Things were clouded in February 1997 when the Ecuadorian Congress deposed Bucaram, charging that he was 'mentally incompetent' to serve as president. Bucaram was replaced by interim President Fabián Alarcón Rivera. Alarcón appeared to favor the Indian and colonist plaintiffs against Texaco, but the federal appeals court did not rule on judge Rakoff's decision during his truncated term of office.

On August 10, 1998, Jamil Mahuad succeeded Alarcón as Ecuador's president. Then, on October 7, 1998 the U.S. Court of Appeals for the Second Circuit reversed judge Rakoff's decision and ruled that the lawsuit against Texaco could proceed in the U.S. federal court. In December 1999, it was reported that Texaco's attorneys were seeking to settle the case out of court (Carlos Antonio, 1999c).

It is important to emphasize that the natives of the northern Oriente are not inherently antagonistic to the Ecuadorian state. Instead, they seek a better relationship with the government that is based on mutual respect and understanding. Prior to the 1995 war between Ecuador and Peru, Secoya leader Elías Piyauaje initiated discussions with high officials in the Ministries of Defense and Foreign Relations in an attempt to improve native access to the border areas. His hope is to reach an agreement whereby the Secoya living in Ecuador and Peru can visit each other and participate in joint projects to revitalize their cultural traditions. The basic human right of travel across international borders has long been denied to the Secoya and other residents of the northern Oriente. In the case of the Secoya, binational cooperation on this issue may well be essential to their survival as a culture.

Conclusion

Ecuador's military policies toward Amazonian Indians are based on strategic national interests in specific border regions with different perceived risks. In the southern Oriente, the large Shuar-Achuar population has been seen as valuable ally in the long-standing border conflict with Peru, and the Shuar-Achuar have been courted accordingly. But in the northern Oriente the small communities of Kofán, Siona, and Secoya Indians are treated with mistrust or indifference as the armed forces focus their attention on protecting oil fields and fighting crime and leftist subversion.

The prestige of Ecuador's armed forces reached an all time high in 1995 due to the public's perception of their performance against Peruvian troops in the Cenepa Valley. President Sixto Durán Ballén's 'victory' speeches frequently mentioned that the Ecuadorian army and air force shot down four Peruvian warplanes and five helicopters, while only one Ecuadorian fighter suffered damage (it returned to its base at Macas). The modernization of Ecuador's military equipment and the professionalization of the officer corps appeared to have improved dramatically since 1981, when Ecuador lost the battle of Paquisha in the southern Oriente. In large measure, the strengthening of the armed forces had been financed by oil revenues from the northern Oriente.

Hopefully, the October 26, 1998 'Acta de Brasilia' peace accord between Ecuador and Peru will allow both nations to normalize their relations, promote bilateral trade, and reduce their military expenditures. The World Bank, Inter-American Development Bank (IDB), and other lenders have promised three billion dollars for a 'peace fund' to promote economic integration and development projects in the formerly disputed border areas. Undoubtedly, the lives of ordinary Peruvian and Ecuadorian citizens will be improved if the peace agreement holds.

As part of their professionalization program, the Ecuadorian armed forces need to educate their officers and enlisted men about human rights issues and the special problems faced by indigenous communities. While some military personnel are sensitive to these concerns, many are not. The characterization of the Secoya as 'Peruvian spies' by one army colonel and several enlisted men I have interviewed is symptomatic of wide-spread ignorance regarding the true situation of Indian peoples in the northern Oriente.

Major Iván Borja of the Ministry of Defense said that his approach to winning over Indian communities is to give them material assistance while avoiding rhetorical discussions about politics and indigenous rights. He argued that such practical deeds build trust between the natives and the military, whereas political debates are 'fruitless and counterproductive.' His view may be based on the fact that the military has traditionally desired a unified and 'modern' nation, whereas Indian political leaders have pressed for a constitutional amendment which recognizes that Ecuador is a 'multiethnic and plurinational' state (Hoy, 1995c). Many conservative Ecuadorian politicians and business people feared this proposal because they viewed it as a threat to national integration and development.

Between December 1997 and May 1998, a special Constituent Assembly drafted a new constitution for Ecuador which took effect on August 10, 1998 when President Jamil Mahuad was inaugurated (Fraser, 1998, pp. A51–A52). Article 1 of the new Constitution declares that Ecuador is a 'pluricultural and multiethnic state' and Article 3.1 says 'It is the primordial duty of the State to strengthen national unity in diversity' (Republic of Ecuador, 1998). In my view, the adoption of the new Constitution is an important symbolic and political act that signifies greater respect for the ancient traditions of Ecuador's indigenous peoples and the important contributions they make to national life. Earlier fears that the 'multiethnic' amendment would weaken the state were belied by the 1995 war with Peru, when the vast majority of Ecuadorians rallied behind their nation's cause regardless of their ethnic or regional differences. However, due to a severe economic crisis, including rampant inflation, many bank failures, and charges of corruption, mid-level military officers attempted a coup on January 21, 2000. This action was supported by some indigenous leaders and organizations. The coup forced President Jamil Mahuad from office, but it quickly collapsed as the United States and other nations expressed their strong disapproval of the military takeover. The Ecuadorian Congress then elevated Vice President Gustavo Noboa to the presidency and 'democracy' was saved for the time being (Oppenheimer, 2000).

Despite the current economic and political crisis in Ecuador, the 1998 peace agreement with Peru promises to relieve some of the problems experienced by indigenous peoples on both sides of the border. Divided families and ethnic groups should once again be able to visit one another and reestablish their social relations and rebuild their cultural traditions. Peace should also lessen the concern about Indian 'spies' and the questioning of people's 'loyalties' to this or that nation. Unfortunately, many Ecuadorians and Peruvians are unhappy with the terms and compromises of the October 26, 1998 Acta de Brasilia. Some on each side, for various reasons, see the treaty as a 'diplomatic defeat' for their respective nations. Hopefully, both Ecuadorians and Peruvians will learn to live with the agreement and begin to enjoy the dividends of peaceful relations.

Acknowledgments

My fieldwork among the Siona-Secoya and Kofán peoples of northeastern Ecuador over the past 26 years has been supported at various times by the Henry L. and Grace Doherty Foundation, the National Institute of Mental Health, the Florida International University Foundation, Inc., Cultural Survival, Inc., the Latin American and Caribbean Center and College of Arts and Sciences of Florida International University, the Institute for Science and Interdisciplinary Studies, and a Fulbright Scholar award. Fieldwork among the Secoya of Peru in 1984 was supported by the Florida International University Foundation, Inc. and the Amazon Research and Training Program of the University of Florida. Sabbatical research in 1985–86 was supported by a National Endowment for the Humanities Fellowship and the School of American Research. My brief fieldwork among the Shuar in 1995 was funded by the Pontificia Universidad Católica del Ecuador. I thank all of these foundations and institutions for their valuable assistance. Most importantly, I thank all of the native people who have helped me and put up with me.

References

Ankuash, D. (1995), 'Personal Communication'.
Bonifaz, C. (1995), 'Personal Communication'.
Borja, I. (1995), 'Personal Communication'.
Carlos Antonio, S. (1999a), 'Liberados ocho rehenes tras 79 dias de cautiverio', Hoy 1 de diciembre de 1999, Quito, Ecuador.
Carlos Antonio, S. (1999b), 'Plagio deja incógnitas', *Hoy*, 21 de diciembre de 1999, Quito, Ecuador.
Carlos Antonio, S. (1999c), 'Vigilan juicio contra Texaco', *Hoy*, 19 de diciembre de 1999, Quito, Ecuador.
Descola, P. (1989), *La selva culta: Simbolismo y praxis en la ecología de los Achuar*, Ediciones Abya-Yala: Quito, Ecuador.
El Comercio (1999a), 'Operativo en la frontera con Colombia', *El Comercio*, 12 de

septiembre de 1999, Quito, Ecuador.

El Comercio (1999b), '3 comunicados oficiales', *El Comercio*, 12 de septiembre de 1999, Quito, Ecuador.

El Comercio (1999c), 'El secuestro de 12 extranjeros en la Amazonía', *El Comercio*, 13 de septiembre de 1999, Quito, Ecuador.

Erickson, E. E., et al. (1966), *Area Handbook for Ecuador*, U. S. Government Printing Office: Washington, D.C.

Espinosa, S. (1995), 'Solidaridades sociales y reconocimiento', *Hoy* (Quito), 7 de marzo de 1995, p. 4A, Quito, Ecuador.

Fernández, E. (1995a), 'Los Iwias, a la vanguardia', *El Comercio* (Quito), 8 de marzo de 1995, p. A6, Quito, Ecuador.

Fernández, E. (1995b), 'Iwias: recibidos como héroes', *El Comercio* (Quito), 9 de marzo de 1995, p. A7, Quito, Ecaudor.

Fraser, B. J. (1998), 'Ecuador's New President Gives Academics Hope for Brighter Future', *The Chronicle of Higher Education*, September 18, pp. A51–A52.

Galarza, J. (1972), *El festín del petróleo, segunda edición*, Ediciones Solitierra: Quito, Ecuador.

Harner, M. J. (1972), *The Jívaro: People of the Sacred Waterfalls*, Doubleday/Natural History Press: Garden City, NY.

Hoy (1995a), 'Iwias, "demonios" de la selva', *Hoy*, 4 de febrero de 1995, Quito, Ecuador.

Hoy (1995b), 'Shuaras en difícil situación', *Hoy*, 6 de febrero de 1995, Quito, Ecuador.

Hoy (1995c), 'Indígenas por un país pluricultural', *Hoy*, 24 de febrero de 1995, Quito, Ecuador.

The Miami Herald (1990), 'Boss Reportedly Ties Ex-Aide to Ecuadorian Kidnapping Case', June 17, p. 11A.

Moreno Mendoza, C. (1995), 'Diablos de la selva', *Vistazo*, 16 de febrero de 1995, pp. 20–22, Quito, Ecuador.

The New York Times (1993), 'Colombia Rebels Suspected in Ecuador Ambush', December 19, p. 11.

Oppenheimer, A. (2000), 'Ecuador's President Under the Gun', *The Miami Herald*, May 4, p. 10A.

Republic of Ecuador (1998), *Constitución Política de la República del Ecuador*, Quito, Ecuador.

Salpukas, A. (1993), 'Ecuadorean Indians Suing Texaco', *The New York Times*, November 4, p. C3.

Tsenkush, F. (1995), 'Personal Communication'.

Vickers, W. T. (1989), *Los Sionas y Secoyas: Su adaptación al ambiente amazónico*, Ediciones Abya-Yala: Quito, Ecuador.

9

Let Smiles Return to My Motherland:[1] The Sikh Diaspora and Homeland Politics

My heroes! O, Lions! O, brave men! Recover your senses. How long will you continue to sleep? How long will you consent to be shoe-beaten by others and put up with their tyrannies.

Rise O, Lions! Pluck your courage. Serve your country and do your duty. The enemy is eating you up. Shoe-beat him out of your country ... come brave men!

Har Dayal, founding member of the Ghadar Movement

****

The land of Punjab is shackled
terror loose and our motherland cries
where are my red-faced sons? where are them?
The angry and rebellious ones to restore my honor?

Ravinder Ravi, Canadian Punjabi poet writing of Operation Blue Star

Introduction

The post-Cold War era has been witness to a rise in increasingly strident proclamations for self-determination among numerous nationalist factions around the world. The abrupt fragmentation of the Soviet Union and Yugoslavia, and the sectarian violence that followed, starkly evince the notion held by many ethno-national groups that political maps should coincide with ethnic ones. At the cusp of the new millenium, virulent nationalism in the form of ethnoseparatist armed conflict and ritual ethnic cleansing have become permanent political problems that remain resistant to facile solutions.

In their attempts to counter nascent nationalist tendencies, many regimes have deployed both militant and non-militant strategies to maintain legitimacy and harness their more 'rebellious' ethnic, linguistic, and religious minorities. While there is a burgeoning literature that examines the domestic context of ethnic conflict and ethnonationalism, there has, until recently, been little analysis of transnational factors that affect the dynamics of nationalist movements.[2] Scholars of ethnic conflict (most notably political scientists) have assumed closed political systems and paid scant attention to the activities of coethnic groups operating outside a state's territorial boundaries. Such a restricted approach has sorely limited our understanding of the role transnational networks play in shaping and sustaining nationalist and ethnopolitical conflicts.

However, as recent news headlines indicate, numerous ethno-separatist movements, from the Kurds to the Kashmiris, enjoy considerable support from overseas coethnic groups sympathetic to their cause. Overseas support has taken many forms, including raising and remitting funds to support armed insurrections, highlighting state repression and human rights abuses in the homeland, and lobbying host country and other governments to adopt foreign policies favorable to the respective group's agenda. A corollary of this has been that the concept of 'diaspora' (defined broadly as international migrants and their progeny who preserve strong material and emotional ties to their lands of origin) has more recently enjoyed somewhat of a resurgence in the social sciences. Recognition of the importance of diasporan involvement in ethnonationalist movements has led some scholars (Tatla, 1999; Cohen, 1997; Dusenbery, 1995; Constas and Platias, 1993; Shain, 1991, 1989; Sheffer, 1986) to investigate the 'complex triadic relationship'[3] that exists between migrant communities, their homelands, and their host countries.

This study attempts to add to this emergent literature and focuses on the North American Sikh diaspora and the role it has played and continues to play in the politics of its homeland.[4] Specifically, this chapter traces the development of two political movements—Ghadar and Khalistan—in order to highlight the motivations behind diasporan sympathies and mechanisms of diasporan support.[5] The Ghadar (meaning 'mutiny' or 'revolution') struggle was an early twentieth century emigrant effort to oust the British from colonial India, while the Khalistan ('the land of the pure,' 'the nation of the Khalsa') agitation is an ongoing movement to carve out a separate Sikh state out of territory that presently constitutes the Indian Punjab. Although there are a number of similarities between the two movements, there is one key difference—while the Ghadar movement was a pan-Indian nationalist coalition uniting Sikhs, Hindus, and Muslims, the Khalistan movement is one that is supported exclusively by Sikh nationalists.[6] Ironically, as this chapter highlights, Sikh involvement in Ghadar—a movement that was designed to advance the cause of Indian sovereignty—would half a century later set the stage for the Khalistan struggle, a movement whose *raison d'être* is the ultimate destruction of India in its present territorial form.

Karen Leonard (1989) and W. H. McLeod (1989a) contend that the specifics of the chronology of migration make it untenable to theoretically engage the concept of a 'Sikh diaspora' in analyzing migration identity politics over time.[7] Cautioning against the careless adoption of labels, McLeod (1989a, p. 32) states: '[W]e need to be aware that when we talk of Sikh migration we are choosing to use an imprecise adjective.' Both Leonard and he argue that for early twentieth century migrants, what was most meaningful was their common culture, 'their place of origin,' 'their mother tongue,' in essence, their 'Punjabi identity.' According to them, it was only in the later period, that the Sikh aspect of their identity gained salience and served to forge a sense of pan-Sikh consciousness. While conceding the point that the Sikh aspect of early migrant identity may have been subsumed within a broader Punjabi identity, for ease of classification I define the migrants as 'Sikh' rather than 'Punjabi' in my analysis of early settlement patterns. This assumption derives some legitimacy from the fact that several accounts (Tatla, 1999; Buchignani and Indra, 1989; Dusenbery, 1989; Helweg, 1989; Johnston, 1988) indicate that the majority of early Punjabi migrants belonged to the Sikh faith. Norman Buchignani and Doreen Marie Indra (1989, p. 142) for example, claim that because of patterns associated with chain migration, the early Indian emigrant population in North America was extremely homogenous, with Sikhs constituting 90–95 percent of the total migrant community.

In chronicling the evolution of Sikh diasporan political mobilization, this chapter explores the following questions: First, why do diasporan groups (many of whose members have resided outside for generations) have an interest in gaining political autonomy in their homeland? Second, what kinds of institutions heighten and/or sustain diasporan identity-formation and provide a sense of group cohesion in the migrants' host countries? Third, what type of tactics do diasporan groups employ in order to achieve their political objectives? And finally, what role does the political situation in both the homeland and the hostland play in the development of a migrant nationalist ethos?

Sikh identity, migration, and settlement

Given that this study seeks to analyze the political mobilization strategies of the 'Sikh diaspora,' it is necessary to clarify how the term 'Sikh' is employed in this chapter.[8] According to Robin Cohen (1997, p. 107), the Sikhs may be broadly categorized as an 'ethnoreligious' community akin to the Jews. Somewhat ambiguously, the label 'Sikh' simultaneously refers to an ethnic group, a religious community, a nation, and 'a people.'[9] In order to downplay caste differences and emphasize *Khalsa* (the military brother-hood of Sikhs) unity, all initiated Sikh males are given the name Singh (lion) while all women are named Kaur (princess). *Amrit-dhari* (baptized) Sikhs are enjoined to observe five material articles of faith, also referred to as the five *Kakkas* or five 'Ks': *Kesh*, unshorn hair; *Kanga*, comb; *Kachera*, breeches worn under clothing; *Kara*, steel bangle worn on the right hand; and *Kirpan*, sword. While the Sikh community generally accords great respect for the *Khalsa* brotherhood, not all Sikhs have taken *Amrit*. As in any religion, a continuum of ' Sikh-ness' exists within the community at large. While *Amrit-dhari* Sikhs (also known as *Kes-dhari*[10] or *Khalsa*) vigilantly adhere to the five Ks, uninitiated Sikhs (*Sahajdhar*[11]) are selective in the symbols they choose to observe. Some wear the steel bangle but cut their hair and beards while others eschew all religious symbols while still strongly identifying with their Sikh 'heritage.'

As an ethnoreligious community of approximately sixteen million, Sikhs constitute a relatively small percentage of India's total population, usually estimated at less than two percent (1.8% to 1.9%).[12] However, as several scholars (Tatla, 1999; LaBrack, 1989) point out, they are represented overseas in numbers far exceeding this ratio. Recent estimates indicate that eight to ten percent of the total Sikh population of approximately 16 million live outside India (a figure that includes first and second generation foreign-born Sikhs). In a few countries, they comprise a majority of the South Asian population, as in Great Britain, for example, where Sikhs constitute well over fifty percent of all Indian immigrants (LaBrack, 1989; Helweg, 1986). Of the total overseas Sikh population (of approximately one million), over 75 percent are concentrated in three countries: Great Britain, Canada, and the United States (Tatla, 1999, p. 41). Hugh Tinker (1977, 1976, 1974) has claimed that India's internal and external political relations have historically been, and continue to be, strongly influenced by her emigrant communities. This phenomenon is exemplified in the case of overseas Sikhs whose specific migrant experience highlights the extent to which expatriates can exert leverage on and be influenced by the political conditions in their erstwhile homelands.

As several authors (Tatla, 1999; Singh and Barrier, 1996; Barrier and Dusenbery, 1989; Helweg, 1989) document, the Punjab has historically experienced a long tradition of emigration. Despite the fact that the region is endowed with rich natural resources, a rapidly increasing population coupled with restrictive British policies in the late eighteenth and early nineteenth centuries formed 'push' factors that galvanized migration (Tatla, 1999; Helweg, 1989). The roots of the Sikh community's proclivity towards migration may be traced back to the early period of British colonialism. After a series of battles (the First and Second Anglo-Sikh Wars[13]), the British defeated the Sikhs in 1849 and Punjab was annexed into the colonial Empire. With the imposition of British rule in the Punjab, the predominantly agrarian society underwent a profound transformation that resulted in the progressive integration of its economy into the colonial economic system. As numerous accounts (Tatla, 1999; Angelo, 1997; Mahmood, 1996; Goulbourne, 1991; Fox, 1985) attest, the British were considerably impressed with the military prowess of these 'Lions of the Punjab' whom they had fought and conquered and were eager to formally incorporate them into the British Indian army. Racial theories about physiognomy (on which nineteenth century British colonialism was predicated) further lent credence to the view of Sikhs as a 'martial race.' The co-optation of Sikhs into the British Indian army in the service of the British Empire also fit in nicely with the prevailing colonial policy of 'divide and rule.'[14]

The British had, for the purpose of army recruitment, defined a 'Sikh' as meaning an *Amrit-dhari* Sikh, a member of the *Khalsa*. Relevant to issues pertaining to Sikh identity is the fact that the British did not merely encourage the observance of the five 'Ks' by Sikh soldiers but *compelled* them to adhere to *Khalsa* symbols (Fox, 1985, 141–143). As the Sikh population had become heavily dependent on income from service in the armed forces during this time, the British preference for *Amrit-dhari* Sikhs also led to an increasing number of initiations into the *Khalsa* (Mahmood, 1996, pp. 110–111).[15] British colonial policy thus infused the *Khalsa* Sikh movement with a sense of legitimacy and enabled *Khalsa* identity to acquire its subsequent hegemonic status (Oberoi, 1994; Kapur, 1986; Fox, 1985). As Peter van der Veer claims (1994, p. 55), '[t]he Sikh case is an excellent example of the influence of British colonial policies on the development of communal identity.'

According to Peter Goulbourne (1991), the British *Raj* strove to cultivate 'special relationships' with certain groups of her multi-ethnic, multi-linguistic, and multi-religious subjects as part of broader colonial policy. By according certain groups privileges and denying others, the British intentionally exploited longstanding pre-colonial divisions in some cases and created new ethnic rifts in others. In the first major mutiny against British rule in India in 1857,[16] Sikh troops from the princely states remained loyal to the *Raj* and were instrumental in suppressing the rebellion.[17] This loyalty further reinforced the 'special relationship' shared by the British and the Sikhs and led to two important outcomes. First, the Sikhs were granted fertile farmlands in the newly irrigated region of the Punjab. Second, large-scale Sikh enlistment into the armed forces continued, and the numerous and politically dominant *Jat* (peasant farmer caste) Sikhs in particular were heavily recruited by British military officials.[18] Numerous Sikh contingents were deployed to Burma, Hong Kong, Malaya, and the 'islands'[19] in the service of protecting British Imperial interests. Thus, began the long tradition of Sikh emigration and their subsequent settlement in various far-flung places (Tatla 1999, p. 199). Because of their close links to the British armed services, Sikhs tended to be disproportionately represented within overseas Indian communities during the colonial era.[20]

Sikh settlement in North America

According to N. Gerald Barrier (1989, p. 69), the North American West Coast became one of the last, but in several aspects most important, centers of early Sikh migration.[21] Barrier maintains that Sikh settlement in North

America differed from migration to other parts of the world for a number of inter-related reasons. First, this was the only large-scale Sikh migration to a Western country at the beginning of the nineteenth century. Consequently, the issues confronting the Sikhs and their responses to these challenges diverged considerably from their previous experiences in Africa and South East Asia. Second, largely because of the host society's exclusionist sociopolitical structures and the attendant social isolation and political disenfranchisement, Sikhs mobilized more quickly, formulated a broader set of ethnic institutions, and developed a strong national consciousness. Finally, as several authors (Singh, 1994; Barrier, 1989; Buchignani and Indra, 1989; LaBrack, 1988; Juergensmeyer, 1979) contend, the hostile environment that the early migrants faced fueled a strong interest and subsequent involvement in both local and Indian politics.

Most of the early sojourners had arrived in North America through service in the British army and were predominantly from the agrarian region of central Punjab (Chadney, 1984).[22] In the period between 1902–1908, Sikhs settled on the Pacific Coast, mainly in Oregon, Washington, and British Columbia and were employed as unskilled labor in the lumber industry. During these early years, some Sikh pioneers also migrated south to California and worked in the fruit orchards and farmlands in the San Joaquin Valley, which to them was geographically reminiscent of the Punjab.

Sikh migrants received a uniformly hostile reception from the dominant white community and soon became aware that they were the inheritors of several decades of anti-Asian prejudice (Puri 1983; Jacoby 1979).[23] Although the number of Indian migrants totaled no more than a few thousand, the specter of a 'Hindoo'[24] or 'turban tide,' combined with the then prevailing racial attitudes and fears about Asian immigrants as a whole, caused a violent backlash from certain nativist elements. In most cases, the antagonism was directly related to competition for employment, as the new immigrants were often willing to work for considerably lower wages than their native counterparts. In 1907, there were anti-Asian riots in British Columbia against Asians in general (including the Indians, Chinese and Japanese). Later that same year, the Indians were the specific targets of riots in the Bellingham, Washington lumber camps. By late 1908, the riots had moved south to Oregon, while in California, the Exclusion Movement that originally focused its hostility on other Asian groups (such as the Chinese and Japanese) extended its reach to include Indians.

In both the United States and Canada, organized opposition promptly arose in an effort to curtail this new flow of 'undesirables' into 'white man's country.' Consequently, pressures by powerful exclusionary groups led to a series of stringent administrative and legislative measures that effectively curtailed future migration during the second decade of the century.

Canadian immigration measures

Canada began to successfully curb the flow of East Indian immigrants in 1909 by passing legislation that contained the draconian 'continuous journey' clause (Tatla, 1999; Singh, 1994; Jacoby, 1979).[25] This mandated that entrance to Canada be granted only to those immigrants who had arrived by direct steamship from India on tickets purchased in India. Additionally, the amount of cash that an immigrant was required to possess upon arrival increased from $25 to $200. Considering that this was an amount well beyond the reach of most travelers and that there were no steamship lines directly connecting India with Canada, these measures effectively curbed potential immigration from India and served to pacify the increasingly vociferous Canadian exclusionists.

The 'continuous journey' clause specifically aimed at Indians (mainly Sikhs, given the historical pattern of migration) from the Far East resulted in a stark drop in the number of Indians entering the country. Between 1909 and 1913, only twenty-seven passengers were allowed to disembark and permitted entry into Canada. Frustrated by the blatantly racist immigration policies, Sikhs and other Punjabis organized mass protest rallies, sought judicial recourse, and sent several petitions to then secretary of State for India, John Morley. Although a court deemed the 'continuous journey' provision invalid, the Canadian government issued another Order-in-Council that retained the article. Responding to this, the Khalsa Diwan Society (an organization established by Sikh immigrants) led a delegation to Ottawa requesting that the 'continuous journey 'clause be struck down and that Indians receive equitable treatment in cases pertaining to immigration. Given that the Indians were British subjects and that Canada constituted a British dominion, the British colonial government of India also raised objections to the Canadian government's restrictions on Indians claiming that these constraints violated the 'spirit of free movement within the British Empire' (Tatla, 1999, p. 53).

The Komagata Maru episode

Tensions between Canadian immigration officials and Indian immigrants came to a head in 1914, when a Sikh entrepreneur named Gurdit Singh Sarhali chartered a Japanese steam ship, the *Komagata Maru,* in order to transport Indian emigrants to Canada. The *Komagata Maru* picked up 376 Indian passengers[26] (mostly Sikh) from Hong Kong and Shanghai and made its voyage to Canada. The ship anchored at Victoria harbor on May 23, 1914, but was detained and passengers were prohibited from disembarking (although they fulfilled virtually all immigration entrance requirements). The Canadian government immediately placed a 24-hour armed guard launch in order that the ship be kept under constant surveillance. Additionally, Gurdit Singh was isolated from the other passengers and neither he nor others on board were allowed any contact with the Vancouver Sikh community.

Gurdit Singh adamantly maintained that as British subjects the passengers had the prerogative to visit any part of the British Empire as they so chose. Canadian immigration officials viewed the situation somewhat differently and when the immigration team went aboard the ship, it permitted only twenty passengers (who were returnees) to enter the country. After a series of prolonged negotiations, the remaining passengers were issued deportation orders and the *Komagata Maru* was forcibly repatriated. Upon landing in Calcutta, a violent clash erupted between British police personnel and Indian civilians who were outraged at the racist treatment that the passengers had received at the hands of a white government (also see, Deol, 1969).

According to Harish Puri (1983, pp. 77–81), in the minds of the Punjabi community, the term *'Komagata Maru'* subsequently became synonymous with 'British oppression' (1983, p. 69). The incident indelibly marked the political psyche of many Indians, including Sikh soldiers hitherto loyal to the British Empire. There was widespread consensus that if political control of the Indian State had been in Indian hands, then the Indian government would have fought to protect its citizens abroad. According to several scholars (Tatla, 1999; Chadney, 1989; Puri, 1983; Ganguly, 1980; Deol, 1969), the *Komagata Maru* debacle played a significant role in producing fertile ground for the nationalist ideology of the Ghadar movement and, thereafter, the Indian Congress Party.

American attitudes towards Indian immigration

In the first decade of the twentieth century, with the exception of the Chinese Exclusion Act of 1882 and the quasi-statutory 'Gentlemen's Agreement' of 1908 with Japan (barring Japanese workers), there was no United States immigration legislation aimed at any particular national or racial group (Jacoby, 1979). However, as Harold S. Jacoby (1979, p. 162) claims, immigration law in this period did specify 'a number of physical, psychological, economic, and philosophical characteristics, which rendered individuals *as* individuals unwelcome in this country.' Both the interpretation and enforcement of these laws were left to the discretion of the Bureau of Immigration and Naturalization—and the agency had few reservations about applying these provisos to exclude Indian immigrants. With little encouragement from nativist factions and anti-immigrant groups such as the Asiatic Exclusion League, the Bureau swiftly implemented rigorous screening procedures for all Indian immigrants. A direct consequence of these measures was that there was a drastic reduction in the numbers admitted.[27] Far from it being a covert operation, the Bureau officials openly bragged about their biased methods and the high levels of success they had attained as a result.[28] United States immigration restrictions against Asians culminated in the 1917 Barred Zone Act, which designated most of Asia as a geographic zone from which immigrants were barred (Leonard, 2000, p. 194).

Although over ten thousand Sikhs had settled in California between 1904 and 1923, due to strict immigration controls, their numbers had dwindled to a mere three thousand by 1947. From 1920 to 1947, migrants (some of whom had entered the United States illegally via the Mexican/US border) lived in small, secluded communities and worked as agricultural laborers. As Karen Leonard (2000, 1997, 1996, 1992, 1989) recounts in her extensive ethnographic research on Punjabi-American communities, prevailing anti-miscegenation statutes prohibited the migrants from marrying Anglo women, and subsequently, many Sikhs married Mexican women, raised families, and settled in California's Imperial Valley.

One of the most devastating blows to Sikh settlement in America came in the form of a 1923 United States Supreme Court decision. In the 'Thind' case, the Court ruled that although Indians were racially regarded as Caucasian, they could not be classified as 'free white persons' and, therefore, were ineligible for citizenship. This verdict meant that Sikhs would now fall under the jurisdiction of the 1913 California Alien Land Act which restricted the right to register land to American citizens. The original intent of the California Alien Land Act had been to thwart the land-owning aspirations of Japanese farmers—however, the Thind verdict, by stripping Indians of the right to citizenship, effectively extended the California legislation to dispossess them of land ownership rights as well.

Diasporan Sikh institutions and networks[29]

The founding of many Sikh networks and organizations may be traced to the sociopolitical events that were taking place both in North America and in India at the time. During this early period of settlement, Sikh institutional activities centered around three sets of networks (Barrier, p. 1989). First, the Khalsa Diwan Society of Vancouver, founded in 1907, which coordinated several Sikh religious activities, founded *gurdwaras* (Sikh temples), supplied preachers, and raised monies for a variety of local community and Indian social projects. As Barrier (1989, pp. 69–70) highlights, the establishment of the Society served as the catalyst for the creation of a variety of communication networks within segments of the Sikh immigrant community and between Sikhs and their compatriots in the Punjab.[30] The Diwan was also closely affiliated with Khalsa schools (Sikh educational institutions), service organizations, and *gurdwaras* and these institutions also served to forge ties and foster a sense of solidarity within the Sikh community.

One of the biggest issues confronting Canadian Sikhs was the increasingly hostility they encountered in their interactions with mainstream white society. The Canadian Sikh community's feelings of insecurity were further heightened by officially sanctioned persecution in the form of blatantly prejudicial anti-immigration legislation. In 1907, in response, there were impassioned editorials and correspondence detailing these issues in two prominent Sikh publications, the *Khalsa Samachar* and the *Khalsa Advocate*. Barrier (1989, p. 70) cites, for example, an issue of the *Khalsa Samachar* dated April 1, 1908, in which a Sikh named Kartar Singh recounts in detail the maltreatment of Indian immigrants living in Vancouver. By 1913, it could be surmised that the racial situation had deteriorated even further, for the pleas for assistance had become more frequent and plaintive, and information relating to racial harassment had become the primary focus of many publications. There was extensive reporting on delegations sent to both the Canadian and British governments that presented the Indian immigrant community's grievances. Additionally, a group of Canadian-Indian immigrants also visited the Punjab in order to lobby the

British-Indian administration to put pressure on Canada to reform its inequitable immigration code. The Canadian Khalsa Diwan Society supported several of these activities both directly (by coordinating meetings, drafting resolutions and petitions, and sending representatives to meet with government officials) and indirectly (by lending its resources to other immigrant support groups).

Another concern of paramount importance to Sikh immigrants at this time related to the prevailing political and religious upheaval in their Punjabi homeland (Barrier, 1989, pp. 70–71). Canadian Sikhs were actively involved in fund-raising and generated considerable monies that were remitted to India to support political activists and organizations in addition to maintaining Sikh religious and educational institutions. Funds were raised for the Canadian Khalsa Diwan Society, the Educational Conference, and for particular organizations such as the Sikh *Kanya Mahavidyala* in Ferozepur, primarily through appeals made in publications such as the *Khalsa Advocate* and the *Khalsa Samacha* which circulated widely among Vancouver Sikhs. When sending monies to the Punjab, Canadian Sikhs also dispatched copies of Canadian newspapers and other publications—therefore, Sikhs in the Punjab were thoroughly apprised of the situation of their Sikh brothers in Canada. Responding with indignation to reports of Canadian racism against their kinsmen, numerous Sikh organizations in the Punjab coordinated mass protest rallies and sent back donations to help defray legal costs. A 1913 case concerning three Vancouver students barred from attending school in their turbans attracted much attention in the Punjab and generated considerable support for Canadian Sikhs (Barrier, 1989, p. 71).[31]

Barrier (1989, pp. 70–73) further notes that the preoccupation that many Canadian Sikhs had with education and the fate of their religion in the Punjab, was rooted in their own particularly arduous migrant experience. Canadian Sikhs were distinctly aware of the close link between literacy and survival in an alien country and this theme manifested itself in numerous resolutions, meetings, and discussions; it was also the motivation behind the establishment of a Khalsa school that would serve to guarantee a literate community. Education was viewed as a mechanism of upward mobility—there was a sense that if the Sikh community progressed as a whole, it would enhance their image and improve their position vis-à-vis the white Canadian community. Likewise, there was a feeling that if Sikh religious institutions in the Punjab could be strengthened and revitalized, then this would potentially serve as a powerful spiritual resource for Canadian Sikhs.[32]

An organization closely affiliated with the Khalsa Diwan was the Hindustan Ghadar Party. As many migrants realized, repression in the Punjab and subjugation in North America were not isolated phenomena, but rather situations determined by the prevailing geopolitical status quo. This realization was the motivation behind the initial establishment of the Hindustan Association, which subsequently became the Hindustan Ghadar (Revolutionary) Party. As Mark Juergensmeyer (1979) maintains, while a direct correlation cannot be drawn between the establishment of the organization and the hostility and racism that the migrants encountered, it is possible to surmise that economic and social pressures served as a powerful mobilizing force for the nationalist cause. The Hindustan Ghadar Party was unequivocal in its support of self-rule in India and relied heavily on the Khalsa Diwan's membership and resources. The Ghadar group had its own publications and revolutionary mission and while it drew many of its members from the Sikh community, was primarily a Pan-Indian nationalist organization.

The second type of institutions in which Sikhs participated were the 'pan-Indian' organizations that had emerged in several American and Canadian cities to serve the new migrants' needs. Membership in these clubs was open to all religious groups—Hindus, Muslims, and Sikhs—and social and educational programs were designed to provide a wide range of 'practical' support.

A third set of networks was instituted via the Pacific Coast Khalsa Diwan Society (PCKD) which was founded in 1912 in the San Francisco area. Religious, educational, and social programs coordinated by the PCKD closely resembled those organized by the Canadian Khalsa Diwan. Sikhs in the Stockton area also actively participated in PCKD programs, although they maintained their own separate *diwans* and *gurdwaras*. While its leadership was drawn subsequently from Sikhs in the Stockton area, its prominent founding members included several Sikh visitors from India.

The Ghadar movement

According to Mark Juergensmeye (1979), while the Ghadar movement is historically situated within the context of Indian nationalism, it in fact reveals more about the early Punjabi (and by extension Sikh) migrant experience than it does about the freedom struggle in India. Certain scholars (Juergensmeyer, 1979; Puri, 1983) point out that two separate, albeit inter-related, dialectics worked in tandem to produce the Ghadar militancy—while the movement was unarguably a manifestation of nationalist support, its establishment also represented the anger and insecurity felt by a marginalized immigrant community. The movement served as a conduit for the channeling of frustrations endured by the new migrants increasingly beleaguered by their deteriorating situation. Thus, individual hardships encountered by Indian immigrants in North America became immediately and inextricably linked to the national subjugation of Indians in British-ruled India. The bitterness felt by many migrants in response to the racism they experienced at the hands of white North American employers, landlords, and police officers, was transformed into bitterness against white British rulers in India. The intense passion and level of commitment that the movement invoked in the migrant community (to the extent that many were willing to sacrifice their lives for the nationalist cause) may be attributed to 'the fusion of nationalism with other, more personal, experiences' (Juergensmeyer, 1979, p. 175). The motivation behind the formation of the Ghadar party may thus be found in both the American and Indian contexts of the migrant experience. As Juergensmeyer (1979, pp. 173–174) suggests, in the new North American context, the issues of the old British Imperial context gained a heightened salience. In his analysis, therefore, the struggle against oppression in North America and India became fused into one unified struggle—*Ghadar* or revolution—against white hegemony in general.

Although there were some links between the Ghadar leadership and autochthonous political activists in India, the movement operated independently of the freedom movement in India and was largely autonomous. Emphasizing the distinctly self-contained nature of the movement, Juergensmeyer (1979, p. 173) asserts that '[t]he *Ghadar* movement was not only based in North America, it almost wholly existed within North America....' Both Puri (1983, pp. 85–86) and Juergensmeyer (1979, p. 73) further note that most Ghadarites were markedly more militant than most nationalists back in India. Puri (1983, p. 85) recounts that 'most of the Ghadar men had expected to find their compatriots in the Punjab in a state of readiness' but instead 'their fellowmen in Punjab considered the Ghadar men, to be crazy.' Exile militancy, however, is unsurprising, given that exiles are generally less constrained in their activities than their compatriots in the homeland. According to Benedict Anderson (1994, 1992), this brand of 'long distance nationalism' is inherently more militant than a homegrown variety *precisely* because exile protagonists have the freedom to engage politically while remaining unaccountable for their consequences. Moreover, as Yossi Shain (1989, p. 39) suggests, diasporan insecurity, rooted in perceptions that they have limited control over developments in the motherland, often results in them being more dogmatic and unyielding than their native counterparts. This resonates with Lord Acton's claims that 'exile is the nursery of nationality' and that national consciousness arises from exile because men can no longer dream of easily returning to the motherland in which they had been born.[33]

Ghadar militants, for example, had created a romantic chimera in which they would invade India, mobilize the masses into a spontaneous liberation struggle, and heroically herald the birth of a new independent nation. Ultimately, however, the Ghadar movement did not realize its lofty goal of ending British imperialism. It became susceptible to rampant factionalism rooted in ideological differences (a common malady that plagues political groups in general and exile movements in particular) and split into two separate camps in 1917. While the Party formally came to a demise only at the time of Indian independence, as early as the 1930s, the 'politics of schism' (Shain, 1989) had eroded the last vestiges of its political strength and undermined its legitimacy even among champions of Indian nationalism.

During its early stages, the Ghadar movement's membership was drawn from a broad base of Indian migrants whose political interests and backgrounds were as varied as their professional affiliations (Puri, 1983; Ganguly, 1980; Juergensmeyer, 1979). The revolutionary coalition comprised agricultural laborers, priests, political refugees, students, and visiting intellectuals, whose educational and class status varied considerably. For example, members included, Bab Sohan Singh Bhakna (a founding member of the movement who had previously worked as a laborer in the Oregon lumber industry), Jawala Singh (a Stockton potato farmer who helped finance the movement), Bhagwan Singh (a *gyani* [Sikh priest] who led the party after 1917), and Karatar Singh Sarabha (who had come to the United States in the early 1900s to attend the University of California, Berkeley and was subsequently killed in an uprising in the Punjab).

As numerous scholars (Anderson, 1991; Lal, 1990; Singaravélou, 1990; Tinker, 1990; Helweg, 1989; Juergensmeyer, 1979) posit, the experience of being a foreigner in an alien land frequently has the effect of sharpening ethnonational, linguistic, and religious identities. For non-white immigrants in North America, this sense of being the perennial outsider was further intensified by officially sanctioned xenophobia in the form of blatantly anti-non-white immigrant policies. In understanding the historical evolution of the Ghadar movement, it is thus necessary to examine the chronological framework within which events took place during this period.

Between 1910 and 1913, a series of incidents occurred that served to foster mass support for the movement. The tightening of Canadian immigration rules resulted in Indian migrants increasingly settling in the United States. The last year of large-scale immigration to the United States was 1910, and that same year widespread anti-immigrant riots erupted in both Oregon and California. In 1910, Tarak Nath Das instituted the formal struggle for Indian independence in Washington, and in 1911, Har Dayal (generally considered the founding father of the movement) began coordinating Ghadar activities in California. In 1913, California's notorious Alien Land Laws were established, and that year also saw a visible expansion of Ghadar activities. In May 1913, the Hindi Association of the Pacific Coast was founded in Oregon by Har Dayal and Bab Sohan Singh Bhakna. That same year, Har Dayal established the Ghadar Party's political headquarters in the Yuguntar Ashram in San Francisco. Another watershed in the movement's history was that the Party's official newspaper, the *Ghadar,* began publication on November 1, 1913.

In 1914, Indian immigrants experienced one of the more violent phases in their short settlement history. That year, both European and Asian migrant laborers went on strike in the hop fields of Wheatland, California to protest exploitative working conditions. Strike breakers and anti-labor gangs were brutal in their targeting and treatment of Asian immigrant workers, and Indians in particular, suffered the brunt of the violence. These riots permanently marked the Sikh community and played a pivotal role in forging a sense of group solidarity and raising political consciousness. As Juergensmeyer (1979) notes, the date of the riots is significant—later on that same year, in the aftermath of the riots, the Ghadar party experienced its greatest expansion and consolidated its position within the immigrant community.

Juergensmeyer (1979, p. 76) claims that '[i]n reviewing the history of the development of the Ghadar movement, one notices a sort of rebound effect between acts of racial hostility against the immigrant Punjabis and new developments within the movement. And there is also an interaction between events in the Punjab and the activities of the immigrant Punjabis. The two sets of relationships seem to be the incendiary combination necessary for the militancy of Ghadar.' While there are no conclusive social scientific data that supports a causal relationship between immigrant alienation and nationalist proclivities, it may be surmised as Juergensmeyer contends, that the prevailing anti-non-white immigrant ethos and nativist violence greatly helped mobilize support for the Ghadar movement. Thus, while the movement may be seen as a manifestation of exile nationalist solidarity with their compatriots in India, it also needs to be understood within the context of immigrant identity politics. In addition, this early politicization of the North American Sikh migrant community would, more than half a century later, serve as a model for Khalistani activism (Tatla, 1999, p. 211; Mahmood, 1996, p. 111; Helweg, 1993, pp. 78–79; Juergensmeyer, 1988).

In 1946, the United States rescinded the 1917 Barred Zone Act with the enactment of the Luce-Celler bill that allowed limited immigration (an annual quota of approximately one hundred people) from India. Officially titled the India Immigration and Naturalization Act of 1946, it also made early Sikh settlers eligible for citizenship. Indian immigration was further revitalized by the Immigration and Nationality Act of 1965 that based admission on professional criteria rather than race (Leonard, 2000, 1992; LaBrack, 1989, 1988). A similar situation took place in Canada, which began to dismantle its anti-Asian immigration policies after the Second World War. South Asian immigration rose steadily from a handful in 1947 to a high of 12,868 from India alone in 1974. Most of the arrivals in the 1950s were Sikhs, mostly friends and relatives of the early settlers (Joy, 1989). Even in the 1960s, when immigration laws were changed to encourage highly skilled professionals and non-Sikhs started arriving in larger numbers, Punjabi Sikhs still accounted for roughly half the Indian immigrants. In the 1970s, as the criteria for migration changed to favor semi-skilled labor, Sikhs still constituted almost half of all Indian immigrants because of the chain migration process (O'Connell, 2000, p. 192). The political and social institutions and alliances that had been formed by early Sikh settlers during the Ghadar period, played an instrumental role in the politicization of these later arrivals.

The evolution of Khalistan

While the historical demand for Sikh autonomy may be traced to the aftermath of Indian independence, the immediate antecedents to the expansion of the Khalistan movement for an independent Sikh state are rooted in events that transpired in the Punjab during the early 1980s. Until then, Khalistan was an obscure, fringe movement that was little-known to most Indians, including most Sikhs—the select few who were aware of its existence generally regarded it with derision. If the trajectory of Punjabi politics had taken an alternative route, then the agitation for a separate Sikh state could have been dismissed as the clamoring of a few hyper-nationalist radicals. Khalistani activism would have continued in its original inconspicuous form and the movement would have been considered no more than a minor footnote in history. However, actions taken by the Indian government, particularly during the 1980–1985 period, led to the movement gaining mass support and transmogrifying into a violent guerilla insurrection that was framed in ethnoreligious terms.

Peter Goulbourne (1991, pp. 155–158) suggests that there are two versions of how the concept of Khalistan was initially formulated. According to one account, Sikh separatism was first promulgated by a segment of Sikhs within the Punjab during an All Indian Sikh Students Federation rally on August 15, 1972. The other version of the movement's inception chronicles its diasporan roots and highlights the exile element that shaped the movement during its early stages. In this latter account, a Sikh named Davinder Singh Parmar traveled to London in late 1954 and started championing the idea that a separate Sikh state was essential for Sikhs to survive as a community. Parmar was widely ridiculed by his British Sikh compatriots who, at this time, regarded India with a great deal of affection. It was only in 1970, when Parmar met a newly-arrived Sikh physician by the name of Dr. Jagjit Singh Chohan, that his commitment to Sikh separatism finally received reinforcement. Chohan, an ardent champion of Sikh sovereignty, also possessed some Punjabi political credentials. He had been Secretary of the Master Tara faction of the Akali Dal (the Sikh political party) and had also served as the Finance Minister of the Punjab. With Chohan's support, the formal inauguration of the Khalistan movement took place at a press conference at the Waldorf Hotel in Aldwych (just opposite the Indian High Commissioner's office).

As both Chohan and Parmar recount, in the early years, most fellow Sikhs regarded them as 'madmen' and disapproved of their anti-Indian demonstrations and activities. Citing his 'unpatriotic behavior,' several *gurdwaras* barred Chohan from attending religious services and made a concerted effort to distance themselves from him.[34] Most British Sikhs (including those who considered themselves religiously observant) considered him an outright embarrassment to the community and disdainfully viewed the movement as a manifestation of an expatriate's nostalgic fantasies. The leadership of the Akali Dal both in Great Britain and in India publicly denounced his 'radical' position and unceremoniously banished him from the Party. Chohan subsequently went back to the Punjab in 1977 and returned to England in 1980, at which point, the Indian authorities revoked his passport. Although they did not request Chohan's extradition, the Indian government exhorted Great Britain, Canada, and the United

States to suppress the political activities of the small group of Khalistani activists who were residing within their jurisdiction. The host governments refused, citing their liberal-democratic traditions and the fact that no laws were being broken in their three respective countries (Helweg, 1989).

From 1980–1983 the movement gradually gained momentum and expanded to include a small group of volunteers and supporters. In April 1980, Shri Balbir Singh Sandhu (who had been appointed the Secretary General of the National Council of Khalistan), announced the establishment of an eleven member Council of Khalistan that would serve as the vanguard in the worldwide struggle for Sikh sovereignty. In June, Chohan also sent out press releases under the auspices of the International Council of Sikhs to the British media. The dispatches proclaimed that the Khalistan government would establish Consulates in Great Britain and other parts of Western Europe and also specified the geographical dimensions of the new nation. In the vision of Chohan and his supporters, the state of Khalistan would encompass territory spanning from Porbander on the Arabian Sea to Chamba in Himachal Pradesh and would be 850 miles long. At its widest point it measured 200 miles and the map stated that it was 'approved by the All Parties Sikhs Conference London' (Helweg, 1989, p. 315). The Khalistan leadership's plans included establishing an exile government and organizing a 10,000 strong rebel army in the United States. 'Official' Khalistan state documents such as passports, currency, and stamps were also printed in order to legitimize the movement. Another prime objective was to obtain counselor status in the United Nations, but their bid was subsequently denied in 1987 because there was no consensus on who constituted the group's legitimate leadership. On June 8, 1980, Sandhu made the movement's first formal broadcast proclaiming the creation of the state of Khalistan from a radio transmitter at the Golden Temple in Amritsar (in the Punjab). He also issued press releases announcing the establishment of a government of Khalistan (Helweg, 1989).

In the United States, Shri Ganga Singh Dhillon (a naturalized US citizen and President of the Washington based Sri Nankan Sahib Foundation) was quick to adopt the cause and was instrumental in its promotion. Chohan and Dhillon were also in contact with certain factions of the leadership in Pakistan and had also succeeded in enlisting the support of key US political figures, including Senator Mark Hatfield, Senator Jesse Helms, Senator Sam Nunn, and Representative James C. Corman (see Helweg, 1989, pp. 313–316). However, despite this 'international' base of support, most Sikhs paid scant attention to the issue of Sikh separatism, and even at the beginning of 1984, the Khalistan struggle was still essentially limited to a tightly-knit coterie of activists.

The catastrophic events that took place in India in the post-June 1984 period, however, dramatically altered the course of the movement both inside and outside India. June 1984 marks a milestone in the movement's history—for many Sikhs who had originally criticized the separatist movement for being too radical, now increasingly embraced Sikh self-determination as their only means of ethnopolitical salvation. As several scholars (Tatla, 1999; Mahmood, 1996; Goulbourne, 1991; Helweg, 1989; Singh and Malik, 1985) maintain, the role the Indian government played in contributing to the almost exponential popularity of the movement during the 1980s is indisputable. Mass support for Khalistan during the mid-1980s was a manifestation of the deep-seated fear and insecurity felt by an erstwhile allegiant community that had almost overnight been transformed by the realization that the Indian State viewed it as the 'enemy within.'

Punjab's political situation

The 1980s and early 1990s mark a turbulent phase in the history of Punjabi politics in which Sikhs experienced unprecedented levels of violence at the hands of both the Indian government and Khalistani militants. The multifarious causes of the conflict in the Punjab are deeply rooted in the region's post-independence history and have been thoroughly chronicled in several works (Ahmed, 1999, 1996; Tatla, 1999; Gupta, 1996; Hardgrave, 1994; Mehta, 1994; Oberoi, 1993; Eimbree, 1990; Major, 1985; Jeffrey, 1987, 1986; Singh, 1987; Samiuddin, 1985; Chopra, Mishra, and Singh, 1984; Lal, 1984; Wallace, 1985; Wallace and Chopra, 1981; Rai, 1965). It is adequate to note, within the context of this analysis, that the Akali Dal and the Indian central government had battled on a number of fronts that ranged from water rights to linguistic and religious issues. A crucial precipitating factor of the region's political unrest was Prime Minister Indira Gandhi's cavalier dismissal in 1980 of Punjab's elected state legislature, which was for the first time controlled by the Akali Dal. The Akali leadership's anger and alienation were further exacerbated when Gandhi's Congress Party was elected by a narrow margin in the state elections held in May that same year.

It is widely believed (Tatla, 1999; Wallace, 1998; Ahmed, 1996; Tully and Jacob, 1985) that Indira Gandhi and her advisors (in particular her younger son, Sanjay) attempted to politically divide the Sikh community in order to counter the Akali Dal's growing influence. The manifestation of these efforts took the form of a young charismatic militant preacher by the name of Sant Jarnail Singh Bhindranwale. While Bhindranwale's fiery oratory attracted some of the younger unemployed members of the community, his appeal was by no means widespread (Pettigrew, 1987). Most Sikhs viewed him with varying degrees of trepidation as an extremist or fundamentalist with whom they shared little common ground. His lack of mass appeal is evinced by the fact that despite the Congress Party's large-scale support, the Sant won only four seats during the 1979 *gurdwara* elections (Wallace, 1998). The leadership of the Congress Party soon became aware, however, that they had seriously miscalculated their ability to control Bhindranwale and disagreements between the two became increasingly acrimonious. Far from creating a pliable political puppet, they realized too late, that they had, in fact, created a 'Frankenstein's Monster' (Wallace, 1998). The relationship between Congress and Bhindranwale ultimately culminated in unfeigned hostility and Bhindranwale became more vocal and insistent in his calls for Sikh autonomy.[35] Contrary to their desired effect, the repressive measures employed by the government to contain the militancy of Bhindranwale and his supporters only served to expand his popularity (Banerjee, 1996). As subsequent events would starkly demonstrate, the intrigue spawned by Indira Gandhi's Congress Party in the 1970s would have far- and wide-reaching political consequences in the decades to come.

1984: The reaffirmation of Sikh solidarity

Political violence continued to escalate in the Punjab, with both the police and the militants engaging in increasingly virulent tactics.[36] In October 1983, President's Rule (direct rule by the central government) was imposed and the Punjab was classified as 'a disturbed area.' The following April, militant gangs organized attacks on several railway stations in their campaign to disrupt the region's transportation networks. In response, the Indian government dispatched the Central Reserve Police Force and the Border Security Force to the Punjab. The militant All India Sikh Students Federation was disbanded and there was a wide curtailment of a variety of civil rights and liberties.

By April that year, Bhindranwale and his groups of militants had taken refuge in the Golden Temple, the Sikh's holiest temple, in Amritsar. At this time, it was rumored that the Sant and his associates had heavily armed themselves and were in the process of barricading buildings within the compound (Tully and Jacob, 1985). In May 1984, the Indian Army was deployed to the Punjab ostensibly to aid civil authorities suppress the nascent militancy. Both Bhindranwale and the Akali Dal leader, Harchand Singh Longowal, demanded their immediate withdrawal and threatened massive demonstrations in retaliation if their demands were ignored. Their demands went unheeded, and on June 4, 1984, in an effort to crush the militant movement, Indian armed forces attacked the Sikh's most sacred shrine, the *Akal Tahkt*, and other buildings within the compound of the Golden Temple. Code-named 'Operation Blue Star,' the military assault resulted in the mass destruction of the Golden Temple along with a number of irreplaceable religious artifacts and relics.[37] The attack also resulted in the deaths of hundreds of Sikhs, including Bhindranwale, two of his closest associates (Amrik Singh and Shabegh Singh), militants, and visiting pilgrims. The fact that the military offensive coincided with Guru Arjun's[38] martyrdom commemorations (on June 3), when thousands of pilgrims were visiting the Golden Temple, further served to underscore the magnitude of the sacrilege.

Both Indian and diasporan Sikhs considered the army attack as the ultimate assault against their religion. Sikhs around the globe reacted with profound grief and disbelief at the desecration of a holy site that was in both material and symbolic terms the mainstay of their existence as a religious community. While numerous Sikhs had previously condemned the extremism of Bhindranwale and his supporters, there was now a sense that the militants had been correct in their original assessment of the Indian government. The horror at the atrocity was palpable among all strata within the community regardless of religiosity or political affiliation. Several prominent Sikh public figures were vocal in their condemnation of the attack and publicly returned honors bestowed on them by the Indian government.[39] Likewise, two Sikh Members of Parliament and a few high-ranking Sikh army personnel immediately resigned their position while several Sikh regiments mutinied (Tatla, 1999; Tully and Jacob, 1985). Countless numbers of diasporan Sikhs, who until this point had regarded India as their 'motherland' and retained their Indian passports, began acquiring the citizenship of the countries in which they resided. Statements such as the following were frequently voiced: 'Let us burn our Indian passports, we no longer belong to India... We are Americans and Sikhs and proud to be so. We are not just American Sikhs'[40] (Tatla, 1999, p. 196). The Sikh community, which had hitherto been deeply divided on the issue of separatism, was transformed almost overnight into one that was united in their opposition to the actions of the Indian State. Bhindranwale himself could not have envisioned or engendered the kind of solidarity that Sikhs exhibited in the post-Operation Blue Star period—a solidarity, ironically, that was wrought by the actions of the Indian government.

Operation Blue Star was followed by Operation Woodrose that was designed as a 'clean up' offensive to 'eliminate' any residual elements of the militant movement. As numerous human rights reports attest, in the months that followed, thousands of young Sikh men were arbitrarily arrested (often on trumped-up charges) and brutally tortured. Many of them died while in police custody or alternatively were officially reported as 'missing' or 'disappeared.' In what many (Tatla, 1999; Gupte, 1985; Tully and Jacob, 1985) consider a retaliatory act, Indira Gandhi was assassinated by two of her Sikh bodyguards on October 31, 1984. Gandhi's assassination sparked widespread anti-Sikh riots, one of the most violent episodes in Delhi's recent history (Gupte, 1985; Tambiah, 1996; Kothari and Sethi, 1985).[41] Mobs dragged Sikhs off buses and trains, brutally beat them and tore off their turbans, burned and destroyed their property (and looted any remaining items), and in several cases, poured gasoline on them and burned them alive (Mahmood, 1996; Tambiah, 1996). Ostensibly, the mobs were intent on 'avenging Indira Gandhi's death' and were determined to 'teach the Sikhs a lesson.' However, the pogrom-like quality of the riots has been noted by several scholars (Tatla, 1999; Gupta, 1996; Tambiah, 1996; Mulgrew, 1988; Tully and Jacob, 1985; Singh, 1985), who contend that the massacres were not so much a manifestation of spontaneous grief but rather an organized State-sponsored effort to humiliate the Sikhs as a community. The government's inaction in containing the violence and the overt complicity of certain army and police personnel in aiding and abetting the mobs, further contributed to Sikh alienation.[42]

The Punjabi term *'ghallughara'* (holocaust) is invoked by many Sikhs to describe the events of 1984, which they view as a concerted effort by the Indian government to obliterate them as a community. Similarly, in much of the Sikh-produced literature (Jaijee, 1995) that focused on this period, the word 'genocide' is routinely employed to describe anti-Sikh violence that was committed or condoned by an increasingly 'chauvinist' Indian state. Many Sikhs felt during this time, that separatism, constituted the most logical response to what they perceived as 'Brahminical tyranny' (Mitra, 1996, p. 23). Operation Blue Star, Operation Woodrose, and the Delhi massacres would permanently mark the collective memory of Sikhs both within and without the diaspora. Sikhs in India felt that they could no longer trust the Indian State to safeguard their rights, while overseas Sikhs were frustrated by their impotence in alleviating their compatriots' suffering. These two factors greatly contributed to the mass political mobilization of Sikhs in the mid-1980s and led to the Khalistan movement's largest expansion during that same period.[43] Even moderate Sikhs within and without India now regarded the notion of a separate state, which had previously been eschewed by much of the community, as a reasonable and viable option.

North American Khalistani activism

In the aftermath of Operation Blue Star (which Darshan Singh Tatla [1999] refers to as 'the critical event' that heightened Sikh consciousness), Sikhs in North America were quick to rally around the separatist cause. Numerous pro-Khalistan organizations mushroomed almost overnight, many headed by political neophytes with little or no prior activist experience. Some of the main organizations that were formed during the 1984–1986 period included the Council for Khalistan, International Sikh Organization, the Babbar Khalsa International (which had formed in Vancouver in 1981 but came into prominence in the wake of 1984), International Sikh Youth Federation, National Council of Khalistan, and the Sikh Youth of America. All these groups were encapsulated by the World Sikh Organization, an umbrella organization that purports to represent the entire diasporan Sikh community. While the organizations share the common objective of Sikh sovereignty, their leadership, resources, and methods of mobilization have differed significantly (Tatla, 1999). The Babbar Khalsa International is the most militant in its philosophy, maintains offices in both New York and California (as well as in Canada and Europe), and is viewed as an 'effective but closed organization' (Anand, 1997). The once extremely active World Sikh Organization, based in Yuba City, California, has been more recently marginalized by several newer and more vocal organizations. Many of these groups have attempted to shape American foreign policy towards India, with the Council of Khalistan being the most active.

The long embittered Cold War history of US-Indian diplomatic relations proved advantageous to Khalistani Sikhs in their lobbying efforts in America.[44] Despite the fact that Indo-US relations have improved considerably in recent years, Congress members (especially Republicans) are particularly attentive to charges of Indian human rights violations. Framing the right to Sikh self-determination in terms of a human rights issue, Khalistani activists succeeded in winning over several Congress members to their side. The Council of Khalistan (based in Washington D.C. but with ties to Great Britain and the Punjab) headed by charismatic former physician, Dr. Gurmit Singh Aulakh, has played an important role in obtaining congressional support for the Khalistani cause. The self-proclaimed 'grassroots information center for the Khalistan freedom struggle' publishes newsletters, maintains an e-mail listserve and Internet web site (that provides frequent updates on the human rights situation in the Punjab), and engages in a variety of other public relations and fund-raising activities. The Council has been relatively successful in gaining sympathy from a long list of bipartisan congressional supporters, most notably Congressman Dan Burton (Republican—Indiana), Chair of the Campaign Finance Reform Committee, and Senator Jesse Helms (Republican—North Carolina), Chair of the Senate Foreign Relations Committee. In July 1997 Congressman Burton introduced the 'Burton Amendment' to the Foreign Operations Bill that would limit American development aid to India until human rights violations were investigated and accounted for. Although the bill was subsequently defeated, it received support from a number of prominent members of Congress.[45]

The Council of Khalistan, with the aid of these supporters, has managed to publicize their case in the media on a regular basis.[46] It also publishes a monthly English newsletter that highlights the human rights situation in the Punjab and includes graphic photographs and excerpts from interviews with police torture victims and their families.[47] Another Washington-based lobbying group, the Khalistan Affairs Center also issues media releases highlighting the situation in the Punjab. In addition to the physical presence of these pro-Khalistani groups, there have been increasing efforts to recreate the resistance struggle in cyberspace (Gunawardena, 2000). Both the Khalistan Affairs Center[48] and the Council of Khalistan[49] maintain elaborate web sites on the Internet that contain daily news updates from the Punjab. Supplementing these efforts, numerous other organizations and *gurdwaras* across the United States continue in varying degrees to promote the idea of an independent Sikh homeland and rally diasporan Sikh support for the cause.

While Khalistani Sikhs in the United States have been successful in portraying the struggle as one that is grounded in human rights infringement, their counterparts in Canada have met with more limited success. A selection of Khalistan organizations in Canada include the World Sikh Organization-Canada, based in Ottawa, the International Sikh Youth Federation with branches in both Vancouver and Toronto, and the ultra-militant Bhabbar Khalsa founded in Vancouver. In the post-1984 period, *gurdwara* support for Khalistan mirrored the situation in the United States, with many remitting funds to support the insurgency in the Punjab (O'Connell, 2000, p. 198). These organizations have not been viewed favorably by most Anglo-Canadians who perceive Khalistani Sikhs as an 'irksome minority' that instigates violence and supports terrorism. This is largely due to the 1985 Air India crash in which 374 people (the majority of whom were Canadian citizens of Indian origin) were killed. While some (Mulgrew, 1988; Blaise and Mukherjee, 1985) maintain that Khalistani militants were responsible for the bombing, others (Kashmeri and McAndrew, 1989) allege that Indian intelligence agents themselves may have been the perpetrators. In addition to the Air India tragedy, a number of violent incidents have occurred within the Khalistani community regarding ideology, leadership, and strategy, which have further undermined the movement's credibility with both Sikh- and Anglo-Canadians. By its unrelenting militant stance and proclamations, the Bhabbar Khalsa, in particular, has reinforced the Canadian public's suspicion concerning the movement's militant tendencies. In response to claims that Canada was harboring Khalistani terrorist organizations, an Indo-Canadian extradition treaty was signed in 1987 (Tatla, 1999).

In 1992, the Indian government's violent counter-insurgency (that had been waged since the early 1980s) finally succeeded in crushing the militant movement in the Punjab. As several authors and human rights agencies (Pettigrew, 1998, 1995; Thandi, 1996; Human Rights Watch, 1994) maintain, the campaign was both brutal and indiscriminate in its targeting of 'subversives' and rural Sikhs unduly suffered.[50] In 1992 the government held elections which were considered a farce by many observers and were, therefore, boycotted by all the major political parties (Tatla, 1999; Singh 1992). In 1995, the Central Government permitted the Akali Dal to formally re-enter the political arena. In the 1997 elections, a coalition (regarded by many as strange bed fellows) comprising the Akali Dal and the Hindu nationalist Bharatiya Janata Party (BJP) came to power (Singh, 1997). The resumption of 'normalcy' to the Punjab, and the frequent internecine conflicts that arose among various diasporan Khalistani factions, have together contributed to the movement's waning popularity in North America in recent years (Mann, 2000; O'Connell, 2000; Tatla, 1999; Wallace, 1998; Anand, 1997; Corriea, 1997; Dorgan, 1997). There remains, however, a diehard group of Khalistani activists that aspires to nothing short of a separate state and continues tirelessly in its mobilization efforts.

Conclusion

The wide range of relations that exists (and has historically existed) between North American Sikh migrants and their compatriots in the Punjab is multi-faceted and deserves a much more comprehensive treatment than the one provided in this chapter. However, even a cursory examination of the Ghadar and Khalistan movements reveals how and why diasporas based on enduring ethnic affinities embrace political struggles in their homeland. While the Ghadar movement demonstrates that migrants have historically played a role in homeland politics, the Khalistan agitation illustrates the way in which this role has been expanded in our current age of rampant globalization.

The last two decades' revolutionary advances in travel, information, and communication technologies have the ability to transform the ways in which diasporas conceive of and relate to their homelands. Technologies that transcend conventional notions of time and space (such as the Internet, in particular), with their potential to generate a new kind of transnational civil society with a shared consciousness, have been, and increasingly will be, deployed by various exile and diasporan groups to achieve their particular political objectives. This has significant implications for issues relating to state sovereignty and security in both migrant-sending and migrant-receiving countries. With the dissolution of traditional state boundaries, it will no longer be possible to contain ethnonationalist conflict and its devastation within the confines of any one territorial state. As the Khalistan case demonstrates, ethnic conflict will not be merely something that happens 'out there' in Asia, Africa, or Latin America, but will increasingly be imported 'over here' to Europe and North America. Moreover, as the Ghadar movement evinces, the recent xenophobic ethos that has reared itself in many policies of the 'political right' in Europe, the United States, and Canada, will further serve to propel non-white immigrants towards their homeland for approbation.

Despite the importance of this phenomenon within the context of ethnonationalist conflict and resolution, it has yet to receive commensurate attention from either the academic community or governmental officials. Discussing the Khalistan case, Madhu Kishwar (1998) concludes that the Indian government needs to effectively engage Sikh diasporan groups if it wishes to provide a genuine and enduring solution in the Punjab. This is a charge that might well be extended to other governments entrenched within the chaos rendered by ethnonationalist conflict.

Notes

1. A verse from a popular Canadian Punjabi song composed by Madan Maddi. Quoted in Tatla, 1999, p. 113.
2. Insightful analyses of some of the external factors that impact ethnic conflict are provided in Ganguly and Taras (1998); Brown (1996); Bose (1994); de Silva and May (1991); Phadnis (1989, pp. 210–240); Pellizzi (1988).
3. A phrase employed by Gabriel Sheffer (1986, p. 1) to describe these new transnational relations.
4. Much of the primary data for this chapter was collected as part of a wider doctoral dissertation project that examines Khalistani activism in the United States, Canada, and Great Britain.
5. An earlier version of this study titled 'From Pan-Indianism to Pan-Sikhism: An Analysis of Ghadar and Khalistan' was presented at the 50th Annual Meeting of the Association of Asian Studies, Washington, D.C., March 26–29, 1998.
6. It is important to note that not all Sikhs support Khalistan, and even among those who do, there is disagreement about what strategies to employ. See, for example, the report by Warren Una (1985), the *Statesman*'s Washington, D.C. correspondent.
7. This issue is explored further in Dusenbery's (1995, pp. 17–42) discussion.
8. For obvious reasons, I exclude Western Sikh converts also referred to as *Gora* (white) Sikhs from this discussion.
9. As many scholars note, the development of the teachings of the Sikh gurus into a coherent, distinct whole has been an intensely political process. See, for example, the work of Oberoi (1994, 1987); Goulbourne (1991, pp. 126–169); McLeod (1989b, 1980); Kapur (1986); Fox (1985).
10. Meaning 'a Sikh who has unshorn hair.'
11. Which loosely translated means 'innate, i.e., not marked by outward symbols' (O'Connell, 2000, p. 196).
12. The figure varies between this range, depending on what you read in different kinds of government documents and scholarly articles.
13. A detailed account of these wars is provided in Nijjar (1976).
14. Incidentally, Goulbourne (1991, p. 149) states that when India was granted independence in 1947, the policy of the colonial rulers was no longer 'divide and rule' but to 'divide and quit.'
15. As the Punjab administration report for 1856–1857 highlights, 'Sikhism ... which had previously fallen off so much, seems again to be slightly on the increase. During the past year the baptismal initiations at the Amritsar temple have been more numerous than during the preceding year. Sikhism is not dormant.' Cited in Kapur (1986, pp. 11–12).
16. Also referred to as the 'Sepoy Mutiny.' A detailed account is provided in Watson (1991).
17. This drastically changed with the Jallianwalla Bagh massacre in 1919 when General Dyer of the British colonial army gave orders to fire on an unarmed crowd of protesters. Over four hundred people were killed and over 1,200 were wounded. Many of the victims were Sikhs who had gathered for the rally, which

was a founding episode in the struggle for Indian independence. This event would serve to permanently alienate the Sikhs from the British in later years.

18. A result of this was the subsequent 'punjabization' of the infantry regiments, with Sikh battalions increasing from twenty-eight to fifty-seven during the 1862–1914 period. In the First World War, the numbers of Sikhs fighting under the British flag rose from 35,000 to 100,000.

19. A term that historically denoted essentially all of the islands that comprise South Asia.

20. After completing their contracts with the police and security services in Hong Kong and the Malaya states, some retired Sikhs settled in Australia and New Zealand in the early 1890s. Another group (mainly from the *Ramgarhia* 'artisan' caste) migrated to Africa, primarily to the eastern areas that would subsequently become Kenya, Tanzania, and Uganda. They formed the bulk of Indian indentured labor recruited for the Ugandan Railways Project in the 1890s. Additionally, small groups such as the *Bhatra* (peddler caste) Sikhs chose to settle in Britain, and worked as petty traders in the Midlands and in the North.

21. Although my discussion focuses on Punjabi Sikhs, it should be noted that some Hindu and Muslim Punjabis also migrated to the North American West Coast during this period.

22. Predominantly from the Jalandhar and Hoshiarpur districts.

23. For example, there was widespread prejudice against immigrants from China and Japan, and in many cases, official policies merely reflected prevailing racist attitudes. For a comprehensive analysis of the factors that contributed to this hostile environment, see Roy (1989).

24. At this time, all Indians regardless of their religious affiliation, were referred to as 'Hindoos' or 'ragheads' by the native white population.

25. Immigration Law of 1906, Sections 37 and 38.

26. Of the 376 passengers aboard, there were 340 Sikhs, 24 Muslims, and 12 Hindus.

27. For example, during the years prior to 1907, the percentage of Indian applicants for admission to the United States who were rejected because of some 'defect' was less than ten percent. For the years 1907–1914, the rejection rate rose to thirty-three percent; and, in the years 1909, 1911, and 1913, the rejection rate was fifty percent or higher.

28. The District Commissioner of Seattle claims in this 1910 annual report that: 'A number of Hindus have applied for admission to the United States through this district during the year just passed. Every Hindu has been rejected by a board of special inquiry on the grounds of belief in polygamy, likely to become a public charge, doctor's certificate, or as an assisted immigrant.' Cited in Jacoby (1979, p. 162).

29. In this section, I rely extensively on Barrier's (1989, pp. 49–89) historical data.

30. Important journals and papers of the time include, *The Aryan* (an English monthly edited by Sundar Singh in Victoria), *The Swedeshi Sewak* (published in Vancouver in both Gurmukhi [Punjabi script] and Urdu), the *Khalsa Herald* (a Gurmukhi journal published in Vancouver by Kartar Singh Akali), *The Free Hindustan* and *Sansar* (published in Vancouver in Gurmukhi). See Barrier (1989, p. 69).

31.   It is interesting to note that the issue of turbans continues to be controversial even in contemporary society. See, for example, Somini Sengupta's 'Restaurant Faces Bias Suit for Barring Man in Turban,' in *The New York Times*, April 25, 1997.

32.   According to Barrier (1989), several accounts reveal the kinds of information that the Canadian Sikhs felt important to share with co-religionists back home. In 1907, the Khalsa Diwan of Vancouver held meetings on the topic 'Controversies with Hindus.' A Canadian Brahmin had attempted to get a manager to force 200 Sikhs in a factory to cut their hair, which resulted in a strike and subsequently successful negotiations with the owners. Another series of reports dealt with the infighting among Sikhs over control over *Sansar*. Some wanted the paper to be community property, while others filed a case in court to keep it independent. Incidentally, this kind of conflict continues in the current period. See, for example, Anthony DePalma's account, 'Canada's Torn Sikhs: In a Holy Place, Unholy Rage,' in *The New York Times*, February 20, 1997.

33.   Cited in Anderson (1992, p. 4).

34.   Interview with author in London on June 19, 1998.

35.   However, it should be noted that Bhindranwale did not expressly call for the creation of a separate state of Khalistan.

36.   For more information on some of these insurgent groups, see Major (1987).

37.   During the final stages of combat, a fire broke out in the revered Sikh Reference Library and it was decimated. All its contents including irreplaceable copies of the *Guru Granth Sahib* (Sikh holy book), archives of documents from every period of Sikh history, and artifacts of the lives of the gurus were destroyed beyond recognition. Given the high status accorded the written word in Sikh religious tradition, the destruction of the library was tantamount to an attack on the very recesses of the Sikh 'soul.' Mahmood (1996, p. 92) cites one Sikh man who recalls, 'I stood there watching the smoke, black at first then a kind of gray, curling over the rooftops around the Golden Temple Complex. When I found out later that it was the library that had burnt I kept seeing that smoke, smelling that smoke in my mind. It seemed to me that I could feel the pages burning, the precious pages of my Guru Granth Sahib. It seemed like that smoke was stinging my eyes. I cried and cried when I found out about the library. Many people had died, but I was crying most about my Guru [Granth Sahib].'

38.   The fifth of the ten gurus. Lived: 1563–1606.

39.   Noted writer and scholar, Khushwant Singh (a strong opponent of separatism) returned an award that had been bestowed on him by Indira Ghandhi. Bhagat Puran Singh (known as the 'bearded Mother Theresa' for his efforts on behalf of the homeless) did the same.

40.   I often heard statements like this during my own interviews with diasporan Sikhs.

41.   Describing the organized nature of the massacres, Mark Tully and Satish Jacob (1985, p. 7) state that '[t]he government itself admits that throughout India more than 2,717 people were killed in the anti-Sikh riots. Almost all of them were Sikhs. Some 2,510 of them died in Delhi. There, the rioters were mainly brought in from the slums to the areas they attacked. Many Sikhs said that local Hindu residents sheltered them from the mobs. Still, according to official estimates, 50,000 Sikhs fled from the capital of their country to Punjab for safety. Another

50,000 took refuge in special camps set up by the government and voluntary agencies.'

42. When informed of the anti-Sikh violence, Rajiv Ghandi's (Indira's son) official response was that 'the earth shakes at the fall of a big tree.' Ghandi's unfeeling statement, in the wake of the carnage, further served to estrange an already-disaffected community.

43. For a detailed discussion of Khalistan factions within India, see Pettigrew (1995).

44. During the Cold War, Pakistan was considered a stable ally, and, therefore, India was peripheral to US strategic and political interests in the region—India's policy of non-alignment and support for the Russian bloc also did not endear it to US diplomats.

45. Supporters included: Rules Committee Chairman, Gerald Solomon (R-New York), Vice Chairman of the Foreign Relations Subcommittee on Asia and the Pacific, Peter King (R-New York), Dana Rohrabacher (R-California), Edolphus Towns (D-New York), John T. Doolittle (R-California), Roscoe Bartlett (R-Maryland) Esteban Torrres (D-California), Lincoln Diaz-Balart (R-Florida), Wally Herger (R-California), and Gary Condit (D-California).

46. In March 1997, the Council of Khalistan shot into the limelight when Vice President Al Gore's office sent the organization a letter that appeared to support Khalistan. As Anand (1997) suggests, the ensuing controversy was, in fact, 'a classic case of miscommunication in the age of form letters and automatic signatures.' After writing to the Vice President about the situation in the Punjab, Aulakh received a response which stated: 'Thank you for writing to me regarding the ongoing civil conflict in Khalistan. I appreciate hearing your views on this serious situation.. your views are very important to us as the President and I formulate policies to advance the cause of peace around the world.' Aulakh immediately interpreted this to mean that 'by acknowledging the 'civil conflict' in Khalistan,' the Vice president had provided tacit United States support for an independent Sikh homeland. In the wake of angry protests and condemnation from state authorities in New Delhi, an extremely embarrassed White House immediately issued a formal apology for the *faux pas*. White House spokesman Michael McCurry promptly clarified the official United States position in an unambiguous statement: 'the US does not and never supported the establishment of an independent state of Khalistan.. It was an inadvertent error by the Vice President's staff that led to that letter.' At the State Department, spokesperson Nicholas Burns also attempted to salve the situation with his formal pronouncement that '[t]he US does recognize the Punjab as an integral part of India; always has and, I believe, always will in this case. We do not recognize any kind of Republic of Khalistan.' While these formal statements decried any support for an independent Sikh state, the controversy had successfully generated a great deal of publicity for the Council in the national media. See Anand's 1997 account.

47. For example, in the March 2000 massacre of Sikhs in Kashmir, the Council of Khalistan sent out numerous dispatches via regular and electronic mail, alleging that the killings were sponsored by the Indian government.

48. http://www.khalistan.net

49. http://www.khalistan.com

50.   The brutality of the counter-insurgency is captured by the following narrative by Mark Juergensmeyer (1995, p. 353): 'A resident of Punjab told me that the Indian government's brutal campaign that effectively quelled the Sikh rebellion in 1992 was often indiscriminate in its targets: "anyone could be killed," he explained, if he or she was "accused of being a fundamentalist."'

References

Ahmed, I. (1996), *State, Nation and Ethnicity in Contemporary South Asia*, Pinter: London.

Ahmed, I. (1999), 'The 1947 Partition of Punjab: Arguments Put Forth Before the Punjab Boundary Commission by the Parties Involved', in Talbot, Ian and Singh, G. (eds.), *Region and Partition: Bengal, Punjab and the Partition of the Sub-Continent*, Oxford University Press: Oxford.

Anand, S. (1997), 'Sikhs in the U.S.: Moderate Moves', *India Today*, March 31.

Anderson, B. (1991), *Imagined Communities: Reflections on the Origin and Spread of Nationalism*, Revised Edition, Verso: London.

Anderson, B. (1992), 'Long Distance Nationalism: World Capitalism and the Rise of Identity Politics', Working Paper No. 5.1, presented at the Conference on Nation, National Identity, Nationalism, Washington, D.C., September 10–12.

Anderson, B. (1994), 'Exodus', *Critical Inquiry*, Vol. 20, No. 2 (Winter), pp. 314–327.

Angelo, M. (1997), *The Sikh Diaspora: Tradition and Change in an Immigrant Community*, Garland Publishing: New York.

Bannerjee, S. (1996), 'The Politics of Violence in the Indian State and Society', in Rupesinghe, K. and Mumtaz, K. (eds.), *Internal Conflicts in South Asia*, Sage: London.

Barrier, N. G. (1989), 'Sikh Emigrants and their Homeland: The Transmission of Information, Resources and Values in the Early Twentieth Century', in Barrier, N. G. and Dusenbery, V. A. (eds.), *The Sikh Diaspora: Migration and the Experiences Beyond Punjab*, Chanakya Publications: Delhi, India.

Barrier, N. G. and Dusenbery, V. A. (eds.) (1989), *The Sikh Diaspora: Migration and the Experiences Beyond Punjab*, Chanakya Publications: Delhi, India.

Blaise, C. and Mukherjee, B. (1985), *The Sorrow and the Terror: The Haunting Legacy of the Air India Tragedy*, Penguin: New York.

Bose, S. (1994), *States, Nations, Sovereignty: Sri Lanka, India, and the Tamil Eelam Movement*, Sage: New Delhi, India.

Brown, M. E. (ed.) (1996), *The International Dimensions of Internal Conflict*, MIT Press: Cambridge, MA.

Buchignani, N. and Indra, D. M. (1989), 'Key Issues in Canadian-Sikh Ethnic and Race Relations: Implications for the Study of the Sikh Diaspora', in Barrier, N. G. and Dusenbery, V. A. (eds.), *The Sikh Diaspora: Migration and the Experiences Beyond Punjab*, Chanakya Publications: Delhi, India.

Chadney, J. G. (1984), *The Sikhs of Vancouver*, AMS Press: New York.

Chadney, J. G. (1989), 'The Formation of Ethnic Communities: Lessons from the Vancouver Sikhs', in Barrier, N. G. and Dusenbery, V. A. (eds.), *The Sikh Diaspora: Migration and the Experiences Beyond Punjab*, Chanakya Publications: Delhi, India.

Chopra, V. D., Mishra, R. K. and Singh, N. (1984), *Agony of Punjab*, Patriot Publishers: New Delhi, India.

Cohen, R. (1997), *Global Diasporas: An Introduction*, University of Washington Press: Seattle, WA.

Constas, D. C. and Platias, A. G. (ed.) (1993), *Diasporas in World Politic: The Greeks in Comparative Perspective*, MacMillan: London.

Corriea, E. (1997), 'Change of Faith: Gurdwara Elections Indicate the Decreasing Influence of Supporters of Khalistan Among Canadian Sikhs', *India Today International*, October 20, p. 28.

Deol, G. S. (1969), *The Role of the Ghadar Party in the National Movement*, Sterling Publishers: Delhi, India.

DePalma, A. (1997), 'Canada's Torn Sikhs: In a Holy Place, Unholy Rage', *The New York Times*, February 20.

De Silva, K. M. and May, R. J. (ed.) (1991), *Internationalization of Ethnic Conflict*, Pinter Publishers: London.

Dorgan, M. (1997), 'Status of India's Sikhs is Red-hot Issue', *San Jose Mercury News*, August 28.

Dusenbery, V. A. (1989), 'Introduction: A Century of Sikhs Beyond Punjab', in Barrier, N. G. and Dusenbery, V. A. (eds.), *The Sikh Diaspora: Migration and the Experience Beyond Punjab*, Chanakya: Delhi.

Dusenbery, V. A. (1995), 'A Sikh Diaspora? Contested Identities and Constructed Realities', in Van der Veer, P. (ed.), *The Politics of Space in the South Asian Diaspora*, University of Pennsylvania: Philadelphia, PA.

Embree, A. T. (1990), *Utopias in Conflict: Religion and Nationalism in Modern India*, University of California Press: Berkeley, CA.

Fox, R. (1985), *Lions of the Punjab: Culture in the Making*, University of California Press: Berkeley, CA.

Ganguly, A. B. (1980), *Ghadar Revolution in America*, Metropolitan: Delhi, India.

Ganguly, R. and Taras, R. (eds.) (1998), *Understanding Ethnic Conflict: The International Dimension*, Longman: New York.

Goulborune, H. (1991), 'Diasporic Politics: Sikhs and the Demand for Khalistan', in Goulbourne, H. (ed.), *Ethnicity and Nationalism in Post-Imperial Britain*, Cambridge University Press: Cambridge.

Gunawardena, T. (2000), 'Constructing Cybernationalism: The Internet as Shaper of Sikh Solidarity', Paper presented at the Workshop on Migration, Urban Development and Demographic Change in Punjab 1890s–1990s, February 19–20, Coventry, UK.

Gupta, D. (1996), *The Context of Ethnicity: Sikh Identity in a Comparative Perspective*, Oxford University Press: Delhi, India.

Gupte, P. (1985), *Vengeance: India after the Assassination of Indira Ghandi*, W. W. Norton & Company: London.

Hardgrave, R. L., Jr. (1994), 'India: The Dilemmas of Diversity', in Diamond, L. and Plattner, M. F. (eds.), *Nationalism, Ethnic Conflict, and Democracy*, The Johns Hopkins University Press: Baltimore.

Helweg, A. W. (1986), *Sikhs in England*, Second Edition, Oxford University Press: Delhi.

Helweg, A. W. (1989), 'Sikh Politics in India: The Emigrant Factor', in Barrier, N. G. and Dusenbery, V. A. (eds.), *The Sikh Diaspora: Migration and the Experiences Beyond Punjab*, Chanakya Publications: Delhi, India.

Helweg, A. W. (1993), 'The Sikh Diaspora and Sikh Studies', in Hawley, J. S. and Mann, G. S. (eds.), *Studying the Sikhs: Issues for North America*, SUNY: Albany, NY.

Human Rights Watch (1994), 'India: Arms and Abuses in Indian Punjab and Kashmir', *Human Rights Arms Project*, Vol. 6, No. 10 (September).

Jacoby, H. S. (1979), 'Some Demographic and Social Aspects of Early East Indian Life in the United States', in Juergensmeyer, M. and Barrier, N. G. (eds.), *Sikh Studies: Comparative Perspectives on a Changing Tradition*, Graduate Theological Union: Berkeley, CA.

Jaijee, I. S. (1995), *Politics of Genocide: Punjab 1984–1994*, Baba Publishers: Chandigarh, India.

Jeffrey, R. (1986), *What's Happening to India? Punjab, Ethnic Conflict, Mrs. Gandhi's Death and the Test for Federalism*, Macmillan: London.

Jeffrey, R. (1987), 'Grappling with History: Sikh Politicians and the Past', *Pacific Affairs*, Vol. 60, No. 1 (Spring), pp. 59–72.

Johnson, H. (1988), 'Patterns of Sikh Migration to Canada, 1900–1960', in O'Connell, J. T., Israel, M. and Oxtoby, W. G. (eds.), *Sikh History and Religion in the Twentieth Century*, Center for South Asian Studies, University of Toronto: Toronto.

Joy, A. (1989), *Ethnicity in Canada: Social Accommodation and Cultural Persistence Among the Sikhs and the Portuguese*, AMS Press: New York.

Juergensmeyer, M. (1979), 'The Ghadar Syndrome: Immigrant Sikhs and Nationalist Pride', in Juergensmeyer, M. and Barrier, N. G. (eds.), *Sikh Studies: Comparative Perspectives on a Changing Tradition*, Graduate Theological Union: Berkeley, CA.

Juergensmeyer, M. (1988), 'The Ghadar Syndrome: Nationalism in an Immigrant Community', *Punjab Journal of Politics*, Vol. 1, No. 1 (October), pp. 1–22.

Juergensmeyer, M. (1995), 'Anti-fundamentalism', in Marty, M. E. and Appleyby, R. S. (eds.), *Fundamentalisms Comprehended*, University of Chicago Press: Chicago, IL.

Kapur, R. A. (1986), *Sikh Separatism: The Politics of Faith*, Allen & Unwin: London.

Kashmeri, Z. and McAndrew, B. (1989), *Soft Target: How the Indian Intelligence Service Penetrated Canada*, James Lorimer: Toronto.

Kishwa, M. (1998), 'Need to Establish Links: Some Discussions with Sikh Communities in North America', in Kishwa, M. (ed.), *Religion at the Service of Nationalism and Other Essays*, Oxford University Press: Delhi, India.

Kothari, S. and Sethi, H. (eds.) (1985), *Voices from a Sacred City: The Delhi Carnage in Perspective*, Lokayan: Delhi, India.

LaBrack, B. (1988), *The Sikhs of Northern California: 1904–1975*, AMS Press: New York.

LaBrack, B. (1989), 'The New Patrons: Sikhs Overseas', in Barrier, N. G. and Dusenbery, V. A. (eds.), *The Sikh Diaspora: Migration and the Experience Beyond the Punjab*, Chanakya Publications: Delhi, India.

Lal, P. M. (1984), *Disintegration of the Punjab*, Sameer Prakashan: Chandigarh, India.

Lal, V. (1990), 'The Fiji Indians: Marooned at Home', in Clarke, C., Peach, C. and Vertovec, S. (eds.), *South Asians Overseas*, Cambridge University Press: Cambridge.

Leonard, K. (1989), 'Pioneer Voices from California: Reflections on Race, Religion, and Ehtnicity', in Barrier, N. G. and Dusenbery, V. A. (eds.), *The Sikh Diaspora: Migration and the Experience Beyond the Punjab*, Chanakya Publications: Delhi, India.

Leonard, K. (1992), *Making Ethnic Choices: California's Punjabi Mexican Americans*, Temple University Press: Philadelphia, PA.

Leonard, K. (1996), ''Flawed Transmission?' Punjabi in California', in Singh, P. and Barrier, N. G. (eds.), *The Transmission of Sikh Heritage in the Diaspora*, Manohar: Delhi, India.

Leonard, K. (1997), *The South Asian Americans*, Greenwood Press: Westport, CT.

Leonard, K. (2000), 'Punjabi Mexican American: Experiences of Multiethnicity', in Spickard, P and Burroughs, W. J. (eds.), *We are a People: Narrative and Multiplicity in Constructing Ethnic Identity*, Temple University Press: Philadelphia, PA.

Mahmood, C. K. (1996), *Fighting for Faith and Nation: Dialogues with Sikh Militants*, University of Pennsylvania Press: Philadelphia, PA.

Major, A. J. (1985), 'Sikh Ethno-Nationalism, 1967–1984: Implications for the Congress', *South Asia: Journal of South Asian Studies*, Vol. 8 (June-December), pp. 168–181.

Major, A. J. (1987), 'From Moderates to Secessionists: A Who's Who of the Punjab Crisis', *Pacific Affairs*, Vol. 60, No. 1 (Spring), pp. 43–58.

Mann, G. S. (2000), 'Sikhism in the United States of America', in Coward, H., Hinnells, J. H. and Williams, R. B. (eds.), *The South Asian Religious Diaspora in Britain, Canada, and the United States*, SUNY: Albany, NY.

McLeod, W. H. (1980), *Early Sikh Tradition: A Study of the Janam-sakhis*, Clarendon Press: Oxford.

McLeod, W. H. (1989a), 'The First Forty Years of Sikh Migration: Problems and Some Possible Solutions', in Barrier, N. G. and Dusenbery, V. A. (eds.), *The Sikh Diaspora: Migration and the Experience Beyond the Punjab*, Chanakya Publications: Delhi, India.

McLeod, W. H. (1989b), *Who is Sikh? The Problem of Sikh Identity*, Clarendon Press: Oxford.

Mehta, V. (1994), *Rajiv Gandhi and Rama's Kingdom*, Yale University Press: New Haven, CT.

Mitra, S. K. (1996), 'Sub-National Movements in South Asia: Identity, Collective Action and Political Protest', in Mitra, S. K. and Lewis, R. A. (eds.), *Sub-National Movements in South Asia*, Westview Press: Boulder, CO.

Mulgrew, I. (1988), *Unholy Terror: The Sikhs and International Terrorism*, Key Porter Books, Ltd.: Toronto.

Nijjar, B. S. (1976), *Anglo-Sikh Wars*, K. B. Publications: New Delhi, India.

Oberoi, H. S. (1987), 'From Punjab to 'Khalistan': Territoriality and Metacommentary', *Pacific Affairs*, Vol. 60, No. 1 (Spring), pp. 26–41.

Oberoi, H. S. (1993), 'Sikh Fundamentalism: Translating History into Theory', in Marty, M. E. and Appleby, R. S. (eds.), *Fundamentalisms and the State*, University of Chicago Press: Chicago, IL.

Oberoi, H. S. (1994), *The Construction of Religious Boundaries: Culture, Identity, and Diversity in the Sikh Tradition*, Oxford University Press: Delhi, India.

O'Connell, J. T. (2000), 'Sikh Religio-Ethnic Experience in Canada', in Coward, H., Hinnells, J. H. and Williams, R. B. (eds.), *The South Asian Religious Diaspora in Britain, Canada, and the United States*, SUNY: Albany, NY.

Pellizzi, F. (1988), 'To Seek Refuge: Nation and Ethnicity in Exile', in Guidieri, R., Pellizzi, F. and Tambiah, S. J. (eds.), *Ethnicities and Nations: Processes of Interethnic Relations in Latin America, Southeast Asia, and the Pacific*, Rothko Chapel: Houston, TX.

Pettigrew, J. (1987), 'In Search of a New Kingdom of Lahore', *Pacific Affairs*, Vol. 60, No. 1 (Spring), pp. 1–25.

Pettigrew, J. (1995), *The Sikhs of the Punjab: Unheard Voices of State and Guerilla Violence*, Zed Books: London.

Pettigrew, J. (1998), 'Lives Rich in Terror: Human Rights Abuses in Indian Punjab and the Continuing Suffering of Rural Families', Report presented to the Parliamentary Panjab Human Rights Groups, July 19, London.

Phadnis, U. (1989), 'Ethnic Separatism: External Dimensions', in Pladnis, U. (ed.), *Ethnicity and Nation-Building in South Asia*, Sage: New Delhi, India.

Puri, H. K. (1983), *Ghadar Movement: Ideology, Organization, and Strategy*, Guru Nanak Deve University Press: Amritsar, India.

Rai, S. M. (1965), *Partition of the Punjab: A Study of Its Effects on the Politics and Administration of the Punjab (I) 1947–56*, Asia Publishing House: Bombay.

Roy, P. E. (1989), *A White Man's Province: British Columbia Politicians and Chinese and Japanese Immigrants, 1858–1914*, University of British Columbia Press: Vancouver, BC.

Samiuddin, A. (ed.) (1985), *The Punjab Crisis: Challenge and Response*, Mittal Publications: Delhi, India.

Sengupta, S. (1997), 'Restaurant Faces Bias Suit for Barring Man in Turban', *The New York Times*, April 25.

Shain, Y. (1989), *The Frontier of Loyalty: Political Exiles in the Age of the Nation-State*, University Press of New England: Hanover, NH.

Shain, Y. (ed.) (1991), *Governments-in-Exile in Contemporary World Politics*, Routledge: New York.

Sheffer, G. (1986), 'A New Field of Study: Modern Diasporas in International Politics', in Sheffer, G. (ed.), *Modern Diasporas in International Politics*, Croom and Helm: London.

Singaravélou (1990), 'Indians in the French Overseas Departments: Guadeloupe, Martinique, Reunion', Clarke, C., Peach, C. and Vertovec, S. (eds.), *South Asians Overseas*, Cambridge University Press: Cambridge.

Singh, A. (1985), 'The Delhi Carnage and After', in Singh, A. (ed.), *Punjab in Indian Politics: Issues and Trends*, Ajanta Publications: Delhi, India.

Singh, G. (1987), 'Understanding the Punjab Problem', *Asian Survey*, Vol. XXVII, No. 12 (December), pp. 1268–1277.

Singh, G. (1992), 'The Punjab Elections 1992: Breakthrough or Breakdown?', *Asian Survey*, Vol. XXXII, No. 11 (November), pp. 988–999.

Singh, G. (1997), 'The Punjab Legislative Assembly Elections of February 1997: The BJP's Regional Road to Power', *Contemporary South Asia*, Vol. 6, No. 3, pp. 273–283.

Singh, N. (1994), *Canadian Sikhs: History, Religion, and Culture of Sikhs in North America*, Canadian Sikhs' Studies Institute: Ottawa.

Singh, P. and Barrier, N. G. (eds.) (1996), *The Transmission of Sikh Heritage in the Diaspora*, Manohar: Delhi, India.

Singh, P. and Malik, H. (ed.) (1985), *Punjab: The Fatal Miscalculation*, Patwant Singh: New Delhi.

Tambiah, S. J. (1996), *Leveling Crowds: Ethnonationalist Conflicts and Collective Violence in South Asia*, University of California Press: Berkeley, CA.

Tatla, D. S. (1999), *The Sikh Diaspora: The Search for Statehood*, University of Washington Press: Seattle, WA.

Thandi, S. S. (1996), 'Counterinsurgency and Political Violence in Punjab, 1980–94', in Singh, G. and Talbot, I. (eds.), *Punjabi Identity: Continuity and Change*, Manohar: New Delhi.

Tinker, H. (1974), *A New System of Slavery: The Export of Indian Labor Overseas 1830–1920*, Oxford University Press: Oxford.

Tinker, H. (1976), *Separate and Unequal: India and the Indians in the British Commonwealth 1920–1950*, Hurst & Company: London.

Tinker, H. (1977), *The Banyan Tree: Overseas Emigrants From India, Pakistan, and Bangladesh*, Oxford University Press: Oxford.

Tinker, H. (1990), 'Indians in Southeast Asia: Imperial Auxiliaries', in Clarke, C., Peach, C. and Vertovec, S. (eds.), *South Asian Overseas: Migration and Ethnicity*, Cambridge University Press: Cambridge.

Tully, M. and Jacob, S. (1985), *Amritsar: Mrs. Gandhi's Last Battle*, Jonathan Cape: London.

Una, W. (1985), *Sikhs Abroad: Attitudes and Activities of Sikhs Settled in the USA and Canada*, Statesman Commercial Press: Calcutta.

Van der Veer, P. (1994), *Religious Nationalism: Hindus and Muslims in India*, University of California Press: Berkeley, CA.

Wallace, P. (ed.) (1985), *Region and Nation in India*, Oxford University Press: New Delhi.

Wallace, P. (1998), 'Punjab's Political Violence and the External Factor', Paper presented at the Association for Asian Studies 50th Annual Meeting, March 26–28, Washington, D.C.

Wallace, P. and Chopra, S. (eds.) (1981), *Political Dynamics of Punjab*, Guru Nanak Dev University: Amritsar, India.

Watson, B. (1991), *The Great Indian Mutiny: Colin Campbell and the Campaign at Lucknow*, Praeger: New York.

10

Ethnicity and Governance in the Third World: Case Studies from South and Southeast Asia—Sri Lanka and Malaysia

KINGSLEY M. de SILVA

Nationalism, ethnicity and the colonial legacy

The two countries whose recent history and politics are reviewed here, Sri Lanka and Malaysia in South and Southeast Asia[1] respectively, are excellent case studies on the dual and conflicting roles ethnicity plays, at once a powerful constructive agent in state building and a potent destabilizing one. In its most constructive phase, nationalism in alliance with ethnicity, was one of the principal driving forces in the successful agitation for independence against colonial rule, an integral part of the historical anti-colonial struggles of the post-second world war era. Sri Lanka's independence came in 1948, in the critically important first phase of decolonization; Malaysia's followed in 1957. While ethnicity gave support and provided legitimacy to the nationalist upsurge against colonialism it proved to be a formidable obstacle to the peaceful consolidation of the power of these same nationalist forces in post-colonial state construction, especially because both states were multi-ethnic or multi-religious or both. The contrasting history of the two countries in regard to post-independence state construction is reviewed below.

Nationalist leaders in their moment of triumph in Sri Lanka underestimated or ignored the potency of appeals to ethnic or religious identities. Liberals and Marxists alike believed that ascriptive ethnic identities were generally intrinsically evanescent, and were doomed to disappear in the face of purposeful social change that was expected to accompany the construction of a modern post-colonial state. Those predictions, alas, were not fulfilled and this optimistic phase lasted just under 10 years after independence. The passage to independence was more violent in Malaysia than in Sri Lanka, through the Communist insurgency directed against the colonial government. The fact that the insurgency was led by the country's Chinese minority provided as much evidence of the ubiquity and durability of ethnicity as the conflict between the Sinhalese-dominated governments and representatives of the Tamil minority did in Sri Lanka. There was no great optimism about the future of the country in the early years of Malaysia's independence.

The post-colonial and current ethnic resurgence in the former colonies in Asia and Africa underlines a harsh reality—that ethnic conflict is one of the oldest forces of intergroup strife in human history and one of the most persistent and most destructive. This harsh reality is not restricted to those parts of the world. Despite the fact that the industrialized countries of the West have had their share of ethnic and religious dissension, ethnic conflict was identified, up to very recently, as essentially a Third World phenomenon and generally post-colonial. But the old Irish question, in its recent manifestations, continued to attract attention generally by regular bouts of violence. Canada, Spain and Belgium, among industrialized and urbanized countries have also had their problems; the demands by French Canadians for an independent Quebec; the problems of the Basques and Catalans in Spain, and to these must be added the linguistic divide in Belgium. But it would be true to say that these issues—with the possible exception of the problem of Northern Ireland—paled into insignificance compared to the ethnic conflicts of South Asia and parts of Africa and the Middle East.

For decades, the political establishment in the communist states of Central and Eastern Europe—and the Soviet Union in particular—kept assuring us and themselves that their societies were somehow immune to the appeals of ethnicity, religion and even national identity. That was the message preached by Marxist intellectuals and ideologues in all parts of the world. The sudden and rapid disintegration of the Soviet Union, the nationalist resurgence that brought to an end the Communist regimes of Central and Eastern Europe, the reassertion of the independence of the three Baltic states of Estonia, Latvia and Lithuania, and the disintegration of Yugoslavia put an end to that illusion. The sad story of the disintegration of Tito's Yugoslavia into its component elements, and the violence that has ensued as a result of clashes of ethnic identity based on religion, language, culture and historical memories, is the new reality of ethnicity continuing as a potent driving force in international politics. Serbia and now Kosovo have replaced Lebanon as the worst-case scenarios for nations facing severe ethnic and religious divisions and tensions.

In the post-colonial nations of South and Southeast Asia, the state was generally a colonial inheritance, a structure seized through successful rebellion as in Indonesia, won after prolonged but peaceful negotiation as in Sri Lanka, or transferred after the colonial power successfully defeated a powerful insurgency led by sections of an ethnic minority, as was the case in Malaya. Whatever the process of acquisition, the legatees of the colonial powers have all been engaged in post-colonial consolidation and expansion and of state building and coping with the challenges posed to these processes by assertions of ethnic identity on the part of minority groups.

Sri Lanka in South Asia and Malaysia in Southeast Asia (see Maps in Appendix II), both former British colonies, had two distinctive systems of colonial administration.[2] Ceylon (which became Sri Lanka after 1972) was the premier crown colony in the British empire by the 1930s. Despite its location just off the coast of India, it was not part of the Indian empire administered by the India Office, but was controlled by the Colonial Office. In response to the long and successful tradition of Sinhalese resistance to what may be called serial or sequential colonial rule, Portuguese, Dutch and British, the British, the last in the series, adopted a policy of centralization after the crushing of the great rebellion of 1817–18, and till independence that centralized administrative structure was maintained virtually unchanged. The British put an end to the Kandyan kingdom, the last of the independent Sinhalese kingdoms and brought the whole island under their control. In Malaya, on the other hand, the British in the early stages followed a policy of sustaining a more decentralized form of administration in which the indigenous rulers became an integral part of the government system, under British supervision. After the early and mid-1870s that supervision became more stringent, and behind the apparent independence lurked the reality of control through British officials. The only areas of autonomy left to the indigenous rulers were Malay custom and the Islamic religion. Peninsular Malaya had three distinctive types of *negara* or states generally under a native ruler; the Straits Settlements, consisting of Malacca, Penang and Singapore merged into a single unit in 1826, and were considered quite distinctive; four *negara* Selangor, Perak, Penang and Negri Sembilan, constituted the Federated Malay States (FMS) established in 1896; and lastly, there were the curiously named Unfederated Malay States (UMS), of Johore Perlis, Kedah, Kelantan and Trengganu. At independence the Malay states, eleven in all, formed part of a newly established Federation of Malaya (see Map in Appendix II).

There was greater similarity, however, in the economic system of the two colonies: both were plantation colonies which gave their people a relatively high standard of living even in colonial times. Because of its mineral wealth—tin, which was a mainstay of the economy in colonial times and oil, after independence—Malaya/Malaysia was more richly endowed than Sri Lanka. Besides, peninsular Malaya/Malaysia had twice the land area of Sri Lanka, with a much lower population density. Following on this is a third point, one of similarity of colonial experience in demographic change. In both countries the last phases of colonial rule had seen substantial (in the case of Sri Lanka) and profound (in Malaya) demographic change. Partly this was a natural increase in population under colonial rule, but often natural increase was overshadowed by the additions to the population through migration. Indeed, migration often resulted in dramatic changes in the ethnic composition of the colonial population, changes accepted if not encouraged in the interests of economic growth under British capital. The British colonial governments in the two colonies and the British plantation companies and planters, faced with the reluctance or refusal of the indigenous population to work on the plantations and other enterprises, in the case of Sri Lanka, and a deliberate policy of keeping the indigenous population away from such work in the Malay states, had resorted to the importation of labor, from within the empire (India) as in the case of Sri Lanka, and in Malaya from Southern China apart from India. As a result, Malaya became a classic example of a 'plural society' as defined by J. S. Furnivall in his well-known treatise, *Colonial Policy and Practice*, published in 1948 by Cambridge University Press. Furnivall, describes a plural society as one characterized by compartmentalization of economic activity along ethnic lines, and with little or no social interaction among the ethnic groups. In 1957, the year of Malayan independence, Rupert Emerson, a political scientist, described peninsular Malaya as a 'perfect example of the plural society,' where component elements of the population have little in common except the 'fact that they live in the same country' (Emerson, 1957). Sri Lanka, on the other hand, deviated from this pattern because its indigenous elite, especially its upwardly mobile Sinhalese segment, had large investments in the plantations, and in other commercial ventures.

Encouraged and permitted entry as temporary immigrants generally, in time, many of the migrants preferred to remain behind rather than return to the poverty whence they came. In the course of the 20th century, the census records showed that between 11% and 12% of Sri Lanka's population were Tamil migrants from India (mostly from Madras Presidency, now the state of Tamil Nadu) and had overtaken the indigenous Tamils in numbers. In Malaya, demographic change was far greater than in Sri Lanka, since the indigenous Malays were reduced to a minority (to slightly less than half the population) and to make matters worse were reduced to a position of relative poverty in comparison with the immigrants,[3] the Chinese principally and the Indians[4] (not to mention migrants from Sri Lanka who formed a small but relatively well off group among the 'Indians'). The following extract from an essay by a recent writer, a British scholar, captures the essence of the dilemmas that faced the British and the Malays in the late 1920s.

> According to the treaties and engagements concluded at various times with the rulers, the British recognised the sovereignty of the sultans, the autonomy of their states and the special position of their peoples as 'princes of the soil.' The extraction of tin from circa 1850 and the cultivation of rubber from 1890s added to the revenues and profitability of these dependencies and also led to the emergence of a 'plural society' where the communal differences between Malays and immigrants from China and India were reinforced by their economic functions and the place assigned to them in Malay society. As British administration expanded and the economy developed, so the power of the Malays and their position in 'modern Malaya' receded. Yet the principles underlying the British presence remained the same and became ingrained through reiteration. The high commissioner, Sir Hugh Clifford, declared in 1927 that the Malay states 'were, they are and must remain—unless our duties, our obligations and engagements to the Rajas, the Chiefs and to the people of these countries are to be wholly ignored or forgotten—Malay states.

> In the inter-war period, however, officials were struck by the inadequacies of the system of government for fulfilling British ob-

ligations to Malays and accommodating the growing population of non-Malays who had settled permanently in the country, quite apart from the fact that territorial fragmentation stood in the way of administrative and economic efficiency (Stockwell, 1995, pp. liii–liv).

Thus, changes in the ethnic composition in colonial times affected the processes of governance and the prospects and furtherance of ethnic harmony in both Sri Lanka and Malaysia because of the reluctance of the Sinhalese majority in the former and Malays in Malaya to accept large numbers of immigrants as citizens of the new states that would soon be granted independence. One of the principal challenges both nations faced in the passage to independence was in evolving a policy on the terms on which citizenship would be granted.

In Sri Lanka the debate began as early as 1928, since in that year a British Commission of Inquiry—the Donoughmore Commission—recommended that universal suffrage be introduced in the next phase of constitutional development in the island. That next phase came in 1931 and universal suffrage was an essential part of it—a point that is discussed in greater detail later in this chapter. Before the new constitution was accepted by local politicians, through a debate in the national legislature, a crisis over the terms on which immigrants would be granted citizenship had to be resolved. It was resolved temporarily by tightening the requirements for citizenship. Even so the Sinhalese politicians were distinctly unhappy and very vigilant over attempts to bend the accepted rules. Sri Lanka received a very advanced constitution in 1931 in which there was both genuine power-sharing between popularly elected Sri Lankan ministers and British officials, and a transfer of a substantial measure of power to the Sri Lankan politicians. Whitehall and the Governor of the colony permitted Sri Lankan ministers to take the leadership and the initiative in negotiations with the Indian government on the issue of citizenship rights of Indians resident in the country. Several attempts to do so in the 1940s failed and it was left to the post-independence government to handle the citizenship problem on its own. Suffice it to say, for purposes of this essay, that it took forty years from 1948 to resolve the problem, with citizenship being gradually conceded to just about half the immigrant Indians resident in the country (see, especially, de Silva, 1998a, pp. 272–298).

When the time came for Malayan independence, the British took care to settle the question of citizenship as part of the transfer of power negotiations. Many more Chinese and Indians secured independence than the

Malays would have liked, but immigrants had to accept the entrenchment of a privileged position for the Malays as part of the deal.

As we have seen, Sri Lanka gained its independence from Britain in 1948,[5] and Malaya nearly ten years later in 1957.[6] For the latter, its times of troubles started before independence, with the Japanese invasion, and after re-establishment of British rule, a long period of insurgency led by the Chinese communists (see, e.g., Chapman, 1963; Clutterbuck, 1985, 1973; Gullick, 1963; Short, 1960). While the back of the insurgency was broken only just before independence was granted, nevertheless, the Malay leadership which inherited power from the British had the inestimable advantage of being spared the need to conduct such an anti-guerrilla campaign—with a distinct ethnic content—by themselves after independence. The Chinese minority still remained economically powerful, and continued to be so, but they had ceased to be the threat to the political stability of the post-independence Malay state that they may well have been if the British had not been successful in their anti-guerrilla campaigns. The British, for their part, were in a strong position to determine the terms on which citizenship would be granted.

At the time of independence, Malaya/Malaysia was seen as a high conflict area; and the prognosis for the country in the years following independence was far from encouraging. Yet, the prophets of doom were proved wrong. Sri Lanka, on the other hand reversed this process: from a peaceful transfer of power, and a successful consolidation of democracy, to the present position of a high conflict state.

The Sri Lankan paradox

Sri Lanka, or Ceylon, as it was called during British rule over the island (1796–1948) and until 1972, was often referred to, by British commentators on the decolonization process, in the early years of independence (1948 to the mid-1950s), as the 'model' colony where the national political leadership had preferred a negotiated transfer of power, in contrast to the agitation, sometimes peaceful, sometimes violent, but always very vocal, in India. The main reason for this lay with the policies and political styles of the principal leaders of the Sri Lankan nationalist movement who deliberately eschewed the Indian model and chose to follow the processes of peaceful constitutional evolution of the 'settlement' colonies, Canada, Australia and New Zealand in their passage to independence in the form of Dominion Status.

There were others in Sri Lanka, Marxists and their fellow travelers largely, who would have preferred other methods of agitation, and independence outside the British Commonwealth but a clear majority of the electorate supported the mainstream leadership. In most colonial societies, once the struggle for home rule is over and independence is achieved, contests over who should rule at home tend to follow. These are generally ethnic and religious rather than class conflicts. In British India—or the *raj* as it was called—the two struggles, home rule and who should rule at home, were parallel movements which merged in a denouement of great violence in the final stages and rent asunder the territorial legacy of British conquest. The *raj* was divided between two warring legatees, India and Pakistan. In Sri Lanka on the other hand, where the passage to independence was negotiated rather than fought for, the second struggle was successfully avoided for nearly 10 years after independence. A large part of the credit for this goes to D. S. Senanayake, the island's first Prime Minister (1947–52), and the principal negotiator for Sri Lanka's independence (1942–47). His great achievement was in keeping the country together in the final stages of the passage to independence, where Nehru and Gandhi had so signally failed to do in India. The passage to independence had nothing of the mass agitation and communal violence one saw in the *raj*, or the riots, strikes and student agitation seen in Myanmar. In general, the situation in the country seemed to provide an impressive basis for a solid start in nation-building and national regeneration. The post-independence Sri Lankan governments inherited an efficient administrative system, a dynamic judiciary and a well-established social-welfare system and policy. Above all, it inherited a democratic political system based on universal suffrage. Three general elections had been held in the island before independence; 1931, 1936 and 1947.

The decade of peaceful consolidation of power by the Sri Lankan legatees of the British, the United National Party (UNP) governments of 1947 to 1956, has attracted surprisingly little scholarly attention, unlike the periods and episodes of sporadic conflict that followed. Yet, one has only to examine the policies pursued in the 1940s and early 1950s to see how to get the political management of a multi-ethnic polity right, just as Sri Lanka's record after 1956 provides a multiplicity of clues on how the political stability and ethnic harmony of a multi-ethnic polity could be destroyed by the adoption of the wrong policies (on Sri Lanka's demography and ethnic profile, see Appendix I). That comparison will be made in the paragraphs that follow. Here we need to emphasize a deeply symbolic move made by Senanayake in 1948, a few months after independence, when the Tamil Congress leader, G. G. Ponnambalam, and most of his party MPs, were persuaded to cross over from the opposition to the government, with Ponnambalam being accommodated in the Cabinet. While this caused a split within the Tamil Congress, when a recalcitrant minority decided to remain in the opposition, and to establish the Federal Party which later formed the core of the future Tamil United Liberation Front (TULF), Senanayake's main objective of strengthening the government, by underlining its national and multi-ethnic character, had been served. From the time of the formation of the Tamil Congress in 1944 and even well before that, Ponnambalam had led a vigorous campaign for the rights of the Tamils, indeed for a privileged position for the Tamils and the other minorities, in the Sri Lankan polity. Thus, his entry into the Cabinet was an astute and remarkably successful political maneuver by Senanayake. While the UNP was a multi-ethnic and multi-religious party from the inception, the entry of the Tamil Congress into the government made the latter much more multi-ethnic in appearance and composition than it was without the Tamil Congress.

Sri Lanka's descent to political instability came in three stages, beginning with the period mid-1955 to 1961 when two episodes of communal riots broke out against the background of a unilateral change in language policy. The dominant political influence in the period 1956 to 1977 was the populism of the Sri Lanka Freedom Party (of the Bandaranaikes, S. W. R. D. and Sirimavo) which ruled for all but five years (1965–70), generally with the support of, and sometimes in association with, Marxist parties. Throughout the period of rule of the Bandaranaikes, only once did the Cabinet have a Tamil member (1970–77) and even he was not an elected MP, but an appointed one. In contrast to D. S. Senanayake and his colleagues and successors in the UNP, the Bandaranaikes emphasized majority prerogatives and were generally insensitive to the interests of the minorities. We have seen how a unilateral change in language policy in the mid-1950s heralded the first and earliest phase in Sri Lanka's current ethnic conflict (see, e.g., Russell, 1982; de Silva, 1993, 1996). In his time, Senanayake would not countenance any radical changes in language policy, or in the speed with which the agreement reached in 1943–44 on future language policy—with Sinhala and Tamil replacing English over a period of 10 years—would be implemented.

In association with Marxist parties the Bandaranaikes kept expanding the state apparatus and increased its influence in public life and over the economy. Initially, the objective was the construction of a Sri Lankan version of India's Nehruvian socialist economy but in time this was jettisoned in favor of an emulation of the economies of the Soviet bloc: beginning by encouraging import-substitution industries (generally state-owned and inefficiently run), and eventually nationalizing all the important industrial and commercial ventures and financial institutions; and reducing the role of private capital in Sri Lanka's economy to a bare minimum. Sri Lanka's 'closed economy' became the most state-dominated in the whole of non-communist South and Southeast Asia except for Myanmar. These inward looking policies weakened and reduced Sri Lanka's former links with the world economy at the very time when Southeast Asian nations were strengthening theirs, and reaping the benefits.

When Mrs. Bandaranaike was in power (1960–65 and 1970–77), and especially as the head of a coalition with the Marxists (1970–77), there was enormous pressure on the country's democratic system and traditions: on its legislative, administrative and judicial institutions no less than on its economy. She began a process of politicizing the bureaucracy and in 1974, her government brought the national press under state control after a long and vitriolic campaign (see, de Silva, 1997a, pp. 241–263).

In the mid- and late-1960s, there was a second phase of harmonious ethnic relations, till 1972 or so when tensions broke out once more, culminating in the riots of 1977. After 1977, the efforts of another UNP government to reverse many of the policies associated with the SLFP led to another period of relative quiescence. By then the moderate Tamil parties were being rapidly undermined by separatist groups bent on violence against the state. One such attack, a relatively minor one in retrospect, triggered the most violent episode of ethnic conflict in Sri Lanka's recent history, the anti-Tamil riots of 1983. Thereafter, episodes of violent ethnic conflict have been a regular feature.

The prevalence of high levels of political violence and several episodes of armed conflict constitute a baffling phenomenon in a democracy where governments are regularly changed through the ballot, and where a multi-party system has been in place since independence, where voter participation at regularly held, free and impartial elections has been very high, and where governments are generally multi-ethnic and multi-religious. What the Sri Lankan experience demonstrates is that a democratic political system is no guarantee against episodes of political violence; indeed it demonstrates that resolution of conflicts could be as difficult in a system based on a democratic electorate as in a less democratic one.

The conflicts in Sri Lanka illustrate the operation of some of the most combustible factors in ethnic relations: language, religion, long historical memories of tensions and conflict, and a prolonged separatist agitation.

Nevertheless, the current ethnic conflict in Sri Lanka is a much more complex business than a simple straightforward confrontation between a once well-entrenched minority—the Sri Lanka Tamils—and a now powerful but still insecure majority—the Sinhalese—that it is often portrayed to be. The Sinhalese majority and the Sri Lanka Tamil minority are not the only players in this intricate political drama even though, at present, they play the principal roles. Suffice it to say here that there are two conflicting perceptions of these conflicts. Most Sinhalese believe that the Tamil minority had enjoyed a privileged position under British rule and that the balance has of necessity to shift in favor of the Sinhalese majority who, they emphasize, had borne the brunt of resistance against the Portuguese, the Dutch and the British. In short, the Sinhalese, especially the Buddhists, were the principal losers and victims of Western colonialism. The Sri Lanka Tamil minority is an achievement-oriented, industrious group who still continue to enjoy high status in society, considerable influence in the economy, a significant if diminishing role in the bureaucracy and is well placed in all levels of the education system. The Tamils for their part would claim that they are now a harassed minority, the victims of sporadic acts of communal violence and calculated acts and policies of discrimination directed at them. Nevertheless, they could hardly be described as a beleaguered minority, the victims of regular episodes of violence—though violence admittedly has been frequent enough in recent times—given the impassioned ferocity with which they have fought against the Sinhalese-dominated security forces since 1984–85, and their frequent terrorist attacks against the civilian population, Sinhalese in the main. Most of the Tamil fears and their sense of insecurity stem from the belief that they have lost the advantageous position they enjoyed under British rule in many sectors of public life in the country; in brief, a classic case of a sense of relative deprivation (de Silva, 1998a).

The Sri Lankan experience also illustrates the important point that minorities seeking redress of grievances, and guarantees of protection of their identities are by no means always agents of democratic change or adherents of the very liberalism they advocate for themselves. Minorities could be just as harsh as, and indeed harsher than, anybody else, within the territorial limits over which they have dominance, as the most prominent Tamil separatist group in the island since the 1970s, the Liberation Tigers of Tamil Eelam (LTTE), have demonstrated in recent times in Sri Lanka with their expulsion and killing off of the Sinhalese minority who lived there, and their expulsion of the much larger Muslim minority in a ruthless exercise in ethnic cleansing in 1990 (de Silva, 1998a; Hasbullah, 1995).

The country has always had a higher standard of living than the rest of South Asia, and as late as 1960, it had more or less the same per capita GNP as South Korea and nearly double that of Thailand. Why does it lag so far behind these two countries today? As we had pointed out earlier in this essay, the answer lies in the economic policies of the Bandaranaikes and their Marxist allies. While the purposeful efforts of the UNP governments of 1977–94 did have beneficial results in reviving the economy, the ethnic violence of the period after 1983 reduced the tempo of economic growth, and there was also the lingering influence of Marxist ideology on the working class and sections of the intelligentsia but this was a relatively minor factor. As a result of the economic policies pursued up to 1977, the employment generating capacity of the private sector had been substantially reduced. Everything depended on the state sector, and the latter's perform-ance had been dismally poor. It could never keep up with the rapidly growing demand for employment. Had economic growth been sustained between 1960 and 1977 at twice the prevailing rate it would still not have matched non-communist Southeast Asia's but it would have provided the jobs that mattered to the thousands of young people entering the labor market each year as the Malayan/Malaysian economy had done during this same period and continued to do thereafter. The dominance of the state sector provided increasing opportunities for graft for government Ministers and MPs (the latter as go-betweens and the former as providers of opportu-nities in contracts and employment). A more serious drawback of this system was the exclusion of opposition parties (including the Tamil political parties) and opposition groups from employment in the public sector. Had economic growth provided more jobs, the growing discontent among the young Tamil youth may not have turned to violence; and among the Sinhalese, the ultra left and nationalist Janatha Vimukthi Peramuna (JVP)[7] may not have become the deadly threat to state and society that they turned out to be. Sri Lanka's rural areas are free of the grim poverty seen in many parts of South Asia, and caste oppression seen in many parts of India. Agrarian reform has been more of a success than in other parts of South Asia. Yet the Sri Lankan countryside has spawned the JVP and LTTE, two of the most ferocious radical movements in the world in recent times.

One crucially important feature of Sri Lanka's recent political experi-ence, regionalization if not the internationalization of its ethnic conflict, provides yet another contrast to the Malayan/Malaysian situation. Interna-tionalization of Sri Lanka's ethnic conflict has two phases, of which the Indian intervention in the 1980s, was the principal dividing line (de Silva, 1995). Sri Lanka's ethnic conflict of the mid- and late-1970s and 1980s provided India with the opportunity to intervene in the island's affairs. There was an earlier phase. Throughout the 20th century, those who ruled India, whether they were British Viceroys, or Indian politicians, had been deeply interested in the fate of the Indian community on the island, especially in insisting that the bulk of them be absorbed by Ceylon or Sri Lanka as citizens. The controversies over these issues have been especially acrimonious since 1928. Agreement was reached on the terms of a settlement of this question between India and Sri Lanka in 1964 and 1974 but it was only in 1988 that the residual issues stemming from the earlier agreements were finally settled.

India's interest in the problems of Sri Lanka's larger Tamil minority is a more recent development, something that emerged and grew in the 1970s and 1980s with India reaching out into her neighborhood in the role of regional hegemon, especially after her decisive intervention in the separatist campaign in what is now Bangladesh. The Bangladesh episode has had a profound influence on the thinking of Tamil separatist groups in Sri Lanka both in terms of the ultimate objective, and the process—Indian assistance—through which it could be achieved. India has had three roles in Sri Lanka's ethnic conflict. The first, which was intensified with Mrs. Gandhi's return to power in 1980, was that of a covert supporter of Sri Lankan Tamil separatist activists, several groups of which were operating in India. This covert support continued until 1987. Second, the Tamil Nadu factor forms an important facet of India's complex role in regard to Sri Lankan affairs (see the Map of Sri Lanka and Southern India in Appendix II). Seldom has a constituent unit (a province or a state) of one country influenced the relationship between it and a neighboring country with the same intensity and to the same extent that Tamil Nadu did and continues to do in the case of India's relations with Sri Lanka. The India-Tamil Nadu-Sri Lanka relationship is thus a unique one in international affairs. Admittedly India's own role is more complex than merely reacting to the pressures of domestic politics in Tamil Nadu. Nevertheless, concerns about the latter have been an important consideration. Tamil Nadu governments have provided Sri Lankan Tamil separatist activists with sanctuaries, training and bases. Not only did the central government connive in this, but it also tolerated the provision of training facilities in Tamil Nadu and the existence of camps and bases there and in other parts of the country. These began with Indira Gandhi, and in the early 1980s, that is to say, well before the riots of July 1983, in Sri Lanka.

India's role of mediator—the third of India's roles—began under Mrs. Gandhi as a calculated political response to the anti-Tamil riots of July

1983 in Sri Lanka and continued under her son and successor Rajiv Gandhi. A version of that third role, active participant, began in late 1987 and continued to the middle of 1990. That too is almost unique in the history of mediation in ethnic conflict: never before, or very rarely indeed, has a mediator taken on the role of combatant, and the presumed guardian of an ethnic minority's interests waged a bitter war against sections of that minority, and in a neighboring state at that.

For conflict resolution specialists and international relations experts alike, the Indian intervention in Sri Lanka's ethnic conflict, initiated by Mrs. Gandhi, provides a classic case study. Conflict resolution specialists will see in Mrs. Gandhi's intervention in the Sri Lankan imbroglio, commencing in the last week of July 1983, the beginning of an Indian involvement which went through three phases; of attempts at resolution, management and settlement. In essence, the record of these efforts is a study of the failure of a mediator, in each of these phases. International relations experts will see in it the operation of two themes, the regional-power-small-state relationship in an acute form, and the internationalization of ethnic conflict in all its ramifications. The Sri Lanka-India relationship has few parallels in international affairs unless one looks at the superpowers and the periphery of their spheres of influence if not control: the US in the Caribbean, or Central America, the Soviet Union in the Baltic and Caucasus regions among others. From the outset, Mrs. Gandhi's statements and actions made it clear that she regarded India as a principal mediator rather than a neutral one.

India's intervention in Sri Lanka's ethnic conflict began with giving aid to one or other of the Tamil separatist groups. This assistance was given, in part, to sustain the continuation of the struggle to the point of compelling or persuading the Sri Lanka government to alter its strategy, and to negotiate a settlement under Indian auspices. Secondly, in 1987, the Indian government sought to resolve the conflict itself, by acting as a mediator, applying sanctions to one, some or all parties to the conflict, and underwriting a settlement. In the process, the Indians became a common enemy to all or some of the warring factions. The Indian intervention in the Sri Lanka conflict shows how the consequences of internationalization of an ethnic conflict are not necessarily those which the affected parties generally anticipate; indeed, as the case of the Tamils of Sri Lanka and the Indian involvement on their behalf demonstrated, the intervention was not advantageous to the presumed beneficiaries. On the contrary, internationalization actually prolonged the conflict and made many of the parties to the conflict more intractable; again, when—as in the case of India's intervention in the

Sri Lankan conflict in 1987—large regional or global powers enter a domestic ethnic dispute playing the role of sponsors and suppliers, the original issues in the conflict are superseded by the interests of the external contenders.

The hard lesson that emerges from India's mediation and interventionist role in Sri Lanka's ethnic conflict is that most outside powers have much less to offer by way of examples from their own political system and political experiences than they think they have. To be drawn into an ethnic conflict in a neighboring state is the worst folly for a regional power (no less than for a super power) as Israel learned in Lebanon, and India found out in Sri Lanka soon enough. The reluctance of Sri Lankan governments to consider, much less accept, another episode of external mediation stems from the pronounced failure of Indian mediation, and the heavy political costs it inflicted on Sri Lanka's democratic system.

The Malaysian alternative

The principal question we need to answer here is how Malaya/Malaysia succeeded in maintaining a stable political structure and relatively harmonious relations between potentially antagonistic if not hostile ethnic groups while Sri Lanka failed to do so during many periods of its post-independence history. Malaya's first Prime Minister, Tunku Abdul Rahman, and Sri Lanka's D. S. Senanayake, were very much alike in a common sense approach in problems of government and a shrewd pragmatism in policy making—despite the difference in social background, a scion of a princely house in the case of Rahman, while Senanayake was a landowner and a very efficient manager of the family plantations and properties. They both had the same historic role of managing the transition from colonial to indigenous rule (on Malaya/Malaysia's demography and ethnic profile see Appendix II). As Prime Minister, Senanayake had the advantage of well-established administrative systems and considerable experience in political leadership in a democracy, indeed many more years of such leadership at a very high level than Rahman had in his career as Prime Minister. Senanayake had been Minister of Agriculture for 1931 to 1947, principal negotiator on Sri Lanka's passage to independence from 1942 to 1947, and Prime Minister from 1947 to his death in 1952. Besides, Rahman had a much more difficult political inheritance and political environment in which to establish himself than Senanayake. That he succeeded in consolidating his power and establishing a form of democratic government is a great tribute to his statesmanship.

Moreover, unlike in the case of Senanayake in Sri Lanka, there were two significant political changes of a structural nature in Malaya/Malaysia in the decade after independence—i.e., in the period 1957 to 1966[8]—that Rahman had to cope with after independence. The first of these came in 1963 when the Federation of Malaysia was established bringing together the Malay states in peninsular Malaya, and the British controlled territories of Sarawak, and Sabah, along with the island state of Singapore,[9] to form a new and larger political entity. The next phase in structural change came in 1965. With the establishment of the Federation of Malaysia in 1963, the Malays were reduced to a minority especially because of Singapore's largely Chinese population. The potential tensions in this situation became very real to Rahman and his Malay constituency very quickly when Singapore's political leadership under the dynamic Lee Kuan Yew kept insisting on a multi-racial 'Malaysian Malaysia' rather than an entity reflecting the political dominance of the Malays. This was too much for Rahman and in 1965 he contrived to have Singapore expelled from the federation, thus re-establishing and firmly consolidating the political dominance of the Malays in the polity (Milne, 1966; Soon, 1969; Yew, 1998). The name Malaysia was retained despite the absence of Singapore, a vital component element of the original Malaysia of 1963. Both Malaysia and Singapore weathered the storm. The Malays were now, unmistakably, the dominant element in the new federation.

There were three notable continuities in policy from 1957: the first of these, a coalition of ethnic groups—the main political parties were organized on ethnic lines—was one of Rahman's most constructive political initiatives and the core of the legacy he left behind to his successors. This coalition in its various forms has ruled the country from 1957 to the present day and has succeeded in maintaining the peace in a situation fraught with considerable danger of ethnic conflict.[10] The flip side of this achievement is that Malaysia, unlike Sri Lanka, has yet to see a genuine change of regime or the defeat of the principal Malay party, the United Malays National Organisation (UMNO), at a general election. Secondly, there is the recognition of the special status of the Malays in the Malaysian polity. This special status under the law, a continuity from colonial times, was incorporated in the constitutional arrangements to transfer power to Sri Lankans in 1957 although the Constitutional Commission under Lord Reid recommended that these should not be permanently incorporated in the constitution, and should be reviewed after 15 years. On the contrary, this special status was re-defined and consolidated in the 1960s, and especially after 1969. While a parliamentary system was a central feature of the political structure, there were few pretensions to democratic rule. The third point of continuity was in economic policy, from colonial times specializing in commodity production for export—rubber, palm oil, tin and later, petroleum—with foreign companies (principally British owned up to very recently) controlling more than 60 percent of the modern sector, while Chinese investors owned and operated most of the others. All three of these policies saw their origins under Tunku Abdul Rahman.

The post-election riots of 1969 in which over 600 people, mainly Chinese, were killed are treated as a watershed in Malaysia's development (see, e.g., Gagliano, 1970; Tiek, 1971; Von Vorys, 1976). While the coalition itself was returned to power at the elections that preceded the riots, the small but perceptible shift in the electoral balance was sufficient to trigger the disturbances. These were attributed in the main to the frustrations of the largely rural Malay electorate with its still conspicuously disadvantaged economic position relative to the wealthier urban-based Chinese. The government's response was to enact what it called a New Economic Policy (NEP) in 1970, designed to continue for 20 years and had the twin goals of 'removing the identification of race with economic function' and 'eradicating poverty' (Means, 1972; Esman, 1987; Gullick and Gale, 1986; Jesudasan, 1989; Jomo, 1990, Jomo, 1990–91; Mehmet, 1986; Snodgrass, 1980). Both goals aimed at enhancing Malay rural incomes and helping the Malays to move into the higher income urban-industrial sector. Ethnic quotas were imposed for corporate equity ownership, public and private sector employment, and university admission. State enterprises were set up to develop particular sectors of the economy by and for Malays, and various policies were enacted to create both a Malay bourgeoisie and a Malay industrial proletariat. Over and above all this the special privileged position of Malays in the constitution was strengthened, and placed beyond dispute or even discussion.

Once an ethnic conflict erupts, extraordinary political skills are required to manage if not resolve it. Malaysian politicians have done far better than their Sri Lankan or Indian counterparts in this regard. Needless to say much depends on the extent, duration and levels of violence of the conflict and the impact of these on the country's political structures and institutions. Over the last 30 years, there has been no violent outbursts of ethnic conflict in Malaysia.

Of the many reasons for the relatively peaceful operation of the Malaysian political system, one of the most important has been the evolution of a pragmatic political bargain between the principal ethnic groups in the country, the Malays and the Chinese. First, at the political level, the country accepts a special status for the Malays in the Malaysian polity, while also recognizing the dynamism of the Chinese minority as the source of the country's economic strength (Mauzy, 1993, pp. 112–113). This bargain is more implicit than explicit but acts as a powerful restraining influence on both. The origins of this bargain go back virtually to the early days of independence, and while it has been re-interpreted particularly after May 1969, it has lasted to the present day. The crucial difference between Malaysia and Sri Lanka is that there has been no similar 'agreement' or 'compact' between the Sinhalese and Tamils since the mid-1950s; indeed since the early 1920s. The second part of the bargain is just as important: the dynamic Chinese minority accepts an extensive affirmative action policy, called 'restructuring,' designed to improve the economic position of the Malay majority. The other minority, the Indians, have a more ambiguous position and role.

Malaysia's post-independence economic growth since independence has been phenomenal unlike Sri Lanka's. Although there were fears that the New Economic Policy would retard economic growth, the reality is that economic growth actually accelerated in the 1970s and 1980s and continued into the mid-1990s under the leadership of Mahathir bin Mohammed. Much of it continues to be dependent on the dynamism and business and managerial skills of the Chinese (Gungwu, 1991; Wu and Wu, 1980; Redding, 1990; Mackie, 1989, 1992; Gomez, 1999). The goals of economic redistribution and poverty reduction have been largely met by the 1990s. Nevertheless, although their position has improved substantially since 1971, the Malays are still unhappy. The restructuring has largely ignored intra-ethnic maldistribution of wealth. The rich Chinese and the rich Malays—for the first time in the 20th century there is a numerically significant class of rich Malays—have benefited to a greater extent than the poor of both ethnic groups. The Chinese themselves are frustrated by policies that openly discriminate against them. Nevertheless, these policies have succeeded in keeping the peace, last disturbed in 1969, and permitted the country to concentrate on economic development.

Indeed as a recent Malaysian author of Indian extraction has pointed out:

> If one recounts Malaysia's experience with ethnicity over the past three or four decades, it is possible to say that capitalist development has reduced one axis of ethnic conflict. Capitalist relations of

production have engendered certain common interests among the different ethnic groups, particularly among the elite. There is declining value to the dominant political class in politicising ethnicity. Their greater concern is to generate a high rate of growth for political support and to compete in the international economy. The necessary step for accommodation appears to have been the relative homogenisation of the class structure on ethnic lines. The irony in Malaysia is that it took explicit policies of one-sidedly pursuing the economic interests of the dominant group to effect this change (Jesudasan, 1996, p. 26).

A second factor in helping to sustain a stable and peaceful political system is the nature of Malaysia's electoral system. This first-past-the post electoral system devised in 1954 and parliamentary government based on it depends on and encourages multi-racial co-operation particularly among the racially-based component parties of the ruling coalition.[11] The contrast here between the Malaysian and Sri Lankan electoral systems reflects the difference in the spatial distribution of the various ethnic groups in the two countries. In Sri Lanka, the two national political parties generally take the Muslims and Indian Tamils resident in the Sinhalese areas into consideration in their electoral calculations but the indigenous Tamils who are largely concentrated in the north and east of the country have powerful regional parties of their own and prefer to remain independent of the national parties.[12] While the nearly continuous economic growth and development of the country since 1957 have undoubtedly given the ruling coalition in Malaya/Malaysia the resources to keep all ethnic groups more satisfied with their lot than they may have been without access to such surplus revenues, even so the demographic pattern of the country with its almost even balance between Malays and non-Malays at the time of independence has also contributed substantially to the maintenance of the political bargain referred to earlier, and has acted as a powerful deterrent to any attempt to radically alter the ethnic composition of the ruling coalition for fear of the devastating consequences of a national racial conflagration. This point, the leaders of the coalition, especially the Malays, always emphasize in their appeal to the electorate just before the elections. By and large, the electorate seems to accept the argument.

There is a third reason why the political system in Malaysia remains more stable and peaceful than that of Sri Lanka. While the minorities in Malaysia are much larger numerically than in Sri Lanka, there is no large territory with a Chinese or non-Malay majority in peninsular Malaysia. The nearest to such a situation is the small island of Penang (a state of the federation) where there is a Chinese majority but an independent Penang as a Chinese 'homeland' makes little sense politically or economically. Equally important is the distance between the Chinese in Malaysia and China itself, separated by hundreds of kilometers of land or sea, and not a mere 35 kilometers at the narrowest point as it is between the Tamils of the Jaffna peninsula in the north of Sri Lanka and Tamil Nadu in Southern India. In short, there is no territorial base to encourage aspirations to separation as there was and is in Sri Lanka; nor is there a regional power seeking to exercise its influence on behalf of a minority as India has attempted in Sri Lanka.

Convergence

The emphasis in this essay, so far, has been the contrast between the success with which Malaya/Malaysia has kept the ethnic peace since 1969, and Sri Lanka's failure to do so over any substantial length of time since the 1970s. As we have seen, the first phase of Sri Lanka's post-independence history, 1948–56, were years of solid achievement in state building and the maintenance of ethnic harmony, while the mid- and late-1950s saw the first episodes of violent conflict. One of the significant, if also poignant, features of Sri Lanka's ethnic conflict is that most of the policy options recommended by political scientists and conflict resolution theorists for the maintenance of ethnic harmony in sharply divided societies or for management of ethnic tensions have actually been adopted there. Many of these were adopted in part or in their entirety: beginning with power sharing among ethnic and religious groups within the governing bodies of national political parties; and extending to power sharing among political parties through the formation of coalitions, whether they be coalitions of necessity, of convenience, or coalitions guided by ideological considerations, or electoral arrangements prior to elections. In response to the exaggerated swing of the pendulum which gave governments massive parliamentary majorities in 1970 and 1977, proportional representation was introduced through the constitution of 1978 as a necessary corrective to this and in the hope of giving the minorities greater influence in policy making than under the first-past-the post electoral system. Some of these confidence building measures were adopted from the early days of independence, and some in the late-1950s, and in the late-1970s and 1980s in response to outbreaks of violence. One policy that was never adopted was the establishment, on the Malaysian model, of a grand coalition between the principal national parties charged with a mandate for devising common policies, if not reaching a national consensus on policies, for a resolution of the island's ethnic conflict.

If one of the answers to the question of how it all went wrong in Sri Lanka lies in the adoption of policies which sought to quicken the pace of changes that had already begun, in short-sighted attempts to secure immediate gains—e.g., the language policy of 1956, and the university admission policies of 1970–71, similar changes were made in Malaysia without the dire consequences they had in Sri Lanka. Affirmative action, in Sri Lanka, was a very limited exercise compared to the far more extensive system in operation in Malaysia. Malaysia's commitment to Malay as the national language was much stronger than Sri Lanka's to Sinhalese. Once opposition to these policies in Sri Lanka came up within the national legislature and outside it, and it came soon enough in the case of the language reforms of 1956–58, with ethnic tensions breaking out into violence, attempts were made at modifications of these policies (1958). Two decades later, a new government embarked on a reversal of its predecessor's language policies and modification of university admissions policy (1978–88), the only area in which affirmative action was in operation. Neither modifications of policies or reversals of policies have proved to be effective in repairing the damage. The attempts at removing grievances on a piecemeal basis, resorted to in Sri Lanka in the case of language policy from 1958 and thereafter in the 1970s and 1980s and in the case of university admission policies in the late 1970s and 1980s have had less of a positive impact in regard to reconciliation than was anticipated (de Silva, 1997b, 1997c). An interesting theme in conflict resolution thus emerges in Sri Lanka—even carefully considered and well publicized reversals of controversial policies and indeed their repudiation have had less of an ameliorative effect in a situation of continuing conflict than expected and the original sense of grievance remains only slightly diminished, or is sustained at previous levels by those with a vested interest in prolonging it for their own political ends. In Malaysia, less publicized and less substantial modifications and adjustments have kept the NEP going without strong resistance from the non-Malays (Lim and Gosling, 1997, pp. 125–129).

Part of the answer to the problem is the difference between the two principal minorities in the two countries. To argue as Donald Horowitz does that the difference lies in the fact that the Sri Lanka Tamils are an indigenous minority who had settled in the island for over 1,500 years, unlike the Chinese in Malaysia is not by itself a completely satisfactory explanation, because not all the Chinese in Malaysia are 19th and 20th century migrants.[13] Indeed the Chinese have a very long history of settlement in the Malay states going back several centuries. The difference in the political attitudes of the Sri Lanka Tamils and the Chinese in Malaya needs to be examined in greater depth than is possible in this essay. All we can do here is to point out that in Sri Lanka the 'moderate center' of Tamil opinion has been and continues to be generally reluctant to publicly acknowledge the advantages and benefits of this line of action for fear of being marginalized even further by intransigent Tamil separatist activists. In Malaysia, the 'moderate center' of Chinese and Indian opinion has held firm against the ethnic intransigents in their communities.

The moral of the Sri Lanka story is that it is extremely difficult to restore the *status quo ante* once damage has been done by hastily devised policies. On the basis of the empirical evidence from Sri Lanka, it would be true to say that the ethnic tensions have generally occurred whenever governments have either totally disregarded, or paid less attention than they should have, to the legitimate interests and concerns of minorities. After 1977, tensions have persisted or have erupted in violence despite the efforts of governments to take into consideration the legitimate interest of minorities, in devising new policies, or seeking a reversal of policies which have contributed to the current conflict. What this demonstrates is that it is extremely difficult to reverse a trend during periods of prolonged ethnic conflict. Malaysia has been spared this searing test of political skills after the riots of 1969, that is to say, over the last three decades.

The Malaysian experience demonstrates how political stability is ensured if not guaranteed in societies with sharp ethnic and religious cleavages, by devising political arrangements giving minorities easy access to the highest decision-making processes. By doing so, minorities would have a sense that their opinions have been considered in devising policies, and in their implementation. Sri Lanka's own record in this regard has been more constructive and imaginative than its recent history of the persistence of ethnic tensions and frequent eruptions of violence would lead us to believe.

Even more important, the Malaysian experience has demonstrated how political stability could be ensured in a situation where religious or linguistic divisions have deep historical roots, by a deliberate lowering of expectations on both sides of the divide. Just as a majority group who believe that they have been the principal victims of the imposition of colonial rule—as the Sinhalese do—should do well to resist the temptation to adopt policies that would hasten the redress of historical grievances, so too a minority group should desist from making exaggerated claims and demands. Examples from Sri Lanka would be the '50–50' campaign[14] of the Sri Lankan Tamils in the late 1930s and 1940s, which sought an equalization of representation in the national legislature between the Sinhalese majority (about 70% of the population in the 1940s) and the minorities; and in more recent times the claim to exclusive possession or rights to parts of the country identified as 'the traditional homelands of the Tamils' about a third of the country and half its coast line for less than 12% of the people (de Silva, 1994). As against this a process of mutual lowering of expectations has kept the Malaysian political system stable since independence and helped it to withstand the political tremors set off by the ethnic riots of 1969 in that country. Although the processes of government are then often reduced to a prosaic and humdrum search for areas of agreement between contending groups or factions within those groups, it has had the great benefit of keeping the peace in a sharply divided society. As a result, Malaysia remains a low conflict area, while Sri Lanka has been converted from a low conflict area to one of high conflict.

Finally, in this world of instant communications, most television viewers and newspaper readers are likely to have heard of Sri Lanka because of its recent record of ethnic strife. The core of the Sri Lankan paradox lies in the fact that despite this ethnic strife, Sri Lanka has been a functioning multi-party democracy, and a welfare state of sorts which gives its people a quality of life well above what could be expected of a country with an annual per capita GNP, at present, of about $800.

Sri Lanka is the pioneer in South Asian democracy. In 1931, sixteen years before independence, it became the center of an unusual experiment in preparing a people for independence—the introduction of universal suffrage to a crown colony.[15] Thus, one of the essential ingredients of democracy was established, nearly 70 years ago, more than 20 years before universal suffrage came to India, and only three years after the process was completed in Britain itself. Sri Lanka's first general election under universal suffrage came in 1931, only two years after the first such election in Britain. Women in Sri Lanka had the right to vote, at age 21, long before women in some European countries, France, Belgium and Switzerland, for instance.

Indeed, Sri Lanka, like India, has had a longer history in the working of multi-party democracy than other nations of the developing world, and in many parts of the developed world. Both countries, Sri Lanka in particular, illustrate a dismal truth that very often the compulsions of electoral politics in multi-party democracies help to aggravate ethnic tensions.

There were, of course, other positive features. Traditionally, Sri Lanka had taken pride in its welfare state developed since the late 1930s and early 1940s. The major premise in the decision taken to introduce universal suffrage in 1931 was that it would compel the country's political leadership to be more responsive to the needs of the masses. The form that response took and the speed with which it came were to leave an indelible mark on the post-independence history of the island. The most striking and far-reaching effects of that response was that universal suffrage stimulated a broad impulse towards social welfare beginning in the period 1936–47 and this has continued to the present day. There were four areas of concentration in this, beginning with a program of restoring the irrigation works of the dry zone of the island and the settlement of peasant 'colonists' in that region, transferred from the more crowded parts of the island. The construction of new irrigation works began in the 1950s culminating in the massive Mahaveli project, of the late 1970s and early 1980s, the largest and most complex irrigation scheme in the island's history. The other aspects of this social welfare orientation were: substantial government expenditure on education, health and food subsidies. Together these formed part of Sri Lanka's mini-welfare state. Food subsidies were gradually removed in the 1970s.

The country thus had quite different priorities from her South and Southeast Asian neighbors: between a third and two-fifths of the budget was spent on welfare services—education, health, food subsidies, and the settlement of landless peasants on irrigated land. As late as 1985, an observer of Sri Lanka's welfare policies could point out that the country 'unlike its Asian neighbors or even most countries of the Third World [was] virtually demilitarised' (Bjorkman, 1988, p. 547). Ironically, just at the time these comments were published—1985–86—large sums of money were being diverted to meet the threat posed by the Tamil separatists and the guerrilla and terrorist groups associated with them. While this increased level of defense experience has been maintained since then, and especially since the early 1990s, Sri Lanka's welfare programs have not been seriously affected. Nor has there been any militarization of its politics. Thus Sri Lanka's pronounced failure to keep the social peace has to be set against its excellent PQLI score. Sri Lanka's performance in regard to the latter continues to be superior to that of its neighbors in South Asia, and in many aspects as good as those of Southeast Asia, and parts of East Asia. Certainly, the PQLI score is superior to that of Malaysia where the *per capita* GNP is more than six times that of Sri Lanka.

In the successful working of democratic forms of governance, the Sri Lankan and Indian experiences provide a convincing refutation of the assumptions of the leading theorists of democracy on the essential requirements for establishment and nurturing of democracy—theorists ranging from Robert A Dahl (1989), Barrington Moore (1966), Seymour Martin Lipset, Larry Diamond and Juan Linz (1989)—all of whom assume that a high level of economic prosperity and development is an essential prerequisite for the success of democracy. Adam Przeworski and Fernado Limongi (1997, p. 168) argue, that: 'Bad economic performance in poor countries makes democracy particularly vulnerable: in a declining economy with a per capita income of less than $1,000 democracy can be expected to last on an average less than four years.' This is a new and perverse version, based on a spurious statistical calculation, of the argument made by the more sophisticated theorists of democratization identified earlier in this paragraph. The point, however, is that Sri Lanka's record in the establishment and maintenance of a democratic system provides virtually irrefutable evidence to challenge the validity of this contention. With a per capita GNP of around $800, Sri Lanka has the highest per capita GNP in the whole of South Asia; its economy has not been particularly buoyant. Yet, it has sustained a democratic system for 50 years or more, despite the ethnic tensions and conflicts which have been a prominent feature of Sri Lanka's politics especially since the 1980s. Malaysia has kept ethnic conflicts at bay since 1969, but its political system is much less democratic than Sri Lanka's, and its constitution guarantees a privileged position for its Malay majority—and prohibits public discussion of that privileged status, much less criticisms of it—unlike the Sri Lankan constitution.

In terms of the GNP, Sri Lanka, like all parts of South Asia, has been left far behind by many Southeast Asian states—the per capita GNP in Malaysia is six times that of Sri Lanka—but it ranks well above most, if not all of Southeast Asia, on the physical quality of life index; in literacy, infant mortality and life expectancy. Currently the literacy rate is nearly 90% while infant mortality is around 13 per thousand live births, and life expectancy is over 72 years. As a comparison of these figures with other countries from around the world would make plain, no other low-income country anywhere has achieved Sri Lanka's level of social development and well being. All governments since independence have built upon and consolidated past achievements, a record that is all the more remarkable given the turmoil of the last two decades, and diversion of resources to build up the country's once meager defense system.

Notes

1. Two useful introductory regional surveys on ethnicity and politics in South Asia, are Ghosh, P. S. (1989), *Cooperation and Conflict in South Asia*, Manohar Publishers: Delhi; and Phadnis, U. (1990), *Ethnicity and Nation-building in South Asia*, Sage Publications: New Delhi. On the same themes in Southeast Asia, see Brown, D. (1995), *The State and Ethnic Politics in Southeast Asia*, Routledge: London.

2. For a previous attempt at a comparison between Sri Lanka and Malaya/Malaysia, see Horowitz, D. L. (1991), 'Making Moderation Pay: The Comparative Politics of Ethnic Conflict Management', in Montville, J. V. (ed.), *Conflict and Peacemaking in Multiethnic Societies*, Lexington Books: Lexington, MA and Toronto. See especially, pp. 459–471.

3. This point is made very effectively by Clutterbuck, R. (1985), *Conflict and Violence in Singapore and Malaysia, 1945–1983*, Graham Brash (Pte.) Ltd.: Singapore, pp. 32–37.

4. On immigration to Malaya, see Arasaratnam, S. (1978), *Indians in Malaysia and Singapore*, Revised Edition, Oxford University Press: Kuala Lumpur; Purcell, V. (1967), *The Chinese in Malaya*, 2nd Edition, Oxford University Press: London; Sandhu, K. S. (1969), *Indians in Malaya: Some Aspects of Their Immigration and Settlement, 1786–1957*, Cambridge University Press: Cambridge. Indian immigration to Sri Lanka is not well researched as that to Malaya. A very recent publication is Sahadevan, P. (1995), *India and Overseas Indians: The Case of Sri Lanka*, Kalinga: Delhi. Also see Kodikara, S. U. (1965), *Indo-Ceylon Relations Since Independence*, The Ceylon Institute of World Affairs: Colombo.

5. Sri Lanka's passage to independence is reviewed by the present author in his introduction to the volume on Sri Lanka, edited by him in British Documents on the End of Empire series. Parts I and II, The Stationary Office, London, for the Institute of Commonwealth Studies, University of London, 1997. The introduction is in Part I, pp. xxxi to lxxxvi.

6. For an excellent documentary survey of Malaysia's passage to independence, see Stockwell, A. J. (ed.) (1995), *Malaya*, 3 parts, in the same series, by the same publisher, London, 1995. See particularly the editor's introduction in Part I, pp. xxxi–lxxxiv. See also Milton J. Esman's perceptive chapter titled 'Malaysia: Native Sons and Immigrants', in Esman, M. J. (ed.) (1994), *Ethnic Politics*, Cornell University Press: Ithaca, NY and London, pp. 49–74.

7. On the JVP, the best study is Chandraprema, C. A. (1991), *Sri Lanka: The Years of Terror—The JVP Insurrection, 1987–1989*, Lake House Bookshop: Colombo. The first JVP insurgency of 1971 is reviewed in Alles, A. C. (1976), *Insurgency 1971: An Account of the April Insurrection in Sri Lanka*, Trade Exchange (Ceylon): Colombo. See also Gerald Peiris's very perceptive article titled, 'Insurrection and Youth Unrest in Sri Lanka', in Peiris, G. and de A. Samarasinghe, S. W. R. (eds.) (1999), *History and Politics: Millennial Perspectives: Essays in Honor of Kingsley de Silva*, Law and Society Trust: Colombo, pp. 165–200.

8. On the early years of independence, see Bedlington, S. S. (1978), *Malaysia and Singapore: The Building of New States*, Cornell University Press: Ithaca, NY and London; Ongkili, J. P. (1985), *Nation Building in Malaysia, 1946–1974*, Oxford

University Press: Kuala Lumpur; Sopiee, M. N. (1974), *From Malayan Union Singapore Separation: Political Unification in the Malaysian Union, 1945–1965*, Penerbit Universiti: Kuala Lumpur; Stockwell, A. J. (1979), *British Policy and Malay Politics During the Malayan Union Experiment*, Malaysian Branch of the Royal Asiatic Society: Kuala Lumpur. See also Tunku Abdul Rahman's memoirs, *Looking Back: Monday Musings and Memories*, Pustaka Antara: Kuala Lumpur, 1977.

9.   Singapore was granted independence in 1959.

10.   The Malays were represented by the United Malays National Organization (UMNO), the Chinese by the Malayan Chinese Association (MCA) and the Indians by the Malayan Indian Congress (MIC). The governing coalition, The Alliance, was formed by these parties. The situation changed after 1969. The successor to the pre-1969 Alliance government is the Barisan National which consists of a larger number of parties, but with UMNO still as its core. See, Means, G. P. (1976), *Malaysian Politics*, 2nd Edition, Hodder and Stoughton: London; Means, G. P. and Mauzy, D. K. (1986), *Malaysia: Tradition, Modernity and Islam*, Westview Press: Boulder, CO; Von Vorys, K. (1976), *Democracy Without Consensus: Communalism and Political Stability in Malaysia*, Princeton University Press: Princeton, NJ.

11.   The Committee did think of a system of PR but decided against it for fear that the PR would encourage a large number of small parties at a time when the country needed the stability that only a strong government could provide. See, Rachagan, S. (1978), 'The Development of the Electoral System', in Crouch, H. et al. (eds.), *Malaysian Politics and the 1978 Election*, Oxford University Press: Kuala Lumpur.

12.   For a comparative analysis of the Sri Lankan and Malaysian electoral systems among others, see de Silva, K. M. (1998b), 'Electoral Systems', in Young, C. (ed.), *Ethnic Diversity and Public Policy: A Comparative Inquiry*, Macmillan: London.

13.   See Horowitz, D. L. (1991), 'Making Moderation Pay: The Comparative Politics of Ethnic Conflict Management', in Montville, J. V. (ed.), *Conflict and Peacemaking in Multiethnic Societies*, Lexington Books: Lexington, MA and Toronto. On the migration of Chinese to Malaysia, see Purcell, V. (1967), *The Chinese in Malaya*, 2nd Edition, Oxford University Press: London.

14.   The 'fifty-fifty' campaign was at its height in the later 1930s and 1940s. It was led by G. G. Ponnambalam who later became the founding president of the Tamil Congress (established in 1944). The best study of this subject is Russell, J. (1983), *Communal Politics Under the Donoughmore Constitution*, Tisara Publishers: Colombo.

15.   For a recent discussion of these problems, see, de Silva, K. M. (1997d), 'Sri Lanka: Surviving Ethnic Strife', *Journal of Democracy*, Vol. 8, No. 1 (January), pp. 97–111.

References

Alles, A. C. (1976), *Insurrection 1971: An Account of the April Insurrection in Sri Lanka*, Trade Exchange (Ceylon): Colombo.

Arasaratnam, S. (1978), *Indians in Malaysia and Singapore*, Revised Edition, Oxford University Press: Kuala Lumpur.

Bedlington, S. S. (1978), *Malaysia and Singapore: The Building of New States*, Cornell University Press: Ithaca, NY and London.

Bjorkman, J. W. (1988), 'Health Policy and Politics in Sri Lanka', *Asian Survey*, Vol. 25, No. 5, p. 547.

Brown, D. (1995), *The State and Ethnic Politics in Southeast Asia*, Routledge: London.

Chandraprema, C. A. (1991), *Sri Lanka: The Years of Terror—The JVP Insurrection, 1987–1989*, Lake House Bookstore: Colombo.

Chapman, F. S. (1963), *The Jungle is Neutral*, Chatto and Windus: London.

Clutterbuck, R. (1973), *Riot and Revolution in Singapore and Malaya, 1945–1963*, Faber and Faber: London.

Clutterbuck, R. (1985), *Conflict and Violence in Singapore and Malaysia, 1945–1983*, Graham Brash (Pte.) Ltd.: Singapore.

Furnivall, J. S. (1948), *Colonial Policy and Practice*, Cambridge University Press: Cambridge.

Dahl, R. A. (1989), *Democracy and Its Critics*, Yale University Press: New Haven, CT.

de Silva, K. M. (1993), 'Language, Ethnicity and Politics: The Making of Sri Lanka's Official Language Act No. 33 of 1956', *Ethnic Studies Review*, Vol. 11, No. 1, pp. 1–29.

de Silva, K. M. (1994), *The Traditional Homelands of the Tamils—Separatist Ideology in Sri Lanka: A Historical Appraisal*, 2nd Revised Edition, International Center for Ethnic Studies: Kandy, Sri Lanka.

de Silva, K. M. (1995), *Regional Powers and Small State Security: India and Sri Lanka, 1977–1990*, Woodrow Wilson Center Press: Washington, D.C. and Johns Hopkins University Press: Baltimore, MD.

de Silva, K. M. (1996), 'Coming Full Circle: The Politics of Language in Sri Lanka, 1943–1996', *Ethnic Studies Review*, Vol. 14, No. 1, pp. 11–48.

de Silva, K. M. (1997a), 'The Taming of Sri Lanka's National Press, 1960–1974', in Peiris, G. H. (ed.), *Studies on the Press in Sri Lanka and South Asia*, ICES: Kandy, Sri Lanka.

de Silva, K. M. (1997b), 'Multiculturalism in Sri Lanka: Historical Legacy and Contemporary Reality', *Ethnic Studies Review*, Vol. 15, No. 1 (January), pp. 1–44.

de Silva, K. M. (1997c), 'Affirmative Action Policies: The Sri Lankan Experience', *Ethnic Studies Review*, Vol. 15, No. 2, pp. 245–286.

de Silva, K. M. (1997d), 'Sri Lanka: Surviving Ethnic Strife', *Journal of Democracy*, Vol. 8, No. 1 (January), pp. 97–111.

de Silva, K. M. (1998a), *Reaping the Whirlwind: Ethnic Conflict, Ethnic Politics in Sri Lanka*, Penguin Books: New Delhi.

de Silva, K. M. (1998b), 'Electoral Systems', in Young, C. (ed.), *Ethnic Diversity and Public Policy: A Comparative Inquiry*, Macmillan: London.

Emerson, R. (1957), 'Foreword', in King, F. H. H., *The New Malayan Nation: A Study of Communalism and Nationalism*, Institute of Pacific Relations: New York.

Esman, M. J. (1987), 'Ethnic Politics and Economic Power', *Comparative Politics*, Vol. 19, No. 4 (July), pp. 401–406, 413–414.

Esman, M. J. (1994), 'Malaysia: Native Sons and Immigrants', in Esman, M. J. (ed.), *Ethnic Politics*, Cornell University Press: Ithaca, NY and London.

Gagliano, F. V. (1970), *Communal Violence in Malaysia, 1969: The Political Aftermath*, Ohio University Press: Athens, OH.

Ghosh, P. S. (1989), *Cooperation and Conflict in South Asia*, Manohar Publishers: Delhi.

Gomez, T. E. (1999), *Chinese Business in Malaysia: Accumulation, Accomodation and Ascendance*, Curzon: London.

Gullick, J. M. (1963), *Malaya*, E. Benn: London.

Gullick, J. M. and Gale, B. (1986), *Malaysia: Its Political and Economic Development*, Pelanduk Publications: Petaling Jaya.

Gungwu, W. (1991), *China and the Chinese Overseas*, Times Academic Press: Singapore.

Hasbullah, S. H. (1995), 'The Ethnic Crisis and Internal Displacement: The Muslim Minority of the Northern Province of Sri Lanka', Unpublished seminar paper presented in May, at the International Center for Ethnic Studies, Kanday, Sri Lanka.

Horowitz, D. L. (1991), 'Making Moderation Pay: The Comparative Politics of Ethnic Conflict Management', in Montville, J. (ed.), *Conflict and Peacemaking in Multi-ethnic Societies*, Lexington Book: Lexington, MA and Toronto.

Jesudasan, J. V. (1989), *Ethnicity and the Economy: The State, Chinese Business and Multi-Nationals in Malaysia*, Oxford University Press: Singapore.

Jesudasan, J. V. (1996), *The Management of Segmented Citizenship in Malaysia*, International Center for Ethnic Studies: Kandy, Pamphlet Series, No. 5.

Jomo, K. S. (1990), *Growth and Structural Change in the Malaysian Economy*, St. Martin's Press: New York.

Jomo, K. S. (1990–91), 'Whither Malaysia's New Economic Policy?', *Pacific Affairs*, Vol. 64 (Winter), pp. 469–499.

Kodikara, S. U. (1965), *Indo-Ceylon Relations Since Independence*, The Ceylon Institute of World Affairs: Colombo.

Lim, L. Y. C. and Gosling, L. A. P. (1997), 'Economic Growth and Ethnic Relations: The Chinese and Southeast Asia', in Thompson, W. S. and Jensen, K. M. (eds.), *Rapid Economic Growth, Conflict and Peace in Southeast Asia*, United States Institute of Peace: Washington, D.C.

Lipset, S. M., Diamond, L. and Linz, J. J. (eds.) (1989), *Democracy in Developing Countries*, Vol. 3, Lynne Reinner: Boulder, CO.

Mackie, J. (1989), 'Chinese Businessmen and the Rise of Southeast Asian Capitalism', *Solidarity*, No. 123 (July-September), pp. 96–107.

Mackie, J. (1992), 'Changing Patterns of Chinese Big Business in South East Asia', in MacVey, R. (ed.), *South East Asian Capitalists*, South East Asia Program, Cornell University: Ithaca, NY.

Mauzy, D. (1993), 'Malaysia: Malay Political Hegemony and Coercive Consociationalism', in McGarry, J. and O'Leary, B. (eds.), *The Politics of Ethnic Conflict Regulation*, Routledge: London.

Means, G. P. (1972), 'Special Rights As a Strategy for Development: The Case of Malaysia', *Comparative Politics*, Vol. 1, pp. 29–61.

Means, G. P. (1976), *Malaysian Politics*, 2nd Edition, Hodder and Stoughton: London.

Means, G. P. and Mauzy, D. K. (1986), *Malaysia: Tradition, Modernity and Islam*, Westview Press: Boulder, CO.

Mehmet, O. (1986), *Development in Malaysia*, Croom Helm: London.

Milne, R. S. (1966), 'Singapore's Exit from Malaysia: The Consequences of Ambiguity', *Asian Survey*, Vol. 6 (March), pp. 176–184.

Moore, B. (1966), *Social Origins of Dictatorship and Democracy: Lord and Peasant in the Making of the Modern World*, Beacon Books: Boston.

Ongkili, J. P. (1985), *Nation Building in Malaysia, 1946–1974*, Oxford University Press: Kuala Lumpur.

Peiris, G. (1999), 'Insurrection and Youth Unrest in Sri Lanka', in Peiris, G. and de A. Samarasinghe, S. W. R. (eds.), *History and Politics: Millennial Perspectives, Essays in Honor of Kingsley de Silva*, Law and Society Trust: Colombo.

Phadnis, U. (1990), *Ethnicity and Nation-building in South Asia*, Sage Publications: New Delhi.

Przeworski, A. and Limongi, F. (1997), 'Democracy and Development', in Hadenus, A. (ed.), *Democracy's Victory and Crisis*, Cambridge University Press: Cambridge.

Purcell, V. (1967), *The Chinese in Malaya*, 2nd Edition, Oxford University Press: London.

Rachagan, S. (1978), 'The Development of the Electoral System', in Crouch, H. et al. (eds.), *Malaysian Politics and the 1978 Election*, Oxford University Press: Kuala Lumpur.

Rachman, T. A. (1977), *Looking Back, Monday Musings and Memories*, Pustaka Antara: Kuala Lumpur.

Redding, S. G. (1990), *The Spirit of Chinese Capitalism*, Walter de Gruyer: New York.

Russell, J. (1982), 'Language, Education and Nationalism—The Language Debate of 1944', *The Ceylon Journal of Historical and Social Studies*, New Series, Vol. 8, No. 2, pp. 38–64.

Russell, J. (1983), *Communal Politics Under the Donoughmore Constitution*, Tisara Publishers: Colombo.

Sahadevan, P. (1995), *India and Overseas Indians: The Case of Sri Lanka*, Kalinga: Delhi.

Sandhu, K. S. (1969), *Indians in Malaya: Some Aspects of Their Immigration and Settlement, 1786–1957*, Cambridge University Press: Cambridge.

Short, A. (1960), *The Communist Insurrection in Malaya, 1948–1960*, Muller: London.

Snodgrass, D. R. (1980), *Inequality and Economic Development in Malaysia*, Oxford University Press: Kuala Lumpur.

Soon, L. T. (1969), 'Malaysia-Singapore Relations: Crisis of Adjustment', *Journal of South East Asian Studies*, Vol. X (March), pp. 155–167.

Sopiee, M. N. (1974), *From Malayan Union to Singapore Separation: Political Unification in the Malaysian Union, 1945–1965*, Penerbit Universiti: Kuala Lumpur.

Stockwell, A. J. (1979), *British Policy and Malay Politics During the Malayan Union Experiment*, Malaysian Branch of the Royal Asiatic Society: Kuala Lumpur.

Stockwell, A. J. (ed.) (1995, *Malaya* (3 parts)), The Stationary Office (London), for the Institute of Commonwealth Studies, University of London: London.

Tiek, G. C. (1971), *The May Thirteenth Incident and Democracy in Malaysia*, Oxford University Press: Kuala Lumpur.

Von Vorys, K. (1976), *Democracy Without Consensus: Communalism and Political Stability in Malaysia*, Princeton University Press: Princeton, NJ.

Wu, Y.-L. and Wu, C.-H. (1980), *Chinese Development in South East Asia: The Chinese Dimension*, Hoover Institution Press: Stanford, CA.

Yew, L. K. (19980, *The Singapore Story: The Memoirs of Lee Kuan Yew*, Singapore Press Holdings, Times Edition: Singapore.

Appendix 1

Appendix I–1   Sri Lanka: area (square kilometers)

Total land Area (excluding inland waters)	62,705
Western province	3,593
Central province	5,575
Southern province	5,383
North-Western province	7,406
Sabaragamuwa province	4,921
Northern province	8,290
Eastern province	9,361
Uva province	8,435
North-Central province	9,741

Appendix I–2   Sri Lanka: population

Population		*Population (millions)*	
Census 1981	14,846,750	1995	18.1
Male ('000)	7,568.3	1996	18.3
Females ('000)	7,278.5	1997*	18.5
1994 (Mid Year)	17,865		
Male ('000)	9,107		
Females ('000)	8,758		
Population density (per sq. km) at mid-1996			292

Note: *Provisional.

Sources: Department of Census and Statistics, *Statistical Abstract 1997*; Central Bank of Sri Lanka, *Economic and Social Statistics of Sri Lanka.*

Appendix I-3 Sri Lanka: principal ethnic groups (census 1981)

	Sinhalese	Sri Lankan Tamil	Indian Tamil	Sri Lankan Moor	Burgher*	Malay	Others
Western province	3,321,830	228,516	59,402	238,728	28,542	31,670	11,119
Central province	1,318,530	149,819	380,826	146,937	3,090	4,465	5,581
Southern province	1,789,914	14,454	25,215	46,699	575	4,710	1,094
Northern province	35,128	957,247	63,759	50,831	539	160	1,740
Eastern province	243,701	399,299	10,857	315,436	4,158	1,045	755
North–western province	1,532,979	47,202	8,905	109,791	1,002	2,213	2,242
North–central province	774,799	13,293	843	50,413	287	447	1,410
Uva province	696,596	42,866	138,357	31,912	683	1,612	2,496
Sabaragamuwa province	1,266,091	34,168	130,492	48,180	498	641	1,961
Total	10,979,568	1,886,864	818,656	1,038,927	39,374	46,963	28,398

Note: *People of Dutch or Portuguese extraction.
Sources: Dept. of Census and Statistics, *Statistical Abstract 1997.*

Appendix I-4   Sri Lanka: principal ethnic groups (census 1981)—Percentage distribution of ethnic groups by province

	Sinhalese	Sri Lankan Tamil	Indian Tamil	Sri Lankan Moor	Burgher	Malay	Others
Western province	30.3	12.1	7.3	23.0	72.5	67.4	39.2
Central province	12.0	7.9	46.5	14.1	7.8	9.5	19.7
Southern province	16.3	0.8	3.1	4.5	1.5	10.0	3.9
Northern province	0.3	50.7	7.8	4.9	1.4	0.3	6.1
Eastern province	2.2	21.2	1.3	30.4	10.6	2.2	2.7
North-western province	14.0	2.5	1.1	10.6	2.5	4.7	7.9
North-central province	7.1	0.7	0.1	4.9	0.7	1.0	5.0
Uva province	6.3	2.3	16.9	3.1	1.7	3.4	8.8
Sabaragamuwa province	11.5	1.8	15.9	4.6	1.3	1.4	6.9

Source: Dept. of Census and Statistics, *Statistical Abstract 1997.*

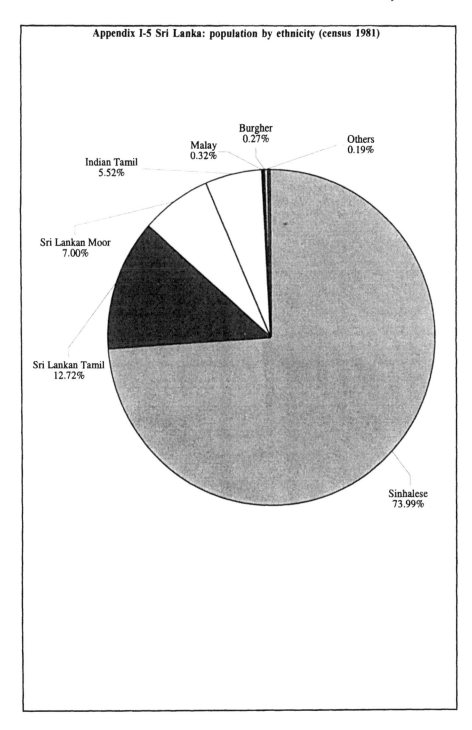

Appendix I-5 Sri Lanka: population by ethnicity (census 1981)

Burgher
0.27%

Others
0.19%

Malay
0.32%

Indian Tamil
5.52%

Sri Lankan Moor
7.00%

Sri Lankan Tamil
12.72%

Sinhalese
73.99%

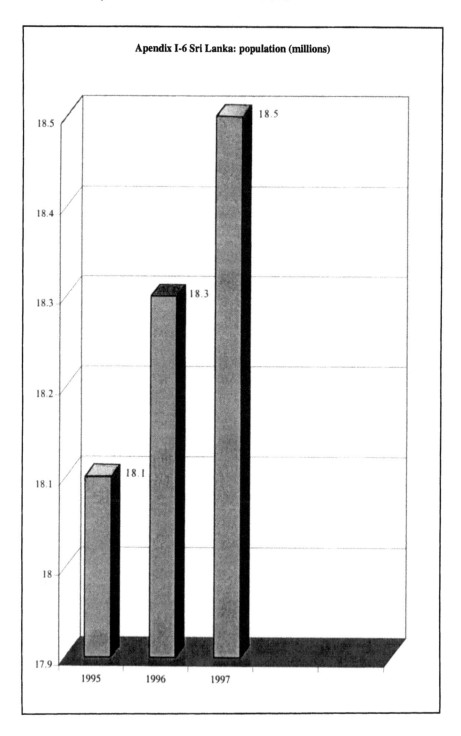

Apendix I-6 Sri Lanka: population (millions)

Appendix II

Appendix II–1 Distribution of Malaysian population in the 1940s

Ethnic group	Population	Population of ethnic group as a percent of total population
Malays	2,600,000	49.0%
Chinese	2,040,000	38.5%
Indians*	578,000	11.0%
European	12,000	0.2%
Other	70,000	1.3%

Note: *Includes Pakistanis and Sri Lankans.
Source: Clutterback, R. (1985), *Conflict and Ethnic Violence in Singapore and Malaysia 1945–1983*, Graham Brash (Pte.) Ltd.: Singapore, p. 33.

Appendix II–2 Malaysia: area

Region	Area (sq. km.)
Peninsular Malaysia	131,573
Sabah (including Labuan)	73,711
Sarawak	124,449
Total	329,733 (127, 311 sq. miles)

Appendix II–3 Malaysia: population

Population (census result)*		Population	
June 10, 1980	13,745,241	1995	20,689,300
August 14, 1991		1996	21,169,000
Male	9,327,519	1997	21,667,500
Female	9,052,136		
Total population	18,379,655	Density (per sq. km.) at mid-1997	65.7

Note: *Including adjustments for under numeration. The enumerated totals were: 13,435,588 in 1980; 17,566,982 in 1991.

Appendix II–4 Malaysia: principal ethnic groups (at census of August 1991)

	Peninsular Malaysia	Sabah*	Sarawak	Total
Malays and other indigenous groups	8,433,826	1,003,540	1,209,118	10,646,484
Chinese	4,250,969	218,233	475,752	4,944,954
Indians	1,380,048	9,310	4,608	1,393,966
Others	410,544	167,790	10,541	588,875
Non-Malaysians	322,229	464,786	18,361	805,376
Total	14,797,616	1,863,659	1,718,380	18,379,655

Notes: *Including the Federal Territory of Labuan. Mid-1997 estimates are as follows (thousands of persons): Malays, 10,233.2; Other indigenous groups, 2,290.9; Chinese, 5,445.1; Others, 685.7; Total, 21,665.5.

Source: Editor, Ms. Lynn Daniel, Europa Press, *Far East and Australasia, 1998,* p. 649.

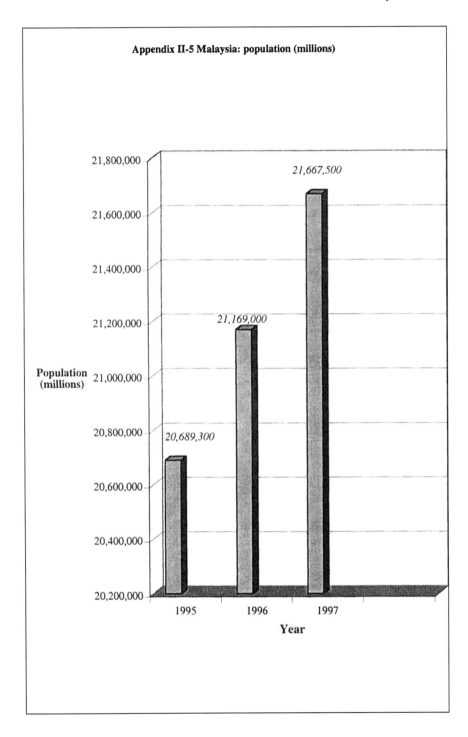

Appendix II-5 Malaysia: population (millions)

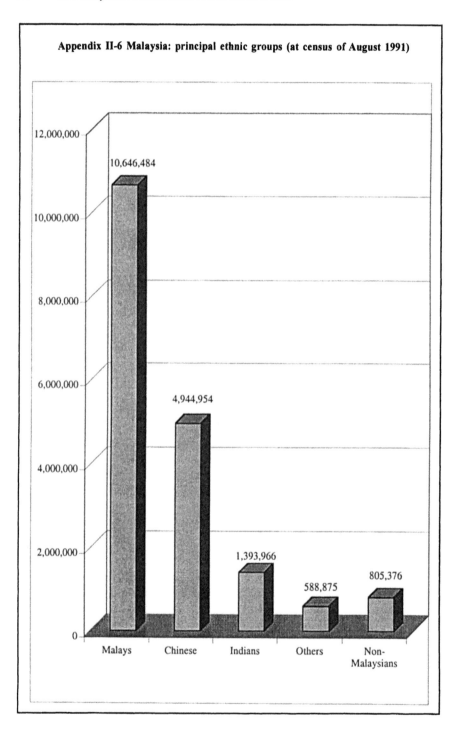

Appendix II-6 Malaysia: principal ethnic groups (at census of August 1991)

Appendix II–7 Provinces of Sri Lanka

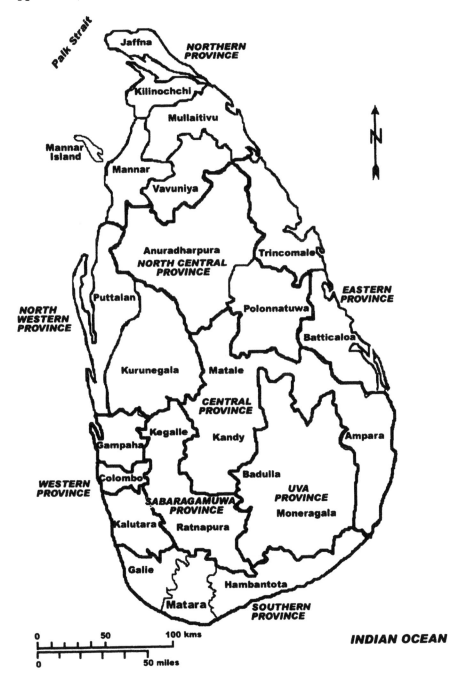

Appendix II–8 Sri Lanka and Southern India

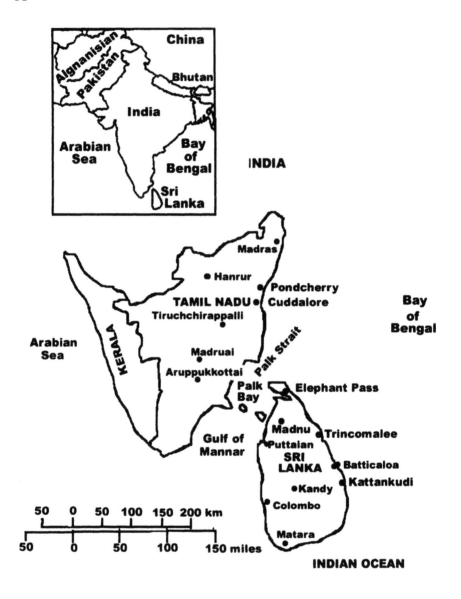

Appendix II–9 Malaysia

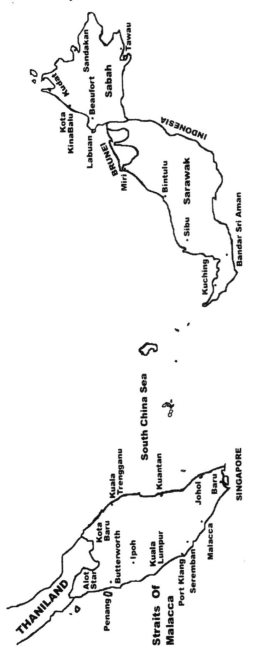

11

Ethnic Conflict and Violence: South Africa, Punjab and Sri Lanka

MOVINDRI REDDY

The starting point of this research are the battlefields of ethnic wars. The spiraling levels of violence, the sustained intensity of 'everyday' brutality, the apparent abiding commitment of 'soldiers' and the salience of identities forms the basis of this comparison. Between 1990 and 1994, the Inkatha Freedom Party (IFP) was the foremost perpetrator of gross human rights violations in KwaZulu-Natal in South Africa, accounting for some 9,000 incidents. The Seven Day War in Edendale in March 1990 is an instance when over 100 people were killed, 3,000 houses destroyed and approximately 30,000 people forced to flee their homes (Truth and Reconciliation Commission, 1999). In Sri Lanka, some 100,000 people have lost their lives in the sustained battle between the Liberation Tigers of Tamil Eelam (LTTE) and the Sinhalese government.[1] Since January 1988, 16,742 people have disappeared and there has been ample evidence of torture and executions by both state forces and the LTTE (Amnesty International, 1998). Thousands have perished in the Sikh battle for secession peaking during some periods, as in 1984 after the assassination of Indira Gandhi by her Sikh security guard when those killed by Hindus were estimated as between

2,212 and 3,879 (Tambiah, 1997, p. 119). In all three countries, sustained conflict has occurred between groups that espouse some sort of ethnic or sectarian political agenda. Another common element among them is their experience of colonial rule, particularly British rule. This comparison attempts to unravel some of the similarities and differences in the experiences of these three countries in order to expose possible elements that could shed light on the causes of ethnic conflicts.

This analysis is organized around three propositions. First, there is a link between constructions of ethnic identities and the ideology and character of authoritarian, despotic or oppressive states. I see these states as being both present and absent. That is, at one level they are highly intrusive and extractive, making deep inroads into civil society in their attempt to control and suppress, frequently using the army, police and judicial system against civilians. At another level, these states are also absent, failing to supply adequate or any welfare benefits, health, education, protection, justice, national identity and so on. It is this absence that leads to the creation of 'indigenous' structures which come to operate in place of the state.

Second, the character and constituent elements of ethnicity before and during violent conflict shifts from being transformative and changing to one that is superficially more rigid, more clearly definable and inflexible. It is this partial consensus, the portrayal of a rigidified identity at the upper levels while multiple characterizations of an ethnic group continue to be hotly debated at the lower levels by the rank and file, that lies at the center of much of the violence within ethnic groups that are engaged in violent combat with other ethnic groups.

This brings us to the third theme, the subject of violence and 'ethnic' wars. Violence becomes the vortex of identity construction, the focal point at which identities are carved out and made more salient for everyday living. Far from assuming the coherence and unity of ethnic organizations is the notion that they are in fact fractured and tensions among members runs high. An important component of this 'disunity' is the multiple interpretations of ethnicity that constituted the debate before 'the war'.

What constitutes an ethnic conflict?

The discourse on definitions of sectarian conflicts covers a wide spectrum of subjects ranging from primordial versus instrumental propositions, rational choice models and post-modern constructions. The primordial perspective proposes that if it is held that members of an ethnic group are of the same blood (Geertz, 1963),[2] then it can be inferred that individuals will be held together by moral obligations tied to primordial affinities (Shils, 1957) or extended ties of nepotism (Vanhanen, 1999, pp. 55–73). Ethnic identities are those one is born into (Isaacs, 1975; Grosby, 1994) and hence are intrinsic givens of everyday reality. Attempts have been made to concretize the concept by applying a socio-biological theory to it (see, Van Den Berghe, 1979, 1986). Critique of these positions coalesce around the 'instrumental' character of ethnicity. Emphasis is placed instead on the 'constructed' disposition of ethnicity and the modifications and remaking of identities in each generation (Eller and Coughlan, 1993). In this view, 'tribalism' entails a 'dynamic rearranging of relations and customs' (Cohen, 1969), and ethnicity is unlike kinship in that it is a 'presumed identity' that has been largely influenced by the political community (Weber, 1978). Both the subjective and objective aspects of ethnic identities are explored to study the process through which ethnic groups are created (Kasfir, 1979). The contexts of ethnicity in terms of space, place, intensities and relevant issues add further depth to these perspectives (Esman, 1977).

In emphasizing difference, John Comaroff (1987) proposes that ethnic identities are not things but relations and hence they can be no theory of ethnicity but rather a theory of history that is capable of capturing the production of difference and identity. The discourses on the role and voice of the 'subaltern' during colonialism have introduced notions that identities forged under colonial rule are oftentime elided or represented in peculiar ways in academic scholarship and texts (Guha and Spivak, 1988). Another perspective in this genre focuses on the multiple positionings that individuals assume in differing situations and relations (Bhaba, 1994; Hall, 1988). In the pursuit for more concise, empirical, 'scientific' and replicatable data and analyses, the rational choice perspective has spawned a host of interesting studies. Hardin, for example, shows that individuals who identify with ethnic groups do not do so because of primordial ties, but because it is rational for them to do so—it is in their interests to join (Hardin, 1995). Hechter proposes that individuals as 'rational egoists' will join a group only if they can receive the benefits of such solidarity unconditionally (Hechter, 1989). Hence every group needs to have some sort of 'sanctioning capacity to ensure compliance' (Hecter, 1989, p. 69).

While some theorists view these conflicts as having multiplied in the post-Cold War era (Huntington, 1993), others see it as a product of western modernity and the rise and fall of industrial empires (Riggs, 1998, pp. 269–288; Huntington, 1993, pp. 22–49). Kakar (1996) sees not a resurgence of religion but rather of communalism which intertwines social, political and economic situations with religions affiliations. We are reminded by others that intercultural conflict is less common than intercultural cooperation (Fearon and Laitin, 1996). The literature on ethnic identities and conflicts is dynamic and this comparative study attempts to add to it by situating ethnic conflicts within the framework of authoritarian states and proposing a linkage between the character of these states and the character of ethnic organizations. It suggests that under these states ethnic interactions and relations are nurtured and deepened, becoming the currency of everyday life. They provide those social and economic responsibilities neglected by the state, and also act as a buffer to and a kind of defiance against the harsh reality of state structures. Oppressive states not only influence the character of ethnic relations, but the ways in which they react to challenges from below directly impact the kinds of challenges that evolve. As Gurr and Harff (1994, p. 85) have suggested, underground organizations that employ terrorism and guerrilla warfare are the more typical responses to states which use deadly force in dealing with challenges. For Arendt (1969/1972, p. 155), when violence is employed by the state it signals a loss of control and power. Marshall (1999) argues that it is wrong to assume that the monopoly use of force by a state over its citizens is necessarily legitimate. Others (see, e.g., Migdal, 1988) have focused on the notion that many of these states are weak states in that they cannot govern civil society on the basis of support and reciprocity, rather they have to resort to force to gain some degree of compliance and order.

This comparison also emphasizes the notion that during violence identities are forged. Herein lies the dilemmas for those who identify with an ethnic community but not with the ideals, political agenda or militant strategies of an ethnic organization. Ethnic mobilization in situations in which communities are essentially disunited, or haven't as yet had an agenda on which to unite, tends to require a distinctive set of mobilizing mechanisms. The desire to inculcate the need for an ethnic political agenda, and to drive home the urgency for action, seems to lend itself to tactics tuned to the creation of an 'atmosphere of fear' and the perpetuation of terror. An environment is created in which the rules of everyday life are constantly changing, where violence against those who fail to cooperate carries with it the threat of death, and where fear becomes pervasive. Individuals are forced to take sides, to kill or be killed.

The absent-present state

The first proposal suggests that as a state becomes more despotic or authoritarian, civil society becomes more removed from it, yet is more controlled by it. At one level these states use a repressive ideology, policies and laws to maintain dominance and control. But at other levels, they are largely absent from the lives of people, providing little in the way of welfare, protection, education, justice, health and national identity.

For those living in such societies in their quest for survival and identity they rely on neighbors, friends, families and local gangs for protection, material support, financial aid and welfare. It is in this space too that ethnic relationships take on a more rigid and lasting character. Alienated by states that undermine a sense of self-worth, ethnic and religious identities are often nurtured. Not only do they provide practical social and economic networks but they also constitute a form of defiance against repressive governments. As has been witnessed in many parts of the world once these oppressive states are removed, virulent ethnic issues are exposed with far-reaching consequences.

Contemporary ethnic conflicts in Africa and South Asia have a dynamism and rhythm that are grounded in the present, tuned to modern trends and circumstances. Despite the proliferation of intense ethnic conflicts in current international politics, the constructions of ethnic identities in specific ways, namely in sectarian and communal ways, have a history. And this history is one that is to a large extent, embedded in the period of colonial conquest when new states were constructed and civil society was beginning to take shape. The character and kinds of organizations created by civilians are to a significant extent, determined by the kind and character of states. The colonial administration was both intrusive and absent, setting the stage for the invention of the ethnic group as an abiding and politically salient entity in modern state systems.

The colonial administration

Colonial conquest dramatically interrupted the lives of people, radically transforming the basic fabric of society. These sublime changes were not the outcomes of coherent and well articulated political policies, but rather, a result of individual manifestations and interpretations of European ideologies, cultural sentiments and languages of conquest and socio-economic expansion. Backed by pre-conceived notions of the 'non-European Other', individual administrators, entrepreneurs and missionaries constructed their own versions of the colonized which influenced the ideology and legislation of administration. As Rothchild (1997, p. 8) states, colonials had an 'authoritarian management style.'

British administrators instituted radical changes by imposing new taxes, demanding labor, creating new laws and legislation and developing the colonies as providers of materials for Europeans. With few personnel and low budgets to efficiently administer these new lands, they took to ruling indirectly via traditional chiefs and headmen. Underlying this policy was the need to preserve the identity and coherence of ethnic groups. One implication was the social and spatial division of colonies along the lines of an ethnic chessboard. People had to operate within these parameters in order to access the government. Those who tried to alter the prescribed boundaries were usually members of the new educated elite, eager to take advantage of new employment opportunities. Realizing that the colonial authorities saw them not as educated and competent individuals but as educated Tamil/Sinhalese/Zulu/Sikh men, many sought to increase their strength by organizing themselves into more coherent ethnic organizations.

In South Africa, it was assumed that all Africans belonged to tribes which were discreet, recognizable units presided over by chiefs. Tribal people were violent, unpredictable, bloodthirsty, passionate, sexually indulgent and uncivilized (Welsh, 1971, p. 19). This is despite the fact that the tribal unit had been battered in the wars prior to and during Shaka's reign. It suffered the same fate during the reign of subsequent royal kings and under colonial rule. These assumptions undermined the dynamic character of tribal affiliations and changes in leadership, membership, character, rituals and so on. Occupying the Cape in 1792, the British gradually expanded their control using indirect rule and instituting a segregated racial system. In Natal, thousands of Zulus were moved off their land into newly designated reserves that were spatially isolated from white towns, cities and farms.[3] By 1900, the reserves were overcrowded and over-utilized and were gradually transformed into labor reservoirs, a process that was institutionalized under the Apartheid regime.

Between 1881 and 1882, of the 173 chiefs and headmen in charge of 102 tribes, 99 were hereditary, 46 were created or appointed and 28 ranked as headmen (Welsh, 1971, p. 111). By 1871, there were only 7 magistrates to administer 300,000 Africans. These measure effectively removed many of the checks and balances on abuses of power that existed prior to colonialism, like the possibility of a disaffected section of a tribe to hive off joining a new chief. The system of *isibalo*, whereby Africans chosen by chiefs had to labor on public works in the colony, contributed towards the growing unpopularity of chiefs. The codification of customary law under the Native Administration Law of 1875, rigidified a nuanced negotiable process. The code was seriously flawed and had a lasting negative impact on the status of women. By Section 94 of the Code, women were considered minors without independent power and could not acquire or hold property independently of their fathers or husbands. British rule lasted until 1910 when the colony gained self rule and segregation became the working ideology of the national government. The precedents for racial segregation and Apartheid had deep roots in the period of colonial conquest.

In Sri Lanka, an island colonized successively by three different European powers, the impact of colonialism was more varied.[4] Each of the colonial powers established a distinctive government leaving behind a specific ideological imprint. At the time of the arrival of the first colonizers, Ceylon was divided along three regional sovereignties: the Tamil Kingdom in the north around Jaffna, and two Sinhalese monarchs with capitals in Kandy and Kotte. The story of the invasion and domination is well documented.[5] What is of interest are the implications of colonial conquest for identity formation and citizenship.[6]

A lasting legacy of early Portuguese rule was the creation of a large category of Ceylonese Roman Catholics who came to play a distinctive role among Tamils and the administrative bureaucracy.[7] The zeal with which public worship in Buddhist and Hindu temples was prevented created a further series of ramifications for later attempts at reviving these religions.[8] British rule lasted the longest, was territorially all-encompassing (a centralized administration was instituted colonizing the entire island), and politically and economically more ambitious. Central to its administration was a reliance on Indirect Rule and chiefly power at district levels was institutionalized.[9] With widespread changes at higher levels, the old systems of status, power, class and caste were preserved at other levels.[10]

Behind this policy also lay the prejudices of colonial officers against processes of assimilation, or 'Europeanization' of the Ceylonese. The growing numbers constituting this new class aroused suspicion and ambivalence.[11] By the middle of the nineteenth century there was already a small group of Ceylonese civil servants and professionals who earned higher salaries and greater prestige than the traditional elites—the *mudaliyas* or the *Kandyan* aristocracy. British officers maintained a social distance between themselves and the former and they also tended to stay aloof from the social and economic problems that were evident in Ceylon. Their presence in Ceylon was further entrenched by the indenture of South Indian Tamil laborers to work in the tea and coffee plantations of Central Ceylon.

Racial theories were central to the construction of 'The-non-European-Other'. Convinced of the superiority of Anglo-Saxon culture, language and religion, the British used racial categories to analyze Sri Lankan society, drawing distinct hierarchical differences between the local peoples along the lines of ethnic differences. Books published in the mid-nineteenth century narrated tales that depicted Tamil-speaking South Indians as the hostile and uncivilized invaders who destroyed the sophisticated indigenous Buddhist civilization (see, Spencer, 1991). In the late ninetieth century, theories about the 'Aryan race' attributed certain structural affinities between Indian and European languages to common racial features. Proponents argued that Sinhala, a derivative of Sanskrit, was actually an Indo-European language and hence, the Sinhala people were Aryans (see, Spencer, 1991; Little, 1994; Tambiah, 1992). This theory had peculiar ramifications for Sinhala identity, which began to surface as prestigious and sacred.[12]

An important element in the colonial discourse was the concept of 'the nation'. In the colonial imagination and relying on the British constitution with its unwritten conventions and precedents, in theory all the natives of Ceylon were treated as the 'Ceylonese nation'. This idea was implicitly behind their intransigence towards communal representation during the era of reform and in the constitution created for post-colonial government.[13] Territorial representation became the basis of the democratic constitution of post-colonial Sri Lanka.[14]

There were two main elements that propelled the construction of a revived Buddhist identity: the Theosophical Society, founded by Madame Blavatsky and Colonel Olcott in 1875; and Anagarika Dharmpala.[15] Dharmpala constructed a novel strand of Buddhist practices and beliefs (dubbed 'Protestant Buddhism') that targeted the layman (Jayawardena, 1990, pp. 18–19).[16] He gave primary significance to the 'Sinhalese nation' as the custodian of Buddhism.[17] This led to a convergence of the Buddhist religion with the idea of a Sri Lankan nation of Sinhalese ethnicity (de Silva, 1988). This notion gained strength in post-colonial Sri Lanka, to constitute a central definition of a Sri Lankan as Sinhalese and Buddhist, and minorities as non-Sri Lankan Tamil/Hindu/Muslim invaders.

The eighteenth century witnessed the end of Mogul domination, the arrival of the British East India Company and consolidation of British rule in Punjab. The construction of Sikh identities follows a fascinating journey throughout this period and into the twentieth century, that encompasses strategic efforts by Sikh leaders to carve out an all-encompassing and definitive logic. Tracing their spiritual master to Guru Nanak (16th century), the period of colonial rule was a time when Sikhs actively sought to create an identity that distinguished them from Hindus and Muslims. The colonial administration did indeed provide a significant impetus towards the desire to construct a specific Sikh identity, but it cannot be thought of as the definitive facilitator. Sikh identity reflects a process that also had its own, very powerful motivations and momentum. At this point I would just like to focus on the colonial impact of Sikh identity formation.

One of the most profound and direct influences was the British army. After the Anglo-Sikh war in 1846, two Sikh regiments were created, and Sikhs were also encouraged to join the Punjab Irregular Force, the Military Police and regiments of John Company.[18] In line with the colonial ideology of maintaining ethnic identities in the face of radical and rapid changes, Sikh regiments were forced to dress and behave according to 'Sikhness' as perceived by the British.[19]

Narrowly defined and obscuring a wide spectrum of Sikh sects and beliefs, the army saw a Sikh soldier as:

> The followers of Guru Govind Singh, that is to say Singhs, the members of the khalsa; these are the only Sikhs who are reckoned as true Sikhs now-a-days. The best practical test of a true Sikh is to ascertain whether calling himself a Sikh he wears uncut hair and abstains from smoking.[20]

This identity mainly reflected that of the Khalsa Sikhs, who by the end of the nineteenth century had devised a set of indicators that defined a Sikh from others.[21] Despite religious diversity the 'Singh or Lion' came to represent all Sikhs (Fox, 1985, p. 7).

The management of Sikh shrines under British rule became a significant rally point for the Khalsa movement and a focal point of Sikh militancy. In 1925, the Shiromani Gurdwara Parbandhak Committee (SGPC) and its political party known as the Shiromani Akali Dal, were formed to campaign for the eviction of the 'mahants' (managers) who were in charge of the gurdwaras (shrines).[22] Agreeing to evict the mahants, the British also adopted the definition of a Sikh as espoused by the SGPC in the Sikh Gurdwaras Act of 1925.[23] When India became independent in 1947, the Punjab inherited the Sikh Gurdwaras Acts and its definition of a Sikh as a 'person who professes the Sikh religion, believes and follows the teachings of Sri Guru Granth Sahib and the ten Gurus only and keeps unshorn hair...' (McLeod, 1989, p. 98). Later, the Delhi Gurdwara Act 24 of 1971 and the Delhi Gurdwara Act 82 of 1971 gave further legitimacy to the Khalsa definition. Not only did the British inclusion of a specific Sikh identity solidify it, but the SGPC and the Akali's were to become the hegemonic bodies in Punjab and the basis of Sikh nationalism and militancy.

The post-colonial state

The apartheid sate, which came into power in South Africa in 1948, was highly intrusive. It used repressive legislation, laws and a racist ideology to oppress black people. It further employed the army, police, violence and terror to institute its racist laws and to maintain racial segregation and oppression. It intruded in the lives of people, in their domestic lives (laws regulating marriage, sexual partners, place of residence) and their public lives (laws regulating where people worked, worshipped, traveled and lived). But it was also absent. People had to protect themselves (in the face of a hostile and an inadequate police force); they had to educate themselves (because of under financed, ill-equipped, and few schools and teachers); they had to tend to their own health (with few hospitals located in urban areas, long waiting lists and a chronic shortage of medical practitioners); they had to institute their own forms of justice (due to inadequate access to the courts of law, lawyers and impartial judges); and they had to construct their own group identities (in the face of racist ideology and an alienating white state). The quest for survival, together with the history of apartheid forced people to identify with smaller ethnic, racial and other networks in their everyday lives.

Under apartheid, ethnic segregation was streamlined as part of a coherent and all-encompassing ideology and political agenda. The policy of creating Bantustans or 'homelands' for all the different 'non-white' ethnic groups, of controlling the number of Africans temporarily leaving these reserves and of controlling their movement in towns and cities, were policies designed to keep urban areas white.[24] To further entrench the system, chiefs and headmen continued to operate in black reserves, controlling patronage and access to land, housing, water, grazing land, urban labor markets, pensions and welfare benefits. In the background of rapidly changing relations of production, African people were forced to live within the parameters of 'old tribal' systems. To concretize this fabric of apartheid, the Bantustans were treated as 'independent homelands', having their own government headquarters, administrative structures and parliaments.

It is precisely within this space created by the intrusive/absent state, that Inkatha and its leader found a niche. All chiefs were incorporated into the KwaZulu Legislative Assembly (known as the KLA, the government of the KwaZulu homeland), and all members of the KLA were members of Inkatha. Inkatha was the ethnic organization created by Gatsha Buthelezi to extend the powers and impact of the KLA into those spaces in which the apartheid state was absent (Mzala, 1988). It sought to bring within its realm the patronage networks instituted by chiefs, neighbors, families and friends. It accomplished this by including the chiefs as a central element of government, thereby ensuring that access to essential services and patronage could only be obtained through Inkatha and hence the KLA. It also created its own institutions like the Women's and Youth Brigades. Alternative clubs developed by people to cope with the absent state, like those pertaining to bulk buying, burials, rotating credit, sewing, gardening and church and the youth were incorporated into its framework. Monopolizing power in all facets of life, the strong-arm tactics that came to be the pejorative of chiefs, landlords, shacklords and others who wielded power through control of land and housing resources, also became a prominent feature of Inkatha. Most significant for this study, it was the spatial framework and ideology of apartheid that enabled Inkatha leaders to construct their own version of Zulu identity and to make it the rallying cry of sustained conflict in South Africa.

One of the first pieces of legislation to be passed by Sri Lanka's first prime minister, Don Stephen Senanayake, was to disenfranchise and deny citizenship to nearly one million Indian Tamils. This piece of legislation enabled the Sinhalese to easily gain a two-thirds majority in parliament and effectively dominate the country.[25] An internal colonization scheme was also instituted whereby irrigation systems in the northern and eastern provinces were rebuilt and Sinhalese peasants were encouraged to settle in what had been Tamil dominated areas. The succeeding administration under S. W. R. D. Bandaraniake made a concerted effort to break the back of the Tamil educated elite, the perceived threat to Sinhalese hegemony. On taking power in 1956, the Bandaraniake government enacted the Official Language Act, replacing English with Sinhala as the official language. This clause was to severely hamper the entrance of non-Sinhala speakers, mainly Tamils, into the civil service.[26] In subsequent governments, geographical quotas and higher university entrance requirements were established for Tamil students. As K. M. de Silva (1986, p. 266) states, 'Sinhalese students were now in the same privileged position in the universities as their politicians were in the national legislature in terms of seats there.'[27]

Behind the desire to give the nation a particular character, lay the political dynamics of religious revivalism espoused by the rank and file of the Sri Lanka Freedom Party (SLFP), which won the elections in 1956 with

Bandaranaike as the premier. The *bhikkus* or political Buddhist monks who had formed the Eksath Bhikku Peramuna (United Monks' Front) were driven by a desire to revitalize state patronage of Buddhism, and aimed to gain some influence in those areas previously dominated by the English-speaking elite (see, Jayawardena, 1985, pp. 111–112). The language issue provided the basis of a Sinhalese nationalism which made a connection between 'the land (Sri Lanka), the Race (Sinhalese), and the Faith (Buddhism)' (Bose, 1994, p. 59). Tamils made strong protests to the 'Sinhala Only' bill reflecting the first strains of a Tamil nationalism.[28] With the increasing strength of the Buddhist movement and ambivalence on his part, Bandaranaike concretized a system that was hostile to minorities,[29] a strategy that was streamlined under Mrs. Bandaranaike.[30]

In 1947, Punjab was divided between India and Pakistan. In post-colonial Punjab, Sikhs constituted just 2% of the population and under the central Indian government, they were categorized as Hindus. The call for a Punjabi-speaking state was an agenda propagated by the most prominent Sikh political party, the Akali Dal. Indira Gandhi agreed to divide Punjab into Punjab (a Punjabi speaking state) and Haryana (a Hindi speaking state), albeit in an arbitrary manner leaving issues of the capital and the division of rivers and other resources open to contention.

Given the history of colonialism and the space it created for the construction and nurturing of ethnic identities, a strategy which the Indian government maintained, Sikh political leaders have consistently endeavored to delineate themselves from Hindus and Muslims, as well as to establish themselves as a coherent ethnic group. Ever since its inception in 1925, the Shiromani Gurdwara Prabandhak Committee (SGPC) has been central to Sikh revivalism and nationalism.[31] Control over the *gurdwaras* gave them direct access to funds, patronage and cites from which to mobilize political campaigns.[32]

After Punjab became a state, the Sikhs were in a majority, constituting 54% while Hindus made up 44% of the total population. Of significance was the fact that although Akali leaders assumed they would enjoy dominant power, in the five elections to the Punjab legislative assembly held between 1967 and 1980, the Congress party commanded more support with the Akali Dal unable to get more than 30% of the total vote. That is, although the leaders of the most powerful body among Sikhs based their entire political agenda on the notion of Sikh separateness and identity, the Sikh community saw more in common with the Hindu oriented Congress Party than with the Akalis. The Akali leadership, seeing that they were not as popular as they had assumed and recognizing that the majority of Sikhs did not imagine their Sikhness in accordance with Akali's constructions, sought to inject the idea of the Indian government as an intrusive-absent state.

Ethnicity: the debated terrain

From the time of colonial conquest, Zulu leaders have vacillated between expressing disdain towards 'traditional' Zulu customs and cultural norms, to embracing them as primary mobilizing forces of civil society. Political resistance in South Africa has taken two dominant paths: those organizations following a nationalist political agenda (for example, the ANC, the South African Communist Party, the Black Consciousness Movement and the Pan African Congress) and those organizations that espoused an ethnic political agenda (for example *Inkatha Ya Ka Zulu*—the forerunner to Inkatha—formed in 1922, the Zulu Cultural Society formed in 1937 and Inkatha formed in 1975).

One of the key figures behind the formation of *Inkatha Ya Ka Zulu* was John Dube who was the chief spokesperson of the Christian African community, the *amakholwa* (the converted).[33] Dube's political transition from disdain for the 'tribal system' to employing it as a fundamental building block of organization, is indicative of the ramifications of the intrusive/absent colonial state.[34] The influence of Christianity on the ambitions and aspirations of people, the education it offered and the kind of lifestyle it extolled, were at odds with the oppressive conditions under which people lived. There was much tension and debate among Christians, between them and the 'tribalists', and with white administrators and it was a debate that was to continue into contemporary times.[35] In 1937, the *Zulu Cultural Society* was founded by the Natal Bantu Teachers' Association in its attempt to gain government recognition of Zulu royalty, and to preserve Zulu traditions and customs.[36] In tracing the precedents for ethnic mobilization among Zulus, the revival of Inkatha *Yenkululeko Ye Sizwe* in May 1975 by Gatsha Buthelezi follows as the next significant organization.[37] At the same time as Inkatha was establishing grassroots connections, the ANC was also beginning to establish itself on the national political scene. Zulu people had more options; they could engage in intellectual debates on the politics of apartheid and the complexities of 'Zuluness' and 'blackness' within this system. In the battle for power in the black resistance movement, intense conflict often erupted, the most sustained battle beginning around the mid-1980s when Inkatha took an aggressive stance towards the popular United Democratic Front and the Federation of South African Trade Unions (later known as the Congress Of South African Trade Unions–COSATU).

Inkatha used violent means to transform itself from a small organization concentrating on women's groups, youth organizations and relying on the 'traditional' authority of chiefs in the homelands, into a more highly coordinated fighting unit with support bases throughout the community. Although it had a sizable group of voluntary members, it coerced young men into joining its armed units, often by threatening violence, reprisals and death. Large bands of Inkatha warriors would patrol the streets going from door to door recruiting men. Those who didn't join fled the townships ever fearful of being tracked down. An *impimpi*, or informer, was dealt with publicly and severely by both Inkatha and ANC sympathetic organizations, serving to expose the community to the consequences of such actions. In the years of intense fighting, between 1985 and the early 1990s, fear became all-pervasive (see, Glover, 1991). As one resident explains:

> It is dangerous to walk at night. Look, today I will be knocking off at 8:00 p.m. and how safe will I be? Where I stay, (a tribal area which was under the control of the amaQabne, the comrades of the United Democratic Front—ANC front), you meet someone at night who greets you 'Quabane, Quabane heyta!' Whatever you do, you may receive a bullet hole. Some people who are not comrades now masquerade as comrades. But if you deny you are a quabane then you are in trouble if the strangers are in fact comrades. To be silent is also dangerous because either side interprets that as insolence. To say nothing is futile. It means you are impimpi (informer) for the other group (*Frontline*, February 29, 1988).[38]

In Sri Lanka, intense combat within the Tamil community among the various resistance organizations, as well as violent confrontations with the Sinhalese armed forces, has reached new and more lethal levels in the past few years. Many commentators have argued that the militant and intransigent attitude of the Sri Lankan government towards the guerrilla movements has in fact catalyzed the conflict and contributed to the ascendancy of the Tigers (see, e.g., Bose, 1994, pp. 90–92). As a prominent Tamil politician explains:

> Since 1977 there has been a reign of terror in the north unleashed by the armed forces. Instead of curbing violence, it has escalated

the incidence of violence, as can be seen from the increasing number of killings of army personnel. We need hardly state that the terrorism of the armed forces has been counterproductive ... the reason is that the grievances of the people are far too deep-seated to be smothered by batons and bullets (Ponnambalam, 1993, pp. 204–205).

The impetus to join a guerrilla movement is made more complex by the fear of not joining. To remain aloof exposes one to accusations of being a government informer, eliciting strong punishment and even death.[39] Remaining in a village and unattached to a resistance organization could also ignite the wrath of state forces, exposing oneself to the possibility of torture for information, or for recruitment into state forces. A youth suggested that it was better to die fighting 'than to wait in the village to be picked up and tortured to death' (Swamy, 1994, p. 99). The entire community has become embroiled in the conflict, few families remain untouched by direct violent activity, and as a Tamil woman explains: '...as mothers we often do not approve. But they are our children. If a son does something wrong, we will forgive him, even if we have to do so a hundred times' (Swamy, 1994, p. 127; also quoted in McGowan, 1992, p. 325). The extent of actual support devoid of fear is hard to tell. However, years of oppression and violence under the Sinhalese government have alienated the majority of Tamils, and although all may not agree on tactics of the Tigers, many will be sympathetic to their cause.

Although the Tigers led the Tamil resistance, the community has spawned numerous other political and militant organizations. The gruesome and bloody conflicts among the various groups and between individual Tamils have been an underlying and persistent element in the Tamil-Sinhalese conflict. The most significant of the non-Tiger militant groups were the Eelam Revolutionary Organization of Students (EROS), the Tamil Eelam Liberation Organization (TELO), the People's Liberation Organization of Tamil Eelam (PLOTE), the Eelam People's Revolutionary Liberation Front (EPRLF), and later, the Eelam National Democratic Liberation Front (ENDLF). In 1986, the LTTE virtually eliminated all TELO's political leadership and fighting cadre. Support for the Tigers does not imply complete allegiance and dissidents are many, with up to 3,000 or more in captivity in LTTE prisons (Swamy, 1994). It required aggressive and bloody techniques to silence other organizations and voices in the war of resistance, and this was to an extent successful, at least at a superficial level. Debates and arguments, ideas and thoughts about Tamil identity continue, albeit in whispers.

The 'Indian Tamils' of south-central Sri Lanka are not only geographically separate from the 'Sri Lankan Tamils' (who constitute about 13 percent of the population and live mainly in the northern (around Jaffna) and eastern (Batticaloa) parts of the island, but are culturally and politically a separate group. The Tigers and other militant organizations have concentrated their efforts among the Sri Lankan Tamils. Differences among this latter group are many: about 80 percent are Hindu and 20 percent are Christian, mainly Roman Catholic; caste distinctions between the majority upper castes (the Vellalars) and the minority lower castes (the Karaiyar, Mukkuvar, etc.) and differences in class, economic activities and social and cultural practices. Some have suggested that the militant struggle has had a leveling social effect. For example, Velupillai Prabhakaran, the leader of the Tigers, is from a low-caste fisherman-merchant community of Karaiyar, and has become the undisputed leader of the Tamil nationalist movement (Suryanarayna, 1991, pp. 95–98). In the battle for power in a situation fraught with so many differences, after ousting the main contenders, the Tigers have molded themselves as a highly disciplined military unit demanding allegiance from its members and from the community. An informant explained:

> As a political force among the Tamils of the north and east the LTTE cannot be bypassed because it is the 'boys', as they are still called, sometimes affectionately, at times chidingly, who are seen as the spearhead of the Tamil struggle for equality, security and justice—for all the brutalities that the Tigers have inflicted on their political opponents, on innocent people and on civil society ... the LTTE is unsinkable, at least for the foreseeable future (Quoted in Bose, 1994, p. 89).

The debates with the community have been polarized. The war has demarcated those who fight for the Tigers and the enemy (Lawrence, 1997; Abeysuriya de Silva, 1998). But the underlying fissures and tensions often surface. And the impetus to find novel solutions still throws up new groups, individuals and organizations into the political arena.

Punjab is a good example of the process whereby debate and argument over what constitutes an ethnic identity is replaced by rigid constructions with definitions, rules, codes of behavior and dress. It was a process that occurred from the 16th century onwards, peaking at certain points when

Sikh leaders felt threatened by the influence of other ethnicities and religions. Perhaps the earliest and most definitive phase was the creation by Guru Govind Singh, the tenth Guru, of the Khalsa order in the 17th century. Replacing the old term of Sikh, derived from the Sanskrit word sisya (meaning disciple), with Khalsa (from Arabic-Persian meaning 'pure'), Govind Singh developed a host of practices and rules that was to constitute this new order. He introduced an initiation rite (called the Khande Kipahul); new ceremonies to commemorate births, marriages and deaths; the practice of keeping unshorn hair and the carrying of arms; and new taboos like not smoking tobacco. The ideal Sikh became a Khalsa Sikh who was visible and religious. But not all Sikhs became Khalsa.

The 19th century Sikh identity was dominated by the Sanatanic Sikh tradition. A loosely defined community, they followed many Hindu practices, but distinguished themselves as followers of Guru Nanak (the first Sikh Guru). Constituted mainly with Sikh intellectuals (Udasi, Nirmalas), their establishments enjoyed extensive patronage form the state, the landed aristocracy, and rich peasants. Their definition of Sikhism was elitist, having few connections with the peasants and the urban poor.

But this fluid definition was to be underscored by the revivalist Singh Sabha movement of the late nineteenth century. Opening the floor to a whole new strata of young entrepreneurs, intellectuals and civil servants, the revivalists started a fresh debate. Using printing technology, the Sabhas were able to coordinate and propagate the debate. For example, in 1886, Avtar Singh Vahiria, editor of the Sri Gurumat Prakasak, issued the following urgent appeal:

> Be it known by all Sikhs that we receive a lot of mail inquiring about the precise rituals that Sikhs ought to follow at the time of birth, marriage and death. If any scholar possesses a manuscript or otherwise knows how these rituals should be performed he should immediately write to us. We will then proceed with publishing an edited version of the same in the Sri Gurumat Prakasak (Oberoi, 1994, pp. 244–245).

It was the Singh Sabha in Lahore (formed in the 1880s) that set about creating a more rigid definition for Sikhs. Formulating a powerful discourse of the Tat Khalsa, they created a new orthodoxy that clearly delineated Sikhs from each other and, more significantly, from Hindus. At the time, the large majority of Sikhs were only distinguishable from Hindus by their reverence to Guru Nanak. Other than that, they prayed to the same Gods, celebrated similar festivals, married using similar ceremonies and embraced similar religious tenets. The Sabha launched a campaign to 'Sikhinize' the Sikhs. They redefined the entire phenomenology of Sikhism and what it implied to be part of that tradition.

The cornerstone of this new tradition were the three doctrines of Guru/Granth/Gurdwara. The Adi Granth came to be regarded as the sacred 'bible' of the Sikhs. Sikh shrines were cleared of Hindu symbols, temple management was changed and Hindu festivals at these shrines were prohibited. The Tat Khalsa Sikhs had to also abide by the Five Ks which made them visible and clearly separated them from 'Others'. The Sabhas formed the basis of the SGPC which was to make the Khalsa identity hegemonic among Sikhs. It is a section from this group that has engaged in militant action to bring about an independent Sikh state. However, although the Khalsa identity dominates, other Sikh identities continue to exist and debate is still maintained.

The initiative to organize a *dharm Yudh* (religious war) against the central government was taken at an All World Sikh Convention in August 1981. The highpoint of a wave of mass demonstrations, work stoppages and protest marches was the siege of the Golden Temple by Jarnail Singh Bhindranwale.[40] A vigorous campaigner for Sikh orthodoxy, Bhindranwale portrayed the Indian government as a 'Hindu state' which was oppressive and discriminatory:

> The Hindus are trying to enslave us; atrocities against the Sikhs are increasing day by day under the Hindu imperialist rulers of New Delhi; the Sikhs have never felt so humiliated, not even during the reign of the Mogul emperors and British colonialists. How long can the Sikhs tolerate injustice? (Quoted in Kapur, 1986, p. 227).

On June 2, 1984, executing Operation Bluestar, the Indian government sealed off Punjab and armed troops stormed the Golden Temple killing Bhindranwale and many of his followers. In the months that followed, repressive measures were used to curb political violence.[41] Under guard, the Golden Temple was repaired and handed back to the SGPC in October 1984. It was also the month when Prime Minister Indira Gandhi was assassinated by two Sikh bodyguards precipitating violent reprisals against Sikhs in India.

Conclusion

In all three cases, identity forms the basis of violence within the ethnic group. The questions of 'what makes a Zulu a Zulu, a Sikh a Sikh and a Tamil a Tamil' form the axis around which identity is pivoted. Intrinsic to the racial ideology of South Africa was the construction of the ethnic other which took numerous forms: Zulus, Xhosas, Pondos, Ndebeles, Indians and 'Coloreds'. It was in the province of Natal in which Zulus constitute more than 80 percent of the population that 'ethnic' violence was most widespread and sustained.

Zulu identity was never a single definable category. On the contrary, it was the 'arena for the sharpest social and political division.'[42] The fervent and often aggressive and violent internal disputes among the Zulus has resulted in the production and creation of divergent ethnic identities. These debates contributed to the disjuncture between Inkatha and the ANC, the questions of Zuluness being at the center of conflict. To fight on the side of Inkatha or to side with the ANC represented differing interpretations of Zulu history and of the role of the great Zulu leaders like King Shaka. It represented different interpretations of the role of Zulus in politics, it represented different views on the value of Zulu myths, codes of conduct and cultural elements and it represented different views on what makes a Zulu a Zulu.

The Zulus have had to reconstruct their identity through generations of domination and oppression. They had to be creative in the face of the destruction of the Kingdom, the assault of Christianity on their old beliefs and culture, the sudden intrusion of Western oppressive rulers and their racist ideologies, the apartheid laws which forcibly moved them away from old home lands into crowded reserves, the dramatic changes of moving from a rural-based subsistence economy to a subsistence-cum-capitalist one and the onslaught of the migrant labor system on the family, culture and coherence of the community. Most importantly, they had to cope with the imposition of two separate worlds in their everyday lives: of 'old tribal systems' and modern industrial, westernized economies. This was the legacy of the absent-present colonial state and the inclusion of the tribal unit as an intrinsic and necessary part of government.

It was only when Inkatha first engaged in a violent attack on university students who were beginning to find the Black Consciousness ideology of Steve Biko attractive, that Zulu identity began to loose its fluidity. Soon, the Zulu community was divided along those who were prepared to kill and be killed for Inkatha and those who were not. Buthelezi and Inkatha constructed a Zuluness that envisaged the warrior-like qualities first propagated by King Shaka; that was 'traditional' in culture; that included the elements of respect for chiefs, elders, old values and moral codes of behavior; and that revered the Zulu kings and Zulu history as narrated by Buthelezi. For the ANC in Natal, which was also dominated by its Zulu membership, the nationalist cause was more important than the ethnic agendas of its members. Apartheid was the enemy, and debates about ethnicity were subsumed under the larger and all-encompassing political program to overthrow the regime that practiced it.

A significant implication of the peaceful transference of power in Sri Lanka in 1948, and one which wasn't premeditated by mass action, was that the inheritors of the state were the political and administrative elite that had developed within the colonial administration. The Sri Lanka Freedom Party (SLFP), based as it was on the colonial logic of governance and well established bureaucracy, created a state as imagined by the Sinhala Buddhists.[43] Although in effect the state had as an important objective the desire to balance the intrusive-absent equation, it did so partially and largely along the lines of ethnic difference. For the Tamils, the state was experienced as alienating and intrusive, a state which prevented access to education and employment (by legislating quotas for Tamil university and civil servant entrants, by raising the requirement for Tamil applicants to these institutions), and a state which was repressive (using detentions, terror, the police and army against its Tamil civilians). It was also a state that was absent, whereby welfare, aid for education and heath was low, and where Tamils had little access to a fair and just judicial or police force. It was in this space that Tamils took to mobilization around 'Tamilness', and around the issue of a separate Tamil state. It took 25 years of negotiations and working within the parliamentary system for Tamils to resort to guerrilla warfare. It was to be a period in which Tamil leaders began to create and develop militant political agendas around different kinds of Tamil identities which were to lead to bloody conflict within the Tamil communities themselves, and with the Sinhalese and Indian army.

The followers of Guru Nanak have always been engaged in fervent debate over what distinguished them as followers of his teachings. The ways in which various individuals replied to this question were varied and diverse. At different points in time, a specific strand of the identity construction began to dominate the debate, but not without argument. In 1925, for example, when the Tat Khalsa were maturing and their definitions of Sikhs were included in the Sikh Gurdwaras and Shrines Bill of 1925, the Sahajdhari Sikhs expressed their strong dissatisfaction: 'Sikhism was never a religion but always a Path ... a cult ... embracing Hindu religion through laying particular stress on the devotional attachment towards Gurus...' (Kapur, 1986, p. 189). Sikh identity has been at the heart of intra-Sikh conflict as well as conflict with the central Indian government.

What this chapter suggests is that sustained violent ethnic conflict is not only the result of immediate local causes and conditions. It is also the outcome of certain kinds of states, of the peculiar ways in which some states articulate with civil society. Although the intrusive/absent analytical concept can be thought of as applicable to all states, in the context in which it is used in this chapter the 'intrusive' attributes of the state are distinctive. At one extreme, are states in which excessive violence and force is consistently, and as intrinsically part of the political and ideological agenda, employed against civil society. These can be thought of as violent states, using the army and police to control and suppress, strictly circumscribing the parameter within which civil society can operate. Other states are those which are highly intrusive in terms of initiating drastic and radical changes or transformations, yet, in theory and practice, seek to allow a substantial amount of the 'traditional' social, economic and political arena to continue. Within both these systems, citizenship is narrowly defined, the notion of the other often having an ethnic or racial component. In the space created by the intrusive/absent state, ethnic allegiances take on deep meanings, have abiding structural connections and form an intrinsic part of civil society. Conflict resolution requires active ways of balancing the intrusive-absent equation to facilitate less intrusion (in terms of violence, suppression, force) and less absence (in terms of providing an unbiased police force, military, judicial system, welfare system and a more inclusive national identity and citizenship). In this respect, the post-apartheid South African government has made serious efforts to make the state less intrusive and less absent. Given the long history of oppression, it will take some time before these efforts can be evaluated. Inter- and intra-ethnic violence has decreased substantially although criminal violence has increased.

Another implication of this chapter is that the warring ethnic organizations may, in fact, only be superficially hegemonic. Various and contending ideologies and identities lie beneath and the political ambitions of leaders may not represent those of the people they purport to be fighting for. There is a need to go beneath the rhetoric of the leadership, to unravel the various constructed identities and to uncover their ideas, ambitions and political desires. Only then can lasting settlements be reached.

Notes

1. Estimates vary due to the large number of disappearances, detentions and clandestine activity. See the annual reports of Amnesty International.
2. See Geertz, C. (1963), 'The Integrative Revolution', in Geertz, C. (ed.), *Old Societies and New States*, Free Press: New York.
3. The chief administrator behind this policy was Theophilis Shepstone, the diplomatic Agent to the Tribes in Natal who relocated some eighty thousand Africans in the colony. For a detailed outline of this period, see Morris, D. R. (1966), *The Washing of the Spears*, Oxford University Press: London. The creation of the conditions of these reserves were, at an early stage, being singled out as a crisis by African leaders. The South African Native National Congress (founded in 1902) loudly expressed its objections: 'The location system does not encourage the Natives to migrate with their families to the laboring centers, as the Natives are taxed in the locations ... the result is generally seen, in the lamentable spread of diseases, the high death-rate, and the depraved moral status of the people ...' See, 'Questions Affecting the Natives and Colored People Resident in British South Africa', Statement by the Executive of the South African Native Congress, 1903, in Johns, S. III (ed.), *Protest and Hope, 1882–1934*, Hoover Institution: Stanford, CA, p. 26.
4. The Portuguese arrived in 1505. They were succeeded by the Dutch (1568–1796) and later, the British (1796–1948).
5. The literature is vast, but a few texts stand out. See, for example, Mills, L. A. (1933), *Ceylon Under British Rule, 1795–1932*, Oxford University Press: Oxford; de Silva, K. M. (1981), *A History of Sri Lanka*, Oxford University Press: Delhi.
6. There are also many useful and good sources for this subject: Wriggins, W. H. (1960), *Dilemmas of a New Nation*, Princeton University Press: Princeton, NJ; Kearney, R. N. (1967), *Communalism and Language in the Politics of Ceylon*, Duke University Press: Durham, NC:, R. N. (1973), *The Politics of Ceylon*, Cornell University Press: Ithaca, NY; Wilson, A. J. (1979), *Politics in Sri Lanka, 1947–1979*, Macmillan: London; Farmer, B. H. (1963), *Ceylon: A Divided Nation*, Oxford University Press: London; Phadnis, U. (1976), *Religion and Politics in Sri Lanka*, Manohar Book Service: New Delhi.
7. The Estado, the colonial state under Portuguese rule, was Roman Catholic, while the Vereenigde Oost-Indische Compagnie (V.O.C.), the administration of the Dutch was Protestant. Under the rule of the VOC., Ceylonese were encouraged to adopt Calvinism, and membership of the Dutch Reformed Church was a prerequisite for high office within the administration. They also revitalized many of the schools established by the Portuguese and built two seminaries in Jaffna and Colombo. Both powers restricted their rule to the coastal regions of the island.
8. For details on the methods employed by missionaries, see, Boxer, C. R. (1958), 'Christians and Spices: Portuguese Missionary Methods in Ceylon, 1518–1658', *History Today*, Vol. 111, pp. 346–354.
9. As Governor Gordon explained, 'It is my desire to preserve as long as possible a system which enlists all native local influences in support of authority, instead of arranging them against it; and which shields the government to a great degree from direct friction with those it governs ...', Gordon to Knutsford, 426 of Octo-

ber 31, 1889, quoted in de Silva, K. M. (1981), *A History of Sri Lanka*, Oxford University Press: New Delhi, p. 323.

10. For example, by the end of the nineteenth century, all posts of President of Village Tribunal were in the hands of the Kandyan chiefs and the *mudaliyars* (the traditional elite) in the low-country (K. M. de Silva, 1981, p. 327).

11. '[I]t is precisely the acquisition of European ideas and the adoption of European in preference to Ceylonese civilization that differentiates this class of Ceylonese from their countrymen ... by a wide gulf from the majority of the native inhabitants of the Colony. Their ideas, their aspirations, their interests are distinctively their own, are all molded upon European models, and are no longer those of the majority of their countrymen' (K. M. de Silva, 1981, p. 327). The criteria for entering the civil service were constantly made more stringent, and after 1880, all candidates had to obtain their education in London in order to qualify. Those few Ceylonese who did manage to enter the civil service were usually diverted to the judicial side of the administration—those positions did not constitute policy making or the developing of innovative administration techniques.

12. 'The racial connotations of 'Aryan' were introduced in the late 19th century by Sri Lankan Sinhalese nationalists to differentiate themselves from Tamils. They were aided by 19th century European Indologists, who spoke of the Aryan subjugation of dark-skinned peoples (the aboriginal Dravidians)—a hypothesis no longer acceptable to serious historians. In reality, there is little difference in the ethnic backgrounds of Sinhalese and Tamils. The first colonizers of Sri Lanka were probably north Indians. But according to the chronicles of Sinhalese, even the first King and his followers married women from south India (the ancient kingdom of Madurai), which exists even today as a major Tamil provincial town). Thereafter, the patterns of royal marriage and mass immigration were wholly from southern India, initially from the Tamil country and later (since the 13th century) from Kerala (*The New York Times*, April 24, 1984). Also see Gunawardena, R. A. L. H. (1991), 'The People of the Lion: Sinhala Identity and Ideology in History and Historiography', in Spencer, J. (ed.), *Sri Lanka: History and Roots of Conflict*, Routledge and Kegan Paul: London. Kemper suggests that a further element brought to Ceylon by the British was their tradition of philosophical and historical scholarship, which in turn, created the desire among the Ceylonese to construct their own histories.' See Kemper, S. (1991), *The Presence of the Past: Chronicles, Politics, and Culture in Sinhala Life*, Cornell University Press: Ithaca, NY.

13. In the early 1900s, with increasing pressure from the Ceylon National Congress, the colonial government started to reform the Ceylonese system of rule. Under a new constitution, and the reformed Legislative Council based on territorial representation of the unofficial candidates (Ceylon locals), the results of the first elections had been 13 seats for the Sinhalese and 3 for Tamils. See Blackton, C. T. (1979), 'The Empire at Bay: British Attitudes and the Growth of Nationalism in the Early Twentieth Century', in Roberts, M. (ed.), *Collective Identities: Nationalism and Protest in Modern Sri Lanka*, Marga Institute: Colombo. The Donoghmore Commission, which recommended the constitution adopted in 1931, clearly stated: 'It is our opinion that only by its abolition will it be possible for the diverse communities to develop together as a true national unity ... Communal representation in Ceylon has no great antiquity to commend it, and its introduction into the

constitution with good intentions has had unfortunate results' (Cited in K. M. de Silva, 1981, p. 422; from the Donoughmore Report, pp. 99–100). See Wilson, A. J. (1988), *The Break-Up of Sri Lanka: The Sinhalese-Tamil Conflict*, C. Hurst and Company: London, p. 13.

14.   The Soulbury Commission, which sat on the eve of independence, also strongly resisted demands for communal representation—an ideal which was supported by Senanayake, who was leader of the United National Party (UNP).

15.   The arrival in Ceylon in May 1880 of Madame Helena Blavastsky and Colonel Henry Steele Olcott of the Theosophical Society, served as the impetus to revitalize and re-construct the Buddhist Revivalist movement. The Theosophical Society was founded in New York in 1875, and moved its headquarters to Adyar, near Madras in 1879. Theosophy espoused a belief in universal mysticism strongly oriented towards Buddhism and Hinduism. See Malalgoda, K. (1976), *Buddhism in Sinhalese Society, 1750–1900*, University of California Press: Berkeley, CA, p. 244. Setting up the Buddhist Theosophical Society (BTS), Olcott went on to raise money for Buddhist education, establishing 63 BTS schools and 40 government schools by 1889 with a total of 18,7000 pupils. These schools were modeled on English mission schools, Buddhist teachings taking a central role. Some of the more well known schools were: Ananda College—an English high school in Colombo in 1886; Dharmaraja College in Kandy, founded in 1887; Mahinda College in Galle, founded in 1892. See Gombrich, R. (1988), *Theravada Buddhism: A Social History from Ancient Benares to Modern Colombo*, Routledge and Kegan Paul: New York, p. 187 and Tambiah, S. (1992), *Buddhist Betrayed? Religion, Politics and Violence in Sri Lanka*, University of Chicago Press: Chicago, IL, p. 186.

16.   He created a middle path of a lifetime devotion to Buddhism while remaining active in worldly political activity. Instead of wearing a yellow robe, he wore white and did not shave his head, although he formally undertook a life of chastity and ascetic abstention. He also took the Eight Precepts—these vows could only be taken by Buddhist laymen on Holy days for 24 hours, and a few older men took them permanently—for life as a young man. He used a new title to designate his status, Anagarika, a Pali word meaning 'homeless'.

17.   Drawing on the Pali chronicles: *Dipavamsa* (Island Chronicle); the *Mahavamsa* (Great Chronicle); and the *Culavamsa* (Little Chronicle); *Dharmapala* recreated the past, isolating, emphasizing and re-constructing certain aspects of chronicles to establish a new foundation for the Buddhists of the early 1900s. A popular myth from the *Mahavamsa* was given particular prominence. It goes as follows: Gotama Buddha had visited Ceylon three times to make it a place where his teachings would be nurtured. He banished the original inhabitants of the island, the malevolent Yakkhas and Nagas (sub-human groups), making way for Vijaya, an immigrant from North India who was to become the first king of Sri Lanka. There were several versions of this myth,. In the earliest chronicle, the Dipavamsa, Buddha takes pity on the Yakkhas and Nagas, induces them to leave the island by providing an appealing home for them. Buddha portrays a compassionate and non-violent ruler, rather than a violent and aggressive one. Dharmapala favored the Mahavamsa version, in which Buddha terrorizes the Yakkhas and Nagas with ominous supernatural acts, and violently chases them from the island. This version

is more in line with the exploits of the warrior king, Duttagamani (often cited by Dharmapala) who successfully subdued the Tamil king, Elara. The latter had ruled the sacred city of Anuradhapura (Little, 1994, pp. 27–29). Besides using this myth and its implications to give substance to the notion of a politically active Buddhist, it also served to establish the Sinhalese 'race' as the God-ordained protectors of Buddhism. Ceylon Tamils too appropriated the Vijaya myth to prove their contention that they were the original inhabitants of the island: 'According to tradition, the Tamils of India and Sri Lanka are the lineal descendants of the naga and [Yakkha] people ... Nagadipa in the north of Sri Lanka was an actual kingdom ... and the people who occupied it were all part of an immigrant tribe from South India, Tamil people called nagas ... [T]he ancestors of the present day Tamils were the original occupiers of the island long before 543 BC which the Pali chronicles dates as the earliest human habitation in Sri Lanka' (Cited in Little, 19994, p. 42).

18.   Oberoi, H. (1994), *The Construction of Religious Boundaries*, University of Chicago Press: Chicago, IL, p. 361. Punjab became the army barracks of the Raj, especially after Sikhs fought on the side of the British in the 1857 uprising.

19.   An amendment on Sikh politics prepared by the assistant director of criminal intelligence shows acute awareness of the consequences of the strategies adopted. 'The British Government, more particularly the military administration, has put itself in a queer position as regards the Sikhs .. The glorification of Sikhism flying to the great advantage of the Government, it now appears to be likely to be used as an instrument to scourge us by a section of those for whose good it was primarily undertaken'—Cited in Petrie, D. (1911), *Confidential Report on Developments in Sikh Politics, 1900–1911*, India: Simla, pp. 51–52, quoted in Kapur, R. (1986), *Sikh Separatism: The Politics of Faith*, Allen and Unwin: London, p. 57.

20.   Ibid., p. 362, form a manual written for army officials.

21.   For the Khalsa Sikhs, a Sikh was one who carried out the Five Ks: *kes* (unshorn hair); *kangha* (wooden comb); *kirpan* (sword); *kara* (steel bracelet); *Kachh* (underpants); visited designated Sikh shrines; went through an initiation ceremony; conducted birth, marriage and death rites according to newly constructed practices; and did not eat prohibited foods.

22.   Following Maharaj Ranjit Singh, the British continued with the system of managing Sikh shrines through a committee and manager. See, Oberoi, *The Construction of Religious Boundaries*, op. cit., pp. 326–327.

23.   Other sects, cults and identities were the Udasis, Nirmalas, Sewa Panthis, Sahajdharis, Namdharis and Nirandkaris.

24.   In 1970, the KwaZulu Legislative Assembly was established as part of the 'Homeland' system. These 'homelands' were envisaged as future 'independent states' separate from the Republic of South Africa. Out of the 10 'homelands', 4 were considered independent. These were Transkei, Ciskei, Venda, and Bophuthatswana. Six were 'self-governing' but had not accepted independence. These were Lebowa, Ndebele, Gazankulu, Kangwane, Bosotho-QwaQwa, and KwaZulu. One of the most significant implications of 'independence' was that residents of these 'states' lost their South African citizenship.

25.   In the late 1930s, before he took office, Senanayake made public his support for the disenfranchisement of the Indian Tamils by saying: 'I do not think a greater blow to the national life of a country has been dealt, even by the Germans in Po-

land, than what has been done Up-country by the enfranchisement of so many Indian labourers' (Quoted in Manor, J. (1989), *The Expedient Utopian: Bandaranaike and Ceylon*, Cambridge University Press: Cambriged, p. 133).

26. In 1949 in the general clerical service of government, and when English was the
     official language, 54% of new recruits were Sinhalese and 41% were Tamils. In
     1955, under Sinhalese dominated government, 66% of all new employees were
     Sinhalese and only 39% were Tamils. In 1963, after Sinhala became the official
     language, 92% of new recruits were Sinhalese, and 7% were Tamils (Cited in Lit-
     tle, 1994, p. 145).

27. de Silva, K. M. (1986), *Managing Ethnic Tensions in Multi-Ethnic Societies: Sri
     Lanka, 1880–1985*, University Press of America: Lanham, MD, p. 266. Tamil en-
     trants into the sciences fell from 35.3% in 1970 to 20.9% in 1974 and 19% in
     1875. Sinhaleses students rose to 75.5% in 1974 and 78.0% in 1975.

28. At a convention held in Trincomalee in August 1956, the Tamil Federal Party
     made a new set of demands: autonomy for the Northern and Eastern Provinces un-
     der a federal constitution, parity of status for the Sinhalese and Tamil languages,
     and a satisfactory settlement of the problem of the Indian Tamil plantation work-
     ers in the island. See de Silva, K. M., *A History of Sri Lanka*, op. cit., p. 513.

29. Although Bandaranaike did make efforts to placate the Tamils, he failed to carry
     these efforts through. In a pact with the Tamil leader S. J. V. Chelvanayagam, it
     was agreed that Tamil would be recognized as a national language, the northern
     and eastern provinces were to be administered in Tamil languages and regional
     councils were to be created to alter the centralization of government. *Bhikkhus*
     protested the pact with a highly publicized civil disobedience campaign. Tamils
     too protested and in the violence that ensued, Bandaranaike cracked down on Sin-
     hala rioters and passed a bill authorizing the use of Tamil. The Bhikkhus retali-
     ated, causing dissension within the party, and on September 25, 1959, one of them
     assassinated Bandaranaike. His wife, Sirimavo Bandaranaike took office, and was
     elected Prime Minister as the SLFP candidate in 1960. She was in government for
     two terms—from 1960 to 1965 and from 1970 to 1977.

30. She made Sinhala the language of administration throughout the island from
     January 1, 1961, as envisaged in the 'Sinhala Only' bill of 1956. She also ex-
     tended state control over education, bringing the prestigious Catholic schools un-
     der her wing—covering their curricula and patterns of instruction. See Little
     (1994), op. cit., p. 73 and de Silva, K. M. *A History of Sri Lanka*, op. cit., p. 527.
     Between Mrs. Bandaranaike's two terms was the administration of Dudley
     Senanayake of the United National Party. Dudley was the son of S. W. R. D.
     Senanayake.

31. Initially the SGPC controlled two shrines: Shri Akal Takht Sahib, Amritsar; and
     Sri Takht Keshgarh Sahit, Anandpur Sahib. In 1945, it also came to control the
     Golden Temple, and later over 100 of the gurdwaras in Punjab, Haryana and Hi-
     marchal Predesh. The committee of the SGPC was selected on the basis of adult
     franchise, and elections were organized by the political party called the Shiromani
     Akali Dal. See Singh, A. (1988), 'The Shiromani Gurdawa Prabandhak Commit-
     tee and the Politicization of the Sikhs', in O'Connell, et. al. (eds.), *Sikh History
     and Region in the Twentieth Century*, South Asian Studies, University Of Toronto:
     Toronto.

32.   The annual budget of the SGPC from the gurdwaras amounted to more than US $12 million in 1985. Kapur, R. A. (1986), *Sikh Separatism: The Politics of Faith*, Allen & Unwin, pp. xv–xvi. Soon after becoming hegemonic among Sikhs, the SGPC marginalized all other sects and cults, making the Khalsa the dominant Sikh identity. As one author comments: 'It is therefore often said that for the Sikh politicians the road to Chandigarth or New Delhi lies via Amritsar, the headquarters of the SGPC' (Kapur, 1986, p. 232).

33.   Born in Natal in 1871, the son of Reverend James Dube of the American Zulu Mission, Dube was educated at Inanda and Amanzimtoti Theological School (later known as Adams College). In 1887, he accompanied the missionary W. C. Wilcox to America, studying at Oberlin Collegeover five years. With money collected from the United States between 1896–1899, Dube was able to establish a Zulu industrial school in the Inanda district in 1901 and the Zulu-English newspaper, Ilanga lase Natal. He was a founding member of the Natal Native Congress iin 1901, and Inkatha Ya Ka Zulu in 1922.

34.   By the beginning of the 20th century, most of the larger landlords, and members of the African *Kholwa* elite were involved in a network of political organizations, vigilance associations and welfare societies. Dube's presidential address to the South African Native Congress in 1912 clearly expressed the thinking of the petty-bourgeoisie: 'Upward! Into the higher places of civilization and Christianity—not backward into the slump of darkness not downward into the abyss of the antiquated tribal system. Our salvation is not there, but in preparing ourselves for an honored place amongst the nations.' Cited in Marks, S. (1986), *The Ambiguities of Dependence in South Africa: Class Nationalism, and the State in Twentieth Century Natal*, Johns Hopkins University Press: Baltimore, MD, p. 53. By 1930, Dube had radically changed his ideas, and before the Native Economic Commission, his reply to the question of how he could reconcile the tribal system with progress, he said: 'Well, it is the only thing we have and I think that if it were properly regulated, it would be best. The tribal system has many advantages and I cannot get away from it. It is under the tribal system that the land is held by our Natives ... If I want land, I must associate with the tribal system ...' Cited in Marks, S. (1989), 'Patriotism, Patriarchy and Purity: Natal and the Politics of Zulu Ethnic Consciousness', in Vail, L. (ed.), *The Creation of Tribalism in Southern Africa*, James Currey: London, p. 221.

35.   One of the contributing factors was that the Zulu law and not Roman-Dutch law, was practiced in the reserves. For example, irrespective of whether a person was a Christian or a 'traditionalist', an accusation of sorcery could have resulted in exile and loss of citizenship of the chiefdom. Christians were forced to deal with the *ababusi bomhlaba* (the rulers of the land) or *iziphathi mandla* (those who wield power)—the chiefs and headmen. There existed a constant need to negotiate and engage in reciprocal relations over matters dealing with land, cattle, dipping tank, taxes, pensions and traveling and work permits. Over and above the structural determinants that modified Christian beliefs, were the 'traditional' beliefs that were intrinsic to the Zulu language, mythology, cosmology and generally *sigcina isiZulu* (doing things the Zulu way). See Ngubane, H. (1977), *Body and Mind in Zulu Medicine: An Ethnography of Health and Disease in Nyuswa-Zulu Thought and Practice*, Academic Press: London, p. 5.

36.   The disruptive effects of colonialism on Zulu family cohesion were beginning to take its toll. As early as 1906, African Chiefs, headmen and homestead heads complained bitterly before the Natal Native Commission that: 'young people are getting out of hand, instead of recognizing and obeying their fathers and guardians they disobey and sometimes disown them. Sons who should be working for the house, appropriate all their earnings for themselves, daughters flaunt their elders to their face, and duty disowned, claim a right to go to towns or mission stations.' Cited in Vilakazi, A. (1965), *Zulu Transformations: A Study of the Dynamics of Social Change*, University of Natal Press: Pietermaritzburg, p. 220.

37.   In March 1953, Mangasuthu Buthelezi was installed as acting chief for the regent Chief Maliyamakhanda. He consolidated his position within the tribal system and by 1972, he had become chief minister of the KwaZulu Legislative Assembly. At the lowest level, the 'Tribal Authorities' (chiefs, headmen, and tribal councilors) had administrative, executive and judicial powers. The 'Regional Authorities', chosen from members of two or more tribal authorities, functioned to establish and maintain services in townships. The 'Territorial Authorities' had executive control over two or more areas for which regional authorities had been established. At the apex was the State President, Supreme Chief by the Native Administration Act of 1927. See Temkin, B. (1976), *Gatsha Buthelezi: Zulu Statesman*, Purnell: Cape Town.

38.   *Frontline*, February 29, 1988. UDF activists were known as *amaquabane*, a Xhosa word meaning 'friend' or 'comrade.'

39.   The violent way in which the LTTE gained predominance over all other guerrilla organizations is chronicled in detail in Swamy, M. R. N. (1994), *Tigers of Lanka: From Boys to Guerrillas*, Konark Publishers: New Delhi.

40.   In the 1970s, Bhindranwale had focused his attention on the Nirankari Sikhs, who were unlike orthodox Sikhs, worshipped living gurus. In 1973, they had been declared 'enemies' of the Sikh panth by the priests of the Golden Temple. Bhindranwale had attacked many Nirankari gurus, and murdered a prominent Hindu leader and newspaper editor. See Kapur (1986), op. cit., p. 226.

41.   A rallying point for the Akali Dal was Article 25 of the Indian Constitution. This piece of legislation guarantees freedom of religious worship to all citizens, but subsumes 'Sikhs', 'Jains', and 'Buddhists' under the category, 'Hindu'. For Akali leaders, this was tantamount to denying the 'existence' and specificity of Sikhs. In a pamphlet entitled 'You owe us justice', they explain as follows: 'India is a multi-lingual, multi-religious and multi-national land. In such a land, a microscopic minority, like the Sikhs has genuine foreboding that ... they may also lose their identity in the vast ocean of overwhelming Hindu majority. Their misgivings are heightened by arbitrary manner in which they are defined as Hindus under Article 25 of the Constitution.' See Kapur (1986), op. cit., p. 228.

42.   John Lonsdale highlights this aspect of ethnic identity in his book about the Kikuyu and Mau Mau in Kenya. Lonsdale, J. (1991), 'The Moral Economy of Mau Mau', in Berman, B. and Lonsdale, J. (ed.), *Unhappy Valley*, James Currey: London, p. 4.

43.   The close collaboration between the British and the new government was reflected in the 'Defense Agreement' signed by the new premier in 1947, which allowed the British military to retain control, after independence, of their major naval base at

Trincomalee (on the east coast) and air base at Katunayake, near Colombo. See Bose (1994), op. cit., p. 52.

References

Amnesty International (1998), *Amnesty International Annual Report 1998*, http://www.amnesty.org/ailib/aireport/ar98/index.html.

Arendt, H. (1969/1972), 'On Violencce', in Arendt, H. (ed.), *Crisis of the Republic*, Harvest/Harcout Brace Jovanovich: San Diego, CA.

Bhaba, H. (1994), 'Remembering Fanon: Self, Psyche and the Colonial Condition', in Williams, P. and Chrisman, L. (eds.), *Colonial Discourse and Post-Colonial Theory: A Reader*, Columbia University Press: New York.

Blackton, C. T. (1979), 'The Empire at Bay: British Attitudes and the Growth of Nationalism in the Early Twentieth Century', in Roberts, M. (ed.), *Collective Identities, Nationalisms and Protest in Modern Sri Lanka*, Marga Institute: Colombo.

Bose, S. (1994), *States, Nations, Sovereignty: Sri Lanka, India and the Tamil Eelam Movement*, Sage Books: New Delhi.

Boxer, C. R. (1958), 'Christians and Spices: Portuguese Missionary Methods in Ceylon, 1518–1658', *History Today*, Vol. 8, pp. 346–354.

Cohen, A. (1969), *Customs and Politics in Urban Africa: A Study of Hausa Migrants in Yuroba Towns*, University of California Press: Berkeley, CA.

Comaroff, J. L. (1987), 'Of Totemism and Ethnicity: Consciousness, Practice and the Signs of Inequality', *Ethnos*, Vol. 52, pp. 301–323.

de Silva, K. M. (1981), *A History of Sri Lanka*, Oxford University Press: Delhi.

de Silva, K. M. (1986), *Managing Ethnic Tensions in Multi-Ethnic Societies: Sri Lanka, 1880–1985*, University Press of America: Lanham, MD.

de Silva, K. M. (1988), 'Buddhist Revivalism, Nationalism, and Politics in Modern Sri Lanka', in Bjorkman, J. W. (ed.), *Fundamentalism, Revivalism and Violence in South Asia*, Manohar Publications: New Delhi.

de Silva, N. A. (1998), 'Anti-State Militant Mobilization, Sri Lanka: 1965–1991', Ph.D. Dissertation, Department of Sociology, State University of New York.

Eller, J. and Coughlan, R. (1993), 'The Poverty of Primordialism: The Demystification of Ethnic Attachments', *Ethnic and Racial Studies*, Vol. 16, No. 2, pp. 187–192.

Esman, M. (1977), *Ethnic Groups in the Western World*, Cornell University Press: Ithaca, NY.

Farmer, B. H. (1963), *Ceylon: A Divided Nation*, Oxford University Press: London.

Fearon, J. and Laitin, D. (1996), 'Explaining Interethnic Cooperation', *American Political Science Review*, Vol. 90, pp. 715–735.

Fox, R. G. (1985), *Lions of Punjab: Culture in the Making*, University of California Press: Berkeley, CA.

Geertz, C. (1963), 'The Integrative Revolution', in Geertz, C. (ed.), *Old Societies and New States*, Free Press: New York.

Glover, J. (1991), 'State Terrorism', in Grey, R. G. and Morris, C. E. (eds.), *Violence, Terrorism and Justice*, Cambridge University Press: Cambridge.

Gombrich, R. F. (1988), *Theravade Buddhism: A Social History from Ancient Bernares to Modern Colombo*, Routledge and Kegan Paul: New York.

Grosby, S. (1994), 'The Verdict of History: The Inexpungeable Tie of Primordiality: A Response to Eller and Coughlan', *Ethnic and Racial Studies*, Vol. 17, No. 2, pp. 164–171.

Guha, R. and Spivak, G. C. (1988), *Selected Subaltern Studies*, Oxford University Press: New York.

Gunawardena, R. A. L. H. (1991), 'The People of the Lion: Sinhala Identity and Ideology in History and Historiography', in Spencer, J. (ed.), *Sri Lanka: History and Roots of Conflict*, Routledge and Kegan Paul: London.

Gurr, T. R. and Harff, B. (1994), *Ethnic Conflict in World Conflict*, Westview Press: Boulder, CO.

Hall, S. (1994), 'Cultural Identity and Diaspora', in Williams, P. and Chrisman, L. (eds.), *Colonial Discourse and Post–Colonial Theory: A Reader*, Columbia University Press: New York.

Hardin, R. (1995), 'Self–interest, Group Identity', in Breton, A., Galeotti, G., Salmon, P. and Wintrobe, R. (eds.), *Nationalism and Rationality*, Cambridge University Press: Cambridge.

Hecter, M. (1989), 'Rational Choice Foundations in Social Order', in Turner, J. H. (ed.), Theory Building in Sociology: Assessing Theoretical Cumulation, Sage Publishers: Holywood, CA.

Huntington, S. (1993), 'The Clash of Civilizations', *Foreign Affairs*, Vol. 72, No. 3, pp. 22–49.

Isaacs, H. R. (1975), *Idols of the Tribe: Group Identity and Political Change*, Harper and Row Publishers: New York.

Jayawardena, K. (1985), *Ethnic and Class Conflict in Sri Lanka: Some Aspects of Sinhala–Buddhist Consciousness Over the Past 100 Years*, Sanjiva Books: Colombo, Sri Lanka.

Jayawardena, K. (1990), *Ethnic and Class Conflicts in Sri Lanka*, Sanjiva Books: Colombo, Sri Lanka.

Johns, S., III (ed.) (1972), *Protest and Hope, 1882–1934*, Vol. 1, Hoover Institution Press: Stanford, CA.

Kakar, S. (1996), *The Colors of Violence: Cultural Identities, Religion and Conflict*, University of Chicago Press: Chicago, IL.

Kapur, R. (1986), *Sikh Separatism: The Politics of Faith*, Allen and Unwin: London.

Kasfir, N. (1979), 'Explaining Ethnic Political Participation', *World Politics*, Vol. 31, No. 3, pp. 365–388.

Kearney, R. N. (1967), *Communalism and Language in the Politics of Ceylon*, Duke University Press: Durhan, NC.

Kearney, R. N. (1973), *The Politics of Ceylon*, Cornell University Press: Ithaca, NY.

Kemper, S. (1991), *The Presence of the Past: Chronicles, Politics, and Culture in Sinhala Life*, Cornell University Press: Ithaca, NY.

Lawrence, P. B. (1997), 'Work of Oracles, Silence of Terror: Notes on the Injury of War in Eastern Sri Lanka', Ph.D. Dissertation, Department of Anthropology, University of Colorado.

Little, D. (1994), *Sri Lanka: The Invention of Enmity*, United States Institute of Peace Press: Washington, D.C.

Malalgoda, K. (1976), *Buddhism in Sinhalese Society, 1750–1900*, University of California Press: Berkeley, CA.

Manor, J. (1989), *The Expedient Utopian: Bandaranaike and Ceylon*, Cambridge University Press: Cambridge.

Marks, M. (1989), 'Patriotism, Patriarchy and Purity: Natal and the Politics of Zulu Ethnic Consciousness', in Vail, L. (ed.), *The Creation of Tribalism in Southern Africa*, James Currey: London.

Marks, S. (1986), *The Ambiguities of Dependence in South Africa: Class, Nationalism and the State in Twentieth Century Natal*, The Johns Hopkins University Press: Baltimore, MD.

Marshall, M. G. (1999), *Third World War*, Rowman and Littlefield Publishers, Inc.: Oxford.

McGowan, W. (1992), *Only Man is Vile: The Tragedy of Sri Lanka*, Farrar, Strauss and Giroux: New York.

McLeod, W. H. (1989), *Who is a Sikh? The Problem of Sikh Identity*, Clarendon Press: Oxford.

Migdal, J. S. (1988), *Strong Societies and Weak States: State-Society Relations and State Capabilities in the Third World*, Princeton University Press: Princeton, NJ.

Mills, L. A. (1933), *Ceylon Under British Rule, 1795–1932*, Oxford University Press: Oxford.

Morris, D. R. (1966), *The Washing of the Spears*, Oxford University Press: London.

Mzala (1988), *Gatsha Buthelezi: Chief With a Double Agenda*, Zed Books: London.

Ngubane, H. (1977), *Body and Mind in Zulu Medicine: An Ethnography of Health and Disease in Nyuswa—Zulu Thought and Practice*, Academic Press: London.

Oberoi, H. (1994), *The Construction of Religious Boundaries*, University of Chicago Press: Chicago, IL.

Petrie, D. (1911), *Confidential Report on the Development in Sikh Politics, 1900–1911*, Simla: India.

Phadnis, U. (1976), *Religion and Politics in Sri Lanka*, Manohar Book Service: New Delhi.

Ponnambalam, S. (1983), *Sri Lanka: The National Question and the Tamil Liberation Struggle*, Zed Books: London.

Riggs, F. W. (1998), 'The Modernity of Ethnic Identity and Conflict', *International Political Science Review*, Vol. 19, No. 3, pp. 269–288.

Rothchild, D. (1997), *Managing Ethnic Conflict in Africa: Pressure and Incentives for Cooperation*, Brookings Institution Press: Washington, D.C.

Shils, E. (1957), 'Primordial, Personal, Sacred and Civil Ties', *British Journal of Sociology*, Vol. 8, No. 2, pp. 130–145.

Singh, A. (1988), 'The Shiromani Gurdawara Prabandhak Committee and the Politicization of the Sikhs', in O'Connell, J. T. et al. (eds.), *Sikh History and Region in the Twentieth Century*, South Asian Studies, University of Toronto: Toronto, ONT.

Spencer, J. (ed.) (1991), *Sri Lanka: History and Roots of Conflict*, Routledge and Kegan Paul: London.

Suryanarayna, V. (1991), 'Into a Quagmire: Sri Lanka's Political System of Crisis', *Frontline*, July 6–19, pp. 95–98.

Swany, M. R. N. (1994), *Tigers of Lanka: From Boys to Guerrillas*, New Konark Publishers: New Delhi.

Tambiah, S. J. (1992), *Buddhism Betrayed: Religion, Politics and Violence in Sri Lanka*, University of Chicago Press: Chicago.

Tambiah, S. J. (1997), *Leveling Crowds: Environmentalist Conflicts and Collective Violence in South Asia*, University of California Press: Berkeley, CA.

Temkin, B. (1976), *Gatsha Buthelezi: Zulu Statesman*, Purnell: Cape Town.

Truth and Reconciliation Commission (South Africa) (1999), *Truth and Reconciliation Commission of South Africa Report*, Grove's Dictionaries, Inc.: New York.

van den Berghe, P. (1979), *The Ethnic Phenomenon*, Elsevier: New York.

van den Berghe, P. (1986), 'Ethnicity and the Socio-biological Debate', in Rex, J. and Mason, D. (eds.), *Theories of Race and Ethnic Relations*, Cambridge University Press: Cambridge.

Vanhanen, T. (1999), 'Domestic Ethnic Conflict and Ethnic Nepotism: A Comparative Analysis', *Journal of Peace Research*, Vol. 36, No. 1, pp. 55–73.

Vilakazi, A. (1965), *Zulu Transformations: A Study of the Dynamics of Social Change*, University of Natal Press: Pietermartizburg, South Africa.

Weber, M. (1978), *Economy and Society*, 2 volumes, translated and edited by Roth, G. and Wittich, C., University of Calirfornia Press: Berkeley, CA.

Welsh, D. (1971), *Roots of Segregation: Native Policy in Colonial Natal, 1845–1910*, Oxford University Press: Cape Town.

Wilson, A. J. (1979), *Politics in Sri Lanka, 1947–1979*, Macmillan: London.

Wilson, A. J. (1988), *The Break-Up of Sri Lanka: The Sinhalese-Tamil Conflict*, C. Hurst and Company: London.

Wriggins, W. H. (1960), *Dilemmas of a New Nation*, Princeton University Press: Princeton, NJ.

Index